Luton Sixth Form College

Beds. LU2 7EW

Baby Wisdom

DEBORAH JACKSON

Baby Wisdom

The World's Best-Kept
Secrets for the First Year
of Parenting

HODDER

MOBIUS

Copyright © 2002 by Deborah Jackson

First published in Great Britain in 2002 by Hodder and Stoughton
A division of Hodder Headline

The right of Deborah Jackson to be identified as the Author
of the Work has been asserted by her in accordance with the
Copyright, Designs and Patents Act 1988.

2 4 6 8 10 9 7 5 3 1

A CIP catalogue record for this title is available from the British Library

ISBN 0 340 79350 3

Typeset in Bembo by
Palimpsest Book Production Limited, Polmont, Stirlingshire
Printed and bound in Great Britain by
Mackays of Chatham plc, Chatham, Kent

Hodder and Stoughton
A division of Hodder Headline
338 Euston Road
London NW1 3BH

To Paul, Frances, Alice and Joseph

Acknowledgments

I should like to thank:
Sarah Molloy at A.M. Heath for sticking with me and having
the big idea; Rowena Webb at Hodder, for her enthusiasm,
patience and judgment; Professor James J. McKenna, Dr Michel
Odent, Dr Mary Manandhar, Ashisha at *Mothering*, Chrissie
Hardman, Roger Halford, Paul Jackson and Pat Thomas for their
kind help with research and references; Baby Milk Action in
Cambridge for national and international breastfeeding statistics; and Paul, Frances, Alice and Joseph for their understanding
and support.

Permissions:
Thanks to Margaret Stewart and the women of the Werra Werra
Taam (Women's Centre), Warmun, Western Australia who feature
in *Ngalangangpum Jarrakpu Purrurn -- Mother and Child: The Women
of Warmun*, for permission to quote their stories in this text.
Words and music for *Welcome to the World* by Si Kahn. © Joe Hill
Music (ASCAP). Used by permission.

Caution:
Recipes and remedies quoted in this book, while accurate
according to their sources, have not been tested. Neither the
author nor the publisher can accept any responsibility for their
use. Please consult your doctor if in any doubt.

'Now that the world is smaller, we can take the best from all cultures and adapt it to our own lives'

Barbara Wishingrad, childbirth educator

'It's tradition – and you don't monkey with tradition'

From the film *Mystic Pizza*

Contents

Preface

CHILD-REARING BEGINS AT HOME

It is easy for babies. They take hold of life with a yell and a bunch of reflexes and they seem to know exactly what they want. Becoming a mother or a father is an altogether more complicated process. For many of us, the transition from child-free to child-friendly means moments of mess and distress. Until we have been through the experience at least once, we don't really know which end is up.

The problem begins with our own upbringing. Home life is segregated so that only a few adults have extended experience of babies and small children. Schools keep children in strict peer groups. The workplace is surrounded by an invisible infant-repellent. It is possible for new parents never to have held a real, live baby before their own. So, like public school boys entering a world with women in it, we tend to regard newborns as an alien species. When we give birth to our own little alien, we seek simple formulas to help us tame this foreigner with his unrecognisable ways.

At first, we are surprised when our naïve strategies fail. Eventually we recognise that child-rearing means letting go of preconceptions (literally, the ideas we had before pregnancy!) As we unlearn the little we thought we knew, we also start to realise that society has washed its hands of the whole family affair. Following nine highly-scrutinised months of pregnancy, babies arrive with very little in the way of customer service. 'In the US, the medical and insurance establishment treats pregnancy as an illness . . . Once you give birth, you are cured, and on your own' (Margaret St John, journalist).

Depending on your country of residence, there may be maternity nurses, health professionals and the occasional coffee morning to give you courage. But there is also likely to be some isolation, a feeling that you might be getting things wrong and a never-ending stream of media blame.

Even the quickest review of the last twenty years of tabloids will show that they were way ahead of the quality papers in defining, fanning and politicising fears about the crisis in the family . . . The moral of the story as they told it is that the fabric of society was eroding because women were no longer doing what women were put on earth by God to do, and neither were men. They were parenting unnaturally, and the result was a new generation that was lawless, degenerate and monstrous.

Maureen Freely, novelist and journalist

The most unnatural thing about modern parenting is the lack of preparation beforehand and the dearth of community support afterwards. Society tends to ignore the needs of parents and children, only pausing long enough to point out the many mistakes we are making. Few adults feel any collective responsibility for the welfare of the next generation.

Whatever the theory of the moment – whether it's the quality of daycare, the value of a full-fat diet or the effects of corporal punishment – parents are generally held to blame. We have apparently lost the art of good discipline; we over-dress them for bed and under-dress them in the day; we smack and shout in supermarkets; we breastfeed too often, we fail to breastfeed at all. We neglect our children to go to work, yet we are unable to let go. We give them too much freedom and not enough. In short, we don't know what we are about and society feels nervous that children are left in our hands.

If you are not getting support, recognition or meaningful social status, you might wonder exactly where your incentive to be a better parent is. Can it be the sheer joy of child-rearing? The most commonly cited emotion of modern parenting is not joy, nor anything like it. It is something much more pervasive and unwelcome, a feeling that seeps under the nursery door and catches us unawares. It is parental guilt.

Guilt may be felt by 'absent' fathers, 'ever-present' mothers and vice versa. It is a modern malaise, a symptom of the break-down in consensus parenting and community encouragement. While some individuals seem to avoid feeling guilty and all of us enjoy times when we feel we've done something right, the media tell us that chronic, low-level anxiety is the one commodity which parents managed to carry with them into the new millennium. It is a cheerless way to feel about ourselves and our capacity to nurture.

There must be another way to raise parents so that they are well equipped to raise their children. Are we missing something?

WIDENING OUR HORIZONS

We may imagine we are well informed about child-rearing and, in terms of medical care, nutritional awareness and scientific proofs, most of us are. Yet our daily frame of reference is narrow. Many childcare manuals fail to mention the rest of the world, a world so diverse that we can scarcely begin to imagine its patterns, its motivations or its ways of being. Inevitably, we are blinkered by our own struggle and experiences.

Childcare can be a lonely business for the nuclear-family parent. Even when surrounded by friends and family, parents are expected to make a long list of child-rearing decisions alone. From initial sleep management to feeding regimes and the purchase of 'essential' baby equipment, we are forced into early choices which radically alter our relationship with our babies. At some time or another, many of us will feel criticised for these choices – and unsupported when things don't work out as planned. In true post-industrial, western style, it is every parent for him- or herself.

We forget that the biological event of birth connects us to a global community of parents, millions upon millions of mothers, fathers, babies and children all striving, coping and learning from their own mistakes. If we could learn about their lives, we might pick up some new ideas and make more sense of things. Perhaps we could share in a wider perspective which teaches us that there are no 'rights' and few 'wrongs' that can't be mended.

Baby Wisdom is a collection of voices from many different cultures. Each has a different perspective on aspects of babycare in the first year of life. The many-voiced approach moves us away from the idea of one 'guru' handing out tablets for everyone else to swallow and allows us to open up our minds completely. There are too many varied opinions here for you to follow them all, so relax and let the world view flow over you. It is reassuring to realise that all around the world parents share our concerns and struggle with many of the same issues. It makes us realise that almost anything is possible.

JUST FOR THE RECORD

This is a new kind of childcare manual. A survey of inter-continental babycare like this could not have been written before the end of the twentieth century. For hundreds of thousands of years, people have been caring for children without reference to books or other cultures. Only in the past 200 years did writers pay any serious attention to the minutiae of cultural life and, even then, the early travellers wrote scathingly about rituals they observed from a distance and refused to understand. Prior to this, most historians were apparently uninterested in the domestic scene, believing it to be beneath their concern.

For instance, when French historian Philippe Ariès set out to write his influential volume *Centuries of Childhood* in 1960, he hit an immediate stumbling block. Since the advent of the printing press, history books had confined themselves to life's big events: affairs of state, wars and royal accessions, lives of the saints and pious works of instruction for the learned few; '. . . how was I to discover in the documents of the past,' wrote Ariès, 'references to things which were too ordinary, too common-place, too far removed from the memorable incident for contemporary writers to mention them?'

A woman's life, seemingly full of routine, was deemed uninteresting and rarely warranted comment. The rituals of birth and motherhood, protected by taboo and often shielded from men, were even less likely to be written down. In developing countries, girls were also less likely to be educated than boys, and so were unable to write their own historical accounts. As Jane Austen remarked, through the voice of Anne Elliot: 'Men have had every advantage of us in telling their own story. Education has been theirs in so much higher a degree; the pen has been in their hands.'

Even when asked about their life's experiences for the record, many women in traditional cultures hardly know what to say. Here is a conversation between Bey, a seventy-five-year-old !Kung San woman from the Kalahari Desert in Africa, and Marjorie Shostak, a field researcher:

Bey: I certainly remember things from my childhood. I am old and have experienced much. You ask me about something and I'll tell you about it.

MS: . . . That's good. But now, let's talk more specifically about things that happened to you, about any time in your life.

Bey: Yes, we are talking very well. You keep asking me and I'll keep telling you. I am old and I know many things.

Marjorie Shostak, anthropologist, in conversation with Bey, a !Kung San woman

Bey never did come up with any specific memories for the record. Mothers, fathers and grandparents all around the world are so busy doing what they feel is right – what their people have always done – they hardly know how to put the experience into words. They don't stop to analyse their actions, and they believe their wisdom and rituals to be so universal and obvious they do not need explaining.

Until quite recently, the lack of written history was no problem, because people knew their traditions would be handed down through experience and words. But just as white men were busy editing history, so they were instrumental in destroying the ancient cultures they encountered on their march around the world.

DIFFERENCE AND SAMENESS

A book like this, with its multi-cultural view of child care and the family, belongs to the increasingly multi-cultural modern world. Only now that scientists are seriously devoting themselves to the social and evolutionary contexts of child-rearing do we have the possibility of an overview. And an overview is urgently needed. If we don't record some of the many endangered, dying, or forgotten customs surrounding the care of young children, we may lose touch with vital clues to the evolved needs of human babies. The aim is neither to elevate other cultures nor to disrespect our own. It is merely to assist in the long process of opening our eyes.

In this guide book for the new, the experienced and the curious parent, there are two main themes: difference and sameness. Here are some amazing facts from around the world, unusual practices and strange exceptions, which inspire and remind us that there is more than one way to raise a baby. But here are also many practices which are both ancient and universal: recurrent themes which demonstrate the harmony between cultures and a sense of continuity with our evolutionary past. This is the

mainstream of parenting wisdom, connecting us to the expectations of babies and small children – and to the nearly-forgotten
parental satisfaction of knowing that you are doing just fine.

Deborah Jackson
Bath, 2002

1. The Kit List

Can you imagine raising a baby without a cot, a buggy or a three-year supply of disposable nappies? Western babies may be born without belongings, but within minutes they are surrounded by the kit and caboodle which our culture deems absolutely necessary.

The story of baby equipment is a metaphor for changes in child-rearing over thousands of years. Before a baby is born, western parents prepare by decorating a nursery and filling it with an array of new equipment. Expectant couples, many of whom have never even held a human baby, thus enter parenthood in a state of consumer readiness. The coordinated baby room and its contents act as security objects, reassuring novice mothers and fathers that they are geared up for the overwhelming event of birth.

Of course, there was a time when mothers had to manage without Mothercare. Our pregnant ancestors focused merely on practical and spiritual preparation for parenthood. It took many thousands of years before humans invented slings and carry cots, cradles and − finally − the cot, that piece of furniture which offers the baby the least human contact of all. Finally, the baby is alone in a world of kite-marked goodies.

This is the evolution of material parenting. In the West, it has gone almost as far as it can go, and there is a growing backlash against equipment overkill. But in other continents, the process is not yet complete. The cachet of owning a western-style stroller or using disposable nappies means that many of the world's poorest parents now aspire to the paraphernalia we take for granted.

So here they are, those essential items on the baby equipment list, without which most of us assume it is impossible to raise the next generation. Sold – to the parents from post-industrial cultures – items to make child-rearing just that bit more . . . expensive.

BABY'S ESSENTIAL SHOPPING LIST

!Kung San baby (Kalahari Desert, Africa, for hundreds of thousands of years to mid-1980s)	Italian baby (middle-class Florence, 1417)	Modern British baby (England, Year 2001)
one kaross (animal-skin hip sling with grass lining)	lined cloaks little shirts robes, with and without sleeves bibs caps six swaddling bands six pieces of woollen cloth branch of coral with a silver ring old cradle with coverlet and pillow	own nursery with matching wallpaper and curtains cot with safety mattress sheets, blankets, cot duvet decorative mobile baby listening monitor night light temperature gauge for nursery babygrows, vests, hats, scratch-mitts, cardigans, socks, coat, soft shoes disposable nappies changing mat and bag disposable baby wipes top-and-tail bowl, cotton wool breast pump, breast pads L-shaped nursing pillow bottles, teats and a sterilising unit baby lotion, bath lotion, sun protection cream, nappy rash cream, baby oil thermometer, Calpol, Gripe Water, Dettol plastic baby bath muslin squares baby nail scissors baby hairbrush pram, pram sheets and blankets pushchair with sun canopy and rainhood car seat and neck support travel cot play gym and play mat rattles, cuddly toys supply of dummies plastic-lined swim trunks baby towel with hood teething ring plastic dish and spoon high chair, bibs baby bouncer for doorway reclining cloth 'chair' camera and photo albums

Slings and Things

> When I turn my head
> He smiles at me, my baby,
> Hidden deep in my hood.
> Oh, how plump he is!
> Ya, ya! Ya, ya!
>
> Inuit lullaby, Greenland

A very long time ago, people simply carried babies around in their arms. But if they had long distances to cover, they would need a baby carrier. Some anthropologists say that slings were humans' first attempt at clothing. Others say they were our first tools. Either way, the sling is a practical body garment which dates back hundreds of thousands of years. Before hats, gloves, coats or shoes, people started wearing wraps which allowed them to carry things and still keep their arms free.

In some cultures, a sling is the baby's first birth gift. Traditionally, this might be the skin of a calf, lamb or goat which was sacrificed at the child's 'welcome to the world' party. Leg skins are used as straps and the baby sits in a pouch. Skins were the first obvious slings, readily available, warm and comforting to wear. The baby sling was, for thousands of years, the sole piece of baby equipment it occurred to anyone to invent.

(For more on slings around the world, see Chapter 6.)

The Carry Cot

The [Thai] child is taken and gently dropped into a winnowing basket while all the family stand around. As this is being done one of the parents has to shout 'mine' and the first one to do so 'owns' the child. If another member of the family does this he or she becomes like a godparent to the child. It is said that, as the baby is dropped on the basket, the shock 'makes him forget life as a spirit' and therefore anchors him more firmly in his body. When someone shouts 'mine', this also cuts his connection with the spirit world and he becomes fully human.

Jacqueline Vincent Priya, birth researcher

Many, many years after the sling came the carry cot. Perhaps the most traditional form of carrying device is the basket, a form of baby transport made famous by Moses in the biblical bull rushes and still popular as the 'Moses basket' of modern times. Here is a worldwide selection of carrying cots:

* Seri babies of New Mexico are carried in a shallow basket filled with sand and lined with a cloth.

* The ancient Anasazi people of the Four Corners – the point where Utah, Colorado, New Mexico and Arizona meet – carried their babies in baskets made of oval willow rings, tied together with strips of juniper and bound with soft deerskin. Archaeologists have found Anasazi baby baskets dating back up to 1,000 years, each one woven for an anticipated baby by somebody's grandmother.

* In Siberia, the Mansi baby is carried in a tiny birch bark carrying cradle, and kept warm under a soft swan-skin coverlet. Birch bark was used for centuries in basket-making throughout the northern hemisphere.

* A Chinese mother working in the rice fields carries her baby in a deep wicker basket, held on by shoulder straps.

CARRY-COT BLUES

The prehistoric sling bound mother and baby together – but the invention of the carry cot also created consumer choice: should the baby be picked up or not? The aggressive Mundugumor tribe of New Guinea were renowned for leaving their babies in their baskets day and night without physical comfort.

> From birth on the [Mundugumor] infant is carried in a rough-plaited basket, semicircular in profile, suspended from the mother's forehead. The basket is harsh, stiff and opaque . . . When it cries, without touching its body, the mother or other female scratches the outside of the basket with her fingernail, making a harsh grating sound.
>
> **Ashley Montagu, social scientist**

For many cultures, the carry cot came with a set of taboos ensuring that the baby was not left alone. In parts of Australia today, the traditional coolamon (a portable wooden trough, lined with spinifex grass or soft paper bark) must not be placed on the ground. Young mothers who are tempted to put baby down while they work are chastised by older women, who say the baby will get trodden on, or eaten by wild dogs. 'The *coolamons* are made to carry the new baby around in. Lay the baby there to sleep in the *coolamon* too. Young mother mustn't carry her new baby everywhere except in the *coolamon*.' (Polly Widaldjil, Aboriginal woman of Warmun).

The dilemma of the young mother highlights the convenience of a sling over a carry cot. Clever inventions – however progressive they may seem – often make our lives more complicated in the end.

The Cradleboard

> . . . Even those who are with child
> Carrying one child on the back
> Holding another on a cradleboard
> Leading one by the hand
> With yet another going before . . .
>
> Zuñi prayer for mothers, western Pueblos, South America

The cradleboard was a baby-carrying device which famously originated with the native tribes of North America. It was a way of swaddling, securing and transporting the baby all in one. Hand-crafted by a family member and given as a gift at the occasion of the birth, the cradleboard was a treasured item in the baby's life. It might typically be made of wicker, with a foot rest, head canopy and a lining – the soft bark of the cliff rose, for example. It was often decorated with gems, such as turquoise, or hung with feathers and dreamcatchers. The baby was strapped on the board using a long cord, laced in a zig zag between buckskin loops.

Cradleboards have been made for more than 4,000 years. Early Bronze Age pictures show babies tightly swaddled into them and prehistoric statuettes depict mothers carrying babies strapped to backboards. The idea was to keep the baby calm and safe while the mother gathered fruit, or tended crops. He would be completely immobile, bandaged and straight, like the trained branch of a sapling fruit tree.

Each tribe had its own reasons for using the cradleboard. For the Nootka people of the American north-west coast, the emphasis was on baby-moulding. Head-pressing devices were made out of cedar bark and attached to the baby's cradle. Four days of post-natal head-pressing were usual for the Nootkan infant: the aim was to elongate the malleable skull bones and increase the natural slope of his forehead, for reasons of beauty and status. The Makah tribe of the Olympic Peninsula (who were related to the Nootka), flattened babies' heads from the top.

Like swaddling, the cradleboard is a form of comfort for the newborn child. It provides powerful physical reassurance for a body which has developed in the restricted space of the womb. Young babies swiftly become accustomed to the bands and stays which immobilise their limbs, offering a feeling of security to which they long to return for sleep. Bound to the cradleboard rather than to their mothers, it is to the cradleboard that children become attached:

Mrs Calley [a white mother and teacher living in Arizona] states that one of her sons would not go to sleep unless strapped on the cradleboard for the first eight months of his life. He always gratefully acquiesced in going back to the board after his abundant romps, and would voluntarily put his arms to his sides ready to be strapped in. 'Surely,' Mrs Calley remarks, 'the Indians have been ahead of their white brothers in the art of child-rearing.'

Ashley Montagu, social scientist

Also like swaddling, the cradleboard educates the child into passivity. Navaho babies of south-west America would only be taken out of confinement for two hours out of twenty-four, for nursing, cleaning and bathing. So was the baby as snug as a bug in his upright home, or frustrated as a fly in a fly-trap? Experts are divided. The Sioux people of Dakota certainly used the cradleboard as a way of blocking out the toddler tantrum: 'The Sioux baby, when thus filled with rage, was strapped up to his neck in the cradleboard. He could not express his rage by the usual violent motion of the limbs . . .' (Erik Erikson, psychoanalyst).

Cradleboard babies may have been unmoving, but they were still on the go. Strapped to their mothers' shoulders or forehead, they received a similar kinetic education to other carried infants. Anthropologists observed cradleboard use among the Seneca, an Iroquois nation people who were the first inhabitants of New York State and southern Ontario. At family gatherings everyone begged to hold the baby, and a cradleboard typically passed through eleven pairs of hands in under an hour.

This stiffened infancy also provided some protection against injury. For the Cree, a subarctic tribe at the northernmost tip of the Great Plains, the board enabled the baby to survive on nomadic forest journeys. The Arapaho mother, who lived further south around Arkansas, even hung the baby on the pommel of her saddle when she rode on horseback.

The Hammock

[Maya] Babies have almost continuous body contact from the time of birth, at first and for the most part with their mothers, but as time progresses, also with other members of the family. A baby is not put down unless it is asleep, at which point it might be laid into a hammock. At the first sign of awakening, it is picked up again.

Brigitte Jordan, birth researcher in Yucatan, Mexico

The hammock is, of course, a kind of sling, which may be suspended from a person, from trees, the ceiling, or walls of a house. If it is big enough, it can sleep two — for instance, the mother and baby of Brazil. Hammocks are particularly popular in South America, where the climate does not call for many layers of clothing in or out of bed.

Hanging by his own weight in the main room of the house, the baby feels the comfort and security of the net, enjoys the rocking movements created by his own body, hears the sounds and feels the vibrations of the people around him. There is little risk of suffocation through the hammock's open weave.

Miniature hammocks are used by some societies to carry babies around. Arapesh mothers of New Guinea traditionally carried their babies in small net bags suspended from the forehead. While working, bag and baby were hung from a tree or the rafters of the house. In rural Turkey, the mother who returns to work in the cotton fields may hang her baby in a cotton bag nearby. The bag is supported by three poles, with a sackcloth awning to protect the infant from the sun – a kind of makeshift baby swing. Whenever the baby wants to nurse, the mother takes him to the shade of the nearest tree.

The Ancient Anasazi woman of America's Four Corners also made hammock cradles using ropes which hung from the beams of the house. Her baby was tied into a blanket for safety, and an older brother or sister would be given the job of gently swinging the baby to and fro.

The Rocking Chair

Rocking is not only for soothing fussy children. It is for soothing cranky mothers, too.

Tricia Schleifer, American artist

The rocking chair is a perfect accessory for parents looking for baby-friendly furniture. Benjamin Franklin, eighteenth-century statesman and founding father of America, is credited with its invention. Once popular with elderly folk throughout the United States, the 'rocker' is now coming back into vogue in middle-class nurseries. Unlike a cradle or baby-bouncer, it allows baby and carer to snuggle together in mutual comfort – and it gives older children and unsteady grandparents a secure way of cuddling the infant. Its soothing effects work on everyone, baby or no baby.

The Cradle

The baby was in the cradle, and I noticed as I looked down the ward that one squeak out of the baby and up would come the mother's foot, and with her toe she would rock the cradle. On the second squeak, which showed that the baby was really awake, she would reach into the cradle and take the baby into her arms, where a baby is supposed to be most of the time.

Dr Brock Chisholm, psychiatrist and former director
of the World Health Organisation

In the long evolution of babycare, from in-arms carrying to the sling and finally to the cot, the cradle plays a crucial role. While slings, baskets and cradleboards allowed babies to be held, the cradle was a tentative step towards separation. It was a real item of baby furniture and it swiftly became an icon of maternity. In the thirteenth century, European artists started to represent babies in rocking cradles: a cliché for western parenting which has lasted nearly a thousand years.

But use of the cradle differed greatly from the use of the modern cot. There was no idea of setting baby aside in a nursery with his own pretty mobiles and a sleep routine. Swaddled infants were laced into their cradles in much the same way that they were laced into cradleboards, and then set down in the main hub of the house where they could watch the world go by (and the world, of course, could watch them).

Perhaps the most important feature of the cradle was its rocking ability, replicating the human rocking which babies so clearly craved. Bartholomew of England, thirteenth-century child care expert, claimed that cradle-rocking improved the baby's digestion. Physiologists now tell us why: rocking assists the movement of the intestine (which is loosely attached inside the body), improving muscle tone and distributing digestive juices throughout the tract. Gentle rocking after a feed is also said to ease infant colic.

As cradles grew increasingly popular, rocking the baby became a profession in its own right. Upper-class mothers delegated the task to the child-nurse or her junior, an under-nurse called the Rocker. String might be tied to the end of the cradle to allow her to keep the cradle in motion while she moved around. Since rocking was considered vital to infant health, reams were written on how to do it correctly. A French child care manual of 1755 had four pages on cradle-rocking technique. And by the end of the eighteenth century, a self-rocking cradle had been invented:

... someone decided that the fatigue of rocking a refractory infant in this sort of crib could be lessened by the aid of machinery. Sheraton's Cabinet Dictionary (1803) shows such a cot from the workshop of a bedstead-maker named William Holinshade, of King Street, Drury Lane [London]. Just such a piece can be seen in the Victorian and Albert Museum ... Elegantly designed, it is fitted with a clock-spring attachment which, even now, is capable of rocking the cradle for forty-three minutes.

F. Gordon Roe, social historian

Cradles gained status in Europe, as they were associated with the rising cult of the Nativity. Crib-making became a lucrative occupation in seventeenth-century Germany, both for real babies and miniature baby Jesus figurines. A few German families still specialise in the carving of cradles, as they have for hundreds of years.

Ordinary families had cradles made from oak panels, which was hard-wearing enough to be used by successive generations of children. Noble babies slept on feather mattresses with pillows, in gilt-edged cradles topped with covers of fur. The legend of St Elizabeth of Hungary tells how she was laid to sleep in a cradle made of silver. The cradle was viewed as a safe, soothing and healthy way to raise a child and ecclesiastical authorities stipulated that children should sleep in them until the age of three.

But cradle-rocking eventually became too fanatical for its own good. Like every other child care method, its success depended on the way it was done, and some nurses were apparently over-doing it. French philosopher Jean Jacques Rousseau, who led the eighteenth-century crusade against swaddling, also looked down on rocking: 'It is never necessary and often harmful,' he said, 'to rock children in the cradle.' Nurses were accused of neglecting their charges by rocking them all day instead of playing with them; gentle rocking had been replaced in some homes by a violent, uncaring action; and by the nineteenth century, parents were being warned against any practice which might be 'habit forming'.

And so the crib was invented – a static, imposing piece of furniture which was to change the infant sleep environment for ever. Cradles, a relic of old-fashioned days, were consigned to museums and the set-piece nurseries of old stately homes. By the end of the nineteenth century, anyone who still rocked a cradle would have been ashamed to admit to such indulgence.

When World Health Organisation director Brock Chisholm went to visit a large general hospital in Pakistan in the 1950s, his hosts tried to distract him from visiting the neonatal ward. As Dr Chisholm insisted, his guides implored him not to go in: they were embarrassed, they said, to let him see such an old-fashioned ward – it was a pattern hundreds of years old and they hoped the World Health Organisation might be able to grant them funds to bring it up to date.

Dr Chisholm pressed on into the room, which he described as 'the best maternity ward I have ever seen in any country'. The babies were sleeping in cradles, rocked and tended by their mothers who sat close at hand.

They wanted to get rid of that perfectly beautiful arrangement, to put their babies under glass the way we do, and to keep them in inspection wards where they can be seen at a distance by their loving fathers whenever they visit, and taken to their mother if she is good and does as the nurse tells her! They wanted to do all that because we Westerners had given them the impression that all our methods are superior to theirs.

Dr Brock Chisholm, psychiatrist and former director
of the World Health Organisation

The Cot

It is an unnatural achievement for the human baby to have to spend his life in a crib. He is in no way adjusted to the crib; rather, his wish to be carried around

becomes clearly evident again and again. Calming by rocking or pacifiers is reminiscent of the time when mother and child were physically more closely associated.

Albrecht Peiper, former director of the children's clinic, University of Leipzig

The cot is an altogether different species of baby equipment. Although it seems to be just a big cradle with the rocker removed, we have to wonder why – when babies love rocking – some cultures opted instead for a motionless piece of furniture. In fact, the crib bears little relation to the cradle, for it has no soothing function at all. Its role is more like that of the playpen, a cage for keeping babies in (or out, according to your perspective).

By the beginning of the twentieth century, the old-fashioned cradle was on its last rockers. Child care theorists now focused on a more scientific, supposedly less time-consuming regime, and had training programmes at the ready for inducing compliance in even the youngest of babies.

The infant must have its own crib, without rockers, and it must on no account be put to sleep in the same bed with its mother. In its early life it should never be taken out of its crib except to be fed, to have its clothing changed, or to be bathed. There should be no holding on the lap, no dangling, no carrying or fussing over the newborn infant; and the more the baby is let alone, the better and healthier it will be.

Anna M. Galbraith, American doctor and author, 1915

It is hard to do a multi-cultural study of cot use, because cots are not a multi-cultural phenomenon. Most peoples of the world prefer to keep their babies in motion: next to their bodies, or gently rocking nearby in hammocks, cradles and slings. Yet cots and nurseries are so normal in western society, it is hard for many of us to imagine a baby without them. Decorating the nursery and prettifying the cot are the primary ways in which young couples prepare for parenthood. When baby arrives and doesn't seem to want to sleep in his room, it can be a great disappointment. These were the only pre-natal preparations they had made.

The cot entirely changes the way we parent. Many families go through terrible struggles to reconcile babies' needs with this cultural requirement. It might help to realise, as we agonise over our babies and the kind of parents we want to be, that the cot in its own nursery is the extreme of sleep conditions. It constitutes the most complete separation that humans have yet imposed on their vulnerable young.

The Pram

It is painful to notice a babe of a few months in one of those new-fangled carriages. His little head is bobbing about, first on one side and then on another – at one moment it is dropping on his chest, the next it is forcibly jolted behind: he looks and doubtless feels, wretched and uncomfortable.

Dr Pye Henry Chavasse, obstetrician and healthcare author, 1880

The perambulator probably dates back to ancient Greece, since a clay model of a baby cart was discovered by archaeologists in Athens, and pictures survive of fourteenth-century babies being wheeled along in India and Ceylon. But prams were never going to catch on seriously until pavements were invented. Sand, mud and cobblestones are all wrong for those delicate chassis. No baby would relish being bounced right out of his buggy – and have you ever *tried* to push a pushchair along a beach?

No, it was not until Victorian times that perambulators first ambulated in significant quantities along the streets. During the 1850s, the decade when the Singer sewing machine was invented, the first serious pram was patented by one Charles Burton. Queen Victoria gave the baby carriage her blessing and there was no stopping its rise in popularity. By 1856, Burton was one of five pram makers who had opened up shop in Oxford Street,

London. Within a decade, perambulator manufacturers even had their own trade gazette.

Undoubtedly, there were hazards to be faced – lack of springs, arsenic-coated harnesses, and the dangers of increased neglect by nursemaids. But the early prams were things of considerable grace and beauty. Liveried wooden casings were hemmed with miniature balustrades, lined with buttoned leather, and trimmed in gleaming brass. Bassinet versions, especially popular in the United States and the colonies, were reed-woven in shell-coiled arabesques, with parasols or canopies fluttering overhead.

Christina Hardyment, social historian

At the outset, child care experts were uncertain about the flamboyant procession of prams which hogged the pavements and clogged the arteries of suburban parks. Babies were treated like gentry gliding past in their livery, propelled by their highly-starched nannies on walks of ever-increasing length. Just like the cradle in medieval times, the pram spawned a new profession and a spate of activity. Rather than the rocker, one employed a pram-nanny, and rather than rocking, she had a lot of pushing to do.

Over the next few decades, perambulating became a fully-established custom, with its own rites and rituals and cultural variations.

It apparently became socially unacceptable for a smart mother to be seen wheeling her own pram. Mrs Linton [essayist, 1880s] contrasted English mothers with French ones, who promenaded beside their 'bonnes' as a matter of course. 'Here, the woman who once had one nursemaid now has two . . . the shabbiest little wife with her two financial ends gaping, must have her still shabbier little drudge to wheel her perambulator.'

Christina Hardyment, social historian

The pram evolved for a while alongside the motor car (invented in 1865) and reached its apotheosis in the 1920s with the

Dunkley motorised model, complete with standing platform for the nursemaid to enjoy the ride. But the reign of the posh perambulator could not last. It was cumbersome, it was cold, it had been over-used as a day bed at the bottom of the garden (where baby's cries could least be heard), and it enforced even further the separation of mother and baby. The future of baby-pushing was low-tech, not high-tech.

Today's lightweight, foldaway, all-terrain baby buggy is a much more flexible beast. Designed for occasional trundling, not all-day parades, it allows the baby to move from the car to the shops to the sling to his parents' arms with a kick and the flick of a plastic lever. Some parents put the baby in the sling and use the buggy as a kind of shopping trolley. Others allow determined toddlers to use the buggy as a form of baby walker. The modern baby is no longer the passive passenger, jostled along despite his own desires. His personal transport has been reshaped to suit his very own consumer requirements.

The High Chair

A breast-fed or bottle-fed baby, who has been trained to take his broth from a spoon, sitting up in a chair, will not give much trouble at weaning time.

The Motherhood Book, London, c. 1930

At the end of the sixteenth century, a few homes started to sport a new piece of furniture: the elevated infant chair. Following the example of kings and princes, it soon became customary for the infant to dine in his 'high chair', rather than nestled comfortably in someone's lap. 'Prints and paintings of the sixteenth and seventeenth centuries often show a child at table, perched in a little high-chair out of which he cannot fall; it must have been in one of these chairs that [Louis XIII] sat at his mother's table, like other children in other families.' (Philippe Ariès, childhood historian).

The high chair was a way of educating small people to eat at table, to sit upright and to master the mysterious art of table manners. By the eighteenth century, the high chair was a standard piece of equipment in middle-class homes, from the highly fashionable and ornate to the basic 'Windsor' design. Some were more sophisticated than others:

An early eighteenth-century (non-Windsor) example in Christchurch Mansion, Ipswich, has been furnished with a detachable front consisting of a shelf and below it a railed cage to prevent the baby from slipping out. Below that again is a small box with a pierced top which could be used to contain a footwarmer on the same principle as the stool-footwarmers seen in many Dutch pictures of the seventeenth century.

F. Gordon Roe, historian

Wherever he sat, the noble child was not about to get cold toes.

The Baby Walker

When it is stronger, let it not stand too soon, but be held by the nurse, or put into a go-chair, that it may thrust forward itself, and not fall.

Nicholas Culpeper, herbalist, 1651

The original baby walker was not so much a 'go-chair' as a wicker cage, a kind of crinoline which kept babies upright and off the floor. It was to prevent babies from crawling, rather than encouraging them to walk, that the item was first invented. By keeping infants' feet on the ground, their bodies upright and their leg muscles active, the wicker frame probably did seem to produce upright citizens – a goal highly prized by European culture. It made the baby appear less animalistic and it kept him occupied. But, as with every new baby-oriented innovation, the experts were sceptical:

. . . there are stools for children to stand in, in which they can turn around any way, when mothers or nurses see them in it, then they care no more for the child, let it alone, go about their own business, supposing the child to be well provided, but they little think on the pain and misery the poor child is in . . . the poor child . . . must stand maybe hours, whereas half an hour standing is too long . . . I wish that all such standing stools were burned.

Felix Würtz, German physician, 1563

The principle of baby-standing was only a wheel or two away from that of baby-walking. Now came the go-chair, a contraption in which the child – half standing, half sitting – propelled himself forward long before he would have been toddling by himself. Sixteenth-century Italian babies were placed in a 'running stool'; eighteenth-century English babies moved around in a 'baby trotter' and in the 1970s and 80s, the baby walker, a large disc of plastic into which the child was buckled, became a common feature in many western homes. Even in rural India, some children learn to walk this way:

One family had a wooden walker, consisting of a cross T-bar on three wheels, with an upright handle built on the cross bar of the T. We were told that the family had bought this for a boy who was slow in learning to walk. This was the only walker we saw in the village, although they were sold at the spring *mēlā* [market].

Leigh Minturn and John Hitchcock, anthropologists

Unless they are used in highly limited ways, baby walkers can do more harm than good. Physical therapists say young muscles are too weak to support the body. In an effort to maintain balance, babies' feet tend to turn inwards. According to the British Royal Society for the Prevention of Accidents, between twelve and fifty per cent of babies left in walkers end up with injuries – usually to the head and face, as they topple forwards. Collisions with fires, falling downstairs and crashing through plate-glass are just some of the frequently-recorded injuries associated with strapping a baby into his own excessively-mobile unit.

I recall a mother who, many years ago, proudly claimed that her son had been 'walking' since he was six months old, with the aid of his baby walker. Unfortunately, this practice had produced unusual body-use in the child who, at around fifteen months, marched without bending his knees and had a tendency to fall over backwards. Unlike the free-range child, for whom learning to fall is at least as important as learning to walk, the artificially-supported baby does not learn how to save himself. In this case, the mother was forced to run after her boy, picking him up wherever he went.

Despite all the evidence – and repeated warnings from paediatricians – a recent study of American parents revealed that most believe the baby walker to be beneficial to infant development.

The Playpen

A nursery fence two feet high, made to surround a mattress, makes an excellent box stall for the young animal.

> Luther Emmett Holt, American paediatrician, *The Care and Feeding of Children*, 1943, 24th edition)

Babies should not be dandled up and down, said Victorian experts, for fear of injuring the brain or spine. They must be left to kick and play – but this play must be restricted, of course, in a house full of furniture and precious bric-à-brac. And so, the playpen was invented. Domestic historian Christina Hardyment calls the playpen a 'convenient prison' and it is hard to see it any other way, since (like a criminal) the baby is kept behind bars and out of potential mischief. In fact, it is surprising that the playpen has lasted at all, since babies with a gram of curiosity hate to be put in there, no matter how many plastic toys and teddies are thrown in.

Most baby equipment is designed for the convenience of the

child carer, not for the edification of the child, whatever the manufacturers say. In western society, the playpen has survived because parents are willing to put up with children's temporary unhappiness in order to get some momentary peace for themselves. In traditional cultures, where the contentment of the baby is intricately bound to the relaxation of parents, clashes between child and theory are not allowed to endure.

Here is the extremely brief history of the playpen as invented by a Yequana father in the Venezuelan jungle:

It had upright sticks lashed with vines to an upper and lower square frame, like a strip-cartoon version of a prehistoric playpen. It had cost a good deal of labour, and Tududu looked quite pleased with himself … He cast about for Cananasinyuwana, his son, who had taken his first step about a week earlier. No sooner had Tududu sighted the tot than he snatched him up and put him triumphantly in the new invention. Cananasinyuwana stood uncomprehending for a few seconds at the centre, then made a move to one side, turned about and realized that he was trapped. In an instant he was screaming a message of utter horror, a sound rarely heard from children of his society. It was unequivocal. The playpen was wrong, unsuitable for human babies . . . Tududu accepted the failure of his experiment without question; after a moment's last look at his handiwork, he smashed the playpen to bits with an axe.

Jean Liedloff, continuum therapist

Reins and Leading Strings

Her Majesty recommended leading strings – a band round the waist, with a loop on each side, of a length to hold, so as to support the child in case she should stumble, and I immediately attended to this advice.

Charlotte Papendiek, assistant keeper of the wardrobe to Queen Charlotte, consort to King George III of England, 1785

Babies walk, they fall, they pick themselves up again and, all over the world, nobody takes the least bit of notice. But a growing sensibility to infant frailty in seventeenth-century Europe changed all that. It was felt that attaching a pair of braces to the child's clothing was necessary to help teach him to walk. The fashion probably kicked off with the refined needs of royalty: as early as 1602, we discover that the nine-month-old future Louis XIII of France is having leading strings attached to his robe 'to teach him to walk'. And when royals find new ways to be delicate, we can be sure that other classes will follow suit.

In the seventeenth century, leading strings were sewn on to children's outer clothes as soon as they came out of their swaddling bands – which in Britain was at four to six weeks of age. In fashionable homes, these were not strings at all, but wide bands of material, which hung down the back and elegantly matched the child's dress. The fashion grew, and evidently the strings were not meant merely for toddlers. One English mother tells her husband she needs purpose-made reins for their four-year-old son: 'Pray desire cousin Peg to buy me a pair of leading strings for Jack. There is stuff made on purpose that is very strong, for he is so heavy I dare not venture him with common ribbon.' (Catherine Verney, Claydon House, Buckinghamshire, 1715). Even dolls of the period wore leading strings, so that little girls could drag them around as they themselves were dragged, pulled and even swung.

When everyone was satisfied that a child could manage alone, there was a ceremonial cutting of the leading strings (a variation on being tied to the 'apron strings', which meant the child had spent too long under his mother's influence). This was a proud occasion for all concerned. The child probably tottered a little at his new-found freedom, since he, too, was convinced he could not walk without adult assistance: 'Upon the 1st I cut the child's strings off from her coats and made her use togs [wear clothes] alone, so as she had two or three falls at first but had no hurt with them,' writes Lady Anne Clifford of Cumbria in her journal about her daughter Margaret, aged nearly two, in 1615.

Harnessing babies on reins remains popular today, and lively children can often be seen straining at the leash like frustrated puppies. For parents who prefer not to lead their children by their tails, there is still the old-fashioned expedient of holding the child's hand – a tactile connection which allows for greater intimacy and a far subtler range of communication.

The Teddy Bear

He sat down on the floor, holding the bear tightly in his arms, wave after wave of relief washing over him in a warm, relaxing flood. All his life long, ever since he could remember, more than three years now, he had gone to sleep with his big Teddy in his arms. The sight of the faithful pointed face, like no other face, the friendly staring black eyes, the familiar feel of the dear, woolly body close to him – they were saturated with a thousand memories of peace, with a thousand associations of comfort and escape from trouble.

Dorothy Canfield, novelist, 1924

It was D.W. Winnicott, paediatrician and psychiatrist, who made us all appreciate the importance of the transitional object. A transitional object, he said – whether it be a blanket, a teddy bear or a scarf – is invested with magical powers by the baby. The child fixes on the object because he must fix on some reliable comfort source, and the 'blankie' or 'teddy' does not leave him while he sleeps. Adults understand this attachment and they respect it. If you have ever seen a child in panic over a lost teddy bear, notice the seriousness with which everyone takes this loss, and the energy they put into finding the treasured toy.

With an interest in encouraging solitary infant sleep, western culture has for years promoted the use of transitional objects. Attachment to people is judged negatively (the child is deemed 'clingy'), but attachment to things is considered natural and acceptable.

Better than lying with your toddler or young child until he falls asleep at night is for him to fall asleep with a 'transitional object' – a stuffed animal, a doll, a toy, a special blanket. The toy will often help him accept the night-time separation from you and can be a source of reassurance and comfort when he is alone. It will give him a feeling of having a little control over his world because he may have the toy or blanket with him whenever he wants, which he cannot expect from you . . .

But if you always allow yourself to be used in the manner of such an object – to lie with him, to feed or rock him, to be held, cuddled or caressed by him, or let him twirl your hair whenever he tries to fall asleep – he will never take on a transitional object, because he won't need to.

Dr Richard Ferber, American paediatrician

This circular argument is a classic of modern paediatric thinking. The doctor advises parents to help their child 'animate' an object, so that the parents do not become 'objectified' as sources of comfort. We get the sense that Ferber will be disappointed if babies do *not* invest strong emotions in a soft animal. There is no mention of the loss that a child must experience in order to transfer his affections to a piece of material that doesn't argue or love back or, indeed, offer any quality other than that of being tactile. Nor is there any sense that, in encouraging children to choose these special toys, we might be creating an unhealthy and lifelong reliance on inanimate objects.

Psychoanalyst Sigmund Freud said that 'animism' – the transference of human attributes to material objects – is our first system of thought, our first psychology. It is a process which allows ordinary items to hold special meanings, a tendency which lasts throughout our life. Some child care experts reverse this argument to imply that the evolved interactions of parent and baby may somehow steal the limelight from the teddy bear. Have we, like the child, forgotten that the bear is just a bit of fabric with a face sewn on?

Attachment objects are the recourse of babies who are being trained for independence before they are ready to take it.

Whether it is an expensive teddy bear or a ragged bit of stuffing makes no difference to the baby. It is the familiarity he seeks: the same smell, the same feel, the same fibres pressed against his skin, as he tries anxiously to inhale some of the human associations for which he is programmed.

Western babies seek comforters between the ages of nine months and a year – around the time of weaning, according to Winnicott; or 'as babyhood draws to a close', according to zoologist Desmond Morris. In fact, of course, neither babyhood nor breastfeeding are over by nine months in traditional cultures. The attachment object is entirely a symptom of our own child care practices, at this point in our cultural development.

In a study of London mothers whose babies were born at home, birth researcher Dr Michel Odent discovered that one main factor predicted babies' use, or non-use, of security objects. Children who were breastfed at night for more than a year did not need them. At the other end of the scale, children who are severely deprived of human bonding experiences (babies in old-fashioned foundling homes and orphanages, for instance) do not seek comfort objects, either. They have withdrawn too far to attach to anything. Michel Odent suggested that 'the need for a transitional object is a healthy reaction of a normal child to a special situation'.

Needless to say, you can't have transitional teddy bears in a world with minimal possessions. Children evolved to attach primarily to their mothers and secondarily to any other humans who presented themselves with affection. Hunter-gatherer tribes did not have to search the bush for their babies' lost 'blankies' when they should really have been searching for berries.

Babies of rural Egypt, for instance, receiving non-stop nurture and attention, by night and day, have no choice but to attach themselves to people:

In large extended families adults and children, who are consistently loving and nur-turing, surround infants and engage them in almost constant social interaction. These infants do not have toys to play with and do not form attachments to blankets or dolls as do American infants. They learn to play with people, not inanimate objects.

Judy Brink, anthropologist, in Giza, an area one hour's drive from Cairo

Babies who are separated for sleep are likely to become attached to the paraphernalia around them: some Skagit Native American children in Washington, for instance, drag their cradleboards around while they play, in the manner of a security object. But there is absolutely nothing 'fundamental' about the use of mother-substitutes when there is a mother or other willing to play the role. Many children around the world grow up without beanies, bears, blankets and crucial bits of bedding.

BEADS FOR BABIES

The modern baby is distracted by a plethora of plastic and a range of interactional toys. One popular item is the educational baby gym, introduced to England from America in the 1840s. Rogers's Patent Infant Gymnasium arrived around the same time as the new Baby Jumper, a fore-runner of the popular 'baby bouncer'.

The earliest human societies had few toys to offer their children and even fewer for under-ones to play with. The !Kung San infant in Africa's Kalahari Desert plays with his mother's person, her beads, her hair. Later, he will graduate to 'toys' made from twigs and flowers, insects and stones. His imagination must work overtime to create his own, unique fantasy world.

Electric Dreams

You can't be with your baby 24 hours a day. Baby Link can.
                    Advertisement for Tomy's Electronic Baby Link Nursery Monitor

The Baby Link lets parents listen in to their babies, although, as cot death researchers now realise, it might be healthier to let babies listen in to their parents (aural stimulation is one of the routes for promoting steady breathing and lighter, healthier sleep).

The Baby Link advert includes a picture of mother enjoying a romantic dinner with the man in her life, romance being a requirement the western mother may not dodge, if she is to 'keep' or 'save' her relationship with the baby's father. And so baby monitors neatly preserve the nuclear family arrangement, promoting marital romance and infant sleep training with one flick of a switch.

Western culture does not expect parents to be on full-time duty. In fact, a major assumption is that dancing twenty-four-hour attendance on a baby is neither possible nor desirable. Many traditional communities would agree. That is why they share the responsibility for child care, each mother supported by a large circle of willing hands.

A wide range of electric gadgets subtly enhances the sleep environment for western babies. Night lights, for instance, are now an essential part of the kit list, and many children are weaned into solitary sleeping by simply leaving a light on. In some families, the landing light will do, while for others, cartoon lamps deliver a reliable nightly glow, ironing out the shadows of the lonely nursery. Meanwhile, newborn babies are lulled to sleep with an increasingly sophisticated range of 'dream' machines. These send animated lights up to the ceiling, or run a *son et lumière* sequence on the side of the cot.

The problem with night lights is that humans are designed to sleep in darkness. Studies show that babies who regularly sleep with a light on are five times more likely to be short-sighted in later life. It is interesting to speculate that the experience of *not* seeing in the dark might be an evolved aspect of infant development. Darkness is an opportunity for the other senses to take over and be passively honed. The night light steals away the body's chance to exercise these skills.

The Artificial Heartbeat

At last, the product parents would have given anything for since time began . . . The most natural comfort in the world . . .

It could be 3 a.m. or 3 p.m. What wouldn't you give for a product that will calm young children down. Then everyone could get some rest. But the moment you put them down – Waah! It's almost as if they can sense your heartbeat – and of course they can.

Advertisement for 'Heartbeat', a baby sleep-inducing device, 1990s

Nothing more natural indeed – unless you are a parent from Africa, Asia, the Middle East or South America. Then it might seem very unnatural to have to 'invest' (as the advertisement urges you to do) in a gadget to mimic the sound of your heart because your baby is too far away to hear the real thing.

A mother's own heartbeat is music to a baby's ears, and some devices use that music to create a sleep-inducing atmosphere. Babies in the neonatal unit at Derriford Hospital, Plymouth, are, apparently, lulled to sleep by rhythms composed using a synthesiser, the human heartbeat and recorded sounds from the womb.

Meanwhile, parents can buy products like SmartSleep, a CD of classical music designed to pave the way for calmer infant slumber and more intelligent dreams: 'Not only can mothers give their babies important brain stimulation, but at the same time they can help them calm down and go to sleep with this collection of some of the most soothing piano music ever written' (SmartSleep promotion).

Used by hospitals in thirty-two American states, SmartSleep is undoubtedly a pleasant addition to the clinical atmosphere. No researchers have yet demonstrated any harm that can arise from falling asleep to Bach's Aria in G major. Our ears do keep listening while we sleep, and music is one very beautiful way to fill the void.

HOME TRUTHS

Planning a nursery and its equipment is a fascinating occupation . . .
Good Housekeeping's Mothercraft, 1959

Heard the one about the mum and dad packing for their summer holiday? Into their brand-new people mover they cram the travel cot, the buggy, the clip-on high chair and a fortnight's supply of nappies. Then they add a box of baby food, high-factor sun creams, armbands, beach toys, a parasol and a range of unbreakable plastic tableware. Having squeezed in a small suitcase for themselves, they drive away, delighted at a job well done. Only they've forgotten something – the baby, sitting glumly in his multi-coloured car seat, on the drive.

Only in the past few hundred years have we witnessed the equipment explosion which results in this urban fairy-tale. The early Victorian baby had few toys and no special furniture for sleeping, transportation, feeding or playing. He did not even have a nursery in which to listen to his collection of hot-house CDs. The human infant had to satisfy himself through the comfort of his mother's body – her body was his mattress, her arms his carry cot, her skin his very own central heating. Her heartbeat and her lullabies were his first and only music.

Increasingly, parents are expected to protect, train and edu-cate their babies using purpose-made products. And as with so many aspects of child care, the lure of these products is spreading from West to East. Baby equipment is a desirable commodity for the rising middle-classes, an outward symbol of a particular kind of parenting.

In Egypt, for instance, the more educated the mother, the more likely she is to buy a crib, a swing and a stroller. Although the number of 'educated' women in a rural Egyptian village is classed as small, their use of equipment makes a marked impact on local child-rearing decisions. To push a baby around in a buggy rather than carry him in arms is almost as grand as being the first family to own a car.

A move towards baby equipment also creates new choices: child-rearing methods which have survived for millennia are challenged by the sight of the first baby-bouncer or cot. Choice in turn brings self-doubt – and as western parents know from the experience of the past hundred years, the antidote to doubt is to spend more money. The 'best' parents are those with a roomful of plastic toys and a stairgate wedged in the doorway.

One day, perhaps, every country will have its own consumer protection organisation to protect people from their own mate-rial consumption. Babies, meanwhile, will be increasingly restricted to a purposefully manufactured, artificially 'safe' and standardised environment.

When I was expecting my first baby, a friend told me in hushed tones exactly how much it cost her to set up her baby's nursery, kitting him out in all the best clothes, buying bottles and sterilising equipment, three kinds of cot for three kinds of sleep (night-time, day-time and travel-time), and a list of toys to make the Hamleys' manager rub his hands with glee.

I determined to try to do things on the cheap – partly by

buying second-hand (a step in the right direction), but mostly by not buying much at all. My New Baby Budget was a tenth of my friend's original estimate. Oddly enough, not one of my babies put in a customer complaint.

2. Baby Born

It's the moment of birth. Chemical reactions are high as mother and baby simultaneously separate and rendezvous for the first time. Many cultures believe that the newborn is not yet a complete person, but a spiritual creature who will slowly become part of the human community. Birth, they say, is just one phase in a soul's journey through the universe.

Hello Baby

Two newborn babies don't resemble each other any more than an Eskimo and a Papuan do.

And yet . . .

Curiously, during the first moments, all newborn babies are alike. For a brief period, it is still as if they had no identity at all.

Frédérick Leboyer, natural birth pioneer

Ache babies of Paraguay arrive with a full head of hair. Aboriginal babies in central Australia are a pale, pinkish yellow, quite unlike their dark-skinned parents. Rajput babies of Khalapur, India, are said to be born with their hands shut — in other words, they come complete from God and need nothing from the material world. And some Tibetan babies are said to change sex in the few days after birth. Even in infancy, the world is more diverse than many of us might believe.

Throughout history, more than half of the world's population has consisted of people under twenty-one. In the past, young people followed the ways of the old. Traditions bound communities together. But now most babies enter a world where change is the keyword; where traditions cannot be taken for granted and the beliefs of the older generations seem suddenly irrelevant.

Today's children will take their place in the wide spectrum of experience which some call 'global' culture. But at the moment of birth none of this seems significant. For now, all baby knows is you: your face, your touch, your familiar voice and even your aroma. These are the immediate future he desires. You mean all the world to him.

The First Cry

Yossi cried loudly at being thrust out of paradise. Suddenly here was gravity, air, and loving, but clumsy, hands holding him . . . All that was needed to complete the scene was some idiot saying 'Healthy pair of lungs!'

Jenny Goodman, a mother from London, describes the birth of her son

Batangueño babies of the Philippines call to their godparents with their very first cry. If the cry is loud and shrill, then godparents may be chosen from a distant village. But if the birth cry is faint, his godparents are summoned from nearby.

It's easy to see why a baby's spiritual fate is so closely connected to his birth cry. This first inhalation is the moment of truth. A lusty yell is the clearest initial sign that all is well; a weak cry is an alarm. Air itself is the trigger for that first in-breath – it takes the baby five times more effort than ordinary breathing.

Malaysian families say the newborn baby utters three prayers which endow him with three aspects of his spirit. There is the soul, or '*ruh*', which stays with him all his life; '*semgangat*', the spirit of life which fills the universe and the body, but which may be depleted by stress or fear and '*nyawa*', the breath of life, which animates the infant body at birth. Nyawa is related to '*pneuma*', the Greek concept for the human spirit, or breath.

Like the ancient Greeks, Malays believe that the breath of life must be inhaled within seconds of being born.

Air and cold – the natural conditions of emergence from the womb – are usually enough to arouse the baby. Few doctors still hold babies upside down by their feet and smack them. But, as Frédérick Leboyer, passionate advocate of peaceful birth, insisted, there must *be* a birth-cry. 'If the child is born stunned, if it is limp,' he wrote, 'if it is waiting instead of crying, every step should be taken instantly to produce a sharp satisfactory cry.'

It is a powerful moment, whether your baby is born into the bright lights of a modern delivery room, or into a hushed, darkened inner sanctum, like the sacred birth spaces created by women in Korea. Osage Native Americans of Missouri say a baby's first cry is a prayer he learnt before descending to earth, an appeal to Grandfather Sun and the Woman Moon.

Even societies with a calm, unhurried approach to childbirth have emergency measures for stimulating a swift response in a reluctant newborn. Some splash the baby with cold water or blow alcohol onto his heart. Others – like the midwives of the Pacific islands of Samoa – bounce him up and down. Balinese mothers say babies sleep solidly through birth and must be shaken awake.

Noise is another useful agent. During ancient Egyptian birth, a servant would shake the '*sistrum*', an early kind of tambourine. Among the Tausog, a remote Philippine tribe, the newborn emerges to the bang of a gong. They believe this noisy introduction will make the baby immune from fright. Wake up! Wake up! And welcome to the world!

Big, Fat, Beautiful Baby

> You may not call me beautiful or
> the spirits will steal me away,
> especially if I'm fat.
>
> Anonymous, Cambodia

The classic modern birth announcement presents a baby's vital statistics: his names, his date of arrival and – amazingly – his weight at birth. This particular detail means little to the uninitiated. It has greater significance for any woman who has been through childbirth.

The birth weight of baby is the kind of thing we westerners like to know. It's the question people are most likely to ask after establishing the gender and name of the baby. It is as if we can calculate our pride in pounds and ounces. Of course, birth weight was simply not measurable in antiquity and has never been a priority in the middle of the rainforest.

Somehow, however, anthropologists have extracted the information that Efé pygmy mothers (standing four-foot-five inches high and weighing just eighty pounds) routinely give birth to eight-pound babies without analgesic. This one-tenth ratio compares to a 130 lb westerner giving birth to a 13 lb infant, a disproportion few would relish. According to birth researcher Dr Michel Odent, the Efé are not the only women in the world giving birth to bigger babies. 'The plump, chubby-cheeked baby is a human creation,' he says, suggesting that inter-racial marriage and sugary, high-fat diets are to blame.

We in the West have a predisposition towards fat babies. In English folklore, it is said that the midwife is rewarded by the weight of the baby she helps to deliver – and researchers have even tested the hypothesis. Hospital doctors in Somerset discovered that the bigger the baby, the bigger the box of chocolates given to the midwife. There was 'an association between birth weight and net chocolate weight, with a linear correlation equation of $y = 3349 + 0.52058x$', they said.

We don't need maths to tell us that a bonny baby is well nourished. In western culture, the equation is almost blindly positive, with an emphasis on bulk, never mind how we achieve it. In many parts of the world, baby's dimple is considered a sign of good luck: the more folds in his skin, the better. The French have a saying: '*Il n'y a rien de plus beau que la graisse sous la peau*'

(There's nothing more attractive than fat under the skin).

To call a newborn 'scrawny' is the greatest insult to an American or European mother. But not all the world shares this opinion. Some tribeswomen agree with the Okinawan islanders near Japan, who recommend an active pregnancy to keep the birth weight of baby down. 'If you had worked hard, the baby would not be so big, and labour would not be difficult,' older women are apt to scold young mothers. In countries where the 'evil' or jealous eye might threaten the baby's health, fat babies are also a provocation to the gods.

However, many reports confirm the health and well-being of newborn babies around the world. The Hmong people of south-east Asia, for instance, have been the subject of thorough-going obstetric studies since their emigration to America. Hmong women display many of the risk factors for premature or low birth weight babies and Caesarian section: these include immigrant status, advanced age, many previous children, short stature, anaemia and refusing antenatal care until late in the pregnancy. Yet they have surprisingly successful birth outcomes: their babies are a good weight and are not generally born too early.

Babies born in rural Malaysia and among the Gusii people of Kenya, East Africa, also emerge at weights comparable with British and American babies. Clearly, healthy babies are born in a diverse range of backgrounds, despite wide differences in pregnancy diets and beliefs about birth. It is known that nature prioritises the growing foetus, even when there is a shortage of food.

There may also be other clues to a baby's birth weight that we have not considered. Perhaps one key is the community support which many pregnant women receive. A recent study from London showed that mothers who received lots of pregnancy support were more likely to give birth to heavier babies.

'Women who had a good social network with several types of support from different sources during pregnancy had higher birthweight babies compared to those who had fewer people to call on,' said Dr Pamela Feldman of University College. 'It was a definite trend . . . Our findings suggest social support may alter the responses of the nervous system to stress and improve fetal growth . . . It's not a situation where pregnant women need help from family or nurses and GPs – they need practical support from a wide range of people.'

While we proudly record our baby's birth weights and other vital statistics in purpose-made baby books, most of the world is busy trying not to tempt fate. Some babies will never know their own birth date, weight, or ever learn to write their own name. Even a small thing like a baby birth announcement makes us realise just how variable the world can be.

I Only Have Eyes for You . . .

It is a unique moment, that first meeting of a mother and her new-born baby, the first glance at the mysterious creature that for months has been carried and nursed in the secret of the womb, and now has become a different, forever independent human being, with features inherited from generations of ancestors.

I held out my hands. Perfect head, tanned skin, dark golden fuzz of hair, and, extraordinary for a new-born baby, open, direct, intense and knowing blue eyes.

Kuki Gallmann, conservationist in Africa, recalls giving birth

Babies have big eyes, all the better to see you with. At birth, infant vision is not perfect, but it is honed to one specific task: focusing on the nearest face. Distant objects and colours are a hazy blur, but then it would be impossible for a baby to take in so much new information at once. His first aim is to gaze into his mother's pupils, at exactly breastfeeding-distance away.

Eye-contact is vitally important in helping a baby to learn about his world. His eyes gauge every parental reaction, drinking in expressions and noticing small changes. Scientists say that mothers instinctively place themselves where they can see directly into a newborn baby's eyes. But just in case adults should not realise the importance of eye-contact, nature has designed the baby's face so they can't miss the point.

For their body size, babies' eyes are relatively bigger than ours, and so are their pupils, the black centres of the eye which work like a camera lens. Whenever we see people or things we find attractive, our pupils enlarge to take in more light – and babies' pupils do the same when they first gaze at a friendly face. No wonder some cultures believe that looking into a baby's eyes is to see into his soul.

Pale-skinned babies are usually born with blue eyes. A bright-blue iris is the perfect frame to show off baby's large pupils. But African and other infants with dark pigments are born with dark brown eyes. Perhaps eye-appeal was not so crucial in mankind's original African habitat, where a warm climate ensured that most babies were given lots of skin-to-skin contact without having to flutter their eyelids. The further our ancestors moved from the equator, the more need for clothes and the greater the possibility of separation between mother and baby. Could baby blue eyes be a cold-climate appeal to be held tight?

Whatever the evolutionary theory, eye-contact is a deliciously perpetual circle which helps to ensure mutual attraction. It's just one part of the elusive 'bonding' which experts love to argue about. ('Bonding' is a relatively new term, coined by European scientists in the 1930s.) The newborn condition is one of dependency, as the Native American tribes understood and respected – but this does not mean that babies are powerless. On the contrary, their evident vulnerability is their evolved strategy for survival. On the Lakota Medicine Wheel, infancy is the beginning, the east, the sunrise of life.

We all start our lives in the east . . . This is the time of the infant, or new-born . . . the power of an infant is the power of dependency. Though now a separate being, an infant has no ability to provide for itself. Yet it has a power to communicate its needs and compel others to provide for it. Many look upon this dependency as a weakness, yet it is something that we all deal with within our-selves throughout our lives.

Grey Wolf, author and educator, Lakota community

PARTY TIME!

A newly-delivered mother and her brand-new baby are under the influence of a cocktail of chemicals. There's a party going on for the post-partum pair, and no one else is invited.

Much as father may want to play his part and the mother-in-law is ready to have her first hold, mother and baby really only have eyes for each other. This is due to the fact that they are hormone high. A heady complement of the love hormone oxytocin – at levels higher than during labour   and prolactin (the mothering hormone) set the scene. These are stirred with a swift rush of adrenalin during the very last contractions before the delivery of the baby. And finally, there are the endorphins, released by both mother and infant. 'There is no doubt that, for a certain time following birth, both mother and baby are impregnated with opiates. The property of opiates to induce states of dependency is well known, so it easy to anticipate how . . . an attachment will be likely to develop' (Michel Odent, obstetrician and primal health researcher).

Deep in the Ituri rainforest of Zaire in the heart of Africa, the Efé pygmy mother sings a song of pure joy to her newborn baby. All through her labour, she has been singing and walking, supported on either side by midwives whose sole job is to stay in harmony with her as she delivers her baby by the riverside.

After the birth, she has no reason to conceal her overwhelming feelings of rapture:

> My heart is so joyous,
> My heart flies in singing.
> Under the trees of the forest,
> The forest, our home, our mother.
> In my net I have caught
> A little bird,
> And my heart is caught
> In the net with my little bird.
>
> Song of the Efé pygmy mother

Feelings of love, a desire to protect, being alert and highly receptive to attachment − these are the chemically-induced states of the new mother. And since her baby is programmed to be mothered and be utterly dependent, they make a perfect match. Ready or not, they are primed to fall in love.

Don't I Know You?

This is a climactic moment and [the baby] should not be cheated of it by over-efficient professionals − with what could be called *partus interruptus*.

Desmond Morris, zoologist

A mother and her newborn 'recognise' each other in a variety of ways after birth. Of course, visual cues are the first step for parents as they eagerly scan their new baby. But one study of Israeli mothers proved they could identify their own infants merely by touch. Breastfeeding mothers were unexpectedly asked to stroke three newborn babies' hands and, without looking, name their own baby. By chance, thirty-three per cent of guesses should have been correct, but the mothers managed an amazing seventy per cent.

Other research has shown that mothers unconsciously touch

their newborn babies in the same way the first time they meet. They tend to begin by touching the fingers, move across the palms of their tiny hands, along the arms, down the legs and around the baby's trunk. This is one of many untaught processes which have convinced scientists that there really is such a thing as maternal instinct. When babies are born in unstressed circumstances, something propels the mother to hold her baby in preconditioned ways:

It was a beautiful birth, with the mother aiding and comforting her daughter as she gave birth to her own new baby girl. Although the baby had entered the world and become physically separated from her mother, she still had all of the warmth and security her mother could provide. Rosine was laid at her mother's breast, able to rest, nurse and hear her mother's voice and heartbeat. Birth therefore became more of a change in environment than a separation between people.

Jan Reynolds, journalist and photographer, witnesses birth
in the Himalayan mountains

Observers of natural birth have said that, given the choice, most mothers do not immediately place their newborns on their stomach. The instinctive reaction seems to be to cradle the baby to one side, offering the breast, stroking the infant and interacting with words and looks. However, if a baby is placed skinto-skin on to a mother's abdomen, a strange and wonderful thing occurs. In the space of an hour, the baby crawls towards the breast entirely by himself.

If he has not been drugged with labour medication and not removed from his mother, the infant will even initiate his first feed, showing a preference for the unwashed areola, the nipple area which is untouched by perfume. He turns his head towards the natural-smelling breast even before he can see it. In Nashville, Tennessee, scientists demonstrated that mothers also could identify their new babies purely by smell, even when postnatal contact had been limited. This aromatic connection is a strong, silent bond which helps to 'glue' mother and baby together, whether they are awake or asleep.

Zulu women of South Africa consider it essential to hold a newborn baby immediately, so that the infant may learn exactly who his mother is. Among the Hausa people of northern Nigeria, a young mother is ritually compelled by female relatives to touch and suckle her first-born baby. The traditional community takes a collective responsibility for awakening the first strains of maternal behaviour.

However, not every baby is given the chance to reunite with his mother's skin. In what can only be seen as postnatal panic, birth attendants in western-style hospitals sometimes intrude into the first intimate moments between a mother and baby. This has an immediate effect on the baby's early acclimatisation. In one Swedish study, most newborns began to cry when they were taken away from their mothers for just twenty minutes. On their return, half of these babies displayed a 'poor suckle'. It is entirely normal for healthy infants to protest when they are whisked away for their five-point (Apgar) check, plus clean-up-and-weigh session.

Before the cord is cut, before the baby is weighed, before the cup of tea, the phonecalls, the clean nightie or the arrival of a room full of visitors, there is this one precious moment. It is a shame to hurry it.

Enter the Placenta

Treat it as for liver cutting into strips and frying lightly with onions. Alternatively, fry the strips lightly in oil with garlic, add wine and cream. Serve with rice.

Placenta recipe, England 1998

In English, they call it the 'third stage' of labour, a mere number to signify the order of events at a delivery. Sometimes it's the 'afterbirth', a word reminiscent of 'afterthought', which also expresses our culture's apparent lack of interest in the furniture of the womb. At best we have the Latin medical term '*placenta uterina*', which means 'flat cake of the uterus'.

Few cultures treat the placenta with similar disregard. For the Balinese, it is an organ of enormous vitality and deep spiritual significance. They call it the 'life force', and until its arrival, the baby is not considered fully alive. The nomadic people of Gabbra, in north-western Kenya, use the same word, 'aku', for both placenta and midwife, since both assist in bringing a new baby into the world. The Gusii of Kenya call it the 'omogoye' or protective binding, essential for the recovery of ill babies.

Hmong people from Laos in south-east Asia call the placenta 'the jacket' – a person's first and finest garment. When a Hmong dies, his soul retraces the journey of life until it reaches the spot where the jacket was buried. Wearing this precious protective item, the soul goes through many adventures to the place beyond the sky, to be reunited with the ancestors. One day it will be reborn as a new baby. It causes untold heartache to Hmong immigrant parents when the placenta is discarded by American doctors. It may not occur to doctors that the placenta bears enormous spiritual significance – just as it may not occur to a Hmong mother that anyone could dream of throwing the placenta away.

An increasing number of western mothers are also asking to see and to keep their placentas. But this is a privilege not yet enshrined in our philosophy:

Some British women today ask to have their placentas for food or ritual   but are told they can't have them! The placenta is the mother's property – an organ from her body – and should not be disposed of without the mother's consent. In the old days, hospitals used to whip the placentas away so that they could sell them off to cosmetic and face cream manufacturers (though this practice is supposed to have largely died out due to worries about HIV and Hepatitis).

Pat Thomas, editor of *AIMS Journal*, Association for
Improvements in the Maternity Services

Although the third stage of labour is regarded as tricky in western circles, early texts and traditional cultures do not report great anxiety over the process. 'Few of the midwives I talked to in south-east Asia had experienced any problems with the delivery of the placenta,' says birth researcher Jacqueline Vincent Priya, 'although most were aware of the problems which might occur if it did not appear reasonably soon after birth. Generally, they either just waited for it to appear or massaged the mother's stomach to help it on its way.'

Waiting, trusting: these are the skills of traditional midwifery. The placenta has nurtured the unborn child for nine months and most midwives are in no hurry to sever the connection. It is only when the placenta can no longer provide efficient oxygen exchange that birth is triggered. The placenta is both the guardian of the womb and the alarm clock of childbirth.

This is a story of a girl who has just had her baby under a tree. Our mother, grandmother or nursemother would take us to the tree. We would stay under the tree until the bag, or placenta (*jarre*) came out. Someone would make a small hole. The nursemother or grandmother would help us push the bag out, then lay us over the hole so that the bloodclots (*manngu*) and bag (*jarre*) would go into the hole. Then they would wash us, cover us up with warm bush around our body, making us heal up inside quick. The baby would lay next to us near the fire and feed. We would stay there for one or two days.

Mona Ramsay, Aboriginal woman of Warmun, Western Australia

In many traditions, the fate of the placenta is spiritually linked to the fate of the child. The two have cohabited for nine months, and the placenta is often given the status of spiritual sibling. At the very least, it is imbued with the womb's mystery and magic. Each society has its own rituals for handling the placenta, which is deemed to have powers over the well-being of the newborn baby.

* Among the people of Okinawa, a Japanese island, the placenta ritual begins at a magical hour of the ebbing tide. Old

women of the village circle the birth house, clapping, banging pots and pans and calling to each other. 'May this baby always laugh and be pleasant!' they chant. The baby's grandmother wraps the placenta in rice straw and buries it outside, behind the hearth. A stone is placed over the burial spot to ensure that the baby will not jump in his sleep.

* If a newborn Tzotzil baby of Mexico needs reviving after the birth, his placenta is placed in boiling water.

* Nootkans of the north-west coast of America traditionally bury the placenta after four days. An aunt or grandmother parcels it up in shredded cedar bark and sings over the parcel to make the child a good singer. She might add a chisel to the package if he was to be a carpenter, or – more recently – a deck of cards to make the child lucky. A girl's placenta is then buried in a sheltered spot, while a boy's is immersed in a swamp, making him able to endure the cold.

* Balinese families have lifelong rituals associated with the placenta, amniotic fluid, womb-blood and vernix, the grease which covers and protects a newborn baby. These four are known as '*kanda empat*', or four siblings. Just as they stood guard over the womb, so they will protect the child for the rest of his life. Parents offer prayers to the four siblings at the baby's birth and at important life ceremonies, such as weddings. The placenta itself is buried by the front door in a coconut shell.

Few cultures regard the placenta as a source of food. People who consider the placenta to be the baby's little brother (Malaysia) or his best friend (Nepal) are unlikely to serve it up as a postnatal meal. Although other mammals eat the placenta, human mothers seem to have little inclination to do the same:

I often saw women who were still in a profound state of regression after the expulsion of the placenta . . . But I never saw one of them give the slightest hint of wanting to bring the placenta to her mouth. I know of women who ate some placenta, but these were intellectuals who had read that eating the placenta is an instinct shared by every mammal, and that the placenta contains vitamins, minerals and hormones that can help the uterus retract.

Michel Odent, obstetrician and primal health researcher

There is no doubt that the placenta is full of goodness. Being rich in pregnancy hormones, it could give an emotional boost if you are suffering from postnatal depression. Some Welsh mothers have developed a taste for it, according to child care authors Nikki Bradford and Jean Williams: 'If the idea of eating it raw upsets you, mothers in rural north Wales say it's best cooked like liver – lightly fried with chopped onions, garlic and a bit of Bisto gravy. However, this may denature the sex steroid it contains so you're back where you started.'

Although most western women perceive birth as a purely clinical process and display little interest in the placenta, there has been a recent trend towards reclaiming this aspect of the birth ritual. Some parents choose to bury the placenta and plant a tree over the spot, creating sacred spaces for their children in a landscape largely devoid of spiritual meaning. Such rituals connect the baby to a nomadic prehistory, when the placental home was one place a child could always call his own.

The Navel String

Wit good blessing
spirits willing
navel string
soon sing

John Agard, Caribbean poet

It is the original human lifeline, baby's physical connection to the womb. The cord may be 20 cm to 120 cm long. For some reason, boys' cords tend to be 5 cm longer than girls'. Many midwives wait until the cord has finished pulsating before clamping and cutting, as it delivers blood, oxygen and nutrients to the baby at a rate of four miles per hour.

After chewing through the umbilical cord, the traditional Maasai midwife of Tanzania utters a short prayer to the baby: 'You are now responsible for your life,' she says, 'as I am responsible for mine.'

So where, exactly, should the cord be cut?

* 'three fingers breadth from the belly and so knit up' (Richard Jones, *The Byrth of Mankinde*, sixteenth-century best-seller, England)
* to baby's shoulder (Cherokee tradition, North America)
* the length of a finger (Malaysia)
* five inches from the navel (Yaghans of Tierra del Fuego, South America)
* 'a long way out' to stop the baby from being too thirsty (Australian Aboriginal)
* a hand's breadth (traditional Mexican tribes)

After a few days, the cord falls away. Yaghan mothers speed the process by tying the free end of the cord to the baby's ankle. The Karen tribe of northern Thailand believe that a baby has thirty-three souls, which attach themselves at birth. When his cord falls off easily, it is a sign that his souls are firmly fixed.

THE KINDEST CUT

Cutting the umbilical cord is traditionally the job of the midwife, but in early human history, it was simply bitten through by the mother herself. In societies where special instruments are used, the tools themselves may take on magical significance. Indian leatherworkers prize their razor-sharp knives for the purpose and an Inuit mother traditionally uses a sacred stone which she keeps in her clothes bag all her life.

It is a momentous act. The Pon people living in the Himalayas say that this is the moment when 'la', life and consciousness, first enter the baby.

The baby's end of the cord must be tied somehow. In an American or British hospital, you are likely to get a plastic clip. Among the Somali of East Africa, the umbilicus is bound with hairs from a camel's tail and the camel itself becomes a lavish gift for the newborn infant. The Maya midwives of Yucatan, Mexico, cauterise the stump with a candle flame; they say this guards against convulsions, probably a reference to neonatal tetanus.

Interestingly, it now seems that tetanus, a major cause of infant death in many developing countries, was a legacy brought by white settlers. It apparently did not exist in South American communities before the arrival of Spanish conquistadors. After this, tetanus became known as 'seventh day disease', striking babies up to a month old. Guatemalan tribes used 'stick oil' (balsam of the camibar tree), or cotton flowers mixed with camphor to try to sterilise the cord stump.

Modern medicine is also on the trail of a little cord magic. Umbilical blood is a valued treatment for rare but serious conditions like leukaemia. The stem cells in cord blood are dubbed 'pluripotent', which means they have the potential to differentiate into many different kinds of tissue and can be used to treat certain diseases of the blood and immune system.

For many traditional peoples, the cord remains a potent talisman, a source of spiritual strength and an amulet to protect the growing baby. As far as they are concerned, it is the child's spirit which needs protecting.

Cheers!

'I had managed to give birth at home, to a healthy seven-and-a-half-pound boy . . .
It was time for celebration. Mark snapped back into the role of host and re-
emerged bearing sparkling wine, herbal tea and a plate of peeled mangoes oozing
ripeness.'

Natania Jansz, newly-delivered British mother

Many western mothers sip a little champagne after the birth,
not so much for the alcohol content, which is incompatible
with breastfeeding, but for the sociable 'chink, chink, cheers!'
effect. Others crave a welcome cup of tea, the very English
response to any situation which requires parting with blood –
as if tannin somehow works like an instant transfusion.

But tea is the last thing you would offer a Malay mother after
delivery, and here's the reason why. People in many parts of the
world follow 'humoral' theories when diagnosing or treating ill-
health. These are schemes of complementary elements which
exist in dynamic equilibrium throughout the universe. The most
famous is the Chinese idea of 'yin' (dark, female, cold) and 'yang'
(light, male, hot).

Cultures which classify the body as 'hot' or 'cold' believe that
in illness the body enters an extreme state. This must be treated
with its opposite in food, medicine or behaviour. 'Hot' and 'cold'
designations have little to do with actual temperature and are
not static labels – your body humour changes with climate, time
of day and season. There are many different versions of the
system, but one thing seems to be clear: the postnatal woman
is 'cold' and needs warming up. 'Beliefs about the postpartum
period are . . . similar in all humoral systems of which I am
aware: after childbirth a woman enters a "cold" state because
her body has been depleted of blood, the "hot" body fluid'
(Carol Laderman, social anthropologist).

So the Malay mother would not thank you for that freshly
brewed cup of tea. In Malaysia, tea is classified as 'lendir', or

'cold', because it has a particular tropical taste known as '*kelat*'. This is true even though it may be served piping hot. However, a 'nice cup of coffee' would be perfectly acceptable. (Coffee is classed as bitter and is therefore 'hot'.)

Besides all these invisible rules, eastern mothers also take the 'hot' and 'cold' rules literally. American doctors were puzzled to notice that newly-delivered immigrant Asian mothers refused iced drinks, preferring hot tea or hot rice water in the post-natal period. This perfectly accords with their native beliefs: a new mother, having lost a copious amount of blood, is 'yin' (cold) and her balance must be restored with foods and drink that are 'yang' (hot).

Meanwhile, the Gusii woman in Kenya, Africa, is treated to the most luxurious drink her female birth companions can find: a bottle of orange soda. And back in seventeenth-century Europe, the apothecaries recommended an even more unusual after-birth beverage: 'My instructions are these. So soon as she is laid in her bed, let her drink a draught of burnt white wine, in which you have melted a dram of spermaceti' (Nicholas Culpeper, herbalist, 1651). Spermaceti is a white, fatty substance extracted from the head of the sperm whale and still used today in skin ointments and cosmetics. Anyone take milk?

The Twin Set

A woman is strong. But the woman who gives birth to twins, that woman's heart is especially strong; that woman, her heart stands up.

Nisa, !Kung San woman of the Kalahari Desert, Africa

Babies who come in twos, or even threes, are regarded with awe by many cultures. There is something magical about multiples.

In medieval times, it was thought that the uterus was a twin chamber and that this explained the gestation of two babies. 'The womb,' said Aristotle, the fourth-century BC Greek philosopher, 'is always double without exception, just as in males there are always two testes without exception.' Some peoples (the Tarascans of Mexico, for instance) link twin births to the eating of double-yoked eggs or double fruit during pregnancy – or perhaps, they say, the expecting father ate a pair of bananas.

The double oven theory is all very well, but this and other gynaecological gaffes helped to contribute to millennia of mis-understandings about twins. For instance, opposite-sex twins born into low-caste Balinese families are presumed to have enjoyed an indecent level of intimacy in the womb. The result is a disaster for the family and surrounding villages, who must postpone weddings and funerals, isolating the babies and their parents for six weeks. At the end of this time, a massive purification ritual takes place, involving many offerings to appease the gods.

The Miskito people of Nicaragua, central America, used to kill female twins, since they refused to believe that the father could be the parent of more than one baby at a time. They reasoned that the second child must be the result of an infidelity.

This deep-rooted fear of twins has some highly practical origins. Twins are much more likely to be born premature and to require intensive care. In the western clinical view, 'The human female is most successful when carrying only one child. Multiple gestation not only increases the risks of a less than perfect outcome, but, in general, means that the mother cannot continue with her normal life-style' (John P. Elliott, American perinatologist).

In early nomadic hunter-gatherer societies, it was difficult to sustain one baby, let alone two. The carrying and the extra nursing required were often not compatible with the daily struggle for survival. Some of the oldest tribes in the world (the Mbuti pygmies of the central African rainforest for instance) never mention twins and there are none to be seen. Postnatal infanticide of the weakest baby is their way of coping with unwanted arrivals.

Western obstetricians are not terribly worried about twins, most of whom can be carried, born and nurtured without too many complications. It is the sudden increase in triplets and high–order multiples which is causing the headaches. Statistics from Canada demonstrate how multiple births – the over–abundant result of new fertility techniques – have increased throughout the western world. Between 1974 and 1990, the incidence of twins rose by thirty-five per cent, the number of triplets tripled, and the incidence of quadruplets quadrupled.

DOUBLE YOUR ODDS

Fertility procedures are not the only factor in determining the likelihood of twins. There are racial differences, too. The birthrate of identical sets of twins is the same all over the globe – at three or four per 100 births. But the chance of having non-identical twins varies enormously depending on racial origin.

While white parents have a one-in-100 chance of producing non-identical twins, Japanese parents only conceive non-identical twins once in every 200 births. At the other extreme, some African mothers (in Nigeria, for example) have a one in 22 chance of producing non-identical twins. This amazing cross-cultural pattern persists even when ethnic populations migrate to the West.

Perhaps the prevalence of twins in African societies helps to explain why Africa has some of the strongest twin taboos in the world.

Although many traditional cultures shun twins, others celebrate and revere them. Here are some positive twin traditions:

* Tarascan twins of Mexico are thought to be talented healers, especially in curing wounds or injuries. When they become farmers, Tarascan twins find their corn and their squash plants fruit in twos.

* The Yoruba people of south-west Nigeria believe they have a sacred obligation to protect twins, '*ibeji*', during life and even after death. If either twin should die, a small wooden carving is made, which becomes the home of the twin spirit. The '*ibeji*' carving is carried by his mother, 'fed' spoons of food and even given birthday parties. The aim is to appease the twin spirit, the '*orisha ibeji*', who has the power to bring great fortune into the household.
* Among the Ashanti of West Africa, twins are taken to work in the king's court. Boys become 'fly switchers' and girls are viewed as potential royal wives. The mother of triplets is blessed, because three is such a lucky number.

A Grand Day Out

A thousand discourses of pregnancy, children,
    wetnurses, milk, successful deliveries
They boil a pot full of marvels, herbs, roses
Then they show the new born.

Angot de Lespeyronnière, seventeenth-century French poet

Sometimes the world comes to see the baby, sometimes parents take baby out to meet the world. An Akkha mother from south-east Asia waits thirteen days before venturing out with her newborn. Their first journey is always to the rice fields. Once there, she produces a banana leaf containing a little cooked rice. She rubs this on to her baby's lips in a ritual which binds him to nature and to the rest of the rice-eating community.

Hmong babies, whose families live in or come from south-east Asia, never venture out unless they are dressed in an intricately embroidered hat. This is to trick any watching '*dab*' (fairy) into believing the little bundle on his mother's back is actually a bunch of flowers. Hmong parents are very protective about their children's souls. After a trip out, parents call out loudly to the souls of their smallest children to come on home, in case they should be left behind. 'Hmong families in Merced [California] can sometimes be heard doing this when they leave local parks after a picnic,' says author Anne Fadiman.

Traditional Tibetan families also have a number of ancient customs regarding taking babies outside. Some allow baby out on a short outing called '*Go-don*' at around three days old. Arriving at a friend's house, the baby is welcomed with a '*kata*' or blessing, a dab of butter on his head.

Many Tibetan traditions were abruptly interrupted by the Chinese invasion of Tibet in 1959. Until then, newborn Tibetan babies were ritually transported to Jokhang, the biggest temple in Lhasa, so they could pay their very first tribute to Lord Buddha. The two-week-old infant was wrapped in a soft maroon-coloured blanket, with a patch of silk at its centre. Grandmother made the blanket and she also had the privilege of carrying the baby all the way. As spiritual protection, the infant would wear a brocade belt, to which was attached a tortoise shell, gold and silver charm boxes and a picture of the sacred Wheel of the Universe.

From East to West, family visits are an important part of the postnatal ritual. In northern Nigeria, the Hausa mother returns to her parents with her baby on a visit known as '*bangwalle*'. Before she leaves, a Muslim naming ceremony is conducted to protect the child, and a ram is sacrificed. This seventh-day home-coming is a chance for the young woman to be cared for by her mother while she looks after the new baby.

A baby's first trip outside is always a special occasion, whether you are taking him up to the shops, over to granny's or home from hospital. For many tribes, stepping outside with baby requires attention to a little ritual detail. The Ladakh baby of northern India, for instance, is clad in a special woollen dress and his woolly hat has a silver '*om*' attached. For added good luck, his parents rub his head with yak butter (a valuable commodity) and his forehead is painted with a black '*bindi*', a small dot made of soot and oil which protects children against the evil eye. Now he is ready to meet the outside world.

DANCING HOME

For many modern women, postnatal seclusion consists of a three-day sleepless bed rest in a noisy hospital, followed by a shaky home-coming in a car that seems to drive far too fast. If you think that's bad, spare a thought for the 'cable dancing' inhabitants of Los Piños, a village high in the Andes in southern Colombia. The rest of the world – and that includes the nearest hospital – is located across a kilometre-wide, 400-metre deep gorge of the Negro river.

Unless villagers choose the two-hour snake-infested route through steep, muddy rainforest, the only way through is by hanging on to an inch-think metal cable via a small harness and hook. This death-defying, thirty-second journey was constructed fifty years ago by lumber merchants and now serves a community of thirty families. 'For the inhabitants of Los Piños, the wire cable is a lifeline: a surreal umbilical cord, along which everything passes . . . Pregnant mothers, who must get to the nearest clinic, cross the wire during the darkness of night, returning with their new-born infants' (Richard Emblin, photojournalist).

At 100 mph, that's what you could call a home-coming.

HOME TRUTHS

At first, when I heard such explanations I found it difficult to take them seriously and it was tempting to dismiss them as no more than primitive fairy stories. These explanations, however, have a far wider application than the narrowly physical focus of modern medical theories, encompassing as they do natural, social and spiritual forces.

Jacqueline Vincent Priya, cross-cultural birth researcher

When I first read about magical placentas and strange food taboos, I thought I had stepped, like Alice, into Wonderland. This was a world so distant and remote from my own, that it felt a little scary. Yet now, when I compare the richness of ancient birth traditions with the bald practicality of modern childbirth, I'm glad I made the journey. In our quest for scientific values, rational proofs and the perfect buggy, we have almost lost our taste for the wonder of newborn life.

Traditional customs remind us that birth is, first and foremost, the most awesome miracle of them all. Greater than the world's finest architecture, the genius works of art and music, or even the beauty of the landscape, is the moment of our arrival on earth. Mothers, in a state of postnatal intoxication, are motivated to bond from the very start. And their babies, Paraguayan or pygmy, Asian, American or Australian, are wired to do the same.

This is a chance to consider the intricate webs of reverence and baby-ritual which are woven around the globe. In every continent, human babies are greeted with hope and love, but we all have our own ways of showing we care. The prayers and incantations of each culture demonstrate a universal desire to nurture the infant spirit. Whatever we believe as parents – even if we have given up believing in much at all – we also have the power to create rituals and sacred spaces, to weave our own magic threads. And more and more parents are choosing to do just this.

We might make the primary contact of mother and baby a question of ritual importance, so protecting the privacy of the first few hours of maternal contact. We may choose to bury the placenta somewhere special, so creating a 'birth place' the child can forever call his own. Perhaps, one day, we might even learn to hear, in a baby's birth cry, his prayer to Grandfather Sun and Woman Moon . . .

3. Mothercare

Before we focus on the needs of baby, it seems only fair to consider the mother, who, if she survives the ordeal of birth, must start life afresh with every baby she delivers. Most cultures assume that new mothers need lots of rest and physical attention – how else, they argue, will she be ready to nurture?

Me and My Midwife

Women who witnessed birth or who bore a first child in another country and then came here [America] for a subsequent baby were astonished by the lack of care, help and sensitivity to their feelings and needs, physical as well as emotional, and found the ensuing fatigue and sometimes sadness lasting far longer than expected. Women who have not experienced the difference often blame themselves or their partners for how bad they feel, not realizing that the whole system has been in denial about what they need.

Phyllis H. Klaus, co-founder of DONA, Doulas of North America

It seems incredible that western mothers get by with only talk and tablets. In most other cultures it is accepted that body and spirit are in need of special invigoration after childbirth and before embarking on the lifelong path of parenting. 'This is a time of massive readjustment,' says British midwife Lesley Page, 'and the midwife may play a crucial role.'

The role of the midwife is nowhere narrower than in North America, where her activities have been curtailed in favour of the expert obstetrician and medical team. In some American states, independent midwifery is illegal, as it was throughout Canada until quite recently. Fewer than five per cent of North American births are attended by a midwife. A designer delivery, complete with Caesarian option and pain-free epidural, puts the busy career woman right into the hands of her obstetrician. And according to some American writers, that's exactly where she wants to be:

Our unanimous vote is that you go for the traditional hospital birth with a god-like medical doctor for your first go-round on this birthing carousel. Remember we are creatures of popular culture, we revere doctors as if they were the heroes and heroines we grew up watching on TV. It's the doctors who are so honorably portrayed on everything from *Dr Kildare* to *Dr Quinn, Medicine Woman*. Poor innocent midwives never have their own series. In fact, they were tried as witches in colonial Salem!

Vicki Iovine, author and mother

Note the use of the word 'traditional' applied to 'hospital birth', a practice which dates back one or two generations. In ever-adaptable human society, traditions are as swiftly created as they are destroyed.

Maligned and burned as witches, ridiculed for their reliance on ritual, blamed for the lives they lost and unappreciated for the ones they saved, traditional midwives have been little understood in recent centuries. Yet midwifery probably is *the* oldest profession, and we have many ancestral midwives to thank for the survival of the human race today.

In ancient times, when humans still worshipped Mother Earth and other female deities, the midwife was a respected helper of women in their hour of direst need. She was the granny of the community who provided true continuity of care during the massive transition of birth, and she was a respected village elder who had experienced many births including her own.

The remit of today's traditional midwife remains much as it has been for millennia. This makes her role at once broader and more intimate than that of the modern-day health professional. In African villages, the 'granny midwife' is a familiar and much-loved elder of the community, whose wisdom extends into spiritual as well as practical matters. In Malaysia, where the courage needed to be a midwife is said to be inherited and young girls begin their midwifery apprenticeship aged four, even women in their thirties are thought to be a little young for the job. Nami, a Lahu midwife from northern Thailand, describes her qualifications: 'I gave birth to my children on my own and . . . I don't know . . . people used to say that as I'd given birth on my own I'd be able to help others. They started coming to me for my help and I suppose I've been doing it for about twenty years now.'

Wise in the secrets of mothercare before and after delivery, a traditional midwife's tasks range from the esoteric to the mundane. She might be expected to bless the baby as well as bathe, massage and wrap him up in swaddling bands. But she lavishes just as much attention on the newly-delivered mother as on the newborn. After all, traditional societies reason that good mothering is only possible if the mother herself receives the utmost support.

This cherishing of the mother is probably one of the elements in traditional post-natal care that helps her cherish her baby . . . the community acknowledges her enhanced status, celebrates with her and gives warm approval and unstinted practical help. Even in poverty, children are seen as a family's riches, and a woman who has borne a child has produced a welcome harvest.

Sheila Kitzinger, anthropologist and birth campaigner

THE DOULA DOES

As the midwife role became increasingly restricted in some countries, a vacancy was created for someone who could offer dedicated, personal postnatal care. The role of postnatal hand-servant has been re-invented in America, where midwives have suffered the greatest loss of autonomy and status. To have your own 'doula' – a woman who provides hands-on care through birth and beyond – is the latest trend in America, Canada and Britain.

A doula provides precisely the woman-to-woman attention that mothers all over the world expect from their local midwives. Postnatally, she attends to the mother so the mother can attend to her baby, just like traditional midwives do today.

Visiting Time

Little was left to the imagination as all the royal births took place before an audience of witnesses including the Archbishop of Canterbury, the Chancellor and the Prime Minister. Afterwards, intimate details of the birth were spread like wildfire; news was circulated by onlookers, the ladies of the court, the attendants and others surrounding the royal bedside. Then there were the receptions for noble ladies from Britain and the Continent, who came to view the new-born infant. As many as forty at a time would crowd into the bedchamber.

Ann Wallace and Gabrielle Taylor, co-authors, describe
royal birth in eighteenth-century England

Lots of mothers are treated like royalty once a baby arrives. We find ourselves suddenly on display and, for a while, it may seem as if our lives are no longer our own. Take the women of the Pacific island of Okinawa, for instance:

After the birth of a child, the mother sits at home during a short rest period, watching happily as neighbours, friends, and relatives continually drop in to admire the newborn. Sipping tea, the visitors offer bits of advice, exchange the latest gossip, ask to hold the infant, and take their leave with the standard phrase: 'Take care of yourself.'

Thomas and Hatsumi Maretzki, anthropologists

But postnatal pride gradually makes way for irritation, as the 'constant stream' of visitors means increasing expense and a drain on the new parents' energy. Notice that the Okinawan visitor does not stint from offering advice, which can also be wearing, however well meant.

In fact, most cultures discourage the arrival of the entire clan in the first few weeks after birth. In Tibetan tradition, excited friends and family must wait three days before visiting after a boy has been born, and four days after a girl. Families in certain parts of India do not officially inform their friends about the baby's arrival until the forty-day seclusion has ended.

Important transitions such as birth, entering puberty, marriage, soul-searching or death of a loved one are known as 'thresholds' to the anthropologists who study them. At each threshold, a person is usually permitted to withdraw from society for a while, in a phenomenon known as ritual seclusion. Western couples practise seclusion today when they go on honeymoon. Everyone senses that the couple need time out, to readjust to their new status after taking the step of declaring lifelong commitment.

Few newly-weds would imagine spending their honeymoon night in separate beds, much less separate rooms. Most mothers around the world would have an equally hard time allowing their babies to be taken away after birth. Postnatal seclusion – preserving the intimate environment of mother and newborn

– used to be nearly universal practice and is still usual in many continents. It protects the duo's privacy and gives the infant an uninterrupted chance to acclimatise to life outside his mother's body.

PARTY PIECE

Some people treat birth as an excuse for a postnatal party. In Westphalia, Germany, women meet for a 'Kaffeeklatsch', a coffee and a chat, around the time of the christening. In Friesland, another German region, postnatal visitors are served 'Kopp', raisins soaked with brandy. In old France, visitors would come with cakes and eggs and a party mood (seventeenth-century satirical cartoons show adults gathered around the 'childbed' in a state of inebriation, while the baby is quite neglected).

In medieval England, outsiders were kept away from mother and baby with a symbolic warning: a swathe of white linen wound around the front door knocker. 'It is a sign,' wrote the humanist Erasmus, 'that there is a young woman lying-in.' White was the colour of purity and innocence, used for wedding veils and young children. It was also a polite way of saying 'Keep Out'.

In contrast to the busy, communal life to come, the infant's first days were traditionally spent in a shadowy, womb-like environment. Bartholomew of England, who wrote a thirteenth-century encyclopaedia called '*De Proprietatibus Rerum*' (On Matters of the World), insisted newborns must be kept with their mothers in a dark room to protect their eyes. This was already common practice. A peaceful postnatal period was emphasised in Europe until the twentieth century.

Above all, the birthchamber should be warm, dark and snug: a seventeenth-century manual recommended, 'you must lay the woman in a warm place, lest her mind should be distressed with too much light' . . . [After delivery] the woman would remain in bed in the same dark, snug environment, for a period known as 'in the straw'.

Margaret Willes, National Trust historian

Most seclusions are designed to last forty days, a magical period which remain the ideal in rural India, Ecuador, Siberia and many other places. (It is also the fabled length of time Jesus spent in spiritual seclusion in the wilderness, and a typical time-span for ritual seclusions of self-discovery and personal recovery).

Typical seclusion taboos are practised by some nomadic Romany women of Europe, who are not allowed to touch kitchen utensils or prepare food for at least a month after the birth. Fathers are kept at a distance − they may not even kiss the new baby until the baptism is complete. At the end of her seclusion, the mother washes herself in river water and her post-natal clothes are discarded or burned.

A Little Peace and Quiet

For an instance of pleasure: nine months of hard work, forty days of abstinence and five years of rocking the cradle.

Guatemalan proverb

Before the five years begin in earnest, put your feet up. Only the sturdiest hunter-gatherer tribes expect women to give birth alone, without fuss, and soon afterwards to resume their usual duties. Hmong women of south-east Asia make a virtue of a quick recovery and women of the Sioux tribe on the Dakota plains were known to get up and follow the group just hours after giving birth. But even the super-fit women of the nomadic !Kung San in the Kalahari are allowed to rest for a while:

Circumstances of group life permitting, the mother may remain in the village for a number of days after the birth of the child. Although there is no recognized 'lying-in' period, she will also minimize her daily activities until she feels strong enough to resume them.

Marjorie Shostak, anthropologist

Bangladesh is rated as the third poorest country in the world and offers mothers nothing in the way of pain relief for childbirth or labour-saving devices afterwards. However, each birthing woman is surrounded by other women, in an environment of fervent loving care. 'The most attractive custom,' according to midwife Frances McConville, 'is that delivery has traditionally taken place in the home with the supportive company of other women friends or relatives . . .. constant and close physical contact by means of massaging is provided, along with intense emotional support.' In the forty days after the birth, 'The mother is never left to cope on her own, and the baby receives a great deal of attention.'

HANDS THAT DON'T DO DISHES

Moroccan women have a wonderful way of ensuring a mother rests after the baby arrives. Towards the end of the pregnancy, her hands are painted with henna paste in intricate, lacy designs – an art now known as 'Mehndi'. A henna party, with music and dance, may even be thrown for the occasion. The henna plant is said to be full of 'baraka', a positive power which protects against the evil eye.

As long as the design remains visible on her hands, a woman is exempt from all household duties. This gives her at least three weeks' rest. Every day during her postnatal confinement, the mother is massaged with a stimulating mixture of henna, walnut bark and kohl.

Indian tradition stipulates between three and forty days of bed rest. This period, known as 'shilla', depends on the mother's state of health. In old Slovakia, eastern Europe, the Rusyn mother would lie in bed for a week to regain her strength. If the lying-in went on any longer, people might say she was lazy – but even when she did get up, she was only allowed to do a few light chores. Her husband and midwife took over all the hard work, leaving her free to concentrate on the baby.

Among the Tiriki, a Bantu people of western Kenya, a new mother returns home for some postnatal pampering. She gives birth in the husband's compound, attended by women of the village, and devotes herself to the new baby for the first week. Once she has her strength back, she takes the baby and any young siblings back to her mother's house for several weeks. She will need the rest – as soon as she returns home, it's back to farming and gathering wood.

No Sex Please, We're Breastfeeding

Let [the nursing woman] keep a good diet, and abstain from hard wine and copulation, and passions: these chiefly trouble the milk.

Nicholas Culpeper, herbalist, 1651

The idea that breastfeeding and sex are incompatible seems to be etched on the ancient social conscience. People as diverse as seventeenth-century Europeans and the modern Afikpo Ibo of eastern Nigeria have tended to the opinion that the nursing mother should be exempt from any sexual role.

Although the reasons given for this prohibition are varied and not always true, the taboo itself is eminently practical. In nomadic societies, there was a real danger should a second baby be conceived while the first was still suckling. The lives of both were put at risk. A no-sex rule ensured that the first child was not prematurely weaned, nor the next prematurely conceived.

Another benefit, which remains relevant today, is the protection of the new mother from an overly swift return to the sexual role. Many breastfeeding mothers experience a reduced interest in sexual intercourse. In many societies, this is considered a natural reaction which is given some respect. In western society, the sexual function is often given precedence over the maternal – few mothers feel genuinely entitled to sexual 'time out'.

[There is] a basic assumption in western society, which is that it is culturally desirable for women to be libidinous as long as the libido is directed towards their husband. Contemporary researchers record that breastfeeding mothers do not resume 'normal' sexual relations as quickly as bottle-feeding mothers. This is assumed to be a negative fact.

Gabrielle Palmer, nutritionist and breastfeeding counsellor

When mothers become overwhelmed with the difficulties of breastfeeding, they may easily overlook the fact that relaxed suckling was designed to be a satisfyingly sensual experience. Hormones which stimulate a mother to feed her baby also feed back pleasure, allowing her to enjoy her months or years of nurturing. Of course, whether or not a woman really allows herself to experience or enjoy these sensations may depend on her cultural education.

Nursing is designed to be a satisfying experience in itself. Couple this with the sheer physical exertion of parenting, and many mothers feel all 'touched out' by the time they crawl into the marital bed at night. In nuclear-family, monogamous households, postnatal sex can become a battleground for a distracted mother and a frustrated father, who are almost entirely dependent on each other for intimacy and affection.

Polygyny, the marriage of one man to several wives, is an age-old system which allows women to breastfeed and attend to their babies' needs without pressure. It obviously also leaves men free to pursue their sexual needs without recrimination. This once-common domestic arrangement is believed to contribute to the success of long-term breastfeeding and the prehistoric continuance of the human species. Polygyny is, of course, the practice of Mormons in modern-day Utah, America, as well as a variety of other tribes who have yet to be influenced by the exclusivity of modern marriage.

Breastfeeding patterns are changing all over the world, the tendency being for women to nurse for shorter lengths of time. As this trend progresses, so the sexual taboos become truncated. Many cultures limit their sex taboo to the length of postnatal seclusion (around forty days) which also coincides with the magical 'six-week check-up' of Dutch and English medical tradition. Compare this with the ancient five-year sex taboo of the Dani tribe in a remote valley of Irian Jaya, New Guinea: 'Dani men and women sleep apart. In fact the Dani, in spite of many voguish anthropological explanations for their penis gourds, are most unsexy. After a birth, women will avoid sex for around five years, and it is hardly ever discussed by men. All the men of the village slept in the hut I stayed in.' (George Monbiot, journalist.)

ABSTINENCE MAKES THE HEART GROW FONDER?

According to research from the University of Minnesota, forty per cent of women are still having sexual problems three months after their babies are born. Discomfort and a difficulty reaching orgasm are two of the main complaints. 'Many women do not return to "pre-pregnancy levels of sexual experience" even one year after giving birth,' says the report. In this context, abstinence during breastfeeding does not seem so outrageous, after all.

The major paternalistic religions, including early Christianity, Islam and Judaism, depicted childbirth as a time of uncleanliness and pollution. In India, orthodox Brahmins are particularly strict on this point. Women are not supposed to cook, clean or have sex postnatally because their postnatal bleeding is contaminating and especially dangerous to men. Such impositions are often assumed by modern western commentators to be oppressive measures which restrict the freedom and power of women. But the postnatal taboos could be characterised another way.

For women in the developing world, the time of impurity is also a time of respite, of being exempt from duty and generally not being available. From India to Africa, postnatal women eat off the same old plate and wear the same old clothes. They wallow in their special state. Being 'impure' is a device which says: 'I am not on show and do not want to be disturbed'. 'Some Malay women say that the old and unattractive clothing they wear during the forty days following childbirth has a dual function. It preserves their good clothing from blood stains and smoke damage, and it preserves the wearers from the sexual attentions of their husbands.' (Carol Laderman, social anthropologist.)

The Power of Touch

Immediately after childbirth is no time to start proving how tough you are . . . After the birth, more than at any time, is the time when a woman deserves a good massage.

Maggie Tisserand, aromatherapist

We live in a world so generally devoid of human contact that massage has become an esoteric art, a professional skill which we must pay to receive. But in many societies, massage is simply a kindness one does for someone else – like making a cup of tea. Mothers are considered in special need of massage around the time of birth.

In rural Nepal, for instance, all members of the community take it in turns to give a pregnant woman a daily massage. Throughout India, girls learn massage from a young age and frequently massage their mothers and other family members.

Postnatal massage is most certainly part of the prescription in cultures which care deeply for the health and recovery of the new mother. Hawaiian custom is to give a vigorous lomi-lomi massage on the fourth day after delivery. Lomi-lomi uses the thumbs, fingers and elbows in strong, circular movements. Malay mothers are given three one-hour massages by the village midwife for the first three days after birth, with special attention paid to the breasts to encourage the milk supply. It has been calculated that Malay women typically receive an astonishing total of twenty massages in the first weeks after birth.

AT A STRETCH

Gentle massage before and after birth is said to minimise stretch marks. Some people recommend a light carrier oil, such as coconut, calendula or grapeseed. Others say a rich lubricant is best – try rubbing sweet almond oil or cocoa butter into the stomach.

- Almond was the preferred massage oil in ancient Rome.
- In Guatemala, a family member (perhaps a child) massages the new mother's back with seeds from the cubanis plant, which release a comforting oil.
- Mustard seed oil is a favourite with Indian women.
- In Polynesia, a new mother would relax by a coconut-strewn fire while friends massaged her with a moisturising balm of coconut oil.
- Wheatgerm oil, rich in vitamin E, is good for healing Caesarian scars.

The plant world is full of natural oils, many with healing properties, which have been used and understood for thousands of
years. The Egyptians developed a primitive distillation process
for producing essential oils around 5,000 years ago. They used
steam to extract the scent-giving parts of the plant, also known
as its essence, or 'soul'. This vibrant life force penetrates the skin
and starts to work on the bloodstream within an hour of being
applied.

Ancient Greeks and Romans used oils in the bath and believed
that aromatic massage prolonged life. In medieval Europe, cru-
saders returned with a selection of perfumes from Arabia and
some wealthy homes even installed a still for making essential
oils. In seventeenth-century England, both mother and baby
were anointed with oils after birth.

Two thousand years ago, myrrh would have been burned as
incense to sweeten and purify the air of the birthing room.
Myrrh is not suitable for applying directly to babies' skins, but
is both rejuvenating and antiseptic when used in adult massage.
As it happens, myrrh is particularly compatible with frankin-
cense oil, which calms and regulates the female system. Could
it be that the Wise Men's presents to baby Jesus were actually
an aromatherapy gift-pack for a weary Mother Mary?

Bath Time

Once the cord was off we would have a wash (bogie) and go back to our camp.
We would crush the seeds from the soap tree (kankulji) near the river and mix
with water to make a soapy lather to rub on our bodies. We washed ourselves
all over with this.

Mona Ramsay, Aboriginal woman of Warmun, Western Australia

Water rituals have always played an important part in the birth
process, from conception (fresh water is associated with fertility)
to postnatal seclusion (water completes the rites of purification

and baptism). The act of being dipped in water symbolises the washing away of an old life and the embracing of a new one. Indian women take ritual baths on the third, fifth, eleventh, twenty-first and fortieth days after delivery.

Guatemalan women have a steam bath to signify the end of their lying-in. Heat is considered very important to healing. Hausa mothers in northern Nigeria wash their private parts in very hot water every day for five months. Hausa husbands spend the last few months of pregnancy gathering firewood so the water will be hot enough. In Haiti, castor oil leaves, known as palma Christi, are strewn into the postnatal bath. Hot baths are a real treat in rural areas, where people normally bathe in cool water straight from a well, even in the cold monsoon season.

ARE YOU SITTING COMFORTABLY?

Aromatherapist Maggie Tisserand believes postnatal infection in hospitals could be minimised if mothers were given regular sitz baths using essential oils. Oils in the water and in the air – through burners placed around the ward – help to combat airborne bacteria and viruses. She recommends a sitz (or hip) bath using a few drops of cypress and lavender oil: cypress is an astringent which encourages raw blood vessels to close; lavender protects, heals and gently promotes new skin growth. Run a few inches of warm water into a bath or clean plastic bowl, add three or four essence drops, mix well and soak . . .

The Yaghan mother of Tierra del Fuego, South America, does not share in the luxury of the hot tap. As soon as she can stand after delivery, she walks with a chosen friend down to the sea and bathes, whatever the temperature of the water, before drying herself with a ball of moss. Her friend takes charge of bathing and drying the baby. One mother was seen to bathe in this way four times on the day she gave birth. You perhaps need to know that the Yaghans are people of the sea, and some babies are even born on board the family canoe. Some people just don't seem to feel the cold!

Brace Yourself . . .

They wrap a six-inch strip of cotton cloth around her abdomen, beginning in front and passing the ends to each other under the woman's buttocks. Every time the bandage is passed, they brace one foot against the woman's hip and pull, thereby cinching the *faja* (girdle, sash) as tight as the woman can stand it. After about three passes, the ends are knotted several times, forming a sometimes discernable penis-shaped bulge against the abdomen, to which the women would laughingly refer as *pollo* (this word has the same double meaning as the English 'cock').

Brigitte Jordan, birth researcher among the Maya in Yucatan

Just as a baby is still swaddled in many countries, so mothers are often bound in tight swathes of material. The idea is to realign the body to meet pre-pregnancy ideals. Although girdles have gone out of fashion in the West, sagging stomachs, baggy bottoms and unreliable pelvic floors are still with us. Western mothers who have tried binding say it gives them the feeling of being swaddled and secure. In Arctic tradition, the Inuit mother's hips are bound tightly by a cord to bring her bones back into line. Tausog mothers in the Philippines have their lower torso wrapped in a cloth called the '*halat*', which is thought to prevent postpartum haemorrhage.

In Yucatan, Mexico, women believe that 'amarrar' or binding gives them the body strength to carry children and other heavy loads. It also keeps out the cold. For a short while, Maya women also wear breast and head bands, supposedly to close up the bones that opened during labour. The idea was also popular in Tudor England, where 'cross cloths' were worn over the forehead to prevent postnatal wrinkles.

Whether or not postnatal binding really works remains to be proved. However, I have yet to hear of a reliable traditional remedy for the fresh grey hairs which mysteriously appear on some women's heads immediately after childbirth. Don't pluck them out, says an old superstition, or ten more will grow in their place. You might try natural vegetable dyes, or perhaps just adopt the attitude of the Indian continent – there, they say grey hairs give you a certain 'grace and charm'.

Warm as Toast

After the first three children, [my mother] would give birth unattended in the field. She would cut the cord, then carry the baby and the afterbirth home. My father would build a hut and put antiseptic herbs into a pot into which a hot stone had been put. She would sit on the pot and the fumes would heal her uterus.

Paschal Khoo-Thwe, Paduang tribe, Burma

Smoking, roasting, 'fire rest' – the vocabulary is starting to smoulder, as we examine those postnatal rituals which revolve around heat. Roasting is the anthropologists' word, but they should call it 'toasting', really, as it has more to do with warming-your-toes-by-the-fire than spit-and-baste. Flames, like water, have the power to purify. Smoke, like steam, has mystical qualities which protect the newly-delivered woman. The idea is to stop mothers catching 'baby chill', a phenomenon treated in Jamaica by wrapping a turban around the mother's head. Postnatal chill is a fully-documented condition which may occur in the hour after delivery, probably as a result of hyperventilation.

Among the indigenous tribes of south-west America, the new

mother would lie in a sandpit, warmed by hot stones underneath her. Sometimes she would lie half-buried in warm sand, a soothing therapy which should be investigated by health farms in colder climates. In Malaysia, the new mother lies on a '*salaian*' or roasting bed, a wooden structure not unlike a sauna bench. Underneath is a large pot containing a small fire and here she will stay for as long as she feels the benefit. The aim is to speed up healing, keep the blood circulating freely and generally help her to regain her shape. Roasting is also apparently an insurance against a creaky old age:

In the heat of the equatorial climate of south-east Asia, I used to wonder how any woman could bear to do this when it was already so hot. When I asked about this I was told that whether the woman does this or not depends on how she feels . . . if she is very exhausted, at night and at certain times of year, it can be very comforting . . . I caused considerable consternation after the birth of my daughter by walking around the house in bare feet and eating food and drink straight from the refrigerator. Older women friends particularly clicked their teeth and said I would be lucky if I did not suffer from pains in my joints when I got older!

Jacqueline Vincent Priya, birth researcher

Vietnamese mothers place a pan of coals under the bed; Thai fathers prepare a fire from a particular smokeless wood – there are many variations on the theme. Of course, heating the mother also provides an instant central-heating system for the baby, who will receive a great deal of skin-to-skin contact after birth. As one observer suggests, this experience completes the triangle of postpartum care: 'The smoke, the water and the oil are powerful symbols of healing and their use in community gatherings and ceremonies is a natural outpouring of a holistic approach to life, a life in which health and spirituality cannot be separated' (Margaret Stewart, midwife).

Mother's Menu

Payment for my *nanang*'s [grandmother's] midwifery services often came in the form of a chicken – which she would kill and turn into a hearty ginger-rice-chicken soup (*aroze caldo*) to share family-to-family with the new parents.

Robin Lin, granddaughter of a Filipino midwife

Food taboos are an integral part of the birth process for many people of the world. Postnatally, they are a practical and magical attempt to maintain the health of mother and therefore the baby. In most cases, the idea is to keep the menu simple – a common-sense precaution against the possibility of food poisoning. The Thai mother, for instance, bases her diet on rice and other 'safe' ingredients, gradually adding other items as her body settles down. Rice is such an important food in the East that it plays a great part in religious ritual. The Akkha mother of Thailand also eats a meal of rice to purify herself after the birth.

Other prescriptions and proscriptions are more complicated, usually related to 'hot' and 'cold' humoral theories and other ancient wisdoms. But postnatal food rules are not always obeyed. Malay mothers are flexible about their many restrictions, and often prefer to experiment to see which foods actually suit them after birth. Where possible, Malay women are fed a postnatal mix of eggs, honey, black pepper and yeast every day – wealthy families also add beef to the menu. Mothers also drink a special tea of boiled roots at least three times a day. Every attention is paid to the postnatal diet and nutritionists studying Malay mothers' blood values found them to have 'satisfactory or high' results for every essential nutrient.

BUSH TUCKER FOR WEARY MUMS

A list of potential postnatal foods recommended by women of the
Warmun Aboriginal Community, Western Australia:

Boab nut – full of vitamins and energy

Black bream – makes a great stew

Kangaroo – 'gives lots of energy'

Pine-melon – like a long pumpkin, great roasted

Sugarbag – honey found on the snappy gum and bloodwood trees,
  good energy source

Water Lily – boil the root for a tea to strengthen the new mother

Konkerberry/ Greenberry/ Whiteberry – sweet berries containing lots
  of vitamins

Hmong families, originally from south-east Asia but many now living in America, do not rely on hospital food to nourish mothers who have just given birth. Each day, the Hmong husband prepares, cooks and carries in the vital elements of a diet which is prescribed for thirty days: chicken boiled with five special herbs (these have to be grown in good time by each immigrant family) and steamed rice. As with all foreign diets, this one is a matter of taste: 'The Hmong men carried these nice little silver cans to the hospital that always had some kind of chicken soup in them and always smelled great' (Raquel Arias, obstetrician, Merced Community Medical Center, California). 'They always brought some horrible stinking concoction that smelled like the chicken had been dead for weeks' (Robert Small, obstetrician, Merced Community Medical Center, California).

In Ethiopia, the pregnant woman is often responsible for making her own postnatal meal. She grinds the flour and makes a porridge to eat after delivery. But in many parts of the world, the new mother's food is of communal concern. Like all caring peoples, the Yaghans of Tierra del Fuego, southern South America, would never allow a new mother to go hungry. Lots of varieties of fish and duck are taboo but, in emergencies, the negative energy can be removed by a shaman or healer, who holds the forbidden item in his hands and blows on it. The food is now ready for cooking and consumption.

Meat fat and milk, say nutritionists, are the best body-building foods and give resistance to disease. In Siberia, women of the Yakut family melt fat and share it with the newly-delivered mother soon after the birth. The elderly midwife spills a little fat into the fire as an offering of thanks to the goddess Ayisit, who guided the infant and mother safely through childbirth.

Rich foods make acceptable gifts and these have been ritualised by many societies.

* In Friesland, Germany, farmers traditionally prepared a 'Puppkekäse' or Baby Cheese in honour of the new arrival. Of course, this was for the mother and her family, not the baby, to eat. Visitors to a German mother and newborn might also bring the 'Weisat', a parcel containing coffee, eggs, butter and sugar.
* In Glamorgan, Wales, it was the custom to bring a pound or two of sugar to the mother, along with a 'cyflwyno' or present for the new baby.
* Ladakh families of northern India bring rich milk and butter to the new mother when visiting for the first time.
* Mongolian families share a meal of fermented horse milk and meat fat.
* Nomads in Somalia feed postnatal mothers the fat of sheep's tail.

In parts of Europe, it was once the custom to feed the first ripe fruit of the cherry tree to a woman who had just delivered her first baby. People believed this would ensure an abundant crop of cherries. It certainly made sure that the new mother was the first to be served with the freshest, health-giving fruit.

If You Take My Advice . . .

We in the West have lost our ability to trust our instincts. They have not . . .

Anita Roddick, Body Shop founder

Advice-giving is an important part of the package for the modern health professional. We expect obstetric and paediatric experts to know better than us and usually we want them to tell us about it. But not all cultures operate in this way. Mothers in many parts of world would be utterly bewildered by the barrage of conflicting advice western women encounter – and from such a wide range of sources.

Doctors, friends, mothers and mothers-in-law, magazine editors, authors and complete strangers all merrily add their two-pennyworths to the muddle which is modern child-rearing. No wonder the first-time mother feels a little confused. She may never before have encountered a subject which elicits such intrusion and lack of consensus.

Many of us begin our parenting journey feeling lost or 'at sea'. In contrast, mothers who are supported by an entire village and a common view on how to bring up children start out with a feeling of being firmly rooted and secure. In fact, so well understood are the ground rules in traditional societies that there is little need for cold-blooded advice-giving. Instead, there is a safe ritual framework for instructing young parents or parents-to-be. This instruction brings few surprises, it is merely the confirmation of a lifetime's practical experience . . .

How odd it would be to tell Ache or !Kung San women that in this country, we learn our parenting skills from books and from doctors (mostly male). In modern Western culture, it is not their mothers or grandmothers or sisters to whom parents turn for counsel. They turn instead to the pediatrician, an expert in pathology who is trained in detecting organic diseases but who is now being asked about what is 'normal' behavior.

Meredith Small, ethno-paediatrician

Advice can be an unwelcome interference in our stand-alone culture, especially when parents have not specifically requested it. But in a society based on interdependence, the young generation look forward to the rites of passage which include instruction from their elders.

For instance, 'Kija Law' is the belief system of the Kija Aboriginal people of Australia. Its strand of Women's Law is handed down by the only credible experts: mothers, mothers-in-law and grandmothers. After childbirth, the initiate mother is taken to a sacred spot and guided through issues such as breast-feeding and infant crying. 'When they have their babies they must learn to grow them up from the old people. They learn about bush medicines, bush tucker and things to help the baby grow up Aboriginal way. They learn what to do when the baby is sick. What they get is a strong way' (Queenie McKenzie, woman of Warmun, Western Australia).

In other places, advice-giving becomes almost unnecessary. Family participants are clear about their given roles, and yet individuals are given personal choice. It is therefore considered demeaning to volunteer advice. In rural Malaysia, where people are 'loathe to give advice unless it is specifically requested', even village midwives will not offer their opinions. Sometimes this causes problems, as the village midwives are asked to communicate government thinking to new mothers. The midwives, however well-disposed they are towards official guidelines, do not have a tradition of handing out unasked-for opinions and are particularly unwilling to suggest anything which might take a mother away from the support of her community.

It may seem strange, in a book about maternity wisdoms, to discover that many people are reluctant to share them. But wisdom has more to do with understanding, living experience and mutual respect than with dispensing expert opinion. As explorer Jean Liedloff observed among the Yequana of remote Venezuela, there was a complete 'unwillingness of one Yequana ever to cajole another . . . they will not impose their wills on their fellow men – not even . . . on children'.

The support mechanisms in many societies allow for flexibility. Traditions are transmitted through custom, not merely through words, which have the power to destroy instinct and individuality. And within the traditions of the group, each family is allowed its own interpretations. In an atmosphere of complete support, each mother will find her own way.

Baby Blues

In hospital whole wards of women are often weeping at the same time. But it rarely occurs after a home birth . . . If a woman is forcibly separated from her baby she is bound to be sad.

Sheila Kitzinger, anthropologist and birth campaigner

Doctors in the West tell us that between fifty and seventy-five per cent of women go through a transient tearfulness and depression after birth. Victorian writer Jane Ellen Panton described the phenomenon in 1896 as 'that blue feeling'. Classically, 'third-day blues' coincides with hormone changes as breastmilk comes in. And yet, as more than one writer has pointed out, it may be that hormones are not entirely to blame, not by themselves, anyway. Hidden emotions and social stresses can trigger depression at an already sensitive time. 'Why the hormonal state is assumed to precede the emotional state is unexplained. It is well known that fear stimulates adrenalin, not vice versa; why then cannot sorrow stimulate certain measurable hormone states?' (Gabrielle Palmer, nutritionist and breastfeeding researcher). And although postnatal depression can occur in mothers anywhere in the world, only in America and Europe has it reached the epidemic proportions which we consider to be normal.

One apparently simple precaution against 'baby blues' seems to be keeping the baby at the breast. Researchers in Jordan found that mothers who were allowed to hold their newborns and breastfeed from the start were less likely to experience baby blues, or the deeper scars of full-blown postnatal depression (PND). In private (American-style) Jordanian hospitals, babies are taken away from their mothers for twenty-four hours and given a milk substitute. Mothers who have experienced complicated deliveries sometimes do not see their infants for three days. 'On the whole,' said the researchers, 'mothers who could breastfeed their babies early felt better in the postnatal period.'

There may be hormonal reasons why breastfeeding ameliorates baby blues. The more a baby feeds, the higher the maternal levels of oxytocin, the hormone which gives her a maternal glow. The whole postnatal picture is, as we have seen, rather like fitting together pieces of a jigsaw – mother hormonally programmed to hold and bond with her baby; baby programmed to respond and excite the mother, both physically and emotionally. Sometimes, it's not the mother-baby relationship which has pieces missing. Perhaps family or community support has broken down, or perhaps the mother feels she is not receiving the kind of attention she needs or expects from her partner.

In Malaysia, the feeling of '*sakit meroyan*', postnatal irritability, is given a magical explanation – they say it is brought on by the powerful spirits which emanate from the placenta, blood and amniotic fluid. However, the emphasis is on the mother's emotional vulnerability: women are supposed to be more likely to suffer from baby blues if they are made sad or angry. According to birth researcher Carol Laderman, 'Some Malay women use this belief to exact the kind of considerate or even deferential treatment from their husbands, during the postpartum period, which they might like to have, but wouldn't dare to expect, at other times.'

In Tibetan medicine, any postnatal depression, or 'deficiency of life-sustaining wind', is taken very seriously, as the mother's state of mind is pivotal to the well-being of the baby and the rest of the family. The affected mother is treated with body massage using healing herbal oils and herbal steam treatments to remove toxins; visualisations and breathing meditation for spiritual calm; nutritional and herbal supplements and mantra chanting. Repetitions of the mantra 'OM AH HUM' are said to clear the body, voice and mind of all negative energy.

In most traditional societies, a wide range of cherishing treatments is available to any mother feeling down after the birth of her baby. The attention they bring is uplifting to anyone who has been through the perilous and exhilarating journey of giving birth.

Please Be Upsitting

> Coming from the darkness to light,
> This baby was received as a treasure
> And the mother is being celebrated.
>> Song of the 'mansang' celebrations, to mark the end of
>> mother and baby's seclusion in Okinawa, Japan

Eventually – and in most societies this means when it feels right – the mother tires of her womb-like existence and begins to stir. For the woman of Okinawa, there is a visible shift in her scope of interest:

The [Okinawan] mother begins to talk about the approaching feast day and the need to get new clothing for the older children. She asks anxiously about the condition of the firewood market and starts to plan her inevitable resumption of work in the mountains and fields. In spite of her feelings of protectiveness and pity for the young baby, she begins, bit by bit, to reinstate her normal routine.

Thomas and Hatsumi Maretzki, anthropologists

The transition into this new phase of life is usually marked with a ceremony of thanksgiving and welcome – for the mother as well as for her baby. In Roman and Judeo-Christian history, this was the '*dies lustricus*', or Day of Purification.

And when the days of her purifying are fulfilled, for a son or for a daughter, she shall bring a lamb of the first year for a burnt offering, and a young pigeon, or a turtle dove, for a sin offering, unto the door of the tabernacle of the congregation, unto the priest:

Who shall offer it before the Lord, and make an atonement for her; and she shall be cleansed from the issue of her blood. This is the law for her that hath born a male or a female.

Leviticus, the laws of the tribe of Levi, Old Testament

For Orthodox Jewish women, the postnatal bath (the '*mikvah*') is a full-body immersion that symbolises the end of her ritual impurity. She may now enter the synagogue and offer thanks for her safe deliverance. This is her prayer: 'Bestow your blessing upon Your handmaid; strengthen and uphold me together with my husband, that we may rear the child that has been born to us to revere You, to serve You in truth, and to walk in the path of righteousness. Guard the tender babe in all his ways.'

In medieval Christian England, mothers were often still lying-in on their baby's eighth-day baptism, and would only emerge a month after delivery for their purification, or 'churching'. Roman Catholics still bring candles to light at Our Lady's altar, with a thanksgiving to Mother Mary. Unless the family was very pious, medieval churching was an excuse for an elaborate party, for putting on best clothes, dancing and gorging at a table that groaned with meats and sweet puddings. The churching feast or '*kerkgangsmaal*' was carried to such excess by old Dutch families that an edict was sent out limiting the number of people allowed to attend.

Purification is an Indian ritual, too. Like the medieval Europeans, Indian families enjoy a good knees-up to celebrate the survival of mother and baby after the period of postnatal seclusion. That is, if they can get organised . . .

The priest had . . . said the ceremony should start at six o'clock in the evening; but at eight, the women were still preparing food . . . .Not that they had done the things which were meant to be done to mark the end of the eleven days and the pollution brought by the birth: traditionally, the whole house should have been cleaned, the walls whitewashed, the floor redone, and the gods worshipped with offerings and prayers. But all the family had done was to have their baths – men, women and children – and to light a scented stick. That took time enough, along with all the cooking.

Sarah Hobson, documentary film-maker, observes a Gowda family in south India

The wonderful phrase 'upsitting' comes from seventeenth-century England, where mothers who had lain in the straw for long enough were allowed to sit in a chair instead. 'I have never been able to sit up an hour at a time,' wrote Lady Mary of the Verney family at Claydon in Oxfordshire in 1647. Anyone who has been through a modern-day episiotomy will know exactly how she felt.

HOME TRUTHS

The well-being of the whole world depends on the woman. She is the fire . . . However poor a family may be, if the woman is good, it's all right. Man is there because of woman.

Brahmin Indian priest

What is it worth, the postnatal protection of the new mother? Her sanity, her well-being, her self-respect, her full recovery – these are the concerns of everyone around her, and some societies do everything they can to help. If only we had the time – time to belong to the kind of community which cares enough to turn up and do the washing, or make a meal, or take older children off the mother's hands. If only we had the expertise to offer a soothing massage, or could make a special postnatal meal filled with the best ingredients. Just think how different giving birth would be. Of course, with a little effort and a pipette of essential oil, we could at least have a go. It does not take much to make a new mother feel cherished.

I love the idea of mother and baby cuddling by an open fire after a sweet oily massage, warm and snug in a darkened room. Perhaps candles are flickering, perhaps a white ribbon hangs on the front door to keep unnecessary visitors at bay. I like the idea of a taboo on entering the kitchen or doing the washing-up and a pause-button approach to sex for a mutually agreed period of time. And I particularly like the theme of continued attention which keeps the mother feeling special after pregnancy. No wonder so many women feel a touch depressed when their major project – childbirth – is suddenly over. Most societies recognise that the real project has only just begun, and it is supremely important not to hurry the transition from expectancy through to everyday reality.

4. Meet the Team

In a book of child wisdom, we have to put children into context. No child exists alone – he becomes himself in the company of others. By tracing the web of connections around each child, we begin to get a real idea of the difference that culture can make.

It Takes a Village . . .

It's hard to explain to someone in a different culture what family means in my culture – how broadly we define it and how seriously we take it. Where I come from, nothing matters more than family ties. Family is all and everyone is family . . . Anyone related to me by blood, tribe or marriage is family, no matter how distant or convoluted the connection. Say my mother introduces me to a girl I've never met before. 'Fauziya, this is my brother's wife's sister's daughter.' I won't think, How is she related to me? I'll call her my sister.

Fauziya Kassindja of the Tchamba-Kusuntu tribes, Togo, West Africa

Whatever their shape or size, birthplace or parentage, babies bring change. The immediate aftermath is a mountain of work and a seismic shift in the family dynamic. Most babies have parents to care for them, families to support the parents and communities to keep the whole thing together. Unless, of course, you have arranged your society so that the parent-and-baby unit is divorced from practical, emotional and spiritual community care.

Relative isolation is the most glaring feature of parenthood in western society. Parents are expected to deliver a one-to-one baby service in the privacy of their own home. When things go wrong, this isolation may become acute: the independent ethic works best when every individual is able to cope, or at least is 'putting on a brave face'.

Most of the world's parents would be amazed by our reluctance to share our problems, or, indeed, our joys, with others in the community. They would be equally bewildered to see the lack of involvement of local people when it came to child-rearing. You only have to compare the indifference of urban England with the child-friendliness of southern Ireland to notice the difference community makes to parents' self-esteem. In other continents, the warmth is even more marked:

Travelling with children throws such a different light on things. Children are so adored and valued in South America. Babies are viewed as angels. I don't think anything could have prepared me for the amount of attention that Sula-Mae was going to attract. I could barely walk a few feet without someone doting on her.

Rennie Loewenthal, La Leche League breastfeeding support group leader, London, takes fourteen-month-old Sula-Mae to north-east Brazil

This communal interest compares well with the ancient lifestyle of – for instance – the Efé pygmy baby in Zaire, Africa. A baby under four months old spends around fifty per cent of his time in the care of an adult other than his mother. Or consider the security of the village Indian child, to whom every adult is his 'uncle' or auntie'. For these babies, making connections is the ancient strategy for survival.

Babies are community creatures. As we like to say in the West – where our villages sprawl into suburbs and our suburbs into towns – it takes a village to raise a child. In this chapter, we meet the whole village team.

Baby – The Original Status Symbol

'I am Wasse,' he says, speaking through my translator, then introduces me to his wife Jandu. The couple met at a tribal feast. 'She loves me because I am a good hunter who can feed my family,' Wasse explains. 'I love her because she has given me two children and that is how we Bayaka count our riches. When I die, people will still know my name because of my children.'

Paul Raffaele, journalist, among the Bayaka pygmies, Central African Republic

In communally-arranged societies, babies bring social status and the possibility of a comfortable retirement. There is no loss of personal standing – in fact, both mother and father see their rank augmented with each child they produce. Anticipated expenses are not enormous, except in those societies where dowry systems and 'bridewealth' turn children into a financial burden.

In western culture, the arrival of a new baby may mean immediate loss of income and status. 'Down-sizing' and 'slow-tracking' are the buzz-words for working mothers, who are made to feel that raising the next generation is somehow a lesser activity than clocking on. At the same time, babies imply a lot of expense; the child's Essential Equipment List gets longer with every passing year. So there are many practical pressures to return to paid work. The office is where we have located the modern community.

We make life harder for both parents when we fail to give their role any social importance. Other societies do not fail in this regard. In fact for many, the birth of children is the prime way for men and women to gain full adult status.

In the Middle East, as in many other cultures, marriage is very definitely perceived as a first step towards having children. Only after the arrival of babies may newly-weds consider themselves to be full adults and finally join the 'club' of the extended family. This is quite unlike the modern western ethos, which celebrates marriage but considers childbearing to be a private matter, a question of personal preference. Muslims consider procreation to be an issue of social and religious concern: 'Such attitudes towards marriage and children are found among Jewish and Christian groups, but within Islam, they are intensified. "When a man has children he has fulfilled half of his religion, so let him fear God for the remaining half," states one of the hadith, or sayings of the Prophet Muhammad' (Elizabeth Warnock Fernea, professor of Middle-Eastern studies).

This spiritual and emotional endorsement of fatherhood is absent from our culture. For us, Fathers' Day is a commercial afterthought, an attempt to bring appreciation of fathers into line with the ancient celebrations of motherhood (although Mothers' Day has now, also, become a highly commercialised event). We are probably the first society to pin parents' status on the arrival of a greetings card.

However, Bagam parents of the Cameroons on the west coast of Africa also wear emblems of parental pride. Just to make sure no one can mistake her elevated identity, the mother carries a small, square woven grass bag with short handles and the father wears five feathers of the 'ngw' bird in his hair. He also carries two of the special grass bags, bordered with blue strands.

In medieval Holland, meanwhile, the new father would sport his very own 'paternity cap': 'When we returned he was stand-ing in the doorway. "Papa, your cap!" cried Cornelia. The girls ran up to him and tried to snatch off the quilted paternity cap he wore, its ribbons dangling below his ears. He looked both proud and embarrassed' (Tracy Chevalier, historical novelist, paints a postnatal domestic scene in seventeenth-century Delft).

Among the Kayapó people of central Brazil, celebration of fatherhood is not a once-a-year affair. Men rise through the social hierarchy in direct proportion to the number of children they have sired. In fact, the word 'father' in Kayapó is the word for adult male. With the birth of his first child, a man becomes a full husband and moves into his wife's compound. He now belongs to a men's club house and may attend political gather-ings and discussions. At first he is a passive member, a 'father of few children'. He begins to take a more dynamic part in the running of the village only when he is a 'father of many children' and possibly already a grandfather.

Just as fatherhood is given immense social importance by most communities, all over the world women gain status from the children they deliver. In rural Malaysia, it is childbirth (rather than puberty) which turns a girl into a woman. In old Germany, a woman was not called '*Frau*' (Mrs or Mistress) until she had her first child.

In parts of Africa, full wife status is not given until children have survived infancy. Among the Tiriki people of western Kenya, for instance, a wife's acceptance by her husband's family is tentative until she has three children. Then, with great ceremony, she is allowed to set up her own hut and hearth to cook for her husband. The Jie, a small Ugandan tribe, say a woman becomes a full wife when she has raised two children to the walking stage. The emphasis is on producing numerous offspring and keeping as many as possible alive. In societies with high infant mortality, making many babies is the main strategy for survival.

Status rules inevitably bring misery for some, even though they mean better treatment for others. In sixteenth- and seventeenth-century Europe, Christian marriage was designed for the production of 'precious fruit' and the fertile woman was blessed by God. This was not so good for those who remained childless. As historian Olwen Hufton says, 'for married women not to have children carried with it connotations of failure and inadequacy'.

Even today, many of the world's women are expected to give birth every two years or so and childlessness is considered a supernatural curse. But where babies are intensely prized, groups usually arrange it so that nobody, in the end, is left out. Small communities – villages in rural Malaysia for instance – often share out the available children so that no home is completely child-free. 'Except in the case of newlyweds, it is rare to find a household lacking children. Malays consider such a home unbearably lonely. Grandparent and childless couples are often given children to raise by relatives with an abundance at home' (Carol Laderman, social anthropologist).

A Turkish proverb says, 'Angels don't enter a house where there is no child.' So people open up their houses; children are said to belong to the whole community and that way everyone can enjoy a little bit of parental status. After all, procreation evolved as simply the supreme motivation for being alive. 'Childbearing becomes the final common pathway for diverse human motives,' says Robert LeVine, an anthropologist working in Africa, 'conferring wealth, security, prestige and immortality – virtually everything valuable – on parents.'

From Here to Paternity

> One says, 'it's a son' the other 'a daughter'
> The other says, 'he has hair,' 'he's the image of his
>   father' . . .
> Papa come close, my son will kiss you
> He's of your making and look how he understands
>
> Angot de Lespeyronnière, French poet, 1610

Fatherhood is a precarious state. Dads have no equivalent of pregnancy or birth to reassure them of paternity, so it's not surprising that society 'conspires', as anthropologists see it, to convince each new father of the family resemblance. If modern blood tests are anything to go by, the fathers have cause for concern:

Evolutionary psychologists . . . asked people who they thought the newborn in their families most resembled. Overwhelmingly, mothers responded that the baby looked like the father. And the mother did this repeatedly when the father was close at hand . . . Perhaps for good reason: A few studies using blood work to establish true paternity have shown that at least 10 per cent of the men named as the father on the birth certificate could not possibly be the biological father.

Meredith Small, ethno-paediatrician

According to press headlines, western fathers are increasingly seeking DNA blood tests to establish paternity. At the time of writing, there are more than forty major private paternity-testing companies in America and seven in Britain, with mail-order test kits widely available on the net. But American dads are not the only ones with gene troubles. In societies where women are permitted to sleep with a variety of partners, it might be impossible, or impolite, to say exactly who fathered each child.

Fathers in ancient Rome took the question of paternity very seriously. They distinguished between '*pater*' (the man who brought you up) and '*genitor*' (the man who donated his genes). In a ritual which could mean life or death for the newborn, the midwife would place the swaddled baby on the ground at the feet of the paterfamilias − or father of the family. If he accepted paternity, the father would raise the child off the ground, taking it from mother earth into his protective care. If he rejected the baby, its future was fragile, to say the least. From this ancient custom comes the English phrase 'to raise a child'.

SHADES OF PINK

In medieval Europe, they tried to find a biological proof of parenthood on the new father's body. People decided that they could tell from a man's nipples whether or not he had fathered children. Pink nipples indicated the childless state; brown nipples meant he was a dad. Is it possible for male nipples to turn a darker shade in sympathy with the breastfeeding mother? Why not do your own spot-check at home?

Of course, most fathers make it to the conception. I say most, because fathers are such a variable breed, it's hard to pin them down. For a start, they are capable of fathering children from their teens to their seventies (most septuagenarians still produce sperm and average around twenty-two orgasms a year). This gives them a span of about sixty fertile years, compared with a woman's thirty-five.

Besides helping to conceive the baby, !Kung San fathers of the Kalahari Desert are able to get pregnant, and give birth, too. This achievement is not a biological miracle, but a question of verbal gymnastics. The !Kung San, whose hunter-gatherer lifestyle allows for lots of gender equality, are happy to use the verb '//ge', meaning to be pregnant and give birth, when referring to fathers as well as mothers. It's a serious case of reflected glory – why, after all, shouldn't fathers enjoy the full status which parenthood brings? (The // in //ge is one of the tongue-clicks which characterise the !Kung language. The ! in !Kung is another.)

Another amazing feat is performed by Gusii men of Kenya, Africa, who go on fathering children even after death. This miraculous undertaking does not involve being at the conception at all. Gusii fatherhood is a status which is attached to any legitimate marriage. After a man dies, his wives are duty-bound to carry on bearing children in his name. Less than a year after her husband's death, each wife goes through a ritual in which she chooses a 'levir', a brother or cousin of her husband, to continue impregnating her for as long as she is able to conceive. Each of these children is said to be fathered by the husband who died.

Social interpretations of the father-role vary enormously. After all, fathers are created largely by culture, while the physical functions of mothers leave little room for doubt. The Kayapó of central Brazil consider it quite acceptable for a sexually active woman to take different lovers, and be 'the friend of many'. Rather than assign a particular father to her pregnancy and risk jealousy, the woman may instead quickly conceive a 'forest baby', so keeping everyone happy. Body Shop founder Anita Roddick went through the Kayapó impregnation ritual:

One day when I was in the forest with the [Kayapó] medicine man he asked me how old I was and if I would like to get pregnant again. I said I wouldn't mind, and so he said he would show me how. I wondered quite what was coming next, but I needn't have worried. He took me down to the river, told me to strip off to the waist and stroked my back, very gently, with some kind of leaf. Then he mixed up a drink with water and shavings from the bark of a tree and tied a vine around my waist. He told me to wear the vine for three days, after which I would be pregnant with a female child.

Now I knew that you needed sperm to be pregnant, but I was also in awe of the rainforest people and their wisdom . . . I worried about it so much that I went back to the medicine man and asked for an antidote.

Anita Roddick, Body Shop founder in Brazil

The Ache people of Paraguay in South America also enjoy a great deal of sexual freedom and any woman is able to name at least two men who might be the genetic father. Jealousy is not an issue and the tribe accepts this kind of probability parenting as normal. The Ache, like the Canela people of Brazil, say that it takes many inseminations from a variety of men to make a baby and say that the child takes after the father who contributed most semen. Pregnant women thus seek affairs with men whose characteristics they admire. Anthropologists call this concept 'partible paternity'. The belief is held by at least eighteen tribes throughout the Amazonian lowlands of South America and a few groups elsewhere in the world.

For the Canela, the Ache and others, paternity is a shared responsibility. Fatherhood is forged not just through conception, but also through the providing role. Each child is treated to the attentions of a number of father-figures: the mother's husband and anyone who had sexual relations with the mother in the past year. 'Ache children do not lack for fathers . . . Ache recognise the connection between sex and conception but also believe that other males contribute to the growth of the child's "essence" when they bring a woman meat; these males have a responsibility for the child as well' (Meredith Small, ethno-paediatrician).

Responsibility, now that's a whole other subject . . .

Birth Partners

It is all different in this country – as is the difference between the sea and the sky. When [my first baby] was born in India it wasn't my husband's business to be with me. I stayed with my mother for five months; out of this two months were complete rest. Here I started work after three days. Over there I had a special Dhabra made for me with lots of ghee and nuts and raisins. Also my sister-in-law and Bhai [midwife] helped me in looking after the baby – massaging, bathing, feeding and changing. Here my husband helped me a lot otherwise I couldn't have coped . . .
    I must say I like the Indian way.

Graduate Hindu mother, working as a part-time cleaner in England

From the moment of birth, traditional cultures make it clear where a father ought to be, and few consider that place to be the birthing room. In fact, with some notable exceptions, most contrive to keep him away. In areas where women still give birth at home, surrounded by familiar female faces, men may be considered an intrusion. Taboos still surround the ancient mystery of birth, ensuring that for millennia it has remained distinctly women's work.

However, this shroud of secrecy does not mean that fathers have no part to play in the arrival of a new baby. Their roles may be ritualised, protective, designed to keep them busy, but they are also very real. Male birth rites often continue for as long as mother and infant are in ritual seclusion. In supportive communities, it may be considered more important that a father is given his own meaningful tasks, rather than steal upon on the female domain.

- In Cherokee Native American tradition, the father is given serious charge of the placenta, in a ritual which leaves mother and baby in postnatal peace. His job is to carry the placenta over two mountain ridges and bury it with a prayer, requesting that two years will pass before another baby is born. He must also make sure that he is not seen, as if anyone were to dig up the placenta and bury it too deeply, the couple would be unable to have any more children.

- In New Guinea, the new Arapesh father has his own distinct birth rites to perform. While his wife looks after the new baby, he seeks out a mentor, an experienced father of children, to guide him through the initiation process. The older man bathes the younger one in perfumed water and paints his body with white circles and lines. Thus purified and beautifully decorated, the Arapesh father completes his ritual by catching an eel, a symbol of his virility. He is now ready to embrace his new paternal status.

These rituals have little in common with the postnatal activities of the modern, western father, whose role is usually much more practical and connected to the baby. His partner probably gives birth in a strange hospital and needs his protection at close quarters. When the new mother returns home with no community of women to pamper and care for her, it is the father who is most likely to be called upon to cook and clean and help out.

This adaptation works fairly well. When a western father plays Lamaze coach or becomes the designated Birth Support Partner, he is helping his partner prepare for nuclear-family life. When he takes on postnatal tasks which traditionally belonged to generations of women, he reinforces western society's belief in the sanctity of the couple, rather than the importance of the community. However, maternity nurse is a tough role to play by yourself. Fathers are often stretched to provide the range of services which traditional midwives, grandmothers and sisters learn through a lifetime of experience. When society does not even make allowance for paternity leave, 'real' work soon intervenes. The one-man support system is swiftly snatched away. No wonder so many women find they cannot relax in postnatal seclusion, but return prematurely to their household chores.

Anything You Can Do . . .

In its perfect form, the husband observing the couvade takes to his bed and pretends to be lying-in, sometimes even simulating by groans and contortions the pains of labour, and sometimes even dressing in his wife's clothes. Whilst in bed, he is pampered and fed on dainties, nurses the infant, and receives the felicitations of his friends and relatives.

Warren Dawson, historian

One of the stranger aspects of worldwide fatherhood is the tradition of 'couvade', a man's attempts to mirror the female acts of birth and postnatal seclusion. Bizarre as the practice may seem, it has been recorded in a wide variety of societies over many hundreds of years. Simply put, fathers re-enact aspects of pregnancy, labour and lying-in. They may reduce their work load for nine months and/or take to bed at around the time of the birth – for which pains they receive the tender loving care usually reserved for a newly-delivered mother.

Obstetrician Dr Michel Odent believes that couvade emerges in developing societies as they turn the corner from matriarchy into patriarchy. If so, then couvade is a ritualised form of attention-seeking, a blatant attempt to divert people's time and energy from the mother to the father. On the other hand, you could construe couvade as an extreme outpouring of sympathy for the female condition, and a desire to share in the momentous birth experience. Dramatised sympathy or ritualised jealousy? – whatever the interpretation, couvade is an unusual way of showing you care.

Couvade (from the French '*couver*', to hatch) was described by the earliest travel writers, including the Venetian Marco Polo, who witnessed the practice among mountain tribes. It is quite obviously a performance for public consumption, drawing attention to the father and allowing him to rival mother and baby as a recipient of community care. In extreme cases, couvade even supplants maternal birth rites, as though the father had taken on the whole perinatal process:

One of the most curious features of [Corsican] customs is that which they observe at the birth of their children. When a woman becomes a mother she pays no heed to the period of lying-in; but her husband, as though he were an invalid, takes to his bed and is waited upon during the period of accouchement with as much attention as if he were really suffering bodily pain.

Diodorus Siculus, Greek historian, first century BC

The Basques of France and Spain were famous for their couvade rituals, as were some tribes of Siberia, Malaysia and North America. But not all couvade practices aim to steal the limelight. In northern Japan, the new Ainu father would hide in a friend's hut and spend twelve days in peaceful meditation. His spiritual seclusion was considered necessary to feed the newborn baby's soul, just as the mother was absorbed in nurturing his body. Among Nootka families, living in southern British Colombia, both mother and father took to their private quarters after birth, although the mother's womb-like birth hut sounds the cosier prospect: 'For four days after the delivery the mother stayed in her hut beside the fire, sitting with her legs stretched out, and being fed cod broth by her female attendants. The father spent these days sitting in the big house where he normally lived, eating dried fish' (Carleton Coon, anthropologist).

Sympathetic pregnancy is not merely a feature of remote or so-called 'primitive' societies. American researchers tell us that expectant western fathers visit their doctors twice as often as they did before their partners were pregnant, and with uncannily pregnant-seeming symptoms: nausea and bloating, to name but two. One study reported that sixty-five per cent of expectant fathers felt oddly uncomfortable, changed their diets or gave up smoking during their partners' pregnancy.

Postnatally, it can help enormously when fathers show solidarity with new mothers. For instance, Mbuti pygmy families of the Ituri rainforest in central Africa greatly prize meat – hunting takes a great deal of each tribe's time and energy. But both mother and father remain vegetarian until the baby has begun to crawl. Among the Yurok, an ancient fishing and gathering tribe of California, neither parent will taste venison or salmon (their most valued foods) until the baby's navel has fully healed. Failure to observe this rule will, they believe, lead to the baby's illness.

All over the world, fathers sense that their actions around the vulnerable time of birth have the power to undermine or encourage the new mother. They want to play their part in the birth rituals which fascinate and engage the whole community. It's their baby too, and they want to be involved.

Investment Bonding

It is not so strange that I love you with my whole heart, for being a father is not a tie which can be ignored . . . This tie is the source of my consideration for your immature minds, a consideration which causes me to take you often into my arms. This tie is the reason why I regularly fed you cake and gave you ripe apples and fancy pears. This tie is the reason why I used to dress you in silken garments and why I could never endure to hear you cry.

Sir Thomas More, writer and statesman, in a letter to
his children, sixteenth-century England

Is there such a thing as paternal instinct? We live in a culture where we doubt even the existence of biological maternal urges, so it may be hard to imagine that men should qualify. And yet there is no doubt about the attachment of fathers to the very youngest infants; about deep emotional responses which they had never anticipated and the development of bonds which endure for the rest of their lives.

Of course, not all fathers are equally involved with their children and many cultures arrange the domestic scene so that daddy is a distant character during the early years. Usually this distance arises wherever men are needed to be warriors; involvement in infant care is assumed by many cultures to compromise a man's capacity to be cold-blooded. But given the chance, fathers can display a series of traits once mistakenly classified as purely feminine.

For instance, fathers greet their newborns in the same way as mothers: touching their fingers and working around to the palms, arms, legs and body. When fathers talk to babies, they raise the pitch of their voices, using repetitions and short phrases, just like women. When asked about their postnatal emotions, men use the same adjectives that mothers do.

And as for bonding, there is no doubt that many fathers are capable of feeling a super-glue attachment to their babies from the first time they hold them in their arms. On the other hand, there are some important physical differences in the ways that men and women bond. 'The interest which a man has in a newborn baby follows a kind of chronology; it gets stronger as the baby gets older. This is not the same for a woman, who has what is called "the primary maternal preoccupation", which is connected with profound biological changes' (Michel Odent, obstetrician and primal health researcher).

LOOK INTO MY EYES

If you show a woman photos of babies, her eyes reveal an involuntary strong dilation – a measure of unconscious attraction, whether or not she has children. Perform the same test on a childless man, and you will actually see pupil constriction, demonstrating dislike. (These results are for westerners. I am not aware of similar tests on men from traditional cultures and baby-friendly communities). But try the test on a father, and the results are reversed. Even in the West, men who have children show pupil dilations nearly as strong as the women, suggesting an acquired interest in babies once they have their own. It seems that the male urge to nurture develops as a result of personal experience, in contrast with female desire, which is biological and usually pre-dates pregnancy.

This study has implications for those western men who do not bond immediately with their babies. Just because some fathers fall in love from the first day does not mean that all New Men must follow suit. There are also implications for New Women who complain that they have no maternal urges and/or do not connect with their newborn babies. Perhaps they, too, have been raised not to feel that 'primary maternal preoccupation' which doctors describe.

There is no rush. Babies do not fail to bond with mothers or fathers simply because the mothers and fathers doubt their own feelings. The solution is to keep connecting with the baby in positive, physical ways and let the emotions follow on. Skin-to-skin contact is the surest way to elicit strong maternal and paternal reactions. Parents can learn to provide what leading psychoanalyst Erik Erikson called 'a lasting centre of trust'. Holding is good for parents, as well as babies.

A series of unmistakable biological imperatives (pregnancy, birth, breastfeeding and hormonal programming) make it obvious to most cultures that mothers are the ones designed to do the lion's share of early bonding and care-giving. But babies are primed to connect eventually with a large circle of intimates, and fathers do not need to be jealous of the early mother-infant relationship.

In an almost forgotten ritual from Munich, Germany, the midwife wraps the newborn, as soon as he has uttered his first cry, in one of his father's shirts. The infant is then handed back to his mother for breastfeeding. This is done to 'make the baby love his father', without disturbing the vital early mother-baby relationship.

Fathers are needed around the time of birth. They can do so much to encourage and support the mother and child. Homemaking, food-bringing and guarding the door from visitors are the kinds of crucial contributions we see adapted from ancient cultures to our own. Fathers we have already seen, like the firewood-gathering Hausa of northern Nigeria (Chapter 2: Bath Time), the meat-fetching Ache of Paraguay (this chapter: From Here to Paternity), the soup-bearing Hmong from south-east Asia (Chapter 2: Mother's Menu) and the wage-earning westerner, all play crucial roles in the protection of the new family.

In tribe after tribe, we see fathers undertaking practical tasks to ensure the safety and nurture of the mother, so that she is able to nurture the child. Together they form the beating heart of the child-rearing community.

A Grand Old Age

Agostino said he liked to sit at the top of his land and count his children and grandchildren. Rather than wringing his hands at the poverty inflicted by fertility, he could comfort himself with the large number of his descendants.

Robert LeVine, anthropologist, talks to an impoverished Gusii grandfather of Kenya

If children are the currency of community life, then grandchildren are the gold-mark of success. All the status conferred on parents is multiplied for the ageing men and women who see their family line stretching far into the future, bearing their name, carrying on the old customs and respecting the memory of ancestors who went before. Wherever traditional cultures remain intact, we see the same pride expressed by the older generation, and the enormous respect which they earn as heads of an ever-increasing clan.

The quickest route to immortality is through the perpetuation of the family line. From continent to continent, old people utter the same refrain: children and grandchildren are their insurance against a bitter old age. Before the imposition of state education (which often alienates the new generation from the old) and the migration of young workers for better jobs, children grew up to be the backbone of their birth-community, guarantors of comfort for the old and the young.

'I don't believe in Social Security. I consider my sons as my security for my old age. In our *samati* (culture) sons are of great importance. We tell them right from the start what we are doing for them and what in turn is their responsibility' (Hindu parent, first generation Punjabi, living in Britain). This ardently-felt belief is the obvious pay-back for years of high-investment parenting. Unfortunately, younger people, influenced by a western-style world view, are less likely to want to keep to their side of the bargain. They may move away to get educated and never return home. They seek new models of family life, based on the nuclear-family example. And they feel little or no obligation to take care of their aged parents, to support them or invite them to live under the same roof.

One society on the point of such a transition is Singapore, where ninety per cent of grandparents still live with their children and grandchildren. This means only ten per cent live alone or in institutions, but ten per cent is too many, according to the Singapore government. Politicians, anxious that children are failing eastern ideals, have introduced a law allowing the over-sixties to sue children who fail to take them in. Their complaints are heard by a special tribunal in charge of 'filial responsibility'.

The island state's legislators have passed a law to ensure that Singaporean children do not duck out of their responsibility to look after elderly parents – a common enough problem in the West, but, according to the advocates of 'Asian values', something practically unheard of in Asian societies. Old people, they say, are treated with more respect, and tend to be cared for within an extended family.

'There's a lot of evidence that it's not a huge problem, but it's felt that there should not be any of it,' said a retired sociologist in Singapore.

Stephen Vines, foreign correspondent

Like Agostino, the sixty-eight-year-old Gusii grandfather who had no money but was content to count the members of his family, grandparents of the world continue to rely on their children and grandchildren for support. The end of life comes round full circle to the dependency with which it began. Many cultures are happy to support the old and the infirm as they do the young and weak. After all their parents did for them, without question or resentment, they consider it is the least they can do in return. And living in extended families, grandparents feel as wealthy as kings.

Deep in the Ituri forest in central Africa, somewhere in the 50,000 square miles of mud and trees, Ndima, an Mbuti pygmy grandfather, lay dying. He had few possessions, but nor did he have any concept of poverty.

I looked around Ndima's hut and was reminded of how little an Mbuti owns after a lifetime of hard work in the forest ... He did not even have on his tattered bark cloth but lay wrinkled and naked on his side, looking up at me with his gentle eyes ... Except for his traditional temporary one-roomed family hut of sticks and leaves, the bow he had once made with his own hands was the only material thing he owned in the world.

But Ndima was not aware that he had so little. Indeed, he probably thought of himself as having everything an old man could wish to have, for he had his children and grandchildren lying around him.

Kevin Duffy, anthropologist

GENERATION GAME

!Kung San families of the Kalahari Desert in Africa believe there is a spiritual connection between alternate generations, particularly when the child is the grandparent's name-sake. In fact, anyone who shares the same name is bonded in a 'name relationship' for life. Since there are only thirty-five male and thirty-five female names to choose from, that makes for a lot of interconnection.

To reinforce their special bond, grandparents of many cultures may be invited to play important roles at the child's birth. It is often granny who has the honour of naming the baby, or grandad who offers a special birth-day blessing.

As for Everyone Else . . .

A child in India is hardly ever alone.

J Holme, author of *Growing up in Hinduism*

We have met some of the most important people in a baby's life. We have seen that in many close-knit communities, adults other than the mother and father are given rituals and responsibilities which allow an intimate, unique and lifelong connection with the newborn baby. Yet these are not all the attachments a child can expect from a traditional community. We have touched only the surface of the potential for human support.

For in small rural villages and nomadic bands, every member is seen in close relationship to every child. Among the Mbuti pygmies of the Ituri rainforest in the Congo, all friends of your mother are called 'mother', all friends of your father are 'father'. Aboriginal children of Australia say 'mother' to their mother's sisters and 'father' to their father's brothers. A Swahili child of Chole Island, Tanzania, calls his mother's big sister 'big mother' and little sister 'little mother'. There are 'big fathers' and 'little grandmothers', too.

In South America, Navajo, Comanche and Hopi children have an abundance of women to call 'Mom'. Tchambuli children of New Guinea call every woman in the clan '*aiyai*' (mother, of course). In all these cases, adults are accorded at least some of the affection, respect and responsibility of real parents.

The next level of intimacy is one where adults are given the 'uncle' or 'auntie' tag. In India, where even strangers tend to be called 'uncle' or 'aunt', there are ten terms to describe the precise relationship of each father's-sister or mother's-brother-in-law. Examples of child-adult kinship terms like these, real and imagined, can be found in every continent. The fictitious ones are often as important as the others:

The family is very important to Black Americans. Kinship ties are deep and often intergenerational, reflecting their African heritage. Modern blacks place great emphasis on their families, both immediate and extended. . . . It is not uncommon for a couple's young children to address neighbors as (for example) 'Aunt Beth' or 'Godmother Dora'. These individuals are not related genetically to the children, but have been taken in as family members – as substitutes for relatives still living 'down home'. They are what is known as 'fictive kin'.

Meredith Mann Taylor, nursing tutor

There are many other ritualised relationships which connect children to their neighbourhood in ways we might never imagine. The woman-who-nursed-me, the big-sister-who-carried-me – these are the people who figure frequently in the memories of communally-raised children. A Siberian baby will have a special relationship with his 'navel mother', the woman who cuts the cord, and his 'carrying mother', the woman who bears him proudly to his father in a cradle, swathed in a decorative cloth.

For thousands of years of human society, children seem to have been using close kinship terms to relate themselves deliberately and individually to adults in their community. Or – more likely – it is a case of adults creating connective roles with the children. Only recently in western cities do we find the idea of children calling adults by their first names; some liberal parents abandon even the expressions 'mother' and 'father'. It is no coincidence that the last explicit kinship ties are being undone by the members of a nuclear society.

Kinship terms are used by the oldest cultures to bond equal members in unique ways. They help to define the human-to-human role, with children in a position of complete security. This was the model of child–adult relationships the Israeli government had in mind in 1947, when they created the kibbutzim: '. . . it is not only within the nuclear family that the child's sense of security is developed. Within the kibbutz, he grows in an atmosphere of trust and confidence; he learns that not only his parents but almost every adult he meets is friendly and helpful' (Menachem Gerson, kibbutz researcher).

As adults, we may have become accustomed to our nuclear-family privacy; we may be aware that community life brings its share of bickering and irritation; we may not want to go back – but many of us admit that our children would love the community life. Sometimes, despite our preference for privacy, we feel pangs that we are not part of a child-friendly culture. We sense that our society has made hard work of the very simple art of growing up.

'As the extended family network is fragmenting,' say J.S. Dosanjh and Paul Ghuman, researchers in ethnic minority education, 'the strain of rearing children is becoming more acute.'

The strains they refer to are not those in Britain or America, but in the Punjab region of India and Pakistan. '. . . village people are increasingly moving away from their traditional family and caste occupations to seek jobs in the burgeoning industries in urban areas. As a consequence, families are rejecting some of the old-established values and attitudes . . . this . . . has serious implications for the care of young children.'

Almost everyone seems to agree that there are advantages to communal child-rearing. For western parents, having children may be our chance to forge new links, to ask for the support we need and to make other people a part of our children's lives. If we don't have our own kin on the doorstep, we can always invent some. If the point of community is inter-dependence, then the more connections you create for your child, the better protected he will be. The system works like a holistic Neighbourhood Watch programme, ensuring that almost every adult and child feels attached to every other.

The Circle of Life

After all, we are all here, so those parental ancestors must have done something right.

Meredith Small, ethno-paediatrician

It is a theme worth noting, that many cultures see the human lifespan as a circle. Death is not a finality, nor the opposite of birth, but a rejoining of one's soul to the spirit world, from where each newborn baby comes. Many people believe that the soul will be reborn again, most probably in the frame of future generations. Human life, so treasured, so connected to the extended family, is not wasted by evaporating into nothingness.

In the language of Trobriand Islanders from Papua New Guinea, the word 'kopoi' translates into two quite separate English concepts. It is the word which means caring for a person who is dying, but it also means to nurture or nurse a newborn baby. Only a society which visualises life as a resolving circle could make such a connection. Only a strongly nurturing community would define birth and death in terms of the care given and received.

In our own society, those who care for the elderly and the dying know the satisfaction which comes from bringing children and ill or old people together. Just one example comes from south-east London, where St Christopher's Hospice carries out an annual ritual featuring a baby. Many of the residents know this will be their last Christmas. It is Katie's first . . .

The highlight for many at the world's first hospice came on Christmas Eve, when staff and volunteers processed through the candlelit wards, humming carols and carrying Katie, a three-month-old baby, daughter of one of the ward managers. This tradition of carrying the youngest child of a member of staff to the patients' bedsides began in 1970 . . .

'The atmosphere is a very strange, paradoxical mixture of sadness and celebration which, I think, is the reality of Christmas,' said the Rev Len Lunn, the hospice's chaplain for the past 11 years. 'If the patients are well enough we give them a carol sheet, otherwise they listen. They always want to see the baby and sometimes they want to hold the baby. It's a very powerful symbol of life being in the context of death, a juxtaposition which is very welcomed.'

Clare Garner, journalist

Life in the context of death may be a theme which belongs properly to religions which embrace reincarnation (and most religions of the world do), but it also makes perfect sense to this Christian cleric.

FIVE ALIVE

In the Lebanon, when five generations of women gather together, they say '*Ya sette kellme settik*' ('Oh grandmother speak to your grandmother'). Daughter, mother, grandmother, great-grandmother, great-great-grandmother: these are relationships which bring great honour and pride. Such a long lineage is rare, even in western society.

Many exotic rituals around the world connect the living and the dead. What may seem to some an unnatural desire to communicate with family spirits and honour the ancestors is to others just a part of the human continuum. Very old people are seen to be on the brink of the spirit world, so they are assumed to have a natural intimacy with the spirit of the newborn baby.

In early Greek culture, there was a belief that the grandparent was reborn in the grandchild. In Balinese religion, human souls reappear every fourth generation, and people say that great-grandparents should not walk the earth at the same time as their great-grandchildren. The name for great-grandchild is the same as that for great-grandparent and simply refers to being close to heaven. The great-grandparent is teased affectionately for hanging on:

Such lingerers have to pay a penny to their great-grandchildren, chance-met on the street. The newborn child and the aged great-grandparent are both too close to the other world for easy entrance into the temple. The baby cannot enter until after a special feast at three and a half or seven months, and the very aged enter through a special side gate.

Margaret Mead, anthropologist

Among the northern Hutu, a tribe of Rwanda in east central Africa, a circle-of-life play is enacted at the end of a mother and baby's seclusion – and again whenever a grandparent dies. The paternal grandmother calls together all the young children to carry out the mime. Representing the future life of the new-born child, the children till the soil using forked branches (if the baby is a boy) or cut the grass and sweep the yard (if it is a girl).

This little show is interrupted by someone sprinkling the children with water – it has started to rain, they say, and it's time for the children to go home. The young actors are then treated to a celebration meal, and all feel they have taken part in welcoming the new baby into the community. When the ritual is performed after a burial, it signifies the ever-turning circle of life, as each passing generation is replaced by a new one.

HOME TRUTHS

There is no such thing as a single human being, pure and simple, unmixed with other human beings. Each personality is a world in himself, a company of many. That self . . . is a composite structure . . . formed out of countless, never-ending influences and exchanges between ourselves and others. These other persons are in fact therefore part of ourselves . . . we are members of one another.

Joan Riviere, psychoanalyst, 1927

Glancing through this catalogue of human exhibits, there seems to be extraordinary unity around the world. Our languages may be unique, our customs weird and wonderful, our ideologies as variable as our political histories, but people play the same roles the world over.

From the equator to the ice caps, land-locked villages to sea-dwellers in stilt houses, we define ourselves in our direct relationship with our children. Why should this be? Why should

American moms and dads, grandmas and grandpas have so much in common with those from Siberia or the barely-penetrable rainforest? What instinct drives us to create aunts and uncles, godparents and other key figures to be prominent in our babies' lives? We could so easily have chosen different forms of address, relating ourselves to the environment, to political groups or to our leaders. We might have evolved without any sense of special relationships, calling everyone 'friend' and never caring who was our mother's sister's husband's cousin twice-removed.

But we do care, and the answer seems to be that human society evolved to transmit protective care from one generation to the next. Early culture was not an egalitarian enterprise, nor an individualistic struggle, but a complex web of individual human bonds, with hierarchies and inequalities taken into account. And the primary bond was with the baby.

Infants, source of all life, contained the secret code for the survival of the race. Fathers wanted to claim paternity. Grand-parents counted children as the currency of their lives, demanding only to be surrounded by them. And a whole host of other characters sought to share in the birth, the upbringing, the joy of each new child. From birth, Balinese parents are known for-ever more as 'Mother of . . .' or 'Father of . . .' the baby. Only a generation or two ago, northern English couples would, upon becoming parents, refer to each other as 'Mam' and 'Dad'. Conspicuously or unconsciously, we connect ourselves to chil-dren, society's most significant symbol of prosperity. Com-munities are crying out to be child-centred.

Babies evolving in hunter-gatherer communities found them-selves uniquely related to everyone they met. Like the Indian, the African, the South American or the Asian child today, the prehistoric baby was surrounded by concerned people. We know that human infants had to be reared in a context of intimate community, moving around in close-knit bands like the few remaining pygmies of central Africa still do today.

Communities provide a mutually beneficial relationship: people are the baby's context for life, and they define themselves through him. His health and happiness are inextricably wound up in their health and happiness. His survival is their success. Our future lies with him.

5. May We Present . . .

How will your baby be welcomed to the world? Will there be a party or christening, a naming ceremony or a ritual dedication? Earth, wind, fire and water are the elements of the ancient baby announcement. In a culture which has resorted to the duplicated mail-out, we could use a few hints on presentation . . .

A Small Announcement

And the angel said unto them, Fear not: for, behold, I bring you good tidings of great joy, which shall be to all people.
For unto you is born this day in the city of David a Saviour, which is Christ the Lord.
And suddenly there was with the angel a multitude of the heavenly host praising God, and saying,
Glory to God in the highest, and on earth peace, good will toward men.

St Luke recalls Jesus' birth announcement

When your baby is born, you may feel like shouting it from the rooftops. Join the crowd. All over the world, parents like to announce their babies' births in style. In Nigeria, where drumming is used to send messages as well as to entertain, a baby is named to the exuberant rhythms of the village drums.

In India, too, drummers appear after a birth, along with the Brahmin priest, the barber and the washerman, each of whom has a ritual role to perform. Among the Rajputs of northern India, birth announcements are the job of the sweeper, who drums out the message outside the door of the birth house, while Brahmin women gather to sing special songs. This drumming and singing is repeated for the first ten days: a noisy start to life by any standards.

When a child is born in Malawi, south-east Africa, the Ngoni father stands outside the birth hut and calls out his ritual cry: three times for a boy, twice for a girl. For old Breton families in north-west France, three peals on the largest church bell meant a boy had been born; one peal on the small bell signified a baby girl.

Sometimes the birth announcement is silent. Chinese families send red-painted eggs to family and friends: an even number for a girl and an odd number for a baby boy. Maranaw tribes of the Philippines hang a string of small flags over the front door after a birth – yellow for girls, white for boys.

Lots of gift-giving goes on when a baby is born. Birth is an opportunity for the father to be magnanimous with his beer or wine cellar; mother-in-law turns up with a food parcel or two; godparents give out coins to the crowd and everyone celebrates with acts of generosity. In old wealthy German families, a baby's birth was announced to the household staff by presenting them with a bunch of flowers. If tied in a white ribbon, the flowers denoted a baby girl had been born; if red, then a boy. This simple birth announcement was known as the 'Freudemaien', the posy of joy.

Back to My Roots

When a son was born to Abraham and Elizabeth, a tree was planted in the orchard for him. They had fourteen children in all, and each child had its 'birth tree' . . . And each grandchild had its tree, there, also, set out by grandfather when the tidings of its birth reached him; not always an apple tree – perhaps it was a plum, or cherry or pear. But it was always known by the name of the person for whom, or by whom, it was planted . . .

Lucy Maud Montgomery, Canadian romantic author, The Story Girl, c. 1910

Trees, which are rooted in the earth and stretch seemingly to the heavens, have always had great spiritual and symbolic meaning for humans. In Native American mythology, trees are the children of Mother Earth and Father Sky. Ancient people frequently invoked the power of trees in their blessings for new babies.

The ancient Romans would hang an olive branch over the doorway to announce the birth of a boy (and a piece of cloth for a girl). In Nigeria, the Ibo father places the stem of a banana tree outside the front door so everyone knows a baby has been born. Outside the village, there are groves of banana trees, each one named after an Ibo baby.

The planting of a birth tree is an ancient idea which has inspired many western parents looking for a meaningful birth ritual. Oak trees, revered by the Druids and Vikings, were the source of many fertility rituals. In old England, a baby was ceremonially passed through the branches of a maple tree, with a prayer for long life. Ash trees, which were believed to have healing properties, were used in magical attempts to cure childhood illnesses like whooping cough or rickets.

Some plant the placenta beneath the roots of a sapling, combining two old customs at once. Aboriginal women of Warmun, Western Australia, place a piece of the cord in a hole in the boab tree to make the child grow big and strong like the tree. Swiss parents plant an apple tree for a baby girl and a nut tree for a boy – they connect the growth of the tree with the development of the child. In eighteenth-century Frankfurt, Germany, the birth of Johann Wolfgang Goethe (the future scientist, poet and playwright) was celebrated by his grandfather, who planted a birth tree in his back garden. In Guatemala, the cord is buried under the birth tree, and this becomes the child's spiritual home. When living far away, a person can always re-create that 'home' by finding a similar tree to sit under.

Other living plants have potent symbolism as well. Grains of rice are symbolic of new life in the east, just as ears of corn are to Native North Americans. In the Unitarian Church, which welcomes people from a variety of religious backgrounds, a baby's naming ceremony may include the giving of a flower to symbolise the growth, beauty and sweet fragrance of life. Meaningful symbolic gestures are all around us — we have only to pluck them from our own imagination.

Soul Mate

It is a sad truth, but we have lost the faculty of giving lovely names to things. Names are everything.

Lord Henry Wotton in *The Picture of Dorian Gray*, Oscar Wilde, 1891

Of course, we must name the new arrival. So important is a baby's name that many cultures believe it embodies his soul. The Inuit of Canada, for instance, say that your name represents the essence of your being, and even to utter a name somehow conjures that person up. Anyone who shares your name becomes, literally, your soul mate. Among the Kafirs of Afghanistan, to name someone is to 'pour' something into them, in other words the quality of the name fills up the child's spirit. A nameless child is considered to be a vulnerable, wandering thing, a concept repeated in many religions, including early Christianity.

I NAME YOU BASIL THE BARBARIAN ...

Some cultures – the Tungus of Siberia, for instance – believe that names have the power to influence your personality. Their belief has some foundation in reality. A 1991 report to the British Psychological Society found that girls who were given names rated as highly feminine (Sophie, Elizabeth and Emily for instance), grew up into more 'feminine' adults. Whether children were influenced by their own names, or by others' reactions to their names, remained unproven.

Another study of the Ashanti people of West Africa demonstrated a similar effect. The Ashanti say that boys who are born on a Monday, 'Kwadwo', are peaceful types, while those born on a Wednesday, 'Kwaku', have quick tempers. One study showed that more Kwakus than Kwadwos were convicted for juvenile crimes. This sounds like an extreme case of personality labelling, to the detriment of the Wednesday boys.

In England, it was supposed to be unlucky to reveal a baby's name outside the family before the christening had taken place. In old Scottish tradition, the christening of the child was the only sure way to protect him against the wicked intentions of the Fey Folk. As an interim measure, a flaming torch was carried sunwise around the mother and baby soon after birth. This, and the bunches of garlic hung from the cradle, might have given some protection against invading germs.

Names still retain a magical quality in many cultures. There is a Chinese tradition which prevents parents from pronouncing the names of babies, for fear that they will attract witchcraft. Children use temporary names (called 'milk names') until they have grown up, when their real names are revealed to them.

Likewise, the Arunta Aborigines of Australia's Northern Territory are given names which are so sacred and powerful that they remain secret from children. A person only finds out his or her true first name after going through the rites of puberty. Imagine telling your fourteen-year-old that from now on his name was going to be – let's say – Kevin instead of Spike. I wonder how he would take it?

Pick a Name, Any Name

A name was not yet chosen. The priest in passing had said it should start with an 'S' as defined by the position of the planets, but the old lady could not make up her mind. It was she who made the decision, once the men had given their views. The mother was not consulted . . .

The old lady bent over the baby. 'Shardamma,' she whispered, 'Sharda, Shara, Saramma.' She struggled to find the pronunciation and kept interchanging the words. 'Sharda, Shara, Sara.'

Sarah Hobson, documentary film-maker, watches as a Gowda woman
of south India chooses her granddaughter's name

While western parents scour the baby books for names that no one else thought of, but everyone will approve of, some cultures seek divine inspiration. Rituals concerning the choice of a name can be as fascinating as the names themselves. In New Zealand Maori tradition, for instance, ancestors' names are slowly recited until the baby sneezes; this is a sign from the spirit world that the right name has been selected. Other ways of handing over the decision include the Australian Aboriginal custom of reciting suitable names during the final birth contractions: the name on your lips as the placenta is delivered is the final choice.

Being asked to name a child is usually a great distinction. Living among the Mbuti pygmies of the Ituri rainforest in Zaire, American Kevin Duffy was asked to name a new baby by Ndima, the infant's dying grandfather.

It was a rare honor, and several names, some exotic, some personal, occurred to me almost immediately: Alexander, Maxwell, Patrick, Caesar, Homer, Stanley.

These were all fine names, but I rejected them after only a moment's consideration. 'The name I give the child,' I said at last, 'is Ndima Kidogo – Little Ndima.' . . .

Nobody spoke as Ndima sat gently rocking his grandson to and fro. 'Ndima Kidogo,' the old man murmured while tenderly pressing the tiny infant against his worn out, wrinkled body. 'I will make your first bow, and we will hunt together in the forest.'

Kevin Duffy, anthropologist

Kevin Duffy was privileged. Among many tribes, including, for instance, the Thonga of South Africa, the name-giver forges a special relationship with the newborn. Every year the Thonga name-giver must bring a gift for the child he or she has named.

When a name must have religious significance, then it matters which book or oracle you consult. Muslim mothers choose ideally from names of the Prophet Mohammed, his wives and daughters, biblical names, or names of the Caliphs and Imams of Islam, to name a few. Mohammed suggested that the most beautiful names were those which conveyed praise or servitude to Allah, for instance:

Islamic boys' names
- Abd al Ra'uf   Servant of the Most Merciful
- Fadh Al Lah   The Excellence of God
- Nur al Din   Brightness of the Faith

Islamic girls' names
- Aisha   Living / Prosperous (wife of the Prophet Mohammed)
- Rida   Favoured by God
- Shakirah   Grateful to Allah

In former times, Roman Catholics were expected to choose from an approved list of saints' names, while Hindu mothers today obtain a religious horoscope giving lucky letters and sounds which should be contained in the baby's name. Sikh priests find the first letter of the new baby's name by opening their holy book, the Granth Sahib, at random.

Chukchee mothers of Siberia use special divining objects, which wobble when they recite the auspicious baby name. Women of the Pacific island of Okinawa, Japan, consult the 'rice oracle', a ritual conducted by an old woman who informs them which fateful letters from the Japanese script should be used to ensure the baby's well-being. Kwakiutl Native Americans of the north-west coast believe their names have been handed down to them since the beginning of time.

Many ancient cultures thought that dreams were signals from the spirit world. Dreams were taken very seriously and used in decision making. Hawaiian tradition, for instance, encouraged parents to choose a baby name from the pictures or words spoken in a dream. As pregnant women are prone to vivid dreams, this can be an exciting and imaginative way to name your baby. Hawaiian names often have an ethereal, dreamlike quality, for instance, Aheahe means 'soft breeze', Aka is 'shadow' and Ala-ula is the 'glow of the sunset'.

What's in a Name?

A good name is better than precious oil.

Jewish saying

Your baby's name may have religious significance, or be chosen to honour the family ancestors. Perhaps it belongs to an honoured relative, or is descriptive of attributes you wish your child to have. I once met a child whose name was 'Timotei' – her parents had seen it on a bottle of shampoo and thought it sounded exotic. Presumably the Hmong people of Laos, south-east Asia, on arriving in America, were similarly inspired by the new and amazing things around them:

Some Hmong parents in Merced [California] have given their children American names. In addition to many standard ones, these have included Kennedy, Nixon, Pajama, Guitar, Main (after Merced's Main Street), and, until a nurse counseled otherwise, Baby Boy, which one mother, seeing it written on her son's hospital papers, assumed was the name the doctor had already chosen for him.

Anne Fadiman, journalist and author

Whatever our inspiration, children's names are usually the most enduring gifts we shall ever give them. Here are some names with a difference:

* The Ibani, an Ijo tribe on the eastern Niger Delta in Nigeria, give names which indicate that children are more important than possessions. 'Faghafura' means 'family is more important than riches'. 'Bitegeriagh' signifies 'a cloth cannot speak' – cloth is the symbol of Ibani wealth, but it is not as important as human life.

* Old English names often proclaimed the virtues required for battle: boys' names included Archibald (very bold), Earl (nobleman, warrior), Graham (warlike) and Hollis (hero). Anglo Saxon girls' names also reflected strength of character, for instance Alberta (noble and bright), Kendra (understanding, knowledge) and Megan (strong and able). Girls were also called 'happy' names like Bliss, Blithe and Merry.

* In Nigeria, Yoruba names convey much meaning in a few syllables. 'Ajibola' is 'one who wakes up to find honour'; 'Olatunde' means 'fame comes again'; 'Oladunjoye' roughly translates as 'high status is more delightful than a chieftaincy title'.

* Some Puritan settlers in seventeenth-century New England used to close their eyes, open the Bible and point to a word at random. Consequently, their children occasionally ended up with names like 'Notwithstanding' and 'Maybe'. Girls were also given humble names to encourage meekness: for instance,

Obedience, Patience, Silence, Content, Lowly, Thankful and Mindwell.

* Native America Tribes are renowned for their poetic personal names. The Comanche who roamed the southern plains of Colorado, Kansas and Oklahoma, gave themselves nomadic names, e.g. 'Making-Bags-While-Moving'. The Miwok of California used names to connect themselves to nature: Kono was 'tree-squirrel-bites-through-pine-nut-kernel' and Isekemu meant 'water-runs-gently-when-the-creek-dries'.

THE SAME NAME GAME

While the Sioux people of South Dakota invented lyrical names like 'Chase in the Morning' or 'Star-Comes-Out', other cultures are inescapably boring. Baby Wisdom's very own Unimaginative Name Awards, in reverse order, go to:

Third place:
All those ancient Roman families who named their children Primus, Secundus, Tertius (or Prima, Secunda, Tertia for girls). (The equivalent of naming your children First, Second and Third.) Fortunately, free-born children were allowed three names each.

Second place:
The Carpatho-Rusyns (an ethnic group living at the crossroads of Poland, Slovakia, Hungary and the Ukraine) traditionally named their boys after father or grandfather. But girls were named with conveyor-belt monotony: all eldest daughters were called Mary, second daughters were named Anna and third daughters were Helen.

First place:
The seventeenth- and eighteenth-century Bach family from Leipzig in Germany, who, over a period of more than 200 years, demonstrated remarkable lack of invention by naming many generations of boys Johann. One was the genius composer, Johann Sebastian Bach, but there were also Johann and Johann his two big brothers, Johann his father, Johann his father's twin brother, Johann his grandfather and numerous Johanns who were uncles and cousins and – of course – his own children. One biographical dictionary names twenty different Johann Bachs, all close relatives, all famous musicians in their day. It must have been very confusing when the post arrived.

To be fair, the Bachs were typical of European families of this period, who (like some American families today) were inclined to use the same names again and again. The idea was to perpetuate the father's name for posterity. Records from sixteenth- to eighteenth-century England show endless repetitions of Johns, Toms, Annes and Elizabeths. You could call it an early form of recycling.

Wetting the Baby's Head

The baptism . . . was an occasion for generosity and rejoicing. 'Wetting the baby's head' in Lancashire referred not merely to the cross of baptism administered from the font but to the drinks purchased afterwards by the father and godfather for neighbours in the alehouse.

Olwen Hufton, historian, on christenings in sixteenth- and
seventeenth-century Europe

Christenings did not become a part of Christian observance until around AD 200 and were not mentioned in the Bible. They replaced the ancient water blessings which belonged to Indo-European tradition (and are still practised today by Brahmin Hindus). In fact, the Christians probably borrowed the form of ceremony from the Celts, who touched their babies with blessed or sacred water in the first few moments after birth. In parts of Mexico, the washing of newborns would be accompanied by chanting to the water goddess, who was celebrated as the baby's true 'mother'.

Scottish islanders used to baptise their babies with spray from the running wave, or water that was cupped in the fingers from the incoming tide. Baptism was the job of the Gaelic nurse, or '*banghluin*', who would place three drops of water on the baby's forehead and say:

> The little drop of the Sky
> On thy little forehead, beloved one.
> The little drop of the Land
> On thy little forehead, beloved one.
> The little drop of the Sea
> On thy little forehead, beloved one . . .
>
> Blessing of the Gaelic midwife

Sometimes Wisdom, Peace and Purity were substituted for the pagan trinity of Sky, Sea and Land and it was an easy step from there to the Christian trinity of the Father, Son and Holy Spirit. Baptism was the rite which sealed the gate between the spirit world and the earthly one. It also saved vulnerable Catholic babies from an after-life spent eternally drifting around Limbo. For Roman Catholics, Holy Baptism is the first of seven sacraments, the essential spiritual doorway on the path to heaven.

Christening customs vary around the world. European Christians used to put a little salt into the baby's mouth to signify the gift of heavenly wisdom and the baby was also anointed with oil on his forehead, ears and nose. In Ethiopia, priests anoint the infant's head, hands, breast and knees in the sign of the cross, before tying a silk cord of red, blue and white around the baby's neck. In medieval England, an illegitimate baby could not be baptised until his mother had done public penance at the market place or in church, wearing only a white sheet.

Ordinary people regarded all these rituals with fear and reverence and many Britons were not at all happy when Henry VIII's new Church of England modernised the formula in the sixteenth century. Prior to Henry's day, the Catholic baptism included exorcism of the devil, since the human infant was born 'with fallen nature', i.e., the imprint of original sin. The Reformation removed all the devil references, but not without resistance: 'Baptism was popularly viewed as a magical rite ensuring eternal salvation and the changes introduced by the Reformation in this particular sacrament caused considerable popular distress' (Marianne Elliott, historian).

Even after the Reformation, it was commonly believed that when a baby cried at the christening, it was a sign that the devil was escaping from his body. So potent were beliefs surrounding baptism, that people went to extreme measures to carry out the ritual. During birth, a water squirting device was used to baptise the crowning heads of babies who were feared to be dead or dying. Mothers in France took their stillborn babies to *'sanctuaires à répit'*, shrines of respite, where they prayed for a miracle. If the infant was imagined to have gained a little colour, breathed or fluttered an eyelid, the priest might be persuaded to give him a baptism, and subsequently a Christian burial.

BAPTISM BELIEFS

Baptism is an ancient and powerful ritual which evokes many popular superstitions. In past times, it was thought that . . .
* The right arm of a baby boy should not be touched by the holy water, for it must contain enough evil to make him a fearless warrior one day and put his enemy to the sword (Ireland).

- When more than one baby was being baptised at a time, guests raced to the church door – the baby of the winning family would be lucky in love (Philippines).
- The baby's christening cap and white 'chrisom' cloth should be worn for the next three months, to protect him from evil spirits (England).
- If the font water was saved and given to the child later in life, he or she would become a wonderful singer (America).
- If the baby lifted his head up during the service, he would enjoy a long life (Wales).
- Children christened by the light of the same candle would grow up to be fond of each other. Christening candles were made tall and wide so they could be shared by siblings (Germany).

By the Tudor period, christenings had become extremely lavish affairs; prosperity and piety were uncomfortably close cousins in the parties which followed a birth. It was considered bad luck not to send the best presents you could afford. Alcohol was also an important feature of the occasion. In Silesia, Germany, a beer barrel placed outside a house was a sign that a christening party was going on and people should drop in for free booze. In Wales, enormous christening glasses, as big as vases, became fashionable. The 'sponsor', or godparent, was expected to down a christening glass full of the local brew at one gulp.

Here is a description from eighteenth-century Anglesey, an island off north Wales: 'In Christenings, when the christening is over then the Father invites home his friends and ye Parson to drink ye health of ye woman in ye straw, and after dinner this they do for ye first part so plentifully till they can drink no more for that day, money to ye midwife, to ye nurse and to the maid. Home stark drunk' (H. Owen, eighteenth-century Welsh biographer). Christening parties became renowned for being raucous affairs, liable to get out of hand, and a few European countries set legal limits to the number of guests allowed at a christening.

Meanwhile, certain bands of Christians refused to believe that a newborn baby was born into original sin at all, and in the sixteenth century breakaway church movements emerged across Europe. The Anabaptists insisted that adults, not infants, should be baptised because Jesus' love was enough to lead their children to spiritual salvation. This led to their persecution by Catholic, Lutheran and Reformed churches and the emigration of many to America. Today, Quakers and others, such as the Amish people of Pennsylvania, descendants of the Swiss Brethren, are among the few Christians who do not practise any kind of christening, but christenings remain almost as popular as white weddings in western Europe and America. They are, of course, only one way to name a baby.

Signed and Sealed

> And when they name you great warrior
> Then will my eyes be wet with remembering
> And how shall we name you, little warrior?
> See, let us play at naming
>
> Song of the Didinga mother, east Africa

Nearly half the world's parents do not bother with a formal naming ceremony at all. The Rajputs of northern India are, like forty-seven per cent of the world's population, relaxed about the whole process. Like the Gowda grandmother quoted earlier, they simply experiment with an assortment of names for the baby's first six months until settling on the one that fits best.

Even the need to register a birth is a fairly new idea. Of course, it could not be done by a pre-literate society, but now most of the literate ones have made birth registration a legal requirement. As reading and writing entered the popular domain in the sixteenth century, there was great excitement about seeing the infant's name scrawled in ink on the parish register. Carrying a baby down to church for this purpose was a moment of personal pride and communal joy. Literate fathers would also record birth dates in the family Bible or, failing that, in the margin of any other book to hand.

Recording the exact time of birth only became necessary if horoscopes were required, as they are for Hindu and Sikh families. In India, the birth certificate or '*janam patra*' is a semi-sacred document used by astrologers to prepare each baby's fortune-telling charts. These will be consulted at key moments – for instance, when assessing compatibility for an arranged marriage. It is the village Brahmin (priest) who is given the important task of recording the baby's precise time, date and place of birth.

Besides registration, western parents have no obligations regarding their babies' names. Yet as many people drift away from formal religions, they seem once again to be seeking naming ceremonies which have personal and community meaning. Magazines and newspapers are full of ideas for humanist, rationalist and other secular rituals which name children without binding them to any particular religion.

The British Humanist Association says that humanism (a belief in essential human morality without an after-life or a God) dates back 2,500 years. Their leaflet, *New Arrivals*, suggests using 'mentors' instead of godparents and offers ideas for poetry readings and appropriate music. In 1998, the British government went further, creating a civil naming ceremony for use in register offices. Parents were invited to make this pledge: 'We promise to try to be patient with our baby, neither demanding too little nor expecting too much. We will try to offer him/her unconditional love regardless of his/her success or failure' (Civil naming ceremony, United Kingdom).

Unfortunately, this document sounds more like a parent-school contract than a meaningful parental promise. All-purpose naming services have little purpose in a society which has lost touch with its own traditions. Simple, symbolic acts are needed to transform civil ceremonies into expressive ritual. The ancient Romans, for instance, decorated the front room and doorway with flowers on a baby's naming day. Ghanaians beautify the mother and baby in patterns of white clay, while Moroccan mothers decorate their babies' hands with henna for luck before they are named.

A FEATHER AND A NAME

The ancient Anasazi Pueblo Indians, of the Four Corners around Arizona, named their babies in a ritual which used a Corn Mother. It was made for the occasion by the baby's grandmother. Granny would take a perfect ear of white corn (maize), stripping off the outer husk and the silk. She fixed a tuft of white eagle down to the top of the corn, making it look like a headdress. The Anasazi called this the 'breath feather' because it could be blown away by the slightest breath. As soon as the newborn was dressed, the grandmother would pass the Corn Mother four times over his body, and as she did so, she would reveal his name.

The ancient Mayan people, whose empire stretched across the tropical rainforest of Mexico from AD 250 to 900, also believed in the sanctity of corn as a source of fertility and new life. Their great text, the Popol Vuh, says human beings were originally formed from an ear of corn.

Blessing Baby

They do not love these beautiful symbolic actions, these 'ministers', to whom they are superstitions. This old, pagan, sacramental earth-rite is, certainly, beautiful. How could one better be blessed, on coming to life, than to have the kiss of that ancient Mother of whom we are all children?

Fiona MacLeod, Celtic visionary, describes the ritual of Old Mothering

The Celts, like many other ancient cultures, combined a number of blessings to give each newborn baby the best possible start in life. At the start of the twentieth century, Scottish author and poet William Sharp set out to research fading Gaelic traditions. He recorded his findings through the 'Celtic Twilight' writings of his pseudonym, Fiona MacLeod. In the Inner Hebrides, Fiona finds a fisherman's daughter on her first day out of bed with her newborn baby, kneeling in the bracken at the edge of a wood:

The girl was there, and had taken the child from her breast and, kneeling, was touching the earth with the small lint-white head.

I asked her what she was doing. She said it was the right thing to do; that as soon as possible after a child was born, the mother should take it – and best at noon, and facing the sun – and touch its brow to the earth. My friends . . . used an unfamiliar phrase: 'It's the Old Mothering.' . . . I do not doubt the rite is among the most primitive of those practised by the Celtic peoples . . . There must be wisdom in that first touch.

Fiona MacLeod, Celtic visionary

In ancient Rome, as in old Scotland and Alsace and Württenberg, Germany, the midwife would place the new baby on the earth (Mother Earth) for the father to raise symbolically in his arms. This Old Mothering rite was performed facing the sun (Father Sun), an element of ancient worship found in Africa, Native American communities and elsewhere. Among the Gusii people of Kenya, for instance, the party to end mother and baby's seclusion involves a ritual sun blessing.

The sun, the moon and the stars feature in many a baby blessing. One of the first experiences of the Zuñi pueblo Indian infant from the Arizona region was to be presented to the Sun

Father, source of all life. The person entrusted with this task was his maternal grandmother, who would wash him in yucca suds, coat him in deer fat and wrap him in a special blanket. The baby was then taken out of the birth room to meet all his female relatives and receive a name. No men were allowed near until four days had passed.

After this, the Zuñi grandmother would transport her grand-child to the flat roof of their house and show him ceremoni-ally to the north, south, east and west. Holding the little bundle far out in her arms, she told the four corners of the world the new baby's name and asked for the blessings of spirits in both earth and sky.

> Now this is the day.
> Our child,
> Into the daylight you will go out standing.
> Preparing for your day . . .
> Our child, it is your day.
> This day . . .
> May your road be fulfilled.
>
> **Zuñi grandmother's prayer as she presents a new baby to the sun**

There is also a remnant of sun worship in the European belief that Sunday's child is the bonniest, happiest, best behaved and generally luckiest child of all. Originally, the Christian sabbath was on Saturday (as it still is in Jewish observance) and Sunday was literally the Day of the Sun. And in pre-Christian belief, Sunday's Child was blessed above all others.

Other welcoming rituals involve aspects of the natural land-scape, the water which sustains life; trees which give shelter and provide food; outstanding features of the landscape which are regarded as part of the community's soul (in eastern cultures, mountains are often seen as breast-like and caves as womb-like, thus emphasising the human relationship with Mother Earth). In Guatemala, the Mayan people take each baby to greet the spirits of nature:

When a boy or girl child is born . . . we go to the stream and say to it 'Here is a new life which will need your water', we go to the volcano and say to it 'Here is a new being that needs your protection', we go to the trees and say to them 'Here is a new being that needs your shade' . . . and so we go to all of Nature saying 'We present our children to you'.

Maria, a Mayan woman of Guatemala

In return for paying these respects, the child will gain the strength of the natural world: its beauty, its power and its fertility. The baby's soul is now bound to the forces of the earth.

Fire rituals are also found on every continent. A single flame is used as a symbol of the human soul. A candle is lit at Roman Catholic christenings to symbolise enlightenment. The Cachikel people of Peten, Guatemala, have a birth rite which involves passing a flaming candle over the baby's head in the shape of the pagan cross. This invokes protection from the evil eye.

'Smoking' is another birth ritual which was once practised all around the world. This has nothing to do with tobacco, but involves passing a baby once through the smoke of a fire, an act which proclaims the parents' intentions to shield their child and keep him safe. Australian Aboriginal and African babies are passed through smoke to give them spiritual and physical protection. The old Scottish tribes did it to stop the Hidden People from touching or singing to the vulnerable newborn.

The last time I was told of it was of a crofter and his wife in North Uist. The once general custom is remembered in a familiar Gaelic saying, the English of which is 'He got a turn through the smoke'. After baptism, a child was taken from the breast by its mother, and handed (sometimes the child was placed in a basket) to the father, across the fire.

Fiona MacLeod, Celtic visionary

I should like to point out the breastfeeding detail in MacLeod's accounts. In order to perform baptism, earth-touching or smoking, the mother had first to take the baby from the breast. We may speculate that this almost permanent attachment to mother was actually the key to the infant's long-term survival and his greatest blessing of all.

Gossips and Grand Lunches

'I don't believe any of that nonsense about sending them a silver spoon at birth and then keeping in touch just at birthdays and Christmas . . . My policy is to send unbirthday presents . . . When they're about fourteen, I invite them to a very grand lunch and from then on I hope they know I'm really there for them if they need me . . . As far as I'm concerned, being a godparent means you stop being a friend of the parents, and you become a friend of the child.'

Gay Firth, England, veteran godmother of six

Medieval Christians, keen to establish a spiritual parenting role, found the most obvious candidates in the women who attended the birth. These seven or eight women were called God Sibs, meaning sisters in God, a phrase which was soon whittled down to 'gossips'. Well into the eighteenth century, gossips were spiritual guardians whose charges were named after them. Mr Gilbert Jackson of Oxfordshire records the birth of his thirteenth daughter: 'XIII. My dau. Elizabeth Raymond, 26 Sept. 1725. Gossips, Mr Hampton, Mrs Raymond and Mrs Gringo . . .' The task of the gossip was to intercede for the child's vulnerable spirit, providing a Christian example and moral guidance. On a more practical level, medieval godparents also pledged to keep the child safe from fire and water. As baptism rites flourished and an ostentatious christening became a sign of religious piety, godparents would lay on lavish gifts for all.

One inventory from fifteenth-century Florence shows that godparents brought two large cakes, large boxes of spiced cookies, bunches of candles and little torches to the christening. In England, the godfather gave sugared almonds to the godmother and midwife, before handing out coins to the children of the parish.

In medieval Europe, godmothers and fathers were expected to keep in touch with the child's progress and (in rich families, at any rate), to send cumulative gifts – like a complete set of silver cutlery – over the years. German godparents sent their charges beautifully handwritten or copper-engraved letters, called 'Patenbriefen', with personal messages and christening scenes, to keep for ever. Although it was a great honour to be a godparent, it was also an onerous task, involving years of gift-giving and the possibility of a more active role if the child was orphaned.

In times when parents might die young and mothers were at risk through childbirth, the godparent was a real safeguard in children's lives. In old Wales, it was believed that godparents should come from three different parishes, while in seventeenth-century Germany some babies had up to fifty godparents poised to protect them.

Christians are not the only ones to consider the future of the baby in this way. Among the Yaghan people of Tierra del Fuego in South America, a special friend of the birthing woman is selected to be a secondary mother for each baby. Her first task is to 'catch' the baby as it emerges. She retains a lifelong interest in the child and is ready to adopt him if needs be.

Perhaps it is time we reinvented godparents and gave them a few rituals to remind them of their lifelong connection. They could send beautiful hand-written letters, for instance, or offer a little fire and water protection . . .

The First Cut

She was *Jethi* (the first-born), so we took her to the Goddess' Mandir – *Chint purni* – and had her hair shaven there and threw it into a river. Then we had no fear that somebody could get her hair locks and harm her by using it in an evil eye or black magic rituals.

Brahmin housewife, India

In welcoming a new baby into the community, many cultures like to create a change in the child, something which binds him to them in a ritual way. One such change is the formalised haircut or shaving, which is believed to protect the baby spiritually and create a reason for thanksgiving.

Hair has always been a strong source of magic and symbolism for humans. It can be harvested, like a crop growing in the earth, and it continues to grow even after death. Haircutting, in particular, is often connected with rituals of purification. The newborn hair of a baby is thought by some cultures to be contaminated with the fluids of the womb; removing it is a way of cleansing the infant and giving him a fresh start. So a baby's first haircut may entail far more than a trip to the hairdresser. By shearing off the 'birth hair' (as the Tibetans call it), the baby makes a symbolic leap from life in the womb to life on earth.

Haircutting ceremonies are conducted by the Samals of the Philippines, the Aymara of Bolivia in South America, and in rural Taiwan. On the Indonesian island of Roti, the baby's shorn hair is hung from a palm tree and everyone celebrates with a pig roast. But the biggest hair-cutting rituals take place on the Indian subcontinent, where Muslim and Hindu laws require it as a step towards spiritual health.

Strict Muslim observance requires the 'Akika', a seven-day head-shaving for newborns, although some parents prefer to perform the ceremony much later. Prayers of thanksgiving are said and the hair is considered to be an offering to Allah.

Permanent Markers

In the parish church of Saint-Nicolas we can see an early seventeenth-century painting which comes from the Abbey of Saint-Martin-des-Champs. The scene of the Circumcision is surrounded by a crowd of children, some of them with their parents, others climbing the pillars to get a better view. For us, surely, there is something strange, almost shocking, about the choice of the Circumcision as a festival of childhood, depicted in the midst of children. Shocking for us, perhaps, but not for a present-day Moslem or for a man of the sixteenth- or early seventeenth-century.

Philippe Ariès, historian, describes the sixteenth-century European festival which celebrated the circumcision of Jesus

Circumcision, the permanent badge of spiritual belonging, is an important birth ritual for many of the world's cultures. It is one of a number of ways in which communities brand their babies, conferring social membership and spiritual protection at the same time. Although it may be performed at puberty or any time during childhood, most cultures circumcise at birth. Perhaps this is because of a widespread belief that newborn babies are less sensitive to pain. This is certainly the rationale applied by the Maya of Yucatan, Mexico, where midwives pierce the ears of newborn girls:

It was explained to us that so soon after birth [the baby] doesn't feel anything, whereas a day later she would be 'paying attention'. Doña Juana dips a threaded needle in alcohol and draws it through each ear; then she cuts the thread and ties it into a loop. In about three days the baby's first earrings, perhaps tiny family heirlooms, will be inserted.

Brigitte Jordan, birth researcher

There may be a grain of truth in the midwife's words. Both mother and baby release endorphins (natural painkillers) during birth, which is how some women are able to undergo stitches without anaesthetic in the aftermath of delivery. However, this protection is shortlived. Babies are able to feel aches and stings and needle pricks even before they are born, and certainly do so afterwards.

Ancient philosophers had no doubt that babies felt pain: in the fifth-century AD, St Augustine wrote, 'All diseases of Christians are to be ascribed to demons, chiefly do they torment the fresh baptized, yea, even the guiltless newborn infant', a view that was shared by Hippocrates and many others. Only in recent European thought did it become the vogue to deny the hurt felt by (or inflicted upon) babies. Right up to the 1980s, surgeons and parenting manuals were throwing doubt on the need for infant anaesthetic when removing the infant foreskin: 'You may be surprised to learn that circumcision will not be painful to your baby because, at this early stage of development, the penis does not yet have functioning pain nerve endings' (Expectant Parents' Information Kit, Procter and Gamble 1982).

Not as surprised, perhaps, as the circumcised baby. Circumcision and other intrusive procedures result in a brief but quite specific infant pain reaction, a total body movement and crying. In studies, babies who were first given topical anaesthetic before circumcison cried less than those who were not. Without anaesthetic, circumcised babies experienced a sudden rise in blood pressure and heart rate, and a rise in cortisol (the stress hormone) and endorphins (the body's reactive painkiller).

For Jewish parents, the circumcision of boys continues to be an essential element of the Divine Covenant which Abraham made with God. The 'Brit Milah' connects all Jewish males, wherever they may live. Even liberal parents tend to opt for it, although there is a growing movement in America in favour of substituting a non-intrusive naming ceremony. Circumcision is usually performed by a '*mohel*' (trained circumciser) at the child's home before sunset on the eighth day. The occasion is crammed with detail and ritual: for instance, the mother is not expected to hold her son while the removal of the foreskin takes place.

This honour is given to the 'sandek', a grandfather or other male relative.

In Muslim tradition, boys are circumcised within three or four days of the birth, as directed by the Qu'ran. The baby's hands may first be dipped in henna, as a protective charm.

Circumcision is also performed on girls in a few rural societies, although many campaigners are lobbying to eradicate the practice. Sometimes, the operation is a token: a tiny nick in the skin to signify that something has been done. But a number of African tribes still practise full female genital mutilation, which can result in lifelong discomfort, pain and even death.

The Afikpo Ibo of eastern Nigeria, for instance, perform clitoridectomy on their girls in early childhood. In Afikpo custom this is done just before puberty, along with cicatrisation (scarring) and decorative tattooing of the girl's arms and body. In Arab countries, clitoridectomy is not universal (it is not mentioned in the Qu'ran) but it is practised among Christian and Muslim groups along the Nile, from Egypt to Somalia and Kenya.

HOME TRUTHS

> In my mind I see you clear
> Changing with each day and year
> Lord we're glad you're finally here,
> Welcome to the world.
> May you grow up proud and strong
> May your life be rich and long
> May your nights be filled with song
> Welcome to the world
>
> Si Kahn, American singer-songwriter

Birth is the primary human celebration, and no culture allows it to pass unremarked. Whether beating a drum, cutting the baby's hair or wetting his tiny head, people find ways to proclaim their joy at the happy event. And when all the shouting and partying is over, the baby must be named.

A baby's name is like a magical garment, an invisible cloak which he tries on for size. It must be something he feels comfortable in for a very long time. Names forge human connections; they demonstrate human concern. No other young animal is named by its mother or father, or can know that special feeling of being called by its own name. Our names are part of what makes us human and, by using them, we teach our babies to know themselves.

6. Close for Comfort

Touching, holding and human contact are the context for life, teaching children all they need to know about acceptance, intimacy and trust. While some cultures limit the amount of touch and carrying a baby receives, others give unstintingly during the 'in-arms phase'.

Constantly Carried

In the post-industrialised West, where people are more privileged than anywhere else in the world, newborn babies are denied the privilege of using their mothers' bodies as a way-station between womb and world.

Penelope Leach, child care author

Human babies emerge in a state of utter dependency. Nine months of pregnancy are not nearly enough to prepare them for life outside the womb. One palaeontologist and primate anatomist, R.D. Martin of America, worked out that human infants actually need a twenty-one-month gestation period: nine months inside and another twelve months outside the womb. And many cultures provide just that, by keeping the baby firmly attached to mother's and other carers' bodies for the first year or more of life. In recent years, western commentators have started to call this 'close contact nurture'.

Once we admit the need of the immature human baby for a period of intensive care, we can begin to understand why he constantly seeks to be comforted. He gains comfort from sucking, from filling his stomach and from emptying his bladder and bowel. He gains comfort from a passive and gradual introduction to the world, from the safe vantage point of someone's hip or arms. He gains comfort from the sights and sounds around him and from the smell and taste of his first foods. But more than anything else, the human infant gains comfort by using his primary sense: touch.

PASS THE BABY ON THE LEFT-HAND SIDE

Most mothers instinctively cradle their babies on the left-hand side. Studies show that eighty-three per cent of right-handed mothers (and seventy-eight per cent of left-handed) cradle baby on the left, where he can hear her soothing heartbeat. In tests, fathers did not demonstrate the same bias, nor did mothers who had been prevented from holding their babies in the first twenty-four hours after birth. Mothers of the !Kung San people in the Kalahari Desert habitually hold their babies on the left when carrying them, as do our primate cousins, the chimpanzees and gorillas. Ancient Egyptian statuettes of the goddess Isis nursing her son Harpokrates show her presenting her left breast to the infant's mouth. And the Talmud, the ancient book of Jewish law, says, 'A woman who begins to nurse her son should start on the left side, as the source of all understanding is from the left.'

The left-side bias means that most babies present their 'right sides' to their mothers' bodies. This is as nature designed it. In the womb, the baby develops slightly more nerves leading to the brain from the right-hand side of the body. At birth, the baby is equipped with a 'tonic neck reflex', a preference for turning the head to the right. This produces a twist in the body which may help to make the person right-handed. Most babies also develop a right-hand preference by the twenty-ninth week of pregnancy and sixty per cent of unborn babies lie with their right sides closer to the mother's body surface, where they receive more stimulation.

Right-handedness goes along with a certain left-earedness. Scientists say that left-side carrying is an instinctive attempt to reach the baby's left ear – the one that is free when the right side of the head is clamped against the mother's body. When words and lullabies are heard from the left, they are processed by the right brain, the side which responds best to the musical quality of language and gauges emotional meaning. A preference for hearing with the left ear can be seen in the way that many people hold their telephone handsets.

Zoologist Desmond Morris points out that ape and human babies seek experiences which simulate their time in the womb. To meet babies' comfort needs by cuddling, rocking, lulling, or any other form of communication need not be interpreted as 'giving in'. Every act of comforting is good for the baby, both physically and emotionally: for instance, developing his body awareness and sociability. Like many other cultures, we might assume that our task is to meet the baby's needs at this stage of utmost helplessness.

As far as Tibetan parents are concerned, close contact nurture is absolutely essential for infant health. The Dalai Lama says touch is vital for the development of a baby's brain.

Bonding is very important . . . physically, it is simple: babies receive bodily touching from their mothers. Physical touch is a very crucial factor for healthy development, including the development of brain cells in the first few weeks . . . It has nothing to do with religion. It is simply that, as human beings, our physical condition requires touch to develop fully.

Tenzin Gyatso, Dalai Lama, spiritual leader of Tibet

Mary Ainsworth, the attachment theorist, made a famous study of Ganda child-rearing in east Africa in 1967. It seemed to confirm this point of view. She discovered that Ganda babies, held constantly in the day and slept with at night, were more advanced than their American peers when it came to standing, crawling and walking. This research led to some practical conclusions:

It is better for a baby to be held a lot, to be picked up when he cries, to be given what he wants when he wants it, and to be given much opportunity and freedom to interact than it is for a baby to be kept for long periods in his crib apart from other people, where his signals cannot be perceived and consequently where he cannot experience a sense of predictable consequence and control.

Dr Mary Ainsworth, anthropologist

Another study comparing American and urban Zambian babies showed that the child care methods of the African mothers created dramatic differences from the beginning. The Zambian babies were born with inferior muscle tone, but by day five their responsiveness had risen dramatically. After ten days of constant carrying, nursing, massaging and other forms of touch, the Zambian babies' muscle tone was better than average and their alertness and social interaction scores had already outstripped those of the American babies.

Traditional peoples are unlikely to question the benefit of being constantly in touch with their babies. Even though the strong physical tie will be broken one day when the next child comes along, they know that permanent emotional bonds have been forged. The early years of contact bring a lifetime of inner security. Holding a baby is one, very physical, way of transmitting unconditional love. Here are some examples of close-contact nurture around the world:

* Swazi babies of Swaziland are closely bonded to their mothers from birth. Until they are three months old, they may only be held by a few selected women and no men (other than

the village healer). After this, the baby lives on his mother's body and may not be weaned before he has 'teeth to chew' and 'legs to run'.

* Children of the Wadi, a slum area of Amman, Jordan, bond to two 'mothers': their birth mother (old mother) and a big sister or aunt (young mother). Young mother carries and cares for the baby and sleeps with him at night. When he is older, the child may be teased as to which 'mother' he loves best. The Qur'an, the holy book of Islam, endorses overt affection from all family members towards a baby.
* The Ache people, hunter-gatherers of the Paraguayan jungle, enjoy frequent body contact with each other even as adults. Babies spend ninety-three per cent of the day and one hundred per cent of the night being held by their mothers. Even toddlers enjoy forty per cent maternal contact time, on or next to their mothers' laps.
* Carrying is so important to the Maya people of Yucatan, Mexico, that they hold a ceremony to mark the way a baby is held. The celebration, known as '*hets mek*', marks the transition from in-arms 'infant' carrying to hip carrying, a sign that the child is now able to hold himself upright.
* The relationship between a Japanese mother and baby is so complete that it is sometimes called 'skinship'. Anthropologist John Douglas says this results in 'primary identification as a member of a group rather than as an independent person'.
* Zincanteco people of Mexico believe they must continually embrace their babies, so that the infants do not lose their souls.

One memorable example of close contact comes from a small band of food-gathering people who emerged to the glare of world attention in July 1971. The Tasaday, a tribe reduced to thirteen adults and fourteen children, lived uncontacted in southern Mindanao in the Philippines for millennia. Since they had not even learned how to trap animals, the Tasaday lived on gathered fruits and leaves. The most impressive trait of the Tasaday seemed to be their loving sensitivity. Babies were constantly held by their parents and all members openly displayed affection to each other:

Twelve or 15 onlookers did not prevent Balayem from hugging Sindi (his wife) close to him. Lobo, a strikingly beautiful and intelligent boy of 10 or 12, and Balayem, whose extrovert manner contrasts with a mobile, sensitive face, unaffectedly throw their arms around Manda [anthropologist Manuel Elizalde], nuzzle up to him, rub their cheeks against his and sit very quietly next to him for extended periods with an arm around his shoulders . . .

Peggy Durdin, journalist

Busy Going Nowhere

It would help immeasurably if we could see baby care as a non-activity. We should learn to regard it as nothing to do.

Jean Liedloff, continuum therapist

The thought of carrying a baby constantly fills many western parents with horror. We imagine ourselves overburdened, our privacy ruined, our backs breaking, the baby taking over our lives. In fact, the reality of baby-wearing is the opposite of hard work. At nine weeks, a baby feels lighter than he did at nine days. He becomes the passive observer, watching, dozing or feeding as he pleases, without actually intruding.

When babies are kept in the centre of things, the level of parental anxiety is immediately lowered. Paradoxically, they get less attention, or at least, less active attention. Their presence is taken for granted and their needs are met at a body level, without the need for worry, judgment or analysis. In traditional terms, this is the original 'baby-came-too': not a long equipment list and a heap of trouble, but a baby whose presence is as unre-markable as the modern handbag. 'In these tribes, a baby is no big deal. They're just there, with the mother, whatever she is doing. But we definitely sentimentalise babies, which is misplaced because we wrap them up, put them in the pram, separate them from ourselves' (Anita Roddick, Body Shop founder).

When baby is passively attached to his father, mother or other care-giver, his role changes completely. Instead of being the centre of attention, an actor on the stage for all to applaud or criticise, he becomes the spectator of the piece. Parents who constantly wear their babies do not sit around ogling or fussing over them, they get on with their lives. Too much ogling, after all, is boring – and many western parents confess to being bored at home with the baby. Nor are babies on show when they are taken everywhere. The Rajput mother of north India, for instance, does not think of her baby as a collector's item: 'A [Rajput] village mother would no more show off her baby to the admiration of a visitor than an American mother would deliberately expose an infant to a contagious disease' (Leigh Minturn and John T. Hitchcock, anthropologists).

You could call this 'touch nurture', compared with the 'sight-and-sound nurture' of the typical American or European parent. Westerners work hard running to and from their babies, bringing them out and interacting with voice and eyes, before putting them away again. The much-carried baby, always present, is not expected to participate, but may be allowed to relax in his carer's arms. Given much less aural and visual stimulation and soothed quickly, he is at peace to marvel at the 3D motion picture which is his world. Here, the lives of African and American babies are contrasted: '. . . in bodily contact with mother or a child care-giver throughout the day, a Gusii baby is present during most of the family's social interaction *without* becoming the center of its attention. In contrast, the American infant's day is sharply divided into periods of total isolation and periods of infant-directed social excitement' (Robert A. LeVine, anthropologist, among the Gusii of Kenya).

The crib baby experiences long periods of non-interaction, punctuated by bouts of intense parental interest. The carried baby experiences no such contrasts, but probably sees more of the world about him. By being taken everywhere, he will slowly learn to take his place on the family stage. His learning is more passive, streamlined and conducted from the same reliable vantage point: an older person's arms.

In medieval Europe, the cradle would be set in the heart of the house, so baby could be rocked and soothed, and watch the bustle of the day. The Turkish baby is suspended from a wooden tripod in a cotton bag while his mother works in the field. He watches the traffic, birds in the sky, women weighing and bagging cotton. In Jamaica, the baby sits upright in a bucket, while children, chickens and lizards dart around him. Today, all over the globe, babies accompany their mothers to work: 'We think of the child as wanting to play and the adult as having to work, but in many societies the mother takes the baby daily in her shawl or carrying net to the garden or to gather roots, and adult labor is seen even in infancy from the pleasant security of its position in close contact with its mother' (Ruth Benedict, anthropologist).

Life must go on. In fact, the ease of carrying a baby, the reduction of stress on mother and baby and the resulting bond between them are compelling reasons for baby-wearing today. Just as the Tibetan baby rides on his mother's back because 'it is easy for a mother to continue her normal pattern of movement and work' (researchers Anne Hubbell Maiden and Edie Farwell), so the modern western mother is being enticed to baby-wear for eminently practical motives. The 'rebozo' in the following extract is the traditional cloth baby carrier worn in Mexico, Guatemala and other South American states:

The show is a cultural and educational tool demonstrating the beauty and variety of rebozo babywearing in traditional cultures in Latin America. The photos are striking and impressive; they show children from newborn to age 3 or 4, mostly in the quiet alert state that is brought about by being worn in the rebozo; others are nursing or sleeping. The women (and a few girls) are generally active, involved at work, at home or in the marketplace; some are socialising . . . the age-old practice of babywearing is making a comeback among busy, active parents of the '90s . . .

From the internet promotion for 'The Rebozo Way
Babywearing Photography Show'

Who would not appreciate a child who is habitually in a 'quiet, alert state'? Bound to an active body, the baby's contact needs are instantly met. Now he is ready to observe the world; real experience is better than hot-housing any day. Busy parents are starting to realise that the world does not have to stop when they have their children. Strap the baby on: we're going for a ride!

Cache and Carry

Only children older than about ten and infants not yet weaned went on the hunt. Such an infant was slung from its mother's shoulder in a piece of animal skin and could be breast-fed even while its mother moved through the forest with the band of hunters.

Kevin Duffy, anthropologist, with Mbuti pygmies of the
central African rainforest

The history of carrying is the history of humanity. Zoologists divide animals broadly into two categories: 'cache' species and 'carrying' species. This has to do with the way animals raise their children. 'Cache' comes from the French 'cacher', to hide, and refers to the practice of keeping young in a nest while one or both parents hunt for food. Birds are the most obvious example of a 'cache' species. Primates – the group to which we belong – are all carriers. We evolved to transport our young with us while we foraged and hunted for food.

It may even be that the upright stance of the human was an adaptation which came out of our desire to carry objects around. Furless as we are, our babies cannot grip on to our 'naked ape' bodies. The earliest humans simply held their babies in their arms until the sling was invented. Going bipedal was part of a major adaptive change, leaving the hands free to carry provisions, tools – and babies. It allowed men and women to become cooperative in the search for food and to form loyal pair bonds.

The human baby's primitive urge to be carried is betrayed in his birth reflexes. Just consider the grasping ability of the otherwise weak newborn. This is so powerful that for the first few days he is able to support his entire body weight with his own fingers. Even very premature babies have a grasping reflex. Tibetan parents consider this to be a heavenly gift:

Tibetan folklore explains that infants who have a strong grip actually possess a wish-fulfilling gem (a mythological gem that can grant any wish) in their hands and do not want anyone to take it away . . . Even though the newborn is small and helpless at birth, the gem represents the continuity the baby maintains with previous lives and the talents, wisdom, and experiences from other lives that will influence his life.

Anne Hubbell Maiden, psychologist and Edie Farwell, anthropologist

The grasping reflex is an instinct governed by the hypothalamus, the most archaic, primitive part of the brain which connects us all with the earliest forms of human life. In some babies, grasping lasts for months; in most it fades after a day or two. After this, a child cannot support his own weight until he is two years old. This reflex cannot be honed – it is automatic, a vestige of our primate ancestry – just like the 'Moro' reflex, another sign of the human baby's ancient desire to be carried.

Moro was a German doctor who, in 1918, devised a test for examining the balancing abilities of newborn babies. The infant is first placed on a table, which the doctor will jolt suddenly. To 'pass' the test, the baby must fling out his arms and legs symmetrically as if clasping at something. (This is not the same as the startle reflex, which survives into adulthood, becoming more marked.) The Moro reflex demonstrates a baby's vestigial ability to cling and rebalance itself, in order to be carried.

Anyone who has had the opportunity to carry a baby chimpanzee will have met this action many times. With the baby ape clinging to your coat, you sit down and relax. The infant ape relaxes with you, loosening its grip. The moment your body tenses or shifts, as if to rise, you feel the little arms and legs fling themselves instantly around you and the hands clasp to your coat firmly once more. This is the Moro reflex in its full functional form.

Desmond Morris, zoologist

Without the benefit of fur, or a sustained clinging and grasping reflex, the human infant must look to other means of persuasion if he wants to be carried everywhere. He communicates his need through cries and smiles. While crying is a negative communication, a generalised alarm call indicating that something – anything – is not right, the smile is the human baby's unique and positive trump card. It indicates his desire, his innate sociability, his ability to love and be loved.

Monkey babies scream and yell, just like ours do – a necessary mechanism for expressing danger and discomfort. But other primates do not smile. Primatologists believe the human smile is the substitute for fur. While the ape baby clings to his mother for comfort, the human baby must ask to be picked up, and he does this through emotional appeal.

Does this mechanism work? It did for traditional societies. A survey of hunter-gatherer groups in the 1970s revealed that they *all* carried their babies at least fifty per cent of the time, some much more. A survey of non-industrial societies revealed an increased inclination to put babies down, with just fifty-six per cent of cultures baby-carrying for more than fifty per cent of the time. Western cultures carry least of all. The typical American baby spends only up to twenty-five per cent of his day hours in physical contact with his caretakers.

So, we have the hunter-gatherer model of carrying, which is almost constant and usually involves skin-to-skin contact. And at the other extreme we have the western model of sporadic holding, which involves leaving the baby alone to sleep and cry and amuse himself for hours. This mode of nurture found its greatest popularity in developed countries in the 1950s, about the time when breastfeeding was at an all-time low. And there are lots of examples in between.

WHAT A CARRY-ON . . .

In close-contact cultures, carrying baby is often perceived as a privilege. Among the Ache forest people of Paraguay, south America, each baby is designated his or her special 'tapare', a kind of carrying godmother, who must be the first person to hold the newborn. Their special relationship will bind them throughout life. Other family members take their turn, too. In Tibet, for instance, carrying is considered essential to paternal bonding. Fathers carry their babies in shawls on their backs.

In Okinawa, Japan, everyone gets their chance. The list of potential carriers includes all members of the extended family: parents, paternal grandparents, uncles, aunts, brothers and sisters. Grandma is the most usual baby-wearer when mother is working in the sweet potato field, or gathering firewood in the mountains:

> Throughout the morning hours grandmother, with the infant on her back, wanders about the village . . . If the mother is nearby, she hurries so that the infant does not cry for long. When the hour for lunch approaches, the grandmother hurries home to begin preparations for the noonday meal. As she walks, the infant's head bobs up and down, forward and back precariously, but it continues to sleep undisturbed.

Thomas W. and Hatsumi Maretzki, anthropologists

Inter-Continental Baby-Carrying – A Gazetteer

Slings from Africa:
The most famous example of a hunter-gatherer sling is that worn by !Kung San mothers of Africa's Kalahari desert. The 'kaross' or 'chik!na' is a leather cloak made from the hide of a large antelope and worn almost exclusively by women. It is tied at the shoulder and often decorated with beads. Babies sit naked in a hip sling inside the kaross – there is plenty of room for wriggling and free access to the breast. They play with their mothers' bead jewellery, in lieu of toys. Each sling has a grass lining which is replaced as it becomes dirty. Older children are carried in a pouch on the mother's back, or perched on her shoulders.

Slings from Europe:
Slings are the latest chic among well-to-do western parents and their designer babies. In London, England, Brooklyn Beckham, son of footballer David and pop star Victoria 'Posh Spice', was spotted in a baby carrier soon after his birth in 1999. This was no ordinary carrier, it was a Bill Amberg front-carrying papoose, made of leather and sheepskin and retailing at £210. Newspaper reporters were awe-struck to see a baby being carried in animal-skin luxury. No reference was made to the thousands of years of precedence set by nomadic hunter-gatherers.

Slings from the Middle East:
Mothers and nurses in ancient Egypt carried their babies in a front sling, binding mother and baby with a band of material which passed across the shoulder. In modern Egypt, toddlers in rural communities ride astride their mothers' shoulders.

Slings from the Antipodes
Although many traditional Australian groups use a paperbark carrying cradle, some use a skin cloak, a more ancient invention than the cradle or 'coolamon'. The cloak has a pouch in the

back, like a hood, in which the baby is perched, facing forwards. This gives him the same vantage point as his mother.

Slings from South America:
Ancient statuettes show Mayan mothers of southern Mexico carrying their babies in a shawl or blanket on their backs. Today, Mayan mothers hang on to their shawl, or '*rebozo*', for support during labour and later use it to carry their babies around. In fact, the rebozo is worn by many South American women, from Mexico to Guatemala, from the Maya to the Mixtecans. The mother wraps the shawl around her pelvis and shoulders, forming a pouch in the small of her back. She lifts her baby over her head to slip him in to his little nest. This flexible wrap can be worn front or back, too.

Slings from the Arctic:
Adults of Alaska and northern Canada wear a '*parka*', traditionally made of caribou or sealskin. The cut and design of the male parka marks him out as a hunter, while the female version, the '*amoutis*' or '*attiggi*', with its ample hood, symbolises the maternal role. An Inuit, Yup'ik or Netsilik baby is carried deep in the fur-lined pouch, supported by a sash which secures him to his mother's body. Except for a fur hat and a moss-pad nappy, he takes all his warmth through skin-to-skin contact. Many Alaskan babies still ride in their mothers' pouches today. Here, a group leader of La Leche League Canada, the breastfeeding support network, describes parka-wearing mothers arriving at a monthly meeting:

It's -40°C and the winds are gusting at 50 km/h making windchills high and visibility low. Do I cancel tonight's LLLC meeting? Not a chance. This is life in the Canadian Arctic and the weather doesn't get better until spring. People here move around in weather that would shut down cities in the south . . . At the meeting most babies are under one year and they arrive warm and snug, each tucked inside mother's amoutis. An amoutis is a special kind of parka that has extra fabric in the arms and back to form a pouch for an infant or toddler to ride in. With mother's warm back to snuggle against and her coat to keep out the cold, baby doesn't feel the bite of the Arctic winds.

Gina Rozon, LLL breastfeeding counsellor and group leader

Slings from Asia:

The Japanese baby is traditionally strapped to his mother's body at waist level. The sash winds twice around the body and is tied at the front. Today's urban Japanese parent is more likely to buy a front-loading, western-style sling with buckles.

Holding with Confidence

The Average American woman may never hold a little baby until she nurses her own, and even then she often behaves as though she were still afraid that the infant might break in her hands. In New Guinea and Bali, on the contrary, they know all about babies. Small infants are looked after by child nurses as young as 4 years old, and this familiarity is shown in all their movements.

Margaret Mead, anthropologist

So unused are many new parents to handling babies that baby-care books now include diagrams on how to pick them up. It is a sad state of affairs when fundamental human skills like baby-holding have been lost to generations of parents. But it is true, we do need help. It took me years of practice with my first child before I felt confident to handle my second.

I recall once seeing a television documentary in which a Brazilian baby had spent some time in intensive care. When he was brought home from hospital, the main concern of the parents was to massage his tiny body because the enforced bed-rest had made him so stiff. In our society, the stiffness or suppleness of a baby is not one of our main concerns. We are used to babies who lose their flexibility through lying around.

The much-carried baby becomes easier to hold as time goes

on. He moulds himself to the carrier, with a body that is increasingly soft and receptive. Researcher Margaret Mead noticed the prolonged flexibility of the constantly-carried Balinese baby. She identified this as a two-way process between the person holding and the infant being held: 'The Balinese infant has preserved a kind of neonatal flexibility, which in the children who have been studied in western culture tends to disappear very early, so that both the way a baby relaxes in its mother's arms and the way the mother holds it are sharply contrasting to our patterns' (Margaret Mead, anthropologist).

It is almost impossible to put into words the quality of touch that any particular baby might need or expect. However, we do know that, while babies enjoy caresses and tenderness, they do not necessarily want us to treat them as if they were as delicate as fine china.

Babies don't break easily. Despite scary newspaper headlines on the dangers of shaking or other rough treatment, the human infant is actually pretty resilient. For rural people who work the land, rough handling is a way of preparing children for the tough life ahead. Gowda mothers of south India cannot imagine treating their babies like precious gems: '"How can we treat them softly?" said the women, "They wouldn't survive their lives"' (Sarah Hobson, film maker in southern India).

This is not a licence to shake or harm babies – on the contrary, it is a way of saying that human infants are programmed for a lot of energetic movement, harmonious carrying and loving cuddles. In places where child care is a traditional and vital life-skill, baby-holding is a question of responding to infant need. No sensitive care-giver would dream of shaking a baby hard, or throwing him down in a temper. Yet to an outsider, the everyday quality of touch might seem abrasive and off-hand. One birth researcher among the Yucatan Maya of Mexico made these slightly anxious notes: 'Neither the midwife nor the family treat this newborn as particularly delicate. Doña Juana handles the baby matter-of-factly and familiarly as she gives it the routine bath. While holding the newborn, neither she nor the helpers make any special attempts to support its head' (Brigitte Jordan, anthropologist).

Having turned babycare into a science, we tend to mistrust ourselves when handling our own children. If a baby's head drooped alarmingly and it distressed him, rest assured, he would let you know. Detailed written warnings from the experts do little to empower new parents.

If it is difficult to learn baby-holding techniques from the written word, it is maybe even harder to measure up to the vast unbroken experience of traditional cultures when it comes to babycare. Western mothers who try to carry their first babies everywhere sometimes find they just don't measure up to the ancient ideal. In a fascinating article on being an American parent in West Africa, mother Sherri Saines describes how hard it was to copy her African counterparts. Anthropology, she rightly points out, cannot be turned directly into method:

I, too, believe that wearing our babies is a great benefit to mothers and children. I lived for three years with the Lobi people of West Africa. West African babies are carried basically until they are weaned; they are generally calmer, cry less, and squirm less than American babies. But . . . cross-cultural comparisons are much too complex to assume cause and effect so easily.

My first child was born in Africa. He, too, was carried much of his first year, passed around and held constantly, and not allowed to cry if possible. Our pace of life was slow and calm. He was healthy and grew well. But he was just as jumpy as other American babies, and other Americans there had the same experience.

My conclusion from this is that culture forms our most basic being in ways that we do not understand, and we can almost never separate ourselves from it.

Sherri B. Saines, American mother

Culture gets into our bones. It is hard – almost impossible – consciously to shake off our inner tensions just by *wanting* to stay calm. As Sherri Saines noticed, the infant is exquisitely attuned to the mood of the person who carries him. Studies of adults and babies interacting show that babies are not fooled by an adult's outward appearance. They read body language with all the instinctive skill of an animal, seeing through our theories to the people we really are. However, this rather scary thought should not put us off. It just means that instead of being overly conscious of our babies (as our culture keeps telling us we should be), we might instead became more aware of ourselves. The remedy for a jumpy baby is a parent who gives only as much as she is able without putting herself under an unrealistic amount of strain – in other words, a parent who is happy in her own skin.

This takes the focus away from the culturally 'fragile' baby. Familiarity is the key to easy baby-holding. By becoming more familiar with babies, we inevitably reduce our inner anxieties. Instead of treating our babies as breakable objects, we, too, begin to appear a little off-hand. Swiftly, our babies get the message that we trust ourselves and them and they can relax in our arms.

The most obvious remedy for our lack of baby-carrying experience is to go out and get some, preferably before our own babies arrive. Baby-holding sessions for pregnant women and their partners would be a significant step towards the hands-on familiarity which babies receive in other cultures.

Perhaps Sherri Saines' baby jumped around a bit because he was her first child. It is hard to overcome the lack of maternal experience provided by your own culture when faced with the first baby you have ever really known and held. I would guess that Sherri's second and subsequent babies were a lot calmer when she held them because, from birth, she could offer them the familiarity which comes from experience.

Rock Around the Clock

For nine months, the baby has been an eternal traveller. Its shifting world has never ceased to move. Sometimes gently, sometimes violently. Its mother's body was always in motion; and even when she was still or asleep, there was always the great rhythm of her breathing of her diaphragm.

The baby has lived in perpetual motion.

Now, a truly appalling change: everything stops.

For the first time.

Nothing moves.

The world has frozen, died.

This is unknown territory.

Frédérick Leboyer, natural birth pioneer

Why do small children love to keep moving? Some people say that babies should be left alone so they will not be disturbed, but this is thinking from an adult point of view. You know what it is like when you step off a boat after even the shortest of journeys – your equilibrium is suddenly snatched away. It feels as if the floor is swaying. If the journey was very long or rough, this sensation can continue for hours, even days.

A newborn baby has been on a nine-month carousel, suspended in the amniotic fluid of the womb. When he emerges, he is not quite ready for a life of solitary inactivity. Babies cry to be carried, to be rocked and to feel the movement of our bodies. The need to be suspended explains why a baby, sleeping in someone's arms, stirs the second he is put down. Even as they grow, children retain the desire to be swung about and hung upside down.

Stillness is not a child's natural medium: 'Babies seem to be striving for movement. They like riding in fast cars, and cry when you stop at the traffic lights. They like to be trundled around in anything on wheels. They enjoy being carried, provided you don't pause for one moment. They like being patted, rubbed, massaged, swung, bounced and rocked' (Sheila Kitzinger, anthropologist).

In studies, parents have been shown to rock their bodies instinctively at sixty to seventy moves per minute, a gentle repetition which approximates the speed of the beating heart.

Humans are genuinely soothed by this rhythm and gentle movement, from infancy to adulthood:

The next time you see a lecturer or an after-dinner speaker swaying rhythmically from side to side, check his speed for heart-beat time. His discomfort at having to face an audience leads him to perform the most comforting movements his body can offer in the somewhat limited circumstances; and so he switches on the old familiar beat of the womb.

Desmond Morris, zoologist

Apart from soothing anxious minds, rocking has measurable physical benefits for the human body. It increases the heart rate in both babies and adults and stimulates the circulation. It helps to improve muscle tone and promotes healthy breathing. Rocking even helps the muscle tone and workings of a baby's gastro-intestinal tract, improving digestion. Tests show that rocking helps premature babies to gain weight and breathe more steadily.

With most babycare, it is not merely what you do with the baby, but the way you do it that matters. Rocking is the same. In the past, doctors have been forced to denounce the violent rocking of babies, especially when used as a desperate measure, akin to shaking. Since medieval times, European doctors have been suspicious of 'too much' rocking, just as they later worried about 'too much' carrying. But gentle rocking is a tradition which belongs to every culture. All around the world, you will see mothers, fathers and others rocking their babies, soothing them with touch and movement:

* Sioux babies of Dakota are tightly bundled up and then lightly rocked, without interruption, by mother or another care-giver. This is how they spend most of the day.
* When the Australian Aborigine baby gets fretful, he is jiggled up and down in a vertical motion.
* For Mbuti pygmies of the rainforest in central Africa, rocking

the baby is a communication which accompanies singing and nursing – mothers begin rocking in pregnancy and continue after the birth.

● Rocking and jiggling are, in some ways, a substitute for the rhythms of a more active lifestyle. Hunter-gatherer parents do not need to stop and rock their babies when they are on a fifteen-mile trek; field-working mothers do not need to jiggle about when they have their babies strapped to their backs. In South America, the Zinacantan baby is soothed by the rhythm of his mother grinding corn.

● A Japanese baby traditionally rides on mother's or nursemaid's back. Extra body movements soothe the baby, but may unsettle western observers: 'When he is restless his bearer sways or jiggles from one foot to the other. Some writers deem this jiggling a fearsome experience for the infant . . . My own unsystematic observations indicate that most Japanese think it soothes the child. At any rate the infant almost constantly feels the reassuring touch of human skin' (Douglas Haring, anthropologist).

Dances with Babies

Every mother intuitively knows that in order to put her baby to sleep she has to rock it, thereby repeating the nirvanic dance [of the foetus in the womb] . . . in many of us syncopated rhythms, music and counterpoint at regular intervals cause a deep oceanic yearning and a longing for maternal protection, which once was the happy world we lived in.

Dr Joost Meerloo, dance historian

Every culture in the world has its own music, and every culture its own way of moving to the rhythms it creates. Even chimpanzees know how to sway and jig during communal jamming sessions, where stamping, clapping and drumming actions may provide the beat for up to half an hour of monkey dancing.

Our music may contain more complex rhythms, it may have a wider variety of meanings and patterns, but it still emerges from our most primitive impulses. In the 1930s, a film called *Zwei Herzen in Dreiviertel Takt* – Two Hearts in Three-quarter Time – illustrated its point with a waltz for a theme tune. Within the three steady beats of the waltz step, we can hear the baby's heart as if in the womb, beating twice for every single beat of the mother's. The same heartbeat is repeated in dance rhythms all around the world:

All the men sing in unison, as they move with the soft, yet heavy bird tread which is the whole of the dance, with bodies bent a little forward, shoulders and head loose and heavy, feet powerful but soft, the men tread the rhythm into the centre of the earth. The drums keep up the pulsating heart beat and for hours, hours, it goes on.

D.H. Lawrence, novelist, in Mexico

Many parents love to dance with their babies. From the rainforest to urban cities, people take their babies in their arms and just go with the music. Dancing-in-arms is a baby's way of participating in music, long before he learns to sing, or sway on his own two feet, or beat out a rhythm with his own hands. 'In-arms, the Balinese baby learns the graceful rhythm of community life. As the mother pounds rice, the baby on her hip absorbs the tempo of Balinese music' (Gayle Brandeis-McGunigle, American writer).

And babies love to dance with their mothers, just as they danced with them '*in utero*'. Even if they are asleep, much-carried babies may find their way to the dance floor. The Yequana baby of Venezuela is so used to being held during wakefulness and sleep that a late-night bop may not even wake him: 'If there is a party while he is asleep, [the Yequana baby] will be bounced about quite violently while his mother hops and stamps in time to the music' (Jean Liedloff, continuum therapist).

Dancing is one very vivid way in which babies absorb culture.

Here, through body movements no one needs to explain or try to understand, the infant can explore the patterns of his people. Through music, singing, drumming and dance, he learns to participate in his own community. And before long, he is taking his own tentative steps towards joining in.

It was the signal for the Molimo dancing to begin, and the women and children began to reappear from the huts . . .

Next to Makubasi, another elder held his bright-eyed little granddaughter on his lap. She climbed down and began to imitate the dancers with captivating charm. A woman scooped up the naked little girl and danced with her once around the fire before depositing her again into the lap of her grandfather.

Kevin Duffy, anthropologist in central Africa

The ability to dance is in every one of us. It began in babyhood.

HOME TRUTHS

The savage still her clinging babe sustains,
Some, this communicated warmth affirm
Is needful, and that Man's else-drooping Race
Requires the general contact.

Hugh Downman, 'Infancy', 1776

In his endeavour to be held and caressed, to be moved around and kept in the frame of activity, a baby is the world's original pleasure seeker. Babies are born with two main imperatives: to be fed and given an extraordinary amount of human contact.

Comfort is the context of healthy life. The comfort of another person's skin, of sucking on the human breast, of being held in loving arms – these are the basic elements of child care in a wide variety of cultures. Methods of carrying may vary, spiritual beliefs might be wildly different, but the same simple rules for babycare appear again and again. Give, give and give to a baby, say parents in traditional societies, and you won't go far wrong.

I like Hugh Downman's idea of 'communicated warmth' as a primary principle of child care. This metaphor could cover all our dealings with children, from hands-on communication with a newborn to the emotional warmth needed when dealing with older children and teenagers. But his eighteenth-century plea for giving babies more 'general contact' did not catch on in Europe. Generations of parents were on a path towards ever-increasing separation. Babies were perceived as wily and manipulative and western parents put up their collective guard, in order not to be exploited by their own children.

Ancient philosophies on babycare are so simplistic and unpretentious that it is hard to take them seriously in our sophisticated culture. For instance, there's the Jewish saying: 'God could not be everywhere and therefore he made mothers.' The uncynical, traditional view is that mothers *can* be everywhere as far as their babies are concerned, by the simple expedient of carrying their babies around. The sophisticated view is that mothers cannot be everywhere and babies must make do without them for much of the time. It's a simple twist, but it can make all the difference to the way we perceive and treat our infants. Even if we are not available all day long, even if 'others' provide the care when mothers cannot, we can still be ready with open arms to meet our babies' insatiable need to be held.

7. Shall We Begin?

As she begins to breastfeed, a mother embarks on a new relationship – preparing the lines of intimate communication with her baby. The meaning and magic of those early feeds is captured in the beliefs and taboos of every human culture.

Misunderstandings: The Story of Colostrum

While the foetus exists in the womb it is nourished on blood, but at birth nature sends that blood to the breasts to be changed into milk.

Bartholomew of England, c.1230

Bartholomew, the thirteenth-century encyclopaedist, may have had the wrong idea, but he was not alone. Breastmilk, revered around the world for its magical properties, was little understood in ancient times. And it was this lack of understanding which led to probably the first major catastrophe in the history of child-rearing: the assumption that colostrum, a baby's sustenance for the first days of life, was a bad thing.

Not all cultures jumped to this conclusion, of course, but it is easy to see why mothers mistrusted the sticky yellow substance which was all their breasts seemed to produce after birth. Babies were most at risk in this early neonatal period, and many must have died even before the milk came in. Colostrum was held to blame. It did not flow obviously from the breast like later milk, and its invisible magic went unappreciated. It even became associated with postnatal beliefs about witchcraft and evil spells. Mothers were anxious that their 'real' milk would never come. In a taboo which pervaded almost every continent, babies were kept away from the breast for a nerve-racking three days.

The testimony of Nisa, a !Kung San woman in the Kalahari Desert, describes the situation perfectly. It is one of the rare occasions when this hunter-gatherer tribe ignores the needs of a baby. Nisa has been taught not to allow her newborn daughter to feed until the milk comes in, a poignant irony since milk flow is encouraged by the act of suckling. The colostrum, unseen and untapped, is nothing to Nisa – any sign of the yellow stuff and she expresses it away.

My husband . . . went out again and killed a spring hare. When he came back, he cooked it and I drank the gravy. That was supposed to help the milk come into my breasts, but my milk didn't come down.

We lived in the bush and there was no one else to help feed her. She just lay there and didn't eat for three nights. Then milk started to fill one breast, and the same night the other one filled. I spilled out the colostrum, the bad thing, and when my chest was filled with good milk, she nursed and nursed and nursed. When she was full, she went to sleep.

Nisa, !Kung San mother, talks to Marjorie Shostak, anthropologist

There are lots of interesting details in this account. Firstly, the gravy which is supposed to induce lactation: many tribes trust in postnatal preparations, foods and prayers to make the breast-milk flow. While some of these clearly have nutritive or spiritual value for the mother, they may also be a sign of insecurity. Secondly, Nisa says no one else was there to feed her baby. Wet-nursing is the solution practised in many cultures where colostrum is banned. Newborns are nursed by other lactating women, rather than by their own mothers. In medieval England, it was even recommended that a baby should drink the milk of nine women before being allowed to suckle at his own mother's breast.

Thirdly, there is the question of the child lying unfed while her father runs around looking for spring hare. As luck would have it, brand new babies are born with a protective mechanism, brown fat stores in the back and neck, which generate warmth by a chemical process. These reserves, presumably designed for emergencies, would undoubtedly have saved the lives of many. But, as we can tell from Nisa's account, fat reserves do not necessarily stop a baby from becoming hungry. Nisa's daughter is ravenous after three days and nights without food.

The !Kung San people's ideas are mirrored all around the world. American Hispanic families traditionally consider colostrum to be 'unclean'. Zulu, Sotho and Pedi mothers of South Africa express their colostrum and discard it. Tausog women of the Philippines must wait until the baby has passed some meconium before they will suckle – another vicious circle, as colostrum is nature's first laxative. And in Breton tradition, the breast must not be offered before baptism.

Colostrum taboos exist today in India and Sierra Leone, Afghanistan and Guatemala. In history, they were practised in ancient Greece and Rome, Tibet, Japan, Europe and North America. Among the Sioux of the Dakota plains, for instance:

The colostrum (the first watery secretion from the milk glands) was normally considered to be poison for the baby; thus the breast was not offered to him until there seemed to be a good stream of perfect milk. The Indian women maintained that it was not right to let a baby do all the initial work only to be rewarded with a thin, watery substance. The implication was clear: how could he trust a world which greeted him thus?

Erik Erikson, psychoanalyst

It is interesting that Professor Erikson himself refers to colostrum as a 'watery secretion', thus corroborating the views of the Sioux women about their own, somehow unworthy, milk. In fact, studies have shown that mothers, once aware of the enormous value of colostrum, are more likely to describe it as 'creamy' than 'watery'.

Other western observers also tend to offer a negative or uninformed view about the value of early nursing. Thomas and Hatsumi Maretzki, anthropologists observing a traditional Japanese community, describe how the newborn is given a gauze nipple dipped in tea and sugar to suck, adding that this is 'often his only feed for as long as two days if lactation is slow'. Postnatal lactation is not 'slow' while it is producing colostrum; it is working perfectly and immediately to provide the ideal food for a tiny baby while he adjusts to life outside the womb.

Even zoologist Desmond Morris refers to colostrum in one paragraph and the arrival of 'true milk' in the next. Colostrum *is* the true milk. It just happens not to resemble breastmilk or the daily pint, a product extracted from cows and heat-treated by machines. Is kangaroo milk any less real because it happens to be pink? The milk produced by any mammal is intended to feed her young.

Misapprehensions like these persist today and will arise again, for so long as we continue to compare yellow colostrum to more visible white milks, and human milk to the ubiquitous cow's milk that fills our refrigerators. Only in ignorance do we imagine colostrum to be an 'absence of milk' or an absence of anything.

When nature's design is thwarted by keeping baby away from the breast, then all sorts of unnecessary jobs are created for the anxious community. Purges and enemas are given to newborns who have not been allowed to feed from birth and so have trouble passing meconium. Mother's breasts must be massaged and the unwanted colostrum expressed. In old England, a mother's breasts were 'drawn' by the nurse or an older baby. Jicarillo mothers of Mexico prefer their mothers to suck at their breasts to clean them out, rather than let their babies near.

Further, the baby must be fed *something* while he waits. If he is not to be wet-nursed or abandoned to his hunger, then effort must go into preparing a suitable colostrum substitute. Baby's first food, in many cultures for many years, has been a laxative diet designed to purge the immature digestive system. Many recipes also contain sugar, presumably an attempt to rectify the hypo-glycaemia which can occur without nursing, because the baby's blood glucose starts to drop immediately after birth. Still more babies are welcomed with an aperitif of alcohol, an unfortunate way to begin life.

- A Hindu father feeds his baby with clotted milk, honey and clarified butter (ghee) from a pure gold vessel.
- The newborn Zulu baby in South Africa and the Fulani baby in Nigeria are fed the milk of a newly-delivered cow.
- Tausog babies of the Philippines are given juice from the pounded leaves of the ampalaya plant, a local laxative.
- Until the seventeenth century, English babies were fed purging mixtures such as syrup of roses or violets, oil of almonds and chicory with rhubarb.
- Friends and relatives of the Sioux mother gather the best berries and herbs they can find and serve the juice to the baby from a buffalo bladder.
- In Bangladesh, the 'bad milk' may be replaced with mustard oil that has been diluted in warm pond or river water.
- Babies of Ghana, west Africa, are given a 'welcome' herbal or alcoholic drink before being fed on sugary liquids.
- In old Japan, a ritual elixir of roots and herbs called 'jumigokoto' was given.
- In ancient Scotland, babies were fed a mixture of whisky and finely-ground oatmeal.
- Pedi mothers of southern Africa feed their babies a watery porridge for the first two or three days.
- In Cairo, Egypt, many babies still start life on a diet of sugared water.

It is hard to say how long the colostrum taboo has been around. Even the Efé pygmies of the east African Ituri rainforest, who have lived the same way for tens of thousands of years, prefer their newborns to be wet-nursed until mothers' milk comes in. It is the most obvious aspect of child care where modern understanding confidently outstrips ancient wisdom. Luckily, new wisdoms can always be created to replace the old ones. Positive cross-cultural colostrum beliefs will no doubt be one of the triumphal chapters of *Baby Wisdom* when it goes into its third millennium edition.

And Now the Good News

At a time when health services are busily promoting breastfeeding with posters and commercials, a Woodaabe woman casually remarked: 'Our children have always been breastfed from birth onwards and go on with only breastmilk for more than five months. Breastmilk is the best food for a baby!' A very vivid practical lesson for mothers from other communities.

Dr Sani Aliou, Director of the Department of Health for the Agadez Region, Niger, reports on the Wodaabe nomads of west Africa

To be breastfed immediately from birth is a luxury enjoyed by a minority of the world's babies. Muslim mothers have been advised to give their babies colostrum since the Middle Ages. The fifteenth-century Islamic scholar Ibn Kathir said that under no circumstances should the mother deny her infant colostrum, since without its benefit he could die.

The Woodaabe people, who refuse to settle down, but roam the dry lands of the Sahel on the edge of the Sahara Desert, remain tuned in to the needs of the newborn infant. They cannot afford – financially or emotionally – to let themselves get sick. And colostrum is simply the best insurance for keeping their babies alive.

The benefits of colostrum are undoubtedly appreciated by the newborn baby. There is no other biological reason why, if left to his own devices, he should gradually move himself towards the breast and search for the nipple all by himself in the hour after birth. Some babies spend two of the first three hours of life just nursing at the breast.

The positive attributes of mothers' invisible milk, neglected by so many for so long, are now thoroughly appreciated by western scientists. They extol the virtues of both colostrum, which they say lasts for around ten days, and 'transitional milk', which endures for the next eight. In fact, breastmilk is a constantly changing entity and labels are not always helpful. However, it is worth mentioning that colostrum is home to five categories of antibodies, protects against diarrhoea, helps to mature the immune system and naturally purges meconium from the baby's intestinal tract.

PUTTING ON WEIGHT

One assumption in western medicine is that all babies lose weight in the first two or three days after birth. Neonatal weight loss is so usual that we assume it to be physiological fact. However, change the postnatal environment (the 'culture' of birth) and it might be possible to change the medical text books.

Researcher Dr Michel Odent investigated the weight of seventy babies born at home, where mothers and babies were allowed skin-to-skin contact, had unlimited access to the breast and slept near their mothers. One in three of these babies did not lose so much as an ounce after they were born. Instead, they maintained a steady weight before beginning to gain on or around the third day.

The western premise for weight loss is that the newborn dehydrates after birth, as he adjusts to the stresses of his new existence.

Since his body weight is eighty per cent water, there is plenty of weight to lose. Odent speculates that colostrum plays an essential part in rehydrating the baby. The protein-rich colostrum contains IgA antibodies which themselves are able to hold a lot of water. And the more colostrum a baby digests, the better his capacity for water retention.

Societies which allow their babies to drink colostrum include the Maoris of New Zealand, Warmun Aborigines of Australia, the Jackash tribe from the Peruvian rainforest and the ancient Maya people of Yucatan, Mexico. 'Nursing begins early [among the Maya], sometimes within a few minutes after birth, and thereafter the baby is put to the breast whenever it shows signs of being hungry or upset' (Brigitte Jordan, birth researcher).

Now the positive magic of colostrum is being made known, millions of women are freed from a taboo which runs counter to their postnatal inclinations. Having been for so long out of fashion, colostrum is now finding favour amongst the women of traditional societies. In Tibet, for instance, despite the fact that all babies were breastfed, colostrum was for years considered impure. Now western health workers have convinced Tibetan mothers to breastfeed straight after delivery, rather than waiting for three days.

In eighteenth-century England, when new-style paediatrician William Cadogan wrote in glowing terms about the purgative value of colostrum, he initiated a change of heart which swept through the country. By the end of the century, colostrum was back on the menu and neonatal mortality had been reduced by sixteen per cent. We should not underestimate the impact of human milk for saving human lives.

When the Milk Comes In

Breastfeeding the babies fitted into this system [English society before the indus-
trial revolution]. It was simply another task that had to be done, like brewing the
beer, making the bread, getting in the harvest or shoeing the horses.

Gabrielle Palmer, nutritionist and breastfeeding campaigner

The colostrum taboo would never have survived if it jeopar-
dised breastfeeding. But strangely, it seems that a three-day gap
is no impediment to nursing – that is, if you live in a society
which accepts breastfeeding as inevitable and straightforward.
From Japan to Africa, mothers manage to breastfeed despite their
postnatal feeding interval. Some societies wait even longer before
they allow the baby near the breast: the Yurok baby of California
is fed nut soup from a tiny shell for an amazing ten days. And
yet their mothers do breastfeed.

These extreme examples prove to us the astonishing resilience
of most babies and their ability to nurse. At the point where
many western women are thinking about giving up, mothers
from some cultures are just about to start.

We talk a great deal in our culture about the difficulties and
problems of breastfeeding. In *The Naked Ape*, zoologist Desmond
Morris compared monkeys and humans and decided that human
feeding was inherently problematic. 'The act of suckling is more
of a problem for females of our species than for other primates.
The infant is so helpless that the mother has to take a more
active part in the process, holding the baby to the breast and
guiding its actions. Some mothers have difficulty persuading
their offspring to suck efficiently.'

It seems that Morris's view of human nursing may have been
limited here to the struggling modern western mother, with
her lack of breastfeeding experience and social support. This
shows how dangerous it is to make physiological assumptions
based on evidence from a single culture. As it happens, even

gorillas find breastfeeding tricky when they are not raised in a naturally nurturing environment:

A female gorilla, born and raised in a zoo, gave birth to an infant. In an attempt to nurse it, the mother held the infant incorrectly, with the back of the baby's head toward the nipple. The keepers feared for the infant's life and took the baby away. During the gorilla's next pregnancy, the keepers tried an experiment. They lined up a group of breast-feeding humans outside the cage and allowed the mother gorilla to observe. When her next infant was born, the mother gorilla, too, turned the baby toward her breast and everything went fine.

Meredith Small, ethno-paediatrician

Western humans are born and raised in an environment as artificial as any zoo. We do not hunt for our own food; we have heat, light and clean water on tap without regard for the climate, the seasons, the time of day or the proximity of a river; we travel at unbelievable speeds; we communicate instantaneously from one side of the planet to another – and yet we rarely see a human mother breastfeed her own baby. Most of us are protected from the natural elements and, if we choose, we do not even have to live in a community with other humans. Is it any wonder that we also find breastfeeding a difficult thing to do?

We must not be led down the unreliable track of believing that our self-imposed problems are somehow part of the universal human condition. Some of us may find breastfeeding tough, but one hundred per cent breastfeeding is achieved in many cultures other than our own. A physical inability to breast-feed, supposedly so common in our society, is actually quite rare. Whatever size your breasts, whatever shape your nipple, whatever your mother's breastfeeding history, whatever your birth experience, whatever your preconceptions, whatever your income, wherever you live – you can do it. If you can conceive and deliver your baby, it is almost certain you can breastfeed him, too.

All in the Mind?

In traditional societies all mothers breastfeed and there is an assumption that every mother can and will do so. In all the places I visited, I came across no one who had been unable to breastfeed or who knew of anyone who had failed to provide enough breastmilk for their baby. For girls growing up in such a society, breastfeeding is an everyday activity which they see going on around them and so they learn the techniques unconsciously at an early age.

Jacqueline Vincent Priya, birth researcher

In some ways, it can be said that breastfeeding — that most intimate and tactile of communications — is all in the mind. Women in total-breastfeeding cultures cannot imagine not doing it, or not knowing how to do it. When researcher Leslie Conton asked Usino mothers of Papua New Guinea about their knowledge of nursing, they replied in astonishment, 'Why does she ask us all this? All women know how to breastfeed!'

A number of different assumptions are to be found in societies where breastfeeding is habitual:

* There may be linguistic reinforcement. For instance, Ekegusii, the language common to Gusii clans in Kenya, has one word 'okogonkia' to refer to giving birth and breastfeeding. One follows the other as day follows night.

* Breastfeeding is often also given spiritual endorsement. Among the Laguna Pueblo Indians of New Mexico, for instance, who believe that breastfeeding transmits beautiful thoughts to the baby's heart and mind, or the Khmir people of north-west Tunisia, who say breastfeeding fills babies with a magical life force. We also find breastfeeding praised in the Qur'an, the holy book of Islam and in the Old Testament, where the prophet Isaiah is one of many writers who refer to this supreme human bond: 'Can a mother forget the baby at her breast and not have compassion on the child she has borne?' (Isaiah, 49:15).

* When nursing is openly practised and a feature of normal

life, it becomes a feature of children's play. In Native American families, girls would 'nurse' their corn dolls; in the rainforest of Zaire, the Mbuti pygmies have no toys, so girls make do with the 'next best thing':

From where I sat I watched two little girls of about seven playing dolls with a real baby. They took turns alternately holding it in a nursing position against their chest and carrying it in a sling over their shoulder. When the baby became restless, they lay on their backs and bounced it up and down on their stomachs until it squealed with pleasure. It was the only doll the children would ever have, and their play was also a learning experience for when they would have children of their own.

Kevin Duffy, anthropologist

If breastfeeding really is all in the mind, what are the physical processes which allow it to work so easily for some, and not for others? When a baby cries, a message is sent to the mother's brain which stimulates the 'let-down reflex', allowing the secretion of milk. The hormone prolactin is simultaneously released, placing an order for tomorrow's supply of milk. Mothers are also equipped with a 'nipple ejection reflex', which means that even those with inverted nipples are able to breastfeed. Meanwhile, baby is fitted with his own rooting reflexes, guiding him instinctively to nurse from the areola.

All these reflexes explain why women in many societies begin nursing without difficulty, proceed without problem and continue for years. If nursing were not achievable for every woman, our species would not have survived the last million years. However, breastfeeding is an intimate relationship, not a one-way delivery process. When they breastfeed, mother and baby are initiating a subtle two-way communication. And like all relationships, this one is susceptible to negative influences and misunderstandings.

A mother's let-down reflex can be affected by negative thinking ('you'll never be able to breastfeed'); by lack of self-confidence ('I'll never be able to breastfeed'); by well-meant interventions ('here, let me take the baby so you can get a good night's sleep'); by stress and by panic. A baby's inborn reflexes can be confused by unnecessary interventions, which do not wait for him to root, to position himself perfectly, to open his mouth wide enough or to suck on the whole areola.

Never should a baby's first feed be orchestrated by a third party. No helpers are necessary unless as incidental emotional support, and in fact, most mothers and babies prefer peace and privacy. This should be a moment as comfortable and unhurried as a first date. After all, to access oxytocin, the so-called 'hormone of love', we have to treat breastfeeding as the sexual act that it is. Nor is there any need for mother to do all the hard work. Given skin-to-skin contact and access to the breast, the baby will do the rest. He will root, take the areola in his wide open mouth and suckle as if he were born to it. Come to think of it, he *was* born to it.

What's Good for Baby . . .

The psychophysiological benefits which mother and child, the nursing couple, reciprocally confer upon one another in the continuing symbiotic relationship are vitally important for their further development. This is a fact which is only very slowly coming to be recognized in our highly sophisticated, technologized, dehumanized, cubistically dilapidated Western world, a world in which breastfeeding has been considered by many to be beneath human dignity.

Ashley Montagu, social scientist, gets passionate about the
benefits of breastfeeding

The mantra that 'breast is best' has been repeated by English-speaking mothers since the 1970s. Some of us are tired of hearing about the benefits of breastfeeding, and yet other cultures depend on this news for survival. Mothers in traditional societies may not always know why, but the benefits conferred by nursing are directly responsible for saving many vulnerable babies. Long-term frequent breastfeeding has also for many years delayed the population explosion which now threatens the future of the planet. It still prevents many more births around the world than all other contraceptive methods combined.

Even though many western babies do well on bottled formulas, chemical mixes are no substitute for the unique milk produced by every mother for her unique baby. On a global level, we simply cannot afford to undermine our most precious resource for infant nurture. Nature's blessings are always reciprocal – what's good for baby is amazingly good for mother, too. Breastfeeding provides a natural lift to the feeding pair . . .

Breastfeeding: Benefits for Baby

1. Breastfed babies have fewer illnesses. In one longitudinal study, children who had not been breastfed had 4 times as many respiratory infections, 8 times as much eczema, 20 times more diarrhoea, 21 times more asthma, 27 times more hay fever and 22 times as many other infections. This is why the WHO and others regard breastfeeding as baby's first 'immunisation'.

2. Breastfeeding is hygienic and safe. Baby Milk Action campaigners estimate that every 30 seconds, a baby dies somewhere in the world from unclean bottle feeding.

3. Breastfeeding is protective against diarrhoea, the single major threat to infant life – this was proved in the 1920s, but authorities waited 50 years before taking any action to limit the promotion of formula milks to developing countries. In Britain alone, full breastfeeding would save the NHS more than £35m a year in treatments for infant gastroenteritis.

4. Breastmilk puts the least strain on babies' immature kidneys, which cannot deal with a diet high in proteins or other 'wastes'.

5. Breastfeeding is a perfect system of supply-and-demand: the baby regulates his own intake. You cannot overfeed him.

6. Breastfeeding helps to mature the infant's immune system and protects against immune deficiency diseases.

7. Breastfed babies are between two and five times less likely to die from cot death, or Sudden Infant Death Syndrome.

8. Long-term breastfeeding ensures proper development of the jaw. Researchers comparing breastfed African Bantu children with white Americans found that 99.6 per cent of Bantu children had a normal bite, while 30 per cent of white children had orthodontic problems.

9. Breastfeeding is part of a care package which gives babies better scores in cognitive tests.

10. Breastfeeding appears to protect against disease later in life: statistics show reduced risk for juvenile diabetes, breast cancer, malignant lymphoma, inflammatory bowel syndrome, asthma, allergy and ear infections.

11. Breastfeeding cements the bond between mother and baby and is therefore of equal benefit to them both. Oxytocin, the hormone which is released on suckling, enables mother and baby to relax, concentrate on each other and primes them for long-lasting attachment.

Breastfeeding: Benefits for Nursing Mothers

1. At birth, the baby's initial suckling stimulates contraction of the uterus, helping to dispel the placenta and reduce bleeding.

2. Early and frequent breastfeeding prevents breast engorgement and mastitis (inflammation of the breast).

3. Oxytocin, released during suckling, is an opiate which makes a mother naturally drowsy and helps her to get to sleep. Most mothers of the world still sleep alongside their babies as our ancestors did.

4. Breastfeeding is the perfect postnatal diet, using up pregnancy fat at a rate of 700 to 1,000 calories a day.

5. Frequent feeding by day and night is nature's best safeguard against conceiving the next baby too quickly. Postnatal amenorrhoea lasts only two months in non-breastfeeding mothers. In cultures where women universally breastfeed, menstruation returns two-thirds to three-quarters of the way through the nursing span. So mothers who nurse for 18 months are unlikely to conceive in the first year. This is vital in cultures where a mother could not hope to sustain two or more babies in quick succession. African !Kung San hunter-gatherer women, who breastfeed constantly and whose only contraception is prolactin, the hormone secreted as the baby suckles, enjoy a four-year space between each birth.

6. By reducing the number of monthly period cycles, births and miscarriages her body goes through, breastfeeding also protects a woman against iron-deficiency (anaemia), long-term exhaustion and possibly endometrial cancer.

7. Mothers who breastfeed are less likely to develop breast cancer. The longer they feed, the better the effect. In a part of China where boat-women habitually nurse from the left breast, women only seem to develop cancer in the right breast.

8. Lactation may actually make a nursing mother's calcium metabolism more efficient, protecting her against osteoporosis later in life.

9. Breastfeeding helps to ease postnatal depression, by stimulating endorphins.

10. Nursing encourages subtle communication between mother and baby, reducing the infant's need to cry or wait for food and comfort.

11. It boosts maternal confidence and enables the mother to realise that she can provide absolutely everything her small baby needs.

Milk of Human Kindness

> With lots of good fine milk
> our breasts are full.
> To avoid all suspicion,
> let the doctor see it,
> because in it is found
> the life and being of the creature,
> for good milk nourishes
> with no trouble and makes the flesh firm . . .

Song of the 'balie', medieval Italian wet nurses

It truly is magical stuff, this translucent milk which fattens our babies and inspires our poets. Traditional cultures of the world unite in their unequivocal belief that human milk is no ordinary substance. Milk, they say, is more than food – it conveys personality and magical human bonds.

In the Middle East, Syrian parents believe the baby receives his character from his mother's milk. An older child who refuses to listen to adults is said to have a 'dry head' – i.e., he is not drinking in their wisdom. Exiled in India, Tenzin Gyatso, the fourteenth Dalai Lama, spiritual leader of Tibet, has said that nursing is a physical bond in which the child is literally filled with the mother's essence.

It was long ago realised that stress can adversely affect breast-feeding. Families around the world are told not to trouble mother or upset her, in case negative feelings should contaminate the milk. Gyatso emphasises this idea and says that anger can even suppress lactation: 'The first act after birth is the child suckling the mother's milk. If the mother's mood remains angry, I think the milk will not flow properly. The mother's life in this way is reflected in the child' (The Dalai Lama).

In some societies, nursing creates a lifelong bond. It is as if sharing breastmilk confers a blood tie, making a child part of the family. And this is indeed the process in many ways. This story of a mistaken baby swap suggests that familial attachment can be created through the chemical and emotional connections of nursing: 'Two Irish babies were accidentally given to the wrong parents, one mother breastfed the "wrong" child and when the mistake was discovered and the babies exchanged she was devastated. She felt closer to the suckled child than to her biological baby' (Gabrielle Palmer, nutritionist and breastfeeding campaigner).

All sorts of nonsense – much of it disparaging – has been claimed about mothers' milk, from fanciful folklore to the early guesses of philosophers and medics. Nicholas Culpeper recommended herbs to 'correct' the milk; Victorian chemists claimed their brews of cow's milk and wheat starch were equal to the human version; modern doctors still sometimes suggest that mother's milk is somehow not 'enough' for a three- or four-month-old infant. Even today, we have not finished working out the constituents of this amazing baby food.

One thing we do know is that breastmilk is a unique product manufactured for individual babies. From the moment a baby is born to the day he sips his last drop, the milk is constantly changing. This is just one reason why it will never be replicated by bottled milk manufacturers. Established milk is twice as rich in fat and sugar as colostrum, for instance. It changes during each feed, from the low-fat foremilk, stored since the last time the baby nursed (and the longer the interval, the lower fat it will be, as the fat is reabsorbed by the mother's body), to the twenty-five-calories-per-ounce hindmilk, which satisfies the baby's hunger and tickles his taste buds. Breastmilk is also a potent early transmitter of culture, as it conveys the taste of the local diet:

The taste of human milk is never the same. It is not the same in the first days after birth and then later on. Foremilk does not taste the same as hindmilk. Morning milk differs from evening milk. These differences come about as a result of what the mother has been eating. On the other hand, formula milk remains exactly the same from the first drop to the last, whatever the time of day.

Michel Odent, obstetrician and primal health researcher

A mother's diet flavours her milk, which is how an Indian baby comes to be reconciled with a spicy menu and a western baby with a mild one. Researchers from the University of Illinois have even found that formula-fed babies are less willing to accept new foods at weaning.

YOU ARE MY SUNSHINE

The only nutrient missing from breastmilk is Vitamin D, and this is actually a hormone which is activated when sunlight meets the skin. Many northern cultures insist on 'sunbathing' of sorts for their babies: in Tibetan tradition, for instance, mothers give their babies daily naked sun baths, following a real bath and a massage with sesame oil. Thirty minutes' sunlight exposure a week (two hours if clothed but bare-headed) is enough to see most babies through the winter. Of course, sun creams should be applied when fair-skinned babies meet direct sunshine.

Most cultures do not question the constituents of a mother's milk. Only western scientists feel the need to test and pronounce !Kung San milk 'nutritionally adequate' for the task of feeding !Kung San babies. To ancient peoples, mother's milk is a pure miracle. As one Muslim Asian woman put it, 'God makes the breast-milk good for the babies.' And it's good for others, too. Breastmilk has always been used in folk cures and remedies. In Chinese tradition, breastmilk is valued for its ability to restore ailing adults; Culpeper recognises it as a seventeenth-century treatment for consumption: 'Milk digests soon, it being concocted by the nurse, and that's the reason, many in a consumption (whose digestion is weak) are cured by sucking a woman's breast' (Nicholas Culpeper, *A Directory for Midwives*, 1651).

Centuries later, John Steinbeck made the act of nursing a starving man the climactic moment of his masterpiece, *The Grapes of Wrath*.

For a minute Rose of Sharon sat still in the whispering barn. Then she hoisted her tired body up and drew the comforter about her. She moved slowly to the corner and stood looking down at the wasted face, into the wide, frightened eyes. Then slowly she lay down beside him. He shook his head slowly from side to side. Rose of Sharon loosened one side of the blanket and bared her breast. 'You got to,' she said. She squirmed closer and pulled his head close. 'There!' she said. 'There.' Her hand moved gently in his hair. She looked up and across the barn, and her lips came together and smiled mysteriously.

John Steinbeck, American novelist, 1939

Going with the Flow

Take then in her hand milk of a cow of a single colour and then sip it with her mouth and then go to running water and spit the milk into it and take up in the same hand a mouthful of the water and swallow it. Then say these words: 'Everywhere have I carried for me the splendid strong kinsman; with this splendid well nourished one. I will have him for me and go home.' When she goes to the brook then let her not look around, nor again when she goes away; and then let her go into another house than that where she started from and there let her taste food.

Anglo-Saxon spell to ensure a copious milk supply

This spell contains a powerful message of affirmation. The 'splendid strong kinsman' is the baby who has been carried and 'well nourished' by the young mother in her womb. She declares her right to keep the baby, to 'have him for me' and asserts her ability to nurture him as she did throughout pregnancy. The message from our prehistoric ancestors is emphatically to trust in the ability to breastfeed. Special diets and herbs, charms and treatments are a way of reinforcing a mother's confidence and increasing her milk supply.

A question of faith

Ancient Egyptians were amazed by the ability of the mother cat to deliver and suckle up to twenty or more kittens at one time. Bastet the Cat remained the supreme Egyptian mother goddess from around 1570 to 575 BC. Hundreds of thousands of visitors every year converged on Bastet's magnificent temple at Bubastis in the Nile Delta, in search of fertility and a little nurturing magic. Women wore amulets and talismans in blue-green earthenware, displaying cats with exaggerated breasts, often nursing their feline litter. Charms were used during childbirth and afterwards, to ensure that maternal milk would flow in abundance.

In Korea, mothers pray to the Birth Grandmother to 'make the milk flow' and offer up rice, soup and other gifts in her honour. Christian mothers from Jordan wear lucky white pebbles from Bethlehem's Grotto of Milk, believing that drops of the Virgin's Mary's breastmilk were spilled there. In northern India, the Rajput mother has her breasts ritually washed by her husband's sister. The blessing to ensure good milk flow is ideally performed with sacred Ganges water and the new mother is expected to show her gratitude: 'For this she receives a present of jewelry. Sometimes the sister-in-law clamors for a particular piece of expensive jewelry. If that child is a boy, particularly a first-born son, her request is usually granted. If no husband's sister is present, another woman acts as a substitute. She receives only a nominal gift' (Leigh Minturn and John Hitchcock, anthropologists in northern India).

While pure Ganges water may have its own spiritual potency, there is absolutely no need for mothers to wash their breasts before nursing. Research has shown that soaping the nipple area eliminates the natural odours which help to establish breastfeeding. More than two-thirds of newborns showed a preference for the unwashed breast and newborns are even guided towards the breast by maternal odour.

Which brings us neatly back to nursing cats. Cat babies each have their own favourite nipple to feed from. Without confusion or fighting, kittens present themselves to the same maternal teat each time. It seems that each baby leaves its own smell on the preferred nipple, an aromatic imprint to which it will later return. And scientists now believe that human babies do a similar thing, depositing their own smell signature on their mothers' breasts. So nursing mothers should never wash their breasts with anything stronger than water, or they might be removing the baby's personal aromatic signal.

Nourishment for nursing

The notion that nursing mothers need to eat special foods is commonplace in almost every culture. If a mother is to nurture her young, it is a short logical step to the assumption that she must require special nurturance herself. But what exactly is a good lactation diet? On that, few cultures agree. Tausog women of the Philippines are fed '*imbau*' (clams), '*pusu*' (banana heart), '*kilul*' (soup of chicken and malunggay leaves) and the green leaves of sweet potatoes, none of which are currently available in the average western supermarket. Here are some worldwide recipes for human milk production:

* Chinese mothers believe that eating pigs' feet in ginger and vinegar aids lactation.
* Gusii mothers of Kenya eat a mixture of eleusine porridge (called '*oboori*') and '*chinsaga*', a green vegetable, which they say are essential for milk release. Eleusine, a grain known as African 'finger millet', is a rich food and an excellent source of calcium.
* In rural Japan, mothers are fed papaya boiled with flour and noodles to stimulate the milk supply.

* In the Punjab, lactating mothers are fed a special supplement called 'Dhabra', made of 'ghee' (clarified butter), flour, ginger, dried grapes, aniseed, raisins and almonds to build up strength.

Although most cultures engage in feverish food preparation for the nursing mother, few attain the nutritional highs which we have reached in the west today. Even so, worldwide lactation studies reveal that good quality human milk is produced even when the mother is under-nourished.

In Keneba, a Gambian village in west Africa, women eat low energy foods, despite providing heavy agricultural labour and lactating almost continually between the ages of fifteen and forty-five. Average calcium consumption is about twenty-five per cent of the UK recommended daily intake. Yet researchers who tried supplementing mothers' diets concluded that food intake made no difference to milk supply. The unforeseen upshot was that dietary supplements caused a drop in prolactin levels and a return to menstruation, which was not what the women wanted at all.

In India and elsewhere, women are sometimes encouraged to drink cow's milk for lactation. We have, after all, spent many years trying to turn cow's milk into a suitable formula for babies and the nursing woman is sometimes even compared (unflatteringly) to a cow. However, there is no evidence that one mammal needs to drink the milk of another in order to produce milk of her own. Nutritionists are quite clear on this:

Another common myth is that a breast-feeding mother needs to drink milk in order to make milk. This, of course, is nonsense. The move away from breast-feeding led to the substitution of human milk with cow's milk. Cow's milk is designed for calves, and is very different from human milk in a number of respects, including its protein, calcium, phosphorous, iron and essential fatty acid content.

Patrick Holford, nutritionist

Herbal hints

Some herbs are known as 'galactogogues', substances which increase the flow of human milk. These have been discovered and used by rural people for thousands of years – but how useful are they? And is it possible that some herbal preparations could be dangerous to the breastfeeding mother or her baby?

* In the Middle East, nomadic Arab tribes encourage their sheep to graze on rosemary because it perfumes their milk. Breastfeeding mothers also include rosemary in their diet. This is said to act as a tonic for the baby.

* Seventeenth-century English mothers drank boiled compounds of fennel and barley – these herbs, according to herbalist Nicholas Culpeper, would 'breed milk'. Fennel and caraway teas were used to increase the milk yield in dairy cows and in breastfeeding women. Fennel seeds make a gentle liquorice-flavoured tea which passes into the milk and is said to ease the baby's digestive system.

* Many Native American mothers drink the juice from the stem of the dandelion, or an infusion of red raspberry leaves. This is rich in useable calcium, magnesium, iron and vitamin C, all essential for the nursing mother.

* Goat's rue tea, an old herbal galactogogue, is said to increase milk supply by up to fifty per cent and stimulate the development of the mammary glands.

* Italian mothers are given an infusion made from fennel seed, aniseed, *galega officinalis* and liquorice root (a maximum of a teaspoon of the combined herbs to one litre of boiling water). They drink this before and after meals to enhance milk production.

Herbs may be less concentrated than their drug derivatives, but that does not mean they are always less potent. They contain lots of active constituents in small amounts. Side effects and toxic reactions are rare when fresh herbs are taken, although allergic reactions are always possible. Essential oils made from herbs can be quite toxic, however, and should not be ingested or rubbed around the nipple.

Only one per cent of chemicals consumed by the mother enter her milk, but even mild herbal remedies may cause side effects if taken in excess. One report from Italy claimed that mothers who were drinking very large quantities of the fennel and aniseed tea had made their babies sick and lethargic. Meanwhile, one Californian baby who was given chamomile tea to drink for his colic developed botulism, as the herb was contaminated with spores.

For safety's sake, check with a doctor or herbalist before taking strong-acting herbal medicines; do not drink any herbal infusion too often (once or twice a day should be enough, unless you are personally prescribed otherwise); and do not feed self-prescribed herbs or medicines directly to the baby — the best way to reach him is through the breastmilk.

HERBS AND CHEMICALS TO AVOID

1. Sage (*Salvia officinalis*); yarrow (*Achillea milleolium*); black walnut (*julandis regia*); parsley and peppermint are all said to decrease milk production and were traditionally used to help women who needed to dry up their milk.

2. Caffeine, the chemical found in tea, coffee, colas and the South African drink called 'maté': it affects the milk, can irritate the baby's bowel and attacks a mother's stores of iron, potassium and B vitamins.

3. Hops (*Lupuli strobulus*); ginseng (*Panex quinquefolium*) and liquorice (*Glycerrhiza glabra*) — all herbs which have steroid-like properties.

Back to the rainforest

As it happens, nature has supplied a variety of triggers which encourage lactation – and they are all easily available in the modern world. The first trigger is touch. Breast massage is one of the ritual elements of postnatal care in many countries. Warmun Aboriginal women from Western Australia would apply 'bush medicine' – perhaps ground leaves from the snappy gum tree ('*pilinyji*') warmed and massaged into the breast. Clean earth was also used to encourage breastfeeding:

This is a young girl called Mona. When she was having a baby she had some trouble getting the breastmilk supply going. To help get the milk supply she put some mud (*mawundu*) on her breasts. This caused the breasts to swell and make milk. This is not mud from an anthill but is found on the ground. It is yellow-red coloured mud.'

Mona Ramsay, Aboriginal woman of Warmun

In Nigeria, breast massage is vigorously administered by female relatives for weeks before and after birth. All positive touch treatments are known to encourage lactation, but the best possible massage is the contact of the baby's gums with the areola.

Skin-to-skin contact with baby also excites the milk-ejection reflex, as was shown in a study from Texas. Mothers of low birthweight infants in intensive care were invited to hold their babies skin-to-skin for at least thirty minutes every day once they were well enough. This positively influenced the amount of breastmilk they were able to express for their ill babies. Mothers in the control group said they had feelings of inadequacy, and their milk volumes were low. Researchers concluded that both maternal confidence and milk flow were improved by babies' touch.

Besides human contact, there are a number of other well-known physical stimulants to help milk release:

● Bathing – an important aspect of postnatal care around the world. Azande women of central Africa sponge their breasts

while bathing to help release their breastmilk (soap should not be used as this masks the natural aroma of the areola).
- Running water works like a subconscious suggestion, triggering milk release.
- The sound of your own baby's voice (crying or otherwise) may have been evolved to activate the milk ejection reflex.
- Central heating works wonders: women in the Guatemalan border province of Huehuetenango heat rocks and use them to warm their home before they begin nursing. This is a cold mountainous region and the mothers are concerned that their milk does not turn 'sour'. 'A warm atmosphere,' according to researcher Amanda Hopkinson, 'helps the milk to flow freely.'

Add all these elements together, and we could be in the tropical rainforest. Imagine yourself holding your naked infant next to your bare skin, in a constantly humid temperature, near a stream of fresh, running water. You have, perhaps, just bathed yourself and your baby and as you hold him close, he grunts impatiently. He turns his head towards the waiting breast . . . The rest is breakfast.

HOME TRUTHS

A lactating mother and her breast-feeding child are interdependent and exclusive in their relations, to a degree that is unique in postnatal life and exceeded only by the relations between a pregnant woman and her unborn child.

Robert A. LeVine, anthropologist

There is an extraordinary degree of self-sufficiency about a mother breastfeeding her baby. The two are so powerful in their mutual completeness, so absorbed in each other and so unneedful of outside help, that others may only look on in envy. Is jealousy the deep and complex emotion which has driven so many cultures to intrude in the early breastfeeding days and prevent the baby from drinking the rich colostrum which is so good for him? Sexual rivalry certainly seems to be a recurring theme in western paternal-maternal relations today.

Or is there another reason why even the most harmonious of communities prevent a baby from nursing immediately after birth? Some cultures harden their children in preparation for an inevitably harsh life. They want to lessen the mother's boundless generosity towards her offspring and so deliberately interrupt the maternal bond. A host of interventions – from cold baths to temporary abandonment – have been used to evaluate the baby's strength; to make sons warlike and daughters strong of heart.

We may pride ourselves that we do not deliberately harden our babies, and yet we have other means to make sure that infants are hardened and separated from their mothers. In western society, we use sophisticated mockery to diminish the too-devoted parent. We characterise women as fettishly connected to their babies if they breastfeed openly and for as long as nature intended. We seduce them back to work and the marital bed and proclaim them weak if they put her own needs on hold while attending to those of small children.

We assume that breastfeeding will be painful, tedious and time-consuming and that if we continue too long, it will eat away at our brain cells, depriving us of status, income and the chance of a good night out. We are particularly concerned that nursing mothers should not take themselves too seriously.

Even in those cultures where breastfeeding is encouraged, history has revealed a profound lack of trust that mother's milk will ever come. A fearful taboo, spanning thousands of years and many continents, has deprived babies of life-giving colostrum and substituted a range of purgatives which are only likely to do him harm. Jealousy, hardening, mistrust: these are the contexts which have confused the nursing relationship and made it a miracle that many babies are breastfed at all. And yet, amazingly, most human babies of the world still are – for a short time, at least.

Breastfeeding is all about trust. And the trust begins at a societal level. If we don't trust that mothers have all that is required for the nurture of a human baby, then mothers will swiftly lose faith in their own ability to breastfeed. What we need is another generation of little girls (and boys, why not?) with dolls stuffed under their jumpers, nursing them in their imaginative and semiconscious role-play. Then we will know that breastfeeding is once more as normal as the taking of a cup of tea.

8. Tricks of the Trade

In some parts of the world, nursing a baby is as natural as having a conversation with a friend. Few cultures insist on rules and regulations which make breastfeeding an obstacle course. This is the way the world feeds . . .

Free to Feed

The breasts of women with many children may be really flat, going all the way down to the waist . . . Although such 'droopy breasts' may be unattractive from our point of view, to the pygmies it is quite OK because it indicates a woman who has been feeding a lot of children.

Ushanda io Elima, writer, teacher and field researcher, on the
Efé of the central African rainforest

In 1910, an anti-embarrassment nursing device for mothers was patented in England. Its inventor supplied the dotted outline of a mother and baby to explain how the contraption might work. In it, the woman is wearing a hefty harness, rather like a leather brassière attached to a buckled waist belt. Presumably this would be strapped on under her clothes. From the nipple point in each bra cup protrudes a thin pipe with a teat on the end. To one of these pipes, a badly-drawn baby is fixed. For some strange reason, the woman appears to be smiling.

You can't have anti-embarrassment devices unless you have embarrassment. And embarrassment is the major problem facing breastfeeding women in England and America today. Part of the issue is our cultural reverence for the female breast as an object of sexual desire. This is not, as has often been assumed, a universal phenomenon. A 1950s survey found that breasts were used for sexual foreplay in only thirteen out of 191 cultures.

Cross-cultural ideas of femininity are as varied as we might expect, since beauty has always been in the eye of the beholder. Some like a plump body, others prefer slim. Fleshy calves, broad hips, thin ankles, pendulous breasts, a space between the front teeth – these are just a few of the attributes named as desirable or sexy by the world's men. Very few, it appears, prefer the 'pert' or upright pre-maternal breast which has become the obsession of the western male. Most societies recognise the mature female shape as ultimately more desirable than the immature.

Among the Efé pygmies, who have lived for thousands of years undisturbed in the African rainforest, the breasts are 'sacred' – not for sexual contact, but for the nurture of babies and small children. In this highly nurturant society, long flat breasts are a positive female status symbol. And in Papua New Guinea, pert breasts are seen as a curse put on a woman to make her appear like a young girl.

While westerners are not the only society to sexualise breasts, we are unusual in our insistence that men have some kind of 'right' to the breast which takes precedence over the needs of babies. An anonymous *Daily Telegraph* editorial puts this modern male perspective without a blush:

Lady Cumberlege, a junior health minister, has now urged cafés, restaurants and other places of common trade to encourage mothers to breast feed their babies in public.

Why? What business is it of hers? Many men are made to feel uncomfortable by the spectacle, either because they are jealous of the baby or because they would prefer to see the woman's breast as an object of erotic veneration rather than in its less interesting role as a teat or udder. This is especially true where other people's wives, other people's babies are concerned.

Daily Telegraph editorial, London 1994

It seems appropriate to compare the sexual jealousy of the *Telegraph* editorial writer with a comment made to anthropologist Katherine Dettwyler, who has researched the cultural context of the female breast. In Mali, west Africa, where the sexiest part of a woman is her inner thigh, women were astonished to hear that many white men sucked at the female breast during sex. 'You mean the men pretend they are little babies?' asked one mother, in perceptive innocence.

When the sight of a breast is literally titillating, it becomes antisocial to bare it in public. Even feeding in your own front room becomes a problem, lest your father-in-law or a disapproving friend should walk in. Such barriers rarely exist in societies which accept breastfeeding as a prerequisite for nurturing new life. In Norway, for instance, where ninety-eight per cent of mothers breastfeed from birth and sixty per cent are still nursing after six months, the breastfeeding woman is a welcome sight.

I thought I would write and tell you of my experiences breastfeeding my baby in public, as I live in a more enlightened country – Norway.

Frederick is my third child, and I can truly say that I have not felt any negative feelings towards my breastfeeding him, either in cafés, shops, on trams, in the hospital, or at friends' homes; unlike when I fed my other two children . . . in England.

Although I was never asked to stop feeding in public, I did see the expressions on some people's faces (enough to turn the milk sour). My GP even suggested that I was feeding my son beyond three months for my own pleasure. My son, after all, did not need my milk any more.

Here in Oslo . . . no one bats an eyelid, and the mothers do not get embarrassed.

Elizabeth Brendefur, English mother in Norway

It is hard to persist in a practice which your culture finds it difficult to condone, much less applaud. Many American and British women must struggle against their social instincts in order to continue with breastfeeding, and against their maternal instincts if they wish to conform with the expectations of friends and family.

In traditional, rural Japan (where the nape of the neck is considered a woman's sexiest attribute), breastfeeding is encouraged by all. Grandparents – those representing the traditional approach – are especially unwilling to let a baby cry. In Okinawa, babies are carried everywhere and are breastfed in front of family and strangers alike.

In the Middle East, although women's bodies are almost entirely covered for reasons of marital and spiritual modesty, a mother's breasts may be bared when breastfeeding. Although there is a recent trend towards rejecting breastfeeding as 'animalistic' and 'primitive', women of urban Egypt are still able to nurse where they will:'Many younger *baladi* (traditional) women feel free to breastfeed anywhere: on a bus, while chatting to their friends, on their doorsteps, or when they are entertaining guests. In the traditional value system the act of breastfeeding is seen as a natural function, and it does not attract special attention' (Homa Hoodfar, anthropologist).

Breast is Dressed

She only gets a couple more months and that's about it. Then I want to be able to fit back into my shirt.

Pop star Madonna, after the birth of her first baby, Lourdes

The clothes we wear may help to encourage or discourage breastfeeding. When fashion dictates body shape, rather than body shape dictating fashion, nature's needs usually finish a poor second.

One of the biggest stumbling blocks is the modern bra. Nursing bras notoriously come with hooks and eyes and treacherous zips to catch you unawares and make breastfeeding akin to safe-breaking. Sydney Singer, a medical anthropologist, has pointed out that breast cancer is a problem only in cultures where women wear bras. This statistic is unlikely to represent complete 'cause and effect', but breastfeeding may be the missing clue, since a) breastfeeding is known to be protective against breast cancer, b) bras make breastfeeding harder and c) cultures where women wear bras are less likely to be cultures where women universally breastfeed.

Our battle with constricting underwear dates back to six-teenth-century Europe, when the preference was for leather, bone or even metal corsets and stays. Tight bras and corsets can (and did) damage developing breast tissue, as some Chinese women found to their cost in the 1920s. The trend for very tight, chest-flattening dresses left some upper-class Chinese mothers unable to breastfeed.

Women of traditional societies in hot climates rarely dress the breast at all. Their constantly-carried babies have unlimited feeds and swiftly learn to help themselves – accessibility is more impor-tant than accessories. Even in breastfeeding cultures where clothes are worn, the emphasis is usually on the infant's right of way. Here are some worldwide fashions for nursing mothers:

* The Sioux mother traditionally wore a breastfeeding blouse with slits in the sides.
* In fifteenth-century Europe, upper-class mothers and wet nurses wore specially-designed gowns which opened at the bodice.
* The dresses of modern Gusii women from Kenya do not always have an opening for breastfeeding, so they pull their breasts up to the neckline for nursing. With little more than the nipple protruding, the baby still manages to nurse.
* The 'amauti' of the Inuit mother is a fur coat with very wide shoulders. These allow her to move her baby from the back to the breast for nursing, without exposing him to the bitter Arctic air.

* After birth in Siberia, a big party is held, during which the dress the mother wore in labour is torn down the middle, ready for nursing. Small children are told that the new baby dropped out from the mother's stomach and tore the dress!

This Way, That Way

There is no specific or preferred posture for feeding. While the mothers are in confinement for the brief period following delivery, they often lie next to the baby and feed him. Sitting while nursing is the most common posture, but mothers frequently nurse while standing or squatting. The baby is held loosely and the mother is relaxed.

Thomas and Hatsumi Maretzki, anthropologists in Okinawa island, Japan

Reams have been written on how to position a baby so that he takes enough breast into his mouth and milks a large section of the areola. Good breastfeeding textbooks show mothers how to relax, sit comfortably, support their backs and arms with cushions and keep the baby's head and back in line. This helpful blueprint for beginning to breastfeed is just that — a blueprint. As mothers from other cultures would tell us, this is just your starting position.

In our sedentary society, it feels normal to nurse while sitting down. In eighteenth-century England, most nurseries were equipped with a low-level nursing stool, either one that was purpose-designed, or an everyday chair with its legs cut down. This piece of furniture survives until the present day in some well-to-do homes. But it does rather suggest that babies can only be fed while mother is sitting up. How do women manage in cultures where there *are* no chairs?

While we may think of breastfeeding as a fairly static activity, hunter-gatherer tribes have neither chairs, nor cushions, nor the inclination to sit around all day while a baby feeds. Of course, it is different in the very early days after birth, when a baby is learning to latch on and the milk supply is shifting gear dramatically. But even then, mothers are likely to feed lying down, the position of greatest relaxation.

The !Kung San people of the Kalahari Desert in Africa are a hunter-gatherer people whose breastfeeding patterns have been thoroughly documented and analysed. Scientists observe a fluid feeding pattern which does not interfere with work or play, and does not force the mother into a sedentary position. !Kung baby-carrying is designed for easy breastfeeding – it is assumed that the nursing mother needs to be mobile: 'The [!Kung San] mother, wherever she goes, carries her infant tied to her left side, skin to skin, in a little leather sling where it can reach her breast. When she sits, she takes the infant out of its sling, holds it, lets it nurse the other breast' (Lorna Marshall, anthropologist).

'San breasts,' says anthropologist Meredith Small, 'are long and flexible' and immediately we see both the advantages and disadvantages of living without a bra. On the plus side, baby can feed freely from all sides, so milking the breast thoroughly and reducing the chances of engorgement (painful swelling) or mastitis, the infection which often follows when a milk duct becomes blocked. On the other hand, when your breasts are stretched in all directions, you reduce your chances of ever returning to the pert pre-pregnancy western sexual ideal. However, it is pregnancy, not breastfeeding, which alters the shape and direction of the breasts, and even women who bottle-feed find their breasts have changed for ever. Perhaps it is time 'pendulous' replaced 'pert' in the western dictionary of chic motherhood.

FREEZE-FRAME ON BREASTFEEDING

Feeding while on the move is not as tricky as it sounds, once a baby is old enough to latch on in confidence. I have a newspaper photograph of an African woman walking home in Mozambique, following the floods which devastated many homes when cyclone Eline struck in February 2000.

In one hand, she carries a pair of white wellington boots, preferring to wade through the mud and subsiding floodwater in her bare feet. In her other hand is a carrier bag, possibly containing fruit. On her head is balanced an enormous bundle in a checked cloth, tied with a knot on top. And feeding from her left breast is a baby, perhaps nine or ten months old. His legs are slung around his mother's hip, and he is secured by a cloth sling which reaches over his mother's right shoulder. It looks as though her yellow dress has a purposely-designed front opening – she wears no bra.

The mother appears distressed: she does not know what state her home will be in if it has survived at all. But the baby looks utterly content, feeding on the move, as he has so often done before, as all babies are designed to do.

Day and night feeds differ quite dramatically for mothers in furniture-free societies. We are the only ones who insist on sitting comfortably upright by day and by night, thus ensuring we have to wake ourselves up and get out of bed to sit in that nursery chair, or make sure we do not fall asleep with our babies tucked in by our side.

Most mothers of the world do not restrict their night feeds or attempt to nurse sitting up. They feed where they lie and baby swiftly learns to take the breast without fully waking either himself or his mother. The highly relaxed, uninterrupted night feeds are in sharp contrast to a day of mobile feeding. Night feeds are higher in prolactin, which ensures that milk production is perfectly calibrated to each baby's personal requirements. So lying down to feed is possibly one of the most important positions to mothers all around the world.

In western eyes only mothers who have given birth with a Caesarian section are likely to be trying to feed lying down. But it is not necessary to have a Caesarian in order to borrow the idea. Simply turn to the page on post-operative breastfeeding positions in your child care manual and you will find all the practical tips you need.

Given the evolutionary perspective, it is not surprising to find many societies doing everything possible to facilitate breast-feeding and make the process easier for mother and baby. However, some cultures train mothers to breastfeed despite many culturally-imposed obstacles. The aggressive Mundugumor river tribe of New Guinea, for instance, live in a 'state of mutual distrust' according to touch expert Ashley Montagu, and seem to resent most aspects of a baby's nurture. Babies are only fed if they will not stop crying:

If . . . the crying does not stop the infant is suckled – the mother standing up while doing so. There is no playful fondling between mother and child. Children therefore develop a strong fighting attitude, holding on to the nipple as firmly as possible, frequently choking from swallowing too rapidly. The choking angers the mother and infuriates the child, thus further turning the suckling experience into one of anger and frustration, struggle and hostility, rather than one of affection, reassurance, and contentment.

Ashley Montagu, social scientist

In this example, the standing-to-feed position is not a part of a healthy and diverse pattern, which includes many other breast-feeding positions. By refusing ever to sit or lie with her baby, the Mundugumor mother expresses her emotional resentment and her unwillingness to relax and enjoy their physical relationship. Rather like the house-guest who refuses to sit down, she betrays her impatience to be somewhere else.

Bassinets and baskets feature in the breastfeeding positions of some cultures. In Syrian tradition, the baby is bound into a cradle while he breastfeeds. Mother is then obliged to plunge the breast into the passive infant's mouth, a habit which extends to later years, as older children and even adult guests also find food is thrust into their mouths by their parents or hosts.

Some Australian Aboriginal mothers keep their small babies in the '*coolamon*' or cradle while nursing. Among the Anbarra people of north central Arnhem Land, the baby would be carried in his cradle of paperbark until his skin had darkened from newborn pink to a more mature shade of black. Babies were fed in their cradles, balanced on the mother's knee, 'the high breasts of a young mother presented a problem as she had to lean right over the baby to place the nipple (*kungal mipulakidjera;* literally "milk's eye") into his mouth' (Annette Hamilton, anthropologist).

It is amazing how many different ways there are to feed a baby, from easy-access systems to let's-see-how-we-can-complicate-life routines. Even more astonishing is the fact that, despite a range of culturally-condoned efforts to separate mother and infant, breastfeeding was universal in all human societies for millions of years. It had to be. Until very recently, there were simply no other viable options.

BURPING BABY

Burping baby is a favourite theme in western babycare literature. However, the art of burping is relatively new in the repertoire of human parenting skills. Babies who are carried in an upright position, who have frequent access to the breast and are not fed unsuitable liquid substitutes, do not need to be burped. It is the sedentary breast feeding position, coupled with long breastfeeding intervals, which cause most infant digestive problems.

> The notion that nature has evolved one species to suffer from indigestion every time it drinks its mother's milk has, amazingly, not been questioned by civilized experts. 'Burping', patting the baby firmly on the back while he is held against one's shoulder, is advocated to help him 'bring up the air he has swallowed.' The baby often vomits on the shoulder in the process . . . Yequana babies [of Venezuela] never require special treatment after nourishing themselves – any more than do the young of other animals.
>
> **Jean Liedloff, continuum therapist**

!Kung San babies who feed in an upright position do not need to be 'burped' after feeding; nor do the offspring of our evolutionary cousins, the primates. However, if you remove an ape baby from the wild and bottle-feed him every two hours, suddenly his immature system displays all the windy instability of the westernised human baby.

> The mixture of air and milk inside the stomach must have a chance to separate so that the air rises to the top and escapes with ease, in small spontaneous burps. If the baby is too horizontal this does not happen. The air is trapped and causes painful wind. The burping ritual automatically makes the baby more vertical and it is this that solves the problem. The pat on the back may or may not help . . . With tribal babies held more vertically, the baby can resolve the problem for itself, without any special maternal assistance.
>
> **Desmond Morris, zoologist**

In any case, babies should not take their milk lying flat on their backs. The mouth and nasal cavity connect to the back of the throat and lead to the middle ear. Ear infections and chronic nasal discharge may result if the middle ear becomes flooded. Baby's head and body should be always facing the breast, and his head slightly raised.

Clocking On

When the baby awakened, she unwrapped his arms and bent down to nurse him. Physically, she was providing her son with the best possible start in life; spiritually, she was achieving merit in the eyes of God. The Prophet himself, in a collection of writings known as the Hadith, assures the nursing mother that each mouthful of milk and each suckle she gives will be counted and rewarded on Judgement Day. At-Tabari, a tenth-century Koranic scholar, further declares that the mother who is kept awake by her child at night will be rewarded as one who frees 70 slaves for the sake of God.

Pamela Crimmins, photographer, observes a breastfeeding mother in Morocco

What a wonderful concept – breastmilk as a bounty which brings heavenly glory. Islamic law sets no miserly limits on the timing of feeds, or restrictions on night-time nurture – quite the contrary. Mohammed promises that every drop of milk will be counted and add to a mother's honour.

Perhaps this is why women in the Muslim country of Egypt, when asked by researchers, were completely unaware of the intervals they allowed between each breastfeed. While western mothers nervously watch the clock, regarding it as a personal failure if the baby should want to feed before his allotted hours are up, mothers living in the new urban areas of Cairo remain blissfully unaware of the time.

Feeding schedules are a particularly western obsession. Clock-watching was introduced to most ordinary European homes during the seventeenth century. Adherence to daily deadlines was first made possible by the distribution of mechanical time-pieces via churches and workplaces: 'The clock was the central metaphor for this shaping of modern European culture ... Time, hitherto experienced, or calculated roughly by the sun, was increasingly segmented, then standardized. Minutes and hours began to colonize the natural rhythms of the day, the month, the year' (Michael Schwab, social historian).

It must have been a very different world, when people lived

by natural rhythms, responding to the turning seasons, the ebb and flow of day and night, or the workings of their own bodies. Westerners find it hard to imagine 'feeling' their way unhurriedly through each day. Without a clock there can be no timetables. Without some device to measure the ticking of the seconds and the striking of the hour, there can be no infant feeding schedules. We who are willing slaves to the demands and strictures of a clock-bound existence hardly notice how artificially fragmented our lives have become.

In rural India today, by contrast, many people live just as they always have, obeying only those diurnal rhythms which can be measured by human sensing. The absence of time limits defines and protects traditional people more completely than any other barrier. It is why Gitanjali Kolanad, writing a guide book for travellers to India, reminds her readers that 'The villages of India far off the beaten track are another world, in another time.'

Yet India may be on the cusp of a creeping mechanical revolution, as we were three hundred years ago. To own a wristwatch is regarded today in some Indian villages as a serious status symbol. As long as the watch is an item of jewellery, a mere sign of affluence or connection, its effect on people's daily lives will be limited. But once people start using clocks and watches to direct their lives, their priorities change irrevocably.

In Europe, the clock heralded a new theory of life, a philosophy which insisted that the animal body was no more than a machine which required systematic regulation. But it took another 200 years before timetables started to affect the lives of babies. Rules on limiting breastfeeds were supplied by many nineteenth-century child care experts. A typical offering comes from Pye Henry Chavasse, an obstetrician from Birmingham. Here is his advice on 'Stated Times For Suckling':

A mother ought to suckle her baby at stated times. It is a bad habit to give him the bosom every time he cries, regardless of the cause; for be what it may –

overfeeding, griping, 'wind,' or acidity – she is apt to consider the breast a panacea for all his sufferings. A mother generally suckles her infant too often – having him almost constantly at the bosom. This practice is injurious both to parent and to child. For the first month he should be suckled about every hour and a half; for the second month, every two hours; gradually, as he becomes older, increasing the distance of time between, until at length he has the breast about every four hours.

Dr Pye Henry Chavasse, *Advice to a Wife on the Management of Her Own Health*

Chavasse's advice included not allowing the new nursing mother to drink too much fluid! He also insisted that any 'viscid mucus' (colostrum) should be washed away from a first-time mother's nipples and that babies should only be allowed to feed at 'considerable intervals' when milk flow became evident. This sort of disinformation helped to lay the foundations for a generation of interval feeding, with Sir Frederick Truby King at the helm.

Truby King was a British psychologist whose breastfeeding campaign saved many infant lives in New Zealand after 1907. His enthusiasm for breastfeeding was coupled with strict daily schedules, followed earnestly by British mothers between the two world wars. But Truby King babies (note the branding: they were his, not the mother's and each baby was to be treated the same, regardless of size, disposition or culture) were reared on a regime of solitary confinement and long-interval feeding. His daughter Mary wrote of her father's work:

Truby King babies are fed four-hourly from birth, with few exceptions, and they do not have any night feeds. A Truby King baby has as much fresh air and sunshine as possible, and the right amount of sleep. His education begins from the very first week, good habits being established which remain all his life.

A real Truby King baby is not too fat . . .

Mary Truby King, child care author, England 1930s

The intervals may have changed slightly, but the principles of clock-watching are as important to many western mothers today

as they were to their grandmothers. While breastfeeding coun-
sellors reiterate the importance of 'demand-feeding', many
women still long to confine those demands to small, predictable
corners of the day. Unsure where to begin, we find it reassuring
to have a list of times and feed durations to cling to. We have
clocks in every room and keep clinical charts. We consult tables
of averages in child care manuals. We attach safety pins to our
T-shirts to remind ourselves which breast should be next. We
quote our babies' feeding patterns to others in pride or misery,
for reassurance and advice.

Our aim, of course, is to give ourselves some freedom and
time away from the baby, but few mothers notice how much
time and anxiety is consumed trying to persuade a baby to
follow artificial schedules instead of internal impulses. Nor do
we always realise the problems created by strict interval feeding:
it increases the chance of engorgement and breast infection,
makes it more likely that the baby will choke on fast-flowing
milk, does not recognise how quickly breastmilk is digested, nor
how small the infant's stomach is – and it increases the average
amount of time the baby spends crying.

Since the beginning of the hominid line, some 1.5 million
years ago, babies were fed without the benefit of a schedule.
Most cultures in the world today still feed freely on demand.
Anthropologists who have timed the feeding patterns in traditional cultures reveal natural nursing to be a responsive act, not
a regimented one. On average, it was found that the African
!Kung San baby typically nursed for a few minutes at a time,
several times an hour. The longest that one observed !Kung San
newborn went without nursing was a ninety-eight-minute
period when he was asleep. As babies grow older, the interval
between each nursing does lengthen, but there is still no regular timetable: nursing remains completely ad hoc.

How does demand-feeding really work? We use the term
somewhat resentfully in Britain and America, where a baby's
'demands' often seem to outstrip our willingness to supply. But

in cultures where crying is a cue, rather than an irritation, the demand-fed baby only has to indicate the slightest need and the breast is offered. Remember that, in a traditional society, the breastfeeding woman is supported by a community of women – mothers, daughters, grandmothers – who help with domestic and other work. Remember also that breastfeeding can be done on the move: it does not require the mother to be sedentary and alone, in the privacy of her home. This is the situation in Yucatan, Mexico, where breastfeeding is considered to be a powerful and subtle form of early communication:

The notion of keeping a baby on a schedule is foreign to Maya women and the universal response to any sign of distress is to offer the baby the breast. Babies have almost continuous body contact from the time of birth, at first and for the most part with their mothers, but as time progresses, also with other members of the family. A baby is not put down unless it is asleep, at which point it might be laid into a hammock. At first sign of awakening, it is picked up again.

Brigitte Jordan, birth researcher

Similar examples proliferate. Here are just a few societies, some more 'traditional' than others, where babies are breastfed according to their own need, rather than according to a doctor's schedule:

* Young Rajput babies in Khalapur, India, were observed to feed every thirty or thirty-five minutes; toddlers fed three to four times during daylight hours. 'Since the baby sleeps with its mother, night feeding is no problem,' say anthropologists Leigh Minturn and John Hitchcock.
* The Native American Sioux baby is allowed free access to the breast, whether to feed or play with it.
* At five months old, Bangladeshi babies feed on average 6.8 times in an eight-hour period. Ten-month-olds feed 7.8 times in eight hours. They also nurse on and off all night, sleeping with their mothers.

* Indonesian mothers in central Java feed their babies at short intervals throughout the twenty hours.
* Bali babies are, like !Kung babies, encouraged to regulate their own feeding; carried above their mother's breast, they simply reach and help themselves.
* Punjabi mothers, whether Hindu, Muslim or Sikh, traditionally feed their babies as soon as they fuss or cry, by day and by night.

Tricks of the Trade

One time when I had my first girl I got lumpy breasts and had green stuff coming out. I was very sick and nearly passed away. I had to go to the doctor, he gave me medicine to dry out my breasts (*kamu*) and put the baby on the tittie bottle.

Shirley Purdie, Aboriginal woman of Warmun, Western Australia

How can we avoid lumpy breasts and other common problems associated with breastfeeding? In the days before male doctors and tittie bottles, mothers had to find remedies and tricks of their own. Here are a few handy hints from women who are wise in the art of breastfeeding:

Engorgement
Known as 'gathering' to the Victorians, engorgement is the swelling of the breasts which results when milk builds up. It is the result of a vicious cycle, often created when the baby is not able to feed as frequently and for a long as he wants. This makes it harder for him to latch on when he *is* allowed to feed. Engorgement most commonly occurs on the third or fourth day after birth, when the milk flows copiously for the first time.

Black American women use breast massage with camphorated oil to soothe painful, swollen breasts. Some aromatherapists recommend massage with essential oils of geranium or peppermint, but these scents should be kept clear from the nipple and areola. You can massage yourself by cupping the breast in one hand and stroking gently with the other, from the trunk down towards the nipple. Use a light base oil like almond if you do not want to confuse your baby with a strong scent. Mothers from many cultures enjoy postnatal massages like this every day.

But massage does not get to the root cause of engorgement. The best way to prevent the breasts becoming over-full is to allow the baby to feed as often as he needs to from the start. Even three-day engorgement is not inevitable. While frequent sucking stimulates more milk to come tomorrow, it also drains the milk ducts completely today.

A personal, cross-cultural story of engorgement, coupled with (and probably caused by) institutional 'feeding times', comes from Tokyo, Japan. Here, a British mother describes giving birth in a private hospital. Notice how 'virtual' video visiting has replaced real-live contact in this highly controlled, sterile environment. Breastfeeding to a timetable in this city hospital corridor is a world away from the intimate, private and unscheduled suckling of newborns in rural Japan.

Mothers were permitted to hold their new-born children only in the corridor at feeding time. Otherwise babies were confined to a nursery with a glass wall in front of it. A nurse would wheel up the cot and everybody would exclaim and video-tape through the glass.

In the breast-feeding corridor nurses walked up and down massaging engorged naked breasts. Women closed their eyes and submitted with only the occasional grimace of pain. At my turn I screamed, begged for aspirin and burst into tears. 'Is it so different in the West then?' demanded the exasperated nurse.

Harriet Sergeant, British mother in Tokyo

CABBAGE PATCH BABIES

A famous old-English remedy for engorgement is the application of cold cabbage leaves to the afflicted breast. A hole should be cut in the centre of the leaf to allow the nipple to poke through, as this Yorkshire mother describes:

> I would tuck a few fresh leaves (or parts of leaves) inside each bra-cup, two or three times a day and night, during those first nursing weeks. And yes, there was some relief! . . .
>
> Cool cabbage curls fit neatly inside my bra. They're not so messy as a damp flannel. The leaves warm up and, as they soften, they fit better. The leaves are wet and limp when removed at nursing . . . Engorgement is lessened. Nursing is easier to start. Why? . . .
>
> Have the close-fitting cabbage leaves raised my skin temperature? Does this make for local sweating and reduced water retention, and so ease engorgement?
>
> **Alyson Christy, breastfeeding mother from North Yorkshire**

Perhaps cabbage leaves enhance the natural action of sweat glands (see the following section on sore nipples), which the modern bra does not. Certainly, a badly-fitted brassière will only exacerbate engorgement and many mothers prefer to leave their bras off at night or while nursing at home. (Why not float around in a kaftan like the Moroccan mother?)

A study from Johannesburg, South Africa, looked at the effectiveness of cold cabbage leaves applied after each feed and allowed to remain in place until they had warmed up. Mothers who used the leaves reported less engorgement and were more likely to breastfeed exclusively for the first six weeks. The researchers were not sure

whether the application of cabbage leaves had been directly beneficial, or whether using a 'home' remedy had increased women's self-
confidence, an essential component of breastfeeding.

Sore nipples

This is another common symptom of breastfeeding, and one
with a simple cause. If nipples are becoming sore, or even cracked,
it is a sign that the baby is not positioned properly at the breast.
A large part of the areola should disappear into the baby's mouth,
otherwise nipple pain will result. Mothers in traditional societies learn breast positioning from a lifetime of watching other
mothers do it. Few western mothers have the same advantage.

We may presume that midwives are the experts, but many
have never breastfed. Ideally, each mother needs at least one
friend or a breastfeeding counsellor who is sympathetic and has
had good breastfeeding experiences. Mother-to-mother support
at this crucial time is the perfect antidote to pain and lack of
confidence.

The recent belief that 'too much' feeding makes the nipples
sore is actually a myth, since the areola contains sweat-producing
glands to lubricate the area. Nor is it true that nipples need to
become 'hardened' to their task. Frequent nursing is the remedy,
not the cause, as it makes the baby less hungry and aggressive
as he suckles. To get feeding going again when nipples are sore,
tickle the baby's bottom lip and wait until he opens his mouth
like a yawn. As soon as he begins to milk the areola properly,
the nipple will have a chance to heal.

Sore and cracked nipples are so rare in some cultures that
one researcher had trouble finding local remedies. Only the
Karen, a hill tribe from northern Thailand, were able to oblige:
'I came across very few people for whom cracked nipples were
a problem and only one group, the Karen, had a cure for it,
consisting of the fat found under the shell of a land crab which

had to be caught in the rice *padi*' (Jacqueline Vincent Priya, birth researcher). Presumably the fat was to be applied externally.

The Magar people of Nepal use apricot oil to moisturise the nipple and the Taralpe of Brazil cover their nipples in honey. Neither is ideal on a regular basis, as the baby is likely to ingest these extra and unnecessary sugars. But sometimes nipples become cracked because of extreme cold: in this case, it is wise to wear extra underwear for insulation and rub in a light, edible oil. The nipple will heal in a week or two – and of course, breastfeeding must continue if the breast is not to become engorged.

However, the world's best nipple cream is a lubricating substance which works wonders, upsets no one and costs nothing at all. It is breastmilk. Mothers all over the world rub a little milk into nipples as soon as they feel slightly sore.

Inverted nipples

Nipples need not stand to attention in order to suckle. Since the baby works the areola, not the nipple at all, and since the mother is equipped with her very own 'nipple erection reflex' which is activated on suckling, there need be no apprehension beforehand. Our present-day anxieties trace back to the nineteenth century, when impossibly tight stays seem to have injured the nipples of many fashionable women. Of course, unnecessarily tight bras do not help, and you might be interested in this nineteenth-century remedy from Norway. Eliza Warren, author of *How I Managed my Children from Infancy to Marriage*, had a Norwegian friend who 'got two large nutmegs, scooped them out like thimbles, then put them in brandy for a week, and afterwards dried them. The breasts were then rubbed every morning with glycerine, and the nipples washed over with brandy, and, when dry, the nutmegs were placed one on each nipple. This drew them out, and hardened them' (Mrs Eliza Warren, London 1865).

Too much milk or 'not enough' milk

Some women seem to produce more milk than their babies can take, but this imbalance is only ever found with interval feeding. When babies are allowed completely free access to the breast, supply and demand dovetail neatly together. However, if for any reason milk flow is still too strong, try these handy hints:

- Indian mothers apply a poultice of jasmine flowers to suppress excess milk.
- African and other mothers prevent milk leaking by pressing the heel of the hand to the breast after a feed, and holding it there for at least a minute. 'When I trained as a breastfeeding counsellor . . . I solemnly absorbed and disseminated this "new fact". In Africa I noticed women unconsciously performing this action just as I might obliviously scratch my ear' (Gabrielle Palmer, nutritionist and breastfeeding campaigner).
- Norwegian mothers mop up leaks with pure wool breast pads.
- Try feeding your baby more frequently.

The 'problem' of 'not enough' milk has to go in inverted commas because it is based on a misunderstanding of how milk is produced and it is one of the most damaging accusations levelled at the newly breastfeeding woman. Ironically, although every mother can produce enough milk for her baby, one way to undermine milk production is to question the ability to nurture and so cause a slump in self-esteem.

The first step towards producing enough milk is to believe in yourself and your ability to nurture your own child. Imagine yourself in the desert, an environment without bottles or breast-feeding rules. Somehow, you would find the means to feed your own baby. Once mothers realise their enormous power and self-sufficiency, they begin to relax. Relaxing and taking the lead from the baby should allow him to suckle enough to feed as often as necessary to produce the next day's milk. Night feeds, being particularly relaxed, and rich in prolactin production, are especially good for encouraging milk production.

Feeding in a hot climate

Sometimes mothers on holiday are encouraged to take bottles along and to feed their babies with water. Not only are some water supplies unreliable, they are completely unnecessary. As I learned from a trip to Israel with my nine-week-old daughter, I was the one who needed to drink more water, not her. As the World Health Organisation puts it:

Even in hot, dry climates, breastmilk contains sufficient water for a young baby's needs. Additional water or sugary drinks are not needed to quench the baby's thirst. They can also be harmful. If the baby is also given water, or drinks made with water, then the risk of getting diarrhoea and other illnesses increases.

Facts For Life child health booklet

Feeding an ill baby

Breastmilk is so easily digested by the baby that it often becomes the only food he will take when ill. Even toddlers on a mixed diet of breastmilk and solids may revert to the comfort and perfect nurture of the breast. Among the Sukuma people of Tanzania, any thoughts of weaning a child are postponed should he become ill. This is in the belief that breastmilk is the best nutrient for the stricken infant.

Tibetan tradition dictates that a nursing mother take any medicine the baby might need. If the baby is nursing and eating solids, he shares the medicine with his mother. If he has been weaned, he takes all the medicine himself.

Breastfeeding and AIDS

HIV transmission is a serious risk for babies of mothers infected with the AIDS virus. In America, where powdered milks are easy to find and safe to use, HIV-positive mothers are advised against breastfeeding. Mothers in rural Africa face a stark and difficult choice, as formulas are scarce and difficult to administer safely and carry their own risk of mortality. A study of HIV-positive mothers in Malawi, south-east Africa, found that

47 of 672 babies became HIV infected from breastfeeding. One half of these infections occurred in the first five months, and more infection occurred to mothers who were inexperienced breastfeeders.

Another study showed that mothers who developed mastitis were more likely to transmit the AIDS virus to their babies. Older mothers with four or more previous births were less likely to have breast inflammation and to pass on the disease. Rather than issuing a ban on breastfeeding to HIV-positive mothers in developing countries, doctors prefer to counsel each mother according to her situation.

Share and Share Alike

The custom of shared suckling which has existed in many societies and still exists today is a quite different practice from that of hiring another woman to feed a baby. The first is an act of female solidarity and co-operation . . . Wet nursing was like the catering trade . . .

Gabrielle Palmer, nutritionist and breastfeeding campaigner

Breastfeeding, like every other aspect of child-rearing, was once a communal activity. Of course, mother's own milk was a baby's first source of sustenance for as long as she carried him and remained his primary carer. But there was always the possibility that the child might be fed or comforted by another lactating woman. And unless a society developed a taboo against shared nursing, this lactational generosity served to bond the child to other women in the group.

Among the Ongre Negrito, Andaman Islanders in the Bay of Bengal, children are usually breastfed for three or four years by a wide variety of mother–figures: 'The [Andamanese] babies were passed from hand to hand within the camp, were petted by everyone and suckled from all women in milk' (Carleton Coon, anthropologist).

Polygynous marriages, where one husband supports a number of wives, seem to encourage shared suckling. In ancient Egyptian harems, women frequently shared the nursing role. In the Kalahari desert, !Kung San co-wives live in close quarters, sharing a family fire and nursing each other's babies. For the Mbuti pygmies of the Ituri rainforest in Zaire, nursing is just another aspect of interdependent communal life:

Women of the same age help each other with the building of their huts, in gathering and in cooking food ... A mother will frequently give her children over to some other possibly unrelated woman to look after, even to suckle, if she is called elsewhere. The children call all their mother's female age mates 'Mother', and they expect the same privileges from them all and acknowledge the same responsibilities toward them.

Colin Turnbull, anthropologist

In Europe until the seventeenth and eighteenth centuries, ordinary women were equally casual about nursing each other's children and would share this pleasurable duty as they shared all domestic responsibility. Shared suckling was also an essential feature of infant adoption. In the spirit of true community, no lactating woman would deny her friend's baby the occasional suckle if she was the nearest person to provide it.

This sharing ethic was turned into a political principle in the 1930s, when the early kibbutzim pioneers of Palestine insisted that one nursing mother should wet-nurse another's baby when the mother herself could not manage it. But like many political principles, it missed the human point. Rather than feeling supported by her female friends, the mother felt supplanted by the system:

One custom which until the 1930s certainly brought much distress to young mothers was widespread in kibbutzim (apparently in all three federations): a nursing mother was not only responsible for her own baby, but also had to nurse another infant if his mother did not have enough milk. This custom, which now seems absurd to kibbutz mothers, was the outcome of a radical interpretation of the principle of sharing everything. It was abandoned in the early 1940s.

Menachem Gerson, kibbutz education researcher

Kibbutzim mothers sensed what scientists now tell us – that breastfeeding is, in itself, a bonding process. Shared breastfeeding is nature's way of providing kin for a baby who loses his own mother. Shared suckling should never undermine the relationship of the mother and baby, which is essential to their mutual emotional growth.

Early societies recognised the enormous bond created by shared suckling. Among the Tausog people of the Philippines, two babies who have shared the same breast become '*magsaw-duru*', milk-siblings for ever. This filial tie is so strong that boy and girl milk-siblings may never marry.

Perhaps because of the inevitable intimacy and rapidly-forming bond, some mothers find the idea of shared nursing repellent. Gusii mothers of Kenya protect the mother-and-baby breastfeeding relationship by an exclusivity taboo. Another woman's child is said to be 'like cold mucus' and only if a mother dies in childbirth is her baby nursed by the grandmother or adoptive mother. Back in thirteenth-century France, Blanche of Castile, mother of Louis IX, was disgusted when a lady-in-waiting dared to suckle her distressed son. As the story goes, she forced the baby to vomit, so he would not be tainted by inferior milk.

In western society, fear of HIV transmission and confused sexual taboos interfere with any idea of shared suckling, although it is still occasionally practised within families and 'breastfeeding circles'. A few progressive London mothers agree to babysitting-with-breastfeeding arrangements – the breastfeeding element making the friend a very special kind of babysitter. But none of this mammary magnanimity undermines the primary breast-feeding relationship, or the suitability of mother's milk, as recommended by child care experts since the Middle Ages: 'It shall be best, if the mother give her child suck herself, for the mother's milk is more convenient and agreeable to the infant than any other woman's and more doth it nourish it . . . and to be short, the mother's milk is the most wholesome for the child' (Richard Jones, *The Byrth of Mankynde*, 1540, England).

HOME TRUTHS

I have heard my grandfather say of these women [in his native Northamptonshire] that it was no uncommon sight to see a woman suddenly unbutton her blouse in the harvest-field, take out a milky breast, and suckle a child old enough to stand and reach the nipple.

H.E. Bates, English novelist, *The Vanished World*, 1969

Breastfeeding, considered to be a solitary and even an antisocial activity in some places, turns out to be a supremely social act in others. While western women struggle alone to master the natural art of nursing, many mothers are supported by their friends, family and the much wider circle of acquaintance. Tricks of the nursing trade are learnt through informal conversation and observation, begun in childhood and continued throughout the female life cycle. And in former times, babies could expect to be nursed by many 'mothers', each of whom had an interest in promoting communal values and the infant's health.

My father was born in 1929 in a poor area of Birmingham, capital of England's industrial Midlands, a fourth child living with his parents in a one-up-one-down terraced house. He told me that a breastfeeding mother and child was a common sight on a bus. Sometimes a joke was made of it; a man sitting nearby might good-naturedly ask if he could have a sip since he was thirsty and everyone, including the nursing mother, would have a good chuckle.

In the West, we all seem to have lost our sense of humour

over breastfeeding. Women nurse in fear of being spotted and attracting disapproval. As a consequence, many simply do not feel free to feed their babies as often as their babies need feeding. It may come as a shock for us to realise that modern Muslim countries are more broad-minded about the breast than are we. We may be surprised to realise that few cultures sexualise breasts as we do, and that even fewer consider sexual significance to be equal to the nurturing role. Many a western magazine article on women's breasts goes by without the merest mention of breastfeeding; this would be unthinkable in a culture which considered breastfeeding to be remotely important.

Infant nursing is a neglected and sorely undervalued art, which is now viewed as optional in many countries. Whether we like it or not, this is having a massive effect on the ecology of child-rearing around the world:

There is no doubt that formula feeding is a major cause of infant sickness, especially gastroenteritis, and of death, especially in the poorest countries. And the problem appears to be growing. For, despite the overwhelming evidence that breastfeeding is best – nutritionally, psychologically, immunologically, economically – most babies in the postmodern world are now bottlefed with an infant formula.

Michael Schwab, social historian

9. A Lot of Bottle

Breastfeeding is the biological imperative which turns out not to be so imperative any more. To complete our worldwide survey of infant feeding, let's wean ourselves gently from wet-nursing and bottle-feeding to baby's first foods.

Milk for Sale

Of nursing children.

Oh! what a raket do authors make about this, what thwarting and contradicting, not of others only, but of themselves.

Nicholas Culpeper, herbalist, *A Directory for Midwives*, 1651

The 'racket' to which Culpeper refers is not the breast-bottle debate, which was to come 200 years later, but the fashion of sending upper-class babies out to be wet-nursed. In social systems which placed hierarchy above communal equality, it did not take long for prosperous parents to delegate aspects of child-rearing to their servants. Before the 1994 civil war in Rwanda, for instance, wealthy Tutsi mothers did not do all the breastfeeding themselves. Social and material superiority allow some to pay for part-time wet nurses: 'Initially, the solicitous role of the mother was predominant, although among wealthier Tutsi she often shared baby nursing with a nursemaid' (Marcel d'Hertefelt, anthropologist in Africa).

Early civilisations reasoned that breastfeeding was not only time-consuming, but incompatible with sex (most societies adhered to postnatal sex taboos while breastfeeding). With the arrival of monogamous marriage, there was pressure on mothers to resume their marital duties. From the high-class villas of ancient Rome to the four-storey terraces of middle-class Georgian England, wet nurses were a wealthy woman's salvation.

In ancient Greece, babies were fed by slaves called '*titthai*' (an evocative word which, however, does not seem to be connected to the modern 'tit', an Old English term meaning 'teat'). The Roman elite, meanwhile, delegated child care to an army of professional servants and slaves. As early as 200 BC, nurses, minders and teachers were employed to do the brunt of parenting. Freeborn babies were assigned wet nurses to release their mothers for a life of leisure, and slave babies were wet-nursed to release the slave mother for work.

From these upper-class beginnings emerged the idea that noblewomen – being of fair complexion and weak constitution – were too delicate to nurse their own babies. A sedentary lifestyle, coupled with over-indulgence and restrictive undergarments, probably did not help their cause. To be too delicate to breastfeed was pretty much a compliment in some circles. The myth that fine women could not suckle persisted until the early twentieth century, when one English doctor was forced to protest to his well-to-do readers:

What is the reason that wealthy ladies so frequently require wet-nurses? The want of occupation! And from whom do they obtain the supply of wet-nurses? From the poor women who have no lack of occupation, as they have to labour for their daily food, and have in consequence the riches of health, though poor in this world's goods . . .

Bear this in mind, ye wealthy, and indolent, and pampered ladies! and alter your plans of life, or take the consequences, and still let the poor women have the healthy, the chubby, the rosy, the laughing children; and you, ye rich ones, have the unhealthy, the skinny, the sallow, the dismal little old men and women who are constantly under the doctor's care, and who have to struggle for their very existence!

Dr Pye Henry Chavasse, child care expert, mid
nineteenth–early twentieth century

CHOOSE CAREFULLY

... she hath been one of the most unhealthfullest women that I think I ever saw, and so extremely troubled with toothache and rheums and swelling in her face as could be, and one night she fell very ill, and was taken like an ague, so as she had but little milk left, and so I was enforced to send for the next woman that was by to give my child suck ... and I thank God the child agrees so well with her milk as can be, so I mean not to change her any more. It is a miracle to me that the child should prosper so well, considering the change of her milk.

Lady Anne Clifford of Cumbria, diarist,
writes about her baby's wet nurse, 1614

The choice of wet nurse was always a great worry. Like modern western mothers changing the infant formula or the nanny, our anxious ancestors fretted over the milk and the temperament of their selected wet nurse. Mothers and wet nurses alike were believed to pass on temperament and mood through their milk. Wet nurses had to be kept happy, or their milk would 'spoil'.

A suitable woman was in great demand – ideally, she was a placid countrywomen who followed a healthy diet and exercise regime. In reality, she was likely to have recently lost a baby of her own. Experts had their own ideas: redheads were too volatile, but ruddy cheeks were a good thing; she must be neither too tall nor too short and she should speak well. From Roman to Victorian times, moralists offered rich, culturally-fragile women advice on choosing appropriate mother-substitutes:

> . . . and because from weakness the mother sometimes cannot suckle a child, she must have a nurse of good habit of body, and red complexion which is the sign of the best temper, and let her not differ much from the temper of the mother, unless it be for the better: let her be between twenty and thirty, well bred, and peaceable, not angry, melancholy, or foolish, not lecherous nor a drunkard . . . Let her breasts be well fashioned with good nipples, that the child may take to them with pleasure.
>
> Nicholas Culpeper, herbalist, *A Directory for Midwives*, 1651

Wet-nursing grew in popularity because it was an indication of social status. The practice must have had an immediate effect on babies' health and many commentators were against it. When Tacitus toured Europe, he was impressed by the strength of the children in Germanic tribes, compared with those back home: 'The children grow up in every home naked and dirty, to that strength of limb and body which excite our admiration. Every mother feeds her child at the breast and does not depute the task to maids and nurses' (Tacitus, Roman historian, first century AD).

In every century, from Plutarch to Rousseau, scholars, authors and moralists urged mothers to keep their babies at their own breasts. This message was reinforced by medieval Christianity, which pictured the breastfeeding mother as the ideal spiritual model. (Eve and Mother Mary were often painted nursing their babies.) Nevertheless, social ambition won the day. Western women gradually developed a stately distance from all things maternal.

In the eleventh century, nurses were brought to live in the baby's home, but as time passed, the baby was more likely to be sent out to nurse. In fourteenth- and fifteenth-century Italy, the *balia* or wet nurse was a person of immense power, who raised the baby at her own home, presiding over his fragile life and, all too frequently, his premature death. Fate had consigned the European baby two separate mothers.

By the seventeenth and eighteenth centuries, professional wet-nursing had reached the height of popularity, buoyed up by the rise of the middle classes. In the Mediterranean, where each trade had its own songs and dances for special occasions, wet nurses celebrated their profession with nurslings in their arms:

> We're fine in our way of life, prompt and skilful in our
>   trade,
> always when the baby cries we feel our milk returning:
> acting with energy and speed, we do our duty,
> we take him out of the cradle drying his little face.
>
> Song of the balie, medieval Italian wet nurses

Nowhere was wet-nursing so popular as in the French cities. Paris even had its own wet-nursing placement bureau. In 1780, the Parisian police chief estimated that of 21,000 babies born in the capital, 17,000 were sent to the country for wet-nursing, 3,000 were placed in nursery homes and 700 were wet-nursed at home, leaving just 700 to be breastfed by their own mothers. In England, meanwhile, there was a nurse for every class, ranging from the lady of genteel birth, who suckled babies of royal blood, to notorious 'baby-farmers', who took in the infants belonging to factory women.

The eventual decline of wet-nursing was a triumph of common sense over fashion. Babies put out to nurse were more likely to fall sick and die than those breastfed at home. The death of a wet-nursling was usually blamed on the nurse's milk being of 'inferior stock', a bitter irony which no one seemed to spot at the time. One in five boys of noble birth was expected to die in infancy, compared with one in seven in rural communities.

But the most pitiful tragedies were reserved for the urban poor, who were forced to send their babies away so that they could wet-nurse others, work factory shifts, or serve long hours in service. Here is a woeful tale from Lyons, France, where the infants of lace workers were despatched into the hills:

The children were delivered by *meneurs* who strapped them into paniers on the sides of donkeys and stilled their cries with wine or eau de vie on a soaked rag. The dead were thrown out en route. It could be days before the children got to a nurse and when they did she was usually someone from a very poor social level, since a foundling was a risky speculation and believed to be a potential source of syphilis for the nurse . . . A concerned official, M. Prost du Royer, estimated that 6,000 babies left Lyons each year and only 2,000 returned, and those in poor physical shape . . . Birth mothers physically attacked the women who returned their children, claiming they had been ruined for life by physical deformities and diseases they had picked up in the nurse's hovel. No one, not even Prost du Royer, however, suggested that a woman giving birth to a child on a silkmaker's premises could bring up her baby herself.

Olwen Hufton, social historian

In fact, wet-nursing persisted until the arrival of artificial bottle milks, which is to say the end of the nineteenth century, give or take a few years. Long before bottle-feeding arrived on the scene, there was an established European tradition of mothers who considered themselves above breastfeeding.

FAMOUS NURSLINGS

Many well-known babies suckled at the breast of a wet nurse. Here is a small selection:

* Painter and sculptor Michelangelo (born 1475) was nursed by the

wife of a stone cutter. 'With my milk,' he said, 'I sucked in the hammer and chisels I use for my statues.'

⁂ Writer and dictionary author Samuel Johnson (born Lichfield, England 1709).

⁂ The children of Jean-Jacques Rousseau (1712–78) were sent to a Parisian foundling hospital, leaving their father free to write about the dangers of wet-nursing and the virtues of maternal breast-feeding.

⁂ Jane Austen, English novelist (born Hampshire 1775).

⁂ Queen Victoria's babies were all wet-nursed. Nurse to Princess Vicky (born 1840) was a doctor's wife from Cowes on the Isle of Wight, who was paid a handsome £1,000 plus £300-a-year pension. Unfortunately, she had a taste for beer. Vicky became pale and colicky, the milk was blamed and the wet nurse asked to leave.

⁂ Some of Hollywood's celebrity mothers now employ wet nurses. One successful 'wet nurse to the stars' is a woman called D. Barens, whose milk is so popular among her American clients that she has been asked to bottle it and bring out her own brand of breast-milk ice cream.

Animal Magic

> Don't give the infant goat's milk, if you can
>   avoid it,
> And even less, that of bitch or sow,
> And avoid cow's milk; give it yours,
> If not, send it away,
> (But, if necessary, I'll grant you ewe's milk).

Francesco da Barberino, didactic poet, Italy, 1264–1348

Until nineteenth-century chemists came to the rescue, there were only two kinds of milk available to human babies: human, or animal. Motherless infants would normally be breastfed by adoptive mothers, but there were still occasions when a substitute food might be needed. Women who were forced to leave their babies to earn a living and mothers who were ill after childbirth sometimes experimented with species of animal milk instead.

Of all the milks tried on human babies, cow's milk remains the most popular. It is a strange choice, given the incompatibility of bovine milk with the immature human digestive system. The reason human babies are fed by lactating cows is because cattle are easy to domesticate and have been bred over generations to produce the maximum yield. Of course, the cow must first be separated from her own baby calf.

Cow's milk is designed to promote the rapid growth of the calf to maturity in its first year. It is high in volatile fatty acids, which humans find hard to digest. It is also rich in indigestible iron (the human baby absorbs more iron when he drinks breastmilk, though it contains less). The protein, calcium and phosphorus levels are all wrong. It takes a baby twenty minutes to digest breastmilk and four hours to process formula feed made from cow's milk. Early exposure to cow's milk increases the chance of developing cow's milk allergy, with symptoms that include diarrhoea, vomiting, colic, eczema and asthma.

Cow's and goat's milk were considered unfit for human consumption in medieval Europe and did not feature in the general diet, least of all for babies. Since most people (including doctors) believed that personality was conveyed through the milk, no one wanted their babies to grow up like beasts of the field. According to fourteenth-century Tuscan moralist Paolo da Certaldo, 'the child, boy or girl, nourished on animal milk doesn't have perfect wits like one fed on women's milk, but always looks stupid and vacant and not right in the head'.

When Thomas Platter, the sixteenth-century Swiss humanist, described the poverty and destitution of his early life, he reminded his readers that he was raised on nothing but cow's milk. Yet two hundred years later, when aristocratic families wanted to replace a troublesome wet nurse, cow's milk diluted with boiled water suddenly became more acceptable.

Animal milks, diluted or fresh from the animal, are fed to babies all over the world. Goats' milk, used as a substitute in some cultures, is better for babies than cows' milk, but the nearest biological substitute would actually be chimpanzee or gorilla milk.

Occasionally, a baby might be put directly to the teat of a goat, apparently with some success. African mothers use a calabash, or seed gourd, filling its hollow shell with cow's milk or herb drinks. Maasai babies in Kenya are occasionally fed from gourds lovingly decorated with beads. Baby milk bottles of various types have been used since the earliest times – some archaeological finds date back to 2,000 BC. 'Nursing horns' were on the standard equipment list of the twelfth-century European child nurse. These were small cows' horns, pierced at the tip. The milk was sucked through parchment shaped like two fingers.

A CONTRACEPTIVE CATASTROPHE

The use of wet nurses and animal milks in early modern society had an unforeseen side-effect. It led to a collapse of the contraceptive protection traditionally provided by breastfeeding.

The mother became a breeding mare, typically enduring twenty pregnancies in a lifetime. Russian peasant women, whose children sucked for hours on bags containing animal milk, had an average of seventeen babies each. This figure was also common in the aristocratic homes of Britain and France.

One seventeenth-century English heiress, Ann Hatton, gave birth to thirty children: five boys and eight girls who survived, another ten who died in infancy and seven babies who were stillborn. It was a punishing schedule, with inevitable risks for maternal health. As one modern commentator says, for a woman to give birth to twenty children '... is absolutely, utterly and totally unnatural. All mammals breast-feed their babies on demand until their offspring are about one-third of the size of the adult. So normal evolution would be for women to have breast-fed their child on demand until the age of about seven' (Rupert Fawdry, obstetrician).

Throughout human history, breastfeeding and its surrounding taboos ensured that most women gave birth to no more than seven children. Families of twenty or more were only possible in cultures which abandoned breastfeeding. This was what the women of Iceland found when they stopped nursing their babies more than 300 years ago. Icelandic babies were reared on a variety of substitutes including chewed fish, which provide the fatty acids essential to brain growth.

At that time many Icelandic women had more than a dozen children. According to Bishop Oddur Einarsson, many women were giving birth to 20 or 30 children at the end of the six-teenth century. Until the late nineteenth century the death rate of infants was 300–400 per 1,000; Iceland is probably the only country in the world which could maintain its population over a period of several centuries without babies being given any human milk at all. This process of survival of the fittest has been so harsh and pitiless that now the Icelandics are among the healthiest people on the planet.

Dr Michel Odent, obstetrician and primal health researcher

Finding the Formula

If we were to say that this preparation does not agree with newborn babies, such a statement could not be supported on theoretical grounds, since in the food are the very same ingredients as in mother's milk.

Baron Justus von Liebig, nineteenth-century inventor of the soup for nurslings,
'A Complete Substitute for that Provided by Nature'

This was the rebuttal of the German chemist who invented the first baby-milk formula, his astonishing response to complaints that newborn babies were reacting adversely to its ingredients. Since these ingredients were cow's milk, wheat starch, bicarbonate of soda and malt flour, we can see why infants might not have been thriving on their scientific diet.

The early arrogance of milk-substitute manufacturers seems shocking today. Two hundred years on, intensive research has still to invent a formula containing *'the very same ingredients as in mother's milk'* and no longer anticipates doing so. Our improved understanding has only served to underline our respect for nature's own inimitable product.

Victorian scientists may have been optimistic about bottled milk, but a sceptical European public was unenthusiastic. The reason for mothers' reluctance was quite plain: the first baby formulas killed babies. Before bottle milk, there was pap, a mixture of bread or grain in water. Pap could be administered by letting the infant suck on a cloth which had first been dipped in the mixture. Boiled barley or wheat, perhaps sweetened with honey or sugar, was the scant nourishment of society's weakest and most vulnerable members. The method was known as 'dry nursing', a last resort for foundlings and orphans. Mortality rates for these infants ranged from fifty to ninety-nine per cent.

In the nineteenth century, many working-class women who spent their day in the factory could neither afford nor find wet nurses. They were desperate for healthy alternatives. Yet when they fed their babies solutions made from raw cow's milk, their babies died in great numbers. Infant mortality rates dropped only when mothers were allowed to stay at home and nurse.

The race was on to perfect an infant formula which would satisfy working mothers and make someone very rich. Baron von Liebig developed his nursling soup as a result of his daughter's 'inability' to breastfeed her own baby. His grandchildren were raised on it for fifteen months and the soup sold throughout Germany and Britain in the 1860s. When informed that the mixture made newborns unsettled, Liebig replied that mothers were not diluting it according to his instructions.

This is a theme which persists with powdered milks today and which helps to account for many infant deaths in non-industrialised countries. Under- and over-dilution are just two misjudgments people easily make when feeding a baby from a packet, especially when they cannot read or translate the directions on the side.

After Liebig came a clutch of chemists, each one eager to crack the formula of human milk. American babies were offered a rich concoction called 'Meig's Mixture', while in Switzerland, a young chemist was working on condensing and drying cow's milk, using the very latest technology. His name was Henri Nestlé.

The basis of my milk is good Swiss milk, concentrated by an air pump at low temperature, which keeps it fresh as milk straight from the cow. The meal is baked by a new process of my invention. The two [milk and meal] are mixed in correct scientific proportions, and the result is a food which is all that could be desired

Henri Nestlé, Swiss chemist, 1867

By the end of the twentieth century, Nestlé's multinational company had become the world's largest food corporation, with sales of $30 billion a year and an international product boycott trailing in its wake. The company's aggressive selling techniques over many decades seriously undermined breastfeeding – especially in developing countries, where mothers were susceptible to the messages of any westerner in a white coat.

The approach used by Nestlé and other bottle milk manufacturers was to offer free samples to mothers at hospitals and health clinics. Company saleswomen even dressed as nurses to promote their message in rural Africa. Although their marketing activities have now been curtailed by an international code, recent reports suggest that the multinationals have found new ways to get their message across.

In 1992, for instance, the manufacturer Farley's offered British hospitals £18 for every baby fed on Ostermilk, and a lump sum of £24,000 if all mothers were successfully persuaded to use the product by the time they went home. In 1998, a survey of 3,000 women in countries as diverse as Bangladesh, Thailand, South Africa and Poland found that up to fifty per cent of health centres were still receiving free samples of formula and that twenty per cent of health workers had received free gifts from the baby milk giants.

The result of all this commercial energy is that the majority of the world's babies are now fed on chemically-modified cow's milk. By the 1920s, formula milks had improved to a level where most babies could be reared safely in the West, without immediate visible harm. Clean milk campaigns and pasteurisation revolutionised the hygiene crisis in artificial infant feeding. Nevertheless, worldwide, formula milks destroy many infant lives which could have been saved by breastfeeding.

GUILT TRIP

Many a western baby has been rescued from the brink by the bottle, and for every mother who feels guilty for not breastfeeding, there is another who feels finally able to relax and enjoy her baby. Given the cultural context of infant feeding, it seems astonishing that mothers feel blamed for the choices they make or the difficulties they encounter as they try to nurture their young. Why *should* mothers be forced to keep trying, despite prevailing public attitudes, despite poor advice, without community support, despite physical pain and feelings of inadequacy?

Breast and bottle-feeding are not merely a matter of personal

> choice, though that is the way they are presented to new mothers today. They are cultural phenomena which reach far deeper into the maternal psyche than we may ever imagine.

Feelings and Fashions

I don't like breastfeeding. I don't like doing it; I don't like watching it being done; and I feel queasy when women breastfeed their children with teeth. However, I still feel somewhat heroic in not having succumbed to the relentless propaganda from the Breast is Best lobby

India Knight, journalist and novelist, London 1995

Artificial infant feeding has been welcomed by succeeding generations of mothers, most of whom have been culturally primed to hear its message. Formula has a foothold in almost every country, including places where mothers were previously unaware they 'needed' it . In the Third World, bottle-feeding is not seen as a pragmatic necessity, but as yet another enticing western commodity. It has the dual status of being both expensive and 'white' (i.e., modern). As one emigrant Punjabi mother put it, breastfeeding '. . . would spoil my figure. If it [bottle-feeding] is good for them *(meaning white mothers)* it should be good for us too . . .' (First-generation Punjabi mother living in England).

Bottle feeding *is* expensive, although not prohibitive for most western mothers. Costs of up to $2,000 (around £1,500) a year are usual – a significant impact on most domestic budgets. In Uganda, the cost of bottle-feeding is nine times greater than a hospital cleaner's wages. Far from deterring mothers, the expense of bottle-feeding carries its own allure. Like upper-class medieval mothers who could afford a wet nurse, the *'nouvelles riches'* of poorer countries may be proud to say they purchase their baby food.

What we are witnessing is a process which anthropologists call 'acculturation'. This is the phenomenon where the cultural assumptions of one society begin to influence the cultural practices of another. Breastfeeding, being a highly suggestible process, is easily influenced by the attitudes of the dominant society, but trends can go in both directions. Acculturation is like a network of oceans, all feeding into one another, and then feeding slowly back again. Educated urban women – those who read books and listen to the news – often lead the trend. So, in the Punjab during the 1970s, it was women of higher social economic status who first pioneered the fashion for formula feeding. In America and Britain, it was better-off, better-educated women who were simultaneously reclaiming the art of breastfeeding.

When I worked in Cardiff, Wales, in the 1980s, teaching English to expectant Bangladeshi mothers, the influence of a certain strand of white culture was immediately apparent. While I, pregnant with my first baby, hoped to breastfeed, the Bangladeshi mothers aspired to western-style bottle feeding. 'In Bangladesh, I nursed my babies myself,' a pregnant mother of six boys told me. 'Here, I want to bottle-feed.'

She gave birth to her first British baby, a seventh boy, who was duly reared on formula milk. The household had few furnishings: a bed, a sofa, a cooker and a television were the only commodities downstairs. The father had no work, there were nine mouths to feed and yet the opportunity of bottle feeding seemed too good to miss. I had a girl and a comfortable home and I breastfed for two years. My Bangladeshi friend was surprised by my 'old-fashioned' choice, since I obviously had the means to buy formula and there was a ready supply in the shops.

The belief that breastfeeding is animalistic reached a height in industrial nations during the middle of the twentieth century. This attitude is the reverse of medieval fears that only breastfeeding could *prevent* a baby becoming bestial. To feed a baby on cow's milk would, in the medieval eye, make a baby ever likely to behave like a cow. Folk stories in the Middle Ages described the fate of children who were abandoned in the forest, suckled by wild boar, and emerged with swinish characteristics.

In hierarchical cultures, it can take a long time for social classes to adapt to each other's ways. For three hundred years in Europe, only the babies of underprivileged families were fully breastfed by their own mothers from birth. Today, babies of the most needy families in Europe are those least likely to be given the breast. 'Breast' or 'bottle' is not merely a matter of personal choice, but of strong community affiliation, of class systems and localised beliefs. Western society is a patchwork of cultures–within–cultures which only gradually affect each others' behaviour.

STRONG ARMS OF THE LAW

Social policy seems to be the best protector of breastfeeding at a national level. Governments have the power to give priority, and thus status, to the breastfeeding mother. Some laws limit the influence of baby milk companies; others give working mothers the time they need to nurse.

- In 1970, breastfeeding rates in Norway were as low as those in Britain and America. Then Norway banned all advertising of artificial formulas. Mothers are entitled to one year's maternity leave on at least eighty per cent pay and, on their return, an hour's breastfeeding break every day. Now ninety-eight per cent of Norwegian women initiate breastfeeding and ninety per cent are still breastfeeding four months later (see Chapter 8).
- Spanish mothers are entitled to ask for up to three years' 'breast-feeding leave' from work, with the security of returning to the same job position. Both Spanish and German mothers are guaranteed two thirty-minute nursing breaks a day.

* In Papua New Guinea, laws to restrict bottle-feeding promotion were put in place while breastfeeding was still popular. Between 1977 and 1979, bottle-feeding rates in the capital, Port Moresby, fell from thirty-five per cent to twelve per cent. Infant malnutrition was reduced by one-third.
* French mothers are guaranteed a government cash bonus if they choose to breastfeed.
* Denmark, France, Luxembourg, Netherlands and Spain have all banned formula milk ads.
* After three months' paid maternity leave, Belgian mothers may opt for another two years' unpaid leave, in order to breastfeed.

On an individual level, of course, there will always be mothers who, for whatever reason, choose not to breastfeed or find it does not work for them. Even though the possibilities of breastfeeding are infinite, it takes a very special set of conditions for a mother to feel, to know and to explore that potential. Ideally, she needs to be raised and supported by a fully breastfeeding environment. That environment is getting harder to find, wherever she lives in the world.

Like a Weaned Child

> I have stilled and quietened my soul
> like a child who is weaned of his mother,
> like a weaned child is my soul within me.
>
> Psalm 131

Weaning a baby from the breast is a momentous time for mother and child. It signals the end of primary dependency, the completion of the unique mother role and the beginning of new connections. In a very obvious way, it signals a reliance on foods which the rest of the community share.

Mothers in every breastfeeding culture try to ensure the readiness of their babies for weaning, but in reality, external circumstances often dictate the end of nursing. In modern societies, the deadline may be the mother's return to work; in hunter-gatherer cultures, it may be a new pregnancy or birth. In Nigeria, the Ibo people refer to the newly-weaned child as 'the child who brought the child': i.e., when the child stops nursing, the mother may once again resume sexual relations and conceive.

Attitudes to weaning vary enormously around the world, and even from child to child. Also, the speed of weaning varies with each culture. For the Gusii children of Kenya, weaning may be abrupt or gentle, according to birth position. Most children are weaned swiftly at around the age of two (it used to be three) and their pleas entirely ignored. Lastborn children are indulged and allowed to feed for longer. Researchers found that Gusii mothers started to avoid visual and verbal interactions with children months before they anticipated weaning.

Hausa children of Ethiopia are weaned in a single day. In accordance with Muslim law, this must be a Friday. Meanwhile, !Kung San mothers of the Kalahari Desert in Africa believe it is dangerous to breastfeed through pregnancy and that they should wean the previous child as quickly as possible. They say the milk belongs to the foetus. However, weaning can take months to complete, and even then, older children may nurse occasionally. Here, one San woman recalls the gentle self-weaning of Kxamshe, her youngest sibling:

Mother stayed inside the hut for a while, and after Kxamshe had grown a little, she carried her wherever she went. Kxamshe had no younger brothers or sisters, because my mother didn't give birth again. Kxamshe just nursed and nursed and grew up. She gave up nursing on her own, while there was still milk in her mother's chest. The milk stayed for a while, then left.

Nisa, !Kung San mother of the Kalahari Desert

One dramatic way of weaning is to separate mother and baby physically. The Yurok Native Americans of California are a traditional people who enforce weaning by sending the mother away for a few days. Weaning in this society is known simply as 'forgetting mother'. In this case, mother is banished for a while, because the baby (at just six months) is too young to go anywhere.

Other societies wait until the child is two, three or more years old, and then send him to grandma's. Jamaican, Maori and many African children are weaned in this way. Kpelle children of Liberia go to grandma's for a short holiday, while Swazi children of Swaziland move out completely at weaning. They go to the 'great hut' owned by their paternal grandmother and live here until adolescence, when they move into separate girls' and boys' huts.

The Bitter Truth

Babies hate such things as olives, mustard, pepper, beer and coffee – and so they should. Babies are not gourmets. Where food is concerned, they are sucking, growing machines that would be at serious risk if they started experimenting with exotic flavours. Their numerous, undulled taste buds ensure that they are kept strictly to the milky way.

Desmond Morris, zoologist

Babies are born with tastebuds on the roof of the mouth, walls of the throat and insides of the cheeks, as well as the tongue. Every taste is a sensation explosion. Initially, this heightened awareness directs the infant towards the sweetness of his mother's milk, imbued with the flavours of the food she is eating. Later, it will lead the child towards an eager anticipation of his local diet.

The sweetness of breastmilk has a powerful effect on the human baby: it makes him suck strongly. In fact, sweetness is the *only* taste which he finds palatable. The other four main flavour categories can even make him grimace and cry.

Some mothers employ the bitterest flavours they can find to deter their small children from nursing. The following list of breast repellents is strictly for information only. Even mothers in traditional societies use them sparingly, as a last resort when the next baby is imminent and the diet insufficient to nurse two . . .

* In eighteenth- and nineteenth-century Russia, mothers and wet nurses would smear their breasts with garlic.
* Rajput mothers of India do the same as the ancient Aztec mothers of Mexico: they rub crushed chillies around the nipple.
* Many African mothers smear their breasts with a deterrent paste of whichever local 'bitter herbs' are to hand.
* Mothers of Okinawa smear the areola with red pepper or bitter medicine. Failing this, they paste on black paper patches, otherwise used to heal toothache, backache and bruises. The child is told that the breasts are hurting.
* In traditional times, !Kung San mothers of the Kalahari smeared the nipple area with '*dcha*', a bitter root of the crawling vine. Now they use tobacco resin.
* Mothers from Czechoslovakia used to wean their babies with laughter. They would bake a cake and cut a hole in the middle, poking the nipple through the middle. When the child came to nurse, he would laugh so much he simply could not latch on.

A Taste of Life

It was the custom in the northern highlands for an infant immediately after birth . . . to taste butter, often mixed with a little honey.

Richard Pankhurst, historian, on nineteenth-century Ethiopia

The English saying 'You are what you eat' would be appreciated in many cultures. Most people identify themselves with their food, and in turn become famous or infamous for their diet. While the British call the French 'frogs', the French refer to the British as 'les rosbifs' (the roast beefs). And since societies are usually proud of their local delicacies, many parents prove impatient to share it with their babies.

Babies in many cultures are kept on a breastmilk diet for six months, but this does not prevent people around the world from introducing tiny babies – ritually, at least – to the bounty of the land. The aim is twofold: to demonstrate the generosity of the world into which the infant is born, and to initiate him into the human community in which he finds himself. This has nothing to do with weaning. Ritual tasting is a birth ceremony which connects the infant to his extended family and his landscape at a spiritual level.

* In Eskimo tradition, a new baby was not a true human being until he had been offered a tiny morsel of meat. The mother from Greenland talks to the baby using archaic words, the language of the spirits, and ritually pretends to feed him his first solids. As soon as this is done, the baby becomes a part of the meat-eating (human) community and shares in his people's relationship with the game they must hunt for survival. Without the connection, it is thought the baby will grow up wild.
* Malaysian mothers touch the baby's mouth with salt, gold and silver before the baby is first put to the breast. Rice – the staple food of Malaysia – is used in a series of rituals to release the mother and baby from postnatal seclusion.
* Tibetan parents trace the Sanskrit syllable DHIH with a special herb on the newborn baby's tongue. Sometimes it is stamped on with butter blessed by a lama, or priest. The lama holds the butter under his chin, recites a mantra and blows gently: the positive energy of the mantra enters the butter and can be used for birth and postnatal rituals.
* The Muslim father places a piece of date on his baby's tongue to symbolise the sweetness of life.

* The Karen hill people of northern Thailand give their new-born babies a few grains of rice, telling them this is what they will be eating in a year's time.
* In Westphalia, Germany, the grandmother would place a small piece of baked apple in the baby's mouth. This made the new-born human and confirmed his right to life.

May I Introduce . . . ?

My little George is out at [nurse] yet and as fine a Little fellow as ever you saw. You would be diverted to see him at eight months old tied in his chair at table eating fat pork and Indian cake for his dinner. I expect to take him home in April next and I flatter myself he will run about the house by that time. He already has a number of teeth and I hope he will get the rest soon.

Mary Badger, American mother, writes to George's grandmother, 1785

More than 200 years ago, little George could be stuffed with fat pork and Indian cake and everyone – including his absent mother – was delighted. Modern western parents are unlikely to be so relaxed about introducing their baby to solid foods. We have learnt to be domestic scientists in our own kitchens, analysing the suitability of each ingredient, steaming and puréeing selected vegetables in our electric mixers and – when busy, or in doubt – buying powdered, branded meals to reconstitute the perfect infant diet. Introducing solids is, like every other aspect of parenting, a question of cultural taste.

Most cultures take it easy. A typical pattern is demonstrated by the Suku people of south-west Congo in central Africa. Mothers breastfeed exclusively for six months before offering solid foods. The child then enjoys a mixed intake of breastmilk and other foods until he is weaned at around three years old. Western mothers are often advised to drop breastfeeds as they introduce solids, so creating a swift weaning pattern at around four months.

SLOWLY DOES IT

Archaeologists tell us that our ancestors weaned their babies grad-ually. Seventeenth-century skeletons found near the Missouri River in North America show that children were nursed exclusively for one year and weaned between two and six years of age. Hebrew peoples of 3,000 BC breastfed for two to three years. And human remains from South Dakota, dating back to 5,500–2,000 BC reveal twenty-month-old children on a mixed diet of breastmilk and solid food.

As we might expect, many cultures give spiritual meaning to the baby's first solid meal. We have already seen the newborn rituals which acknowledge that the sharing of food binds a baby to his community. Early humans commonly believed that eating was the act which defined humanity.

The Rajputs of India, near the Himalayas, say that until he eats solids, the baby is entirely pure, a holy creature who has committed no sin. The Tibetan baby might go through an ini-tiation, or there will be a recitation recognising his new phase of life. As soon as he eats 'real' food, he joins the family which hunts, gathers, sows and reaps. His life, no longer so precarious, belongs not to the spirit but to the human world, with a depend-ence on human forms of sustenance.

Menu d'Enfants

Healthy babies, like healthy adults, need food that is fresh, unprocessed, additive-free, sugar-free (which includes sucrose, glucose, dextrose, maltose and fructose), salt-free and low in fat. In other words, they should be given food that is close to how it is found in nature.

Patrick Holford, nutrition consultant

What kinds of foods are best for babies? Every local diet produces its variations on the weaning theme. Soft foods are ideal, since they steer the child gradually from liquids to solids. But finger foods are also popular, because they give the child the opportunity to feed himself, to chew and to ease the arrival of teeth. This is what nature provides, with a little help from parents around the world:

- In Israel, babies are weaned on to mashed avocado and sweet potato.
- The Utku of Canada tempt their babies with fish eyes, a local delicacy.
- In Tanzania, the Hadza wean their babies on bone marrow, soft fat and ground baobab berries.
- Yurok babies of California eat salmon and deer meat, preserved in seaweed: essential fatty acids from oily fish are especially important when babies are weaned early, and Yurok babies are weaned at six months.
- A Tibetan baby's first food is 'tsampa', a paste of roast barley flour mixed with boiled water and butter, fed on the tip of the finger as early as the day after birth.
- Kaluli babies of Borneo are taken into the forest to be fed crayfish and sago grubs.
- The Afikpo Ibo of eastern Nigeria consider soft fruit, like banana and papaya, to be children's foods. For Kpelle babies of Liberia, Amele babies of Papua New Guinea and western babies fed by supermarkets, mashed banana is a favourite first food.
- Tudor families gave their babies bread sops, minced capon (fattened cockerel) or partridge, vegetable broth and chicken legs (with meat removed) to gnaw on.

* Babies in modern Cairo, Egypt, are weaned on to thickened rice water, egg yolk, mashed potato, mashed squash and tea. But they begin with '*fuul*', a mash of beans which the baby sucks from his mother's finger.
* Jordanian babies are fed rice pudding, biscuits dunked in tea and meat gravy.

Kiss of Life

[the nurse] chews the child's meat for him when he has no teeth so that he can swallow profitably and without danger.

Le Grand Propriétaire de Toutes Choses, domestic manual, France, 1556

The giving and accepting of baby-food is an obvious sign of familial love. The human kiss, a feature of affection in many cultures, originates with a very old practice called 'kiss-feeding'. In the days before the Magimix and the Moulinex, before cooking utensils and cutlery, this was the way mothers prepared their baby foods . . .

The little [one-year-old] boy had been nursing on [his mother's] breast when he became restless and began to reach up toward her mouth as she ate. At first she appeared to be ignoring the child as she carefully chewed what was in her mouth. Then she leaned down to his upturned, expectant face and seemed to give her son a long, passionate kiss full on the mouth. She did this twice before I realized that she was passing premasticated food from her own mouth into his. Only after she had done this several times did the child seem to be satisfied and again grabbed one of her breasts in his grubby hands to suckle contentedly once more. I must have seen such an occurrence many times at a greater distance and did not realize its significance.

Kevin Duffy among the Mbuti pygmies of the Ituri rainforest, central Africa

Chinese mothers traditionally chew their babies' first solid food and then kiss-feed it into their babies' mouths. Balinese mothers do the same. People from the Philippines, New Guinea and South America kiss-feed and so do many mammals, from monkeys to wolves. In fact, if we look far enough back in human history, this seems to be a universal practice, something most mothers did with most children as they weaned them on to a solid diet.

The food is chewed until it is almost liquid and the mother then places her lips over the baby's. When she pushes her tongue into the baby's mouth, he sucks and receives his first solids. Kiss-feeding not only saves on electric gadgets and washing up, it also provides extra antibodies for the vulnerable child: 'When the baby develops teeth, [Hadza] mothers [of Tanzania] pre-chew meat for them, which may have an added advantage in that the salivary glands are linked into the immunological system, which may give further protection against disease' (Gabrielle Palmer, nutritionist and breastfeeding campaigner).

In medieval Europe, when wet nurses took over the work of wealthy mothers, it became the nurse's duty to pre-chew the baby's food, a fact mentioned by many writers of the time. If wet nurses were kiss-feeding, we can safely assume that ordinary mothers were doing it, too.

Sometimes, babysitters in traditional cultures comfort distressed babies by pressing their lips to the crying infant and passing over a little saliva. Kissing is a sign of affection, whether the intention is to nourish or merely to soothe. It is a primal act of love.

HOME TRUTHS

Early on, Italian mothers begin feeding pasta and other foods and they assume that breast-feeding alone is not enough to build a healthy, happy child. These Italian mothers knew exactly how much their babies had eaten and when (usually with the family), and could answer any questions about the babies' diet . . . Food was such an issue for the Italians, and they were so sure of their strategy, that when the researcher pointed out that the baby was uncomfortable and crying with a big pasta spoon shoved in its mouth, one mother responded, 'He'll get used to it.'

Meredith Small, ethno-paediatrician

Parents' anxiety about children eating enough can result in a range of nervous behaviours. Some African mothers forcefeed their babies by holding their noses and immobilising their limbs. This practice is now dying out, but children in many cultures are handfed long after they are capable of feeding themselves. This is to prevent wastage and ensure the child is getting enough.

Of course, parental apprehension is rarely warranted. Babies are unlikely to starve themselves unless engrossed in a battle of wills. By comparing attitudes in different societies, we can see that food fears are culturally induced. For centuries, European parents would agonise over finding the perfect wet nurse. Another place, another culture, and the worry is which animal milk best suits a human baby. Or take a snapshot of modern times, where millions of pounds or dollars are spent on developing a better chemical formula to pour down babies' throats.

We fret over feeding because, as parents, we understand our role to be primarily one of nurture. This is true of all mothers and fathers, wherever they live and whatever their diet. While the hunter-gatherer father is anxious to bring home meat to feed his starving children, New Man may be equally concerned over whether to buy organic baby food or vitamin supplements. While the Italian mother may introduce too many solids, too soon, the African mother may be more interested in keeping her breastmilk supply going for as long as possible.

It's all a matter of taste.

10. Baby Caring

In some ways, this is the stuff of the standard baby book: how to care for your infant in the first weeks and months after birth. The topics may be familiar, but since we are not limited by western experience, some may stretch your imagination. At the end of it all, your baby will be clean, dressed and ready to face the world – whichever bit of it you live in.

Bathing Beauties

11 November 1601 – his head rubbed for the first time;

17 November 1601 – scalp and forehead rubbed with butter and almond oil, cradle cap extensive;

4 July 1602 – hair combed for the first time;

3 October 1606 – [he was five years old] his legs were washed for the first time in tepid water;

2 August 1608 – [he was almost seven years old] bathed for the first time with Madame, his sister.

Bathing diary of King Louis XIII of France (born 27 September 1601)

Tap water is still a luxury unknown in many parts of the world. Of course, early humans had the even greater luxury of fresh water they could rely on and warm water when they needed it, once they had mastered the art of making or keeping fire. But daily bathing, of the kind most westerners have come to expect, is a relatively new phenomenon. It was almost impossible in cold countries with little firewood: in medieval China, for instance, only women of the court had water and rooms warm enough to give their babies regular baths. Peasants dared not bathe their babies, for fear of them catching a chill.

Well into the seventeenth century in England, bathing a small baby was unheard of. Nicholas Culpeper, the hygienist and herbalist, recommended waiting until the child was at least seven months old before washing his limbs: 'In places where bathing of children is used,' he said, tentatively, 'let it be washed twice a week from the seventh month till it be weaned.'

Historians tell us that baths remained out of vogue in Europe until the eighteenth century, and that children were the dirtiest of a rather dirty lot:

Even upper-class children were not washed much before the end of the seventeenth century and it could be argued that no section of the population embodied to such a degree the deliberate cult of bodily filth which flourished in early modern Europe. According to this orthodoxy, corporal fluids were deemed healthy to the body and so were infrequently removed.

Olwen Hufton, social historian

When a baby was born, therefore, bathing him was not necessarily the first priority. At birth, all babies are covered in a greasy layer known by its Latin name, '*vernix caseosa*', which roughly translates as cheesy varnish. Left on the baby until it is absorbed by the skin, vernix forms a protective barrier against the cold air. In Balinese belief, it is a sacred substance, one of the holy '*kanda empat*' or 'four siblings', which ease birth and guard the baby in the womb.

Quite simply, the Stone Age mother would lick her baby clean, in the manner of most mammals, and there is recent evidence of this prehistoric practice all around the world: among the Inuit of Canada, the Chagga people of East Africa – even in parts of Europe where, in the fifteenth century, the midwife would lick the baby with her 'basting tongue' and rub him in almond oil. A mother of the far northern Ingalik, a Northern

Athapaskan people from the Arctic, having given her newborn an initial bath, will then lick his hands and face every morning with her tongue to keep him clean. She does this until he is old enough to sit up by himself. 'Eskimos are not given over-much to washing, since water is scarce and ice is melted into water only at the great expense of burning the difficult-to-come-by blubber. Urine will sometimes be used as a substitute' (Ashley Montagu, social scientist).

The very first bath does not fully remove the amniotic grease. It takes a concerted effort to rub it away from the delicate newborn skin. Vernix has at least two functions that human biologists can identify. Its first and primary purpose is to facilitate birth, by helping the baby to slither along the birth canal. The second is to give the baby's delicate skin a defence barrier against postnatal infection.

Some cultures do not recognise these functions; they imagine that a heavy coating of vernix is an accumulation of semen, a sign that the mother had sexual intercourse during the last weeks of pregnancy. A traditional Malay midwife, disapproving of such behaviour, removes the vernix by rubbing the baby liberally in coconut oil. Medieval Christians used to scour the vernix away with salt. Vietnamese mothers also consider the newborn to be dirty, and so bathe him immediately.

This is where we come to ritual bathing: the solemn initiation of the infant into water, which has clear connections with baptism and other water blessings. Many cultures make a fuss about the baby's first bath, imbuing it with magical properties. In Togo, West Africa, a ritual bathing woman, the 'nachane', arrives to bathe new babies and brides on the eve of their wedding day.

In China, the baby is not given his first bath until the morning of the third day. The occasion is treated as a solemn ceremony, with the midwife officiating in a roomful of guests. In the birth room, the newly-delivered mother sits on her bed with a mirror, a straw sieve, a padlock, a comb, an onion and a weight. Each has ritual significance; the padlock, for instance, is a magical attempt to 'lock' the child into the human world. Incense is burned as an offering to the god and goddess of the bed, and the baby is bathed in water which has been boiled with sprigs of carob tree and artemis. Red silk ribbons are tied around the bath tub (scraps of red material are often used as baby charms in China and elsewhere). The Chinese baby shares his first bath with pieces of fruit and lucky coloured eggs. Guests also add spoonfuls of cold water to the ritual bath, and give the baby a small gift of silver.

In ancient Scotland, the baptism and first bath would be combined. The nurse held the newborn over the bath with one hand, filling her other palm with the spring water. Nine times she would scoop the water and wash it over the baby, using the blessing of the Nine Waves.

> A small wave for your form
> A small wave for your voice
> A small wave for your speech
> A small wave for your means
> A small wave for your generosity
> A small wave for your appetite
> A small wave for your wealth
> A small wave for your life
> A small wave for your health
> Nine waves of grace upon you,
> Waves of the Giver of Health
>
> **Blessing of the Gaelic midwife**

OUT WITH THE BATH WATER . . .

Water has always been precious, symbolic, the stuff of new life. A baby's first bath is often imbued with spiritual meaning. In rural Taiwan, the baby bathes with two eggs and a stone, to make his face as fine as an eggshell and his head 'as hard as a stone', or wise. Gaelic tradition held that a gold or silver coin must be placed in the baby's first bath. Gold related to the powers of the sun and silver to the moon. In Egerland, Germany, a gold coin in the bath meant the baby would become rich.

The water itself was symbolic for many European families. In Italy and Portugal, the water from a baby girl's first bath was tipped over the hearth to keep her near at home; a boy's bathwater was thrown outside the front door, to symbolise his dealings with the wider world. German families threw the bathwater under a fruit tree, so their children would blossom and grow.

Water is highly valued in places with no village pump or household plumbing system, so the water used to bathe a baby becomes doubly precious. In order to bathe her baby after the birth, a Hmong mother from the hillside villages of Laos in south-east Asia must carry water home in a wood and bamboo barrel strapped to her back. She does this in the early stages of labour, an exercise which probably works wonders for her contractions. She does not expect to find water – or any other modern comfort – on tap.

All Scrubbed Up

Once a day each [Yequana] woman put her gourds and clothing (a small, apron-like *cache-sexe*, and ankle, knee, wrist, upper arm, neck and ear beads) on the bank and bathed herself and her baby. However many women and children participated, the bath had a Roman quality of luxuriousness. Every move bespoke sensual enjoyment, and the babies were handled like objects so marvellous that their owners felt constrained to put a mock-modest face on their pleasure and pride.

Jean Liedloff, continuum therapist, describes
bath time in a remote corner of Venezuela

For the Yequana of the South American jungle, there are very few activities which exclude babies. The communal bath is just one of many sensual experiences in which the infant is expected to participate. Bathing babies in some cultures has somehow become a less pleasurable event. The tactile joy of playing with the baby in water is often diminished when the baby is lowered gingerly into his own tub . . .

* Ashanti babies from West Africa wash their babies in a calabash, a fruit-gourd like a little upturned boat.
* Babies born into the poorer neighbourhoods of Cairo, Egypt, are bathed in metal bowls that are also used for laundry and washing up.
* Western parents usually purchase a special plastic baby bath.

When using a miniature bath tub, the care-giver must concentrate on preventing the infant's head from going under (in the West, the bath water is usually decorated with soap bubbles which might get in his eyes or mouth). Few western parents bathe their babies purely out of sensual enjoyment – the main aim is to keep baby clean. As the child grows, however, we might try to entertain him with some 'educational' plastic toys which bob about on the water. The juggling act between an American baby and his yellow duck was observed by anthropologist Margaret Mead and recorded in a 1956 paper entitled *Cultural*

Differences in the Bathing of Babies. Mead compared the bathing experiences of the Balinese and New Guinean babies with those of American infants. She noticed that the American baby swiftly learnt to direct his attention to the toys rather than to his mother. Another difference was the manner of handling. She saw that the Balinese babies were more relaxed in their mother's hands.

Unless bath time is directed with confidence, it can result in an unsettled, agitated or even fearful baby. Most parents tolerate this momentary misery. After all, we are not the only culture to teach our children a resistance to water. First-hand accounts of bathing infants in India also reveal a disregard for (or perhaps a resigned acceptance of) their protests and discomfort. Life for the Rajput child in northern India is generally stress-free, but bathing is a daily battle:

This is a most distressing experience, which the baby must face twice daily. Babies, like adults, are given 'sponge baths' with water from a bucket or pot. No villager immerses himself in water except when bathing in a river. The mothers ordinarily do not use soap when washing the babies, but they rub the eyes rather vigorously with the heel of the hand and often are not very gentle in their handling of the baby during the bathing process. Babies usually cry and struggle violently while being bathed, and they particularly dislike having their face and eyes washed.

Leigh Minturn and John Hitchcock, anthropologists

There is one obvious way around imposed infant bathing. It is the family bath. In the absence of the sea, or a nearby fresh-water lake, an ordinary bath tub or a warm-water swimming pool will do. In ancient times, Icelandic families would gather to bathe in pools warmed by natural hot springs. The simple expedient of bathing together (in water that is the right temperature for the infant) creates a secure and playful environment. Washing becomes a by-product of the exercise, rather than a struggle with the soap. Eye-contact and confident touch are both increased, so improving the relationship between adult and baby, rather than that between adult, baby and plastic toys.

The Japanese were one of the first civilisations to adopt daily bathing. Once the baby is a month or so old, he joins the whole family at bath time. Mother, father and other adults hold him in the deep family bathtub, the '*furo*', or take him down to the local public baths, or '*sento*'. Shared baths continue almost until the child reaches puberty and are remembered as a lively, enriching experience.

The Dangers of Drool

Prepare the children. Take a few minutes to wash the children's hands and faces (if they are small), comb their hair and, if necessary, change their clothes. They are little treasures and he would like to see them playing the part. Minimise all noise. At the time of his arrival, eliminate noise of the washer, dryer or vacuum. Try to encourage the children to be quiet.

Housekeeping Monthly advises mother on preparing for father's arrival home from work, London 1955

A warning note on babycare. Fathers in a number of cultures have developed taboos to make sure they get out of it. Tiriki men of western Kenya claim that vomit and drool from a nursing baby gives them a violent skin reaction, so refuse to care for babies under a year old. Zulu warriors of South Africa say their manhood would be compromised if even a drop of breastmilk fell on their skin.

And fathers in Russia are, apparently, incapable of changing a baby's nappy. Of course, there are a few exceptions:

In a country where sexism rules supreme and men are unlikely to make so much as a cup of tea for their wives without demanding a medal, here is a Russian man who changes his baby's nappy at least as often as I do, baths her, plays with her while I have a lie-in and cooks supper several times a week. If I am grateful, his countrywomen are astonished.

Miranda Ingram, Moscow correspondent

Women in many cultures, like the mother in the 1950s vignette, protect their men from the messy side of infancy. Baby goo is usually considered to be a matter for mothers, until, of course, the point where society requires women to leave their babies and return to a child-hostile work environment. Then, when older siblings have been sent to school and all available adults are busy in the field or factory, the ever-flexible father must take his turn with the baby. How will he deal with all that saliva, crying, hiccuping, posseting, sneezing and eliminating?

FUNNY YOU SHOULD MENTION IT . . .

Punjabi fathers traditionally find the whole subject of babycare rather amusing: 'Fathers' Participation. This modern European practice is still a matter of mirth and hilarity amongst even the middle-class Punjabis' (J.S. Dosanjh and Paul Ghuman, researchers in ethnic minority education).

Farming the land in India or Pakistan, Punjabi fathers leave the house early and have little time for taking care of babies. They do not usually play a significant role until the child is ready for school. But those who have emigrated to the West find that traditional role-play is compromised by lack of community. When a mother has no supportive women around her, she must call on the nearest supportive man: 'With my first child I didn't even wipe his nose clean, and here I had to do everything – changing nappies, feeding and playing with her. There is nobody else to help her' (Hindu father, first child born in India, second in Britain).

For every uninvolved father there is another who is up to his elbows in baby goo. According to British policy researcher Adrienne Burgess, history is packed with dads who took on mothering roles, it's just that their baby-centred activities were never publicised. She says that artists, novelists and biographers preferred to portray women in the act of mothering and men in the guise of authority, so reinforcing the idea that parental roles were sharply delineated.

A perfect example of this split between the public image and the private person is to be found in Prince Albert, Queen Victoria's consort. At a time when fathers were depicted as figures of distant authority and strict discipline, Prince Albert was privately known to be a more affectionate, involved parent than the Queen. Albert had more influence on the children's nursery than did his wife, and he laid out a grand scheme of education for his babies. When he realised that children do not respond well to elaborate schedules and an upbringing based on scientific principles (what we might now call 'hot-housing'), he relaxed his own over-ambitious plans. Though he himself had a solitary childhood and his parents divorced when he was six, Albert was determined to treat his children with unabashed tenderness: 'His care was like that of a mother nor could [there] be a kinder, wiser, more judicious nurse' (Queen Victoria recalls the parenting skills of Prince Albert, 1840s and 1850s).

Fathers all over the world display a similar desire for intimacy with their babies and children. Men of the Manus island community in the Pacific Ocean care for babies while mother works in the mango grove. Hmong fathers from south-east Asia are happy to attend to children and Mbuti fathers of the Ituri rainforest in Africa observe no taboos which might separate them from their babies:

Filial love is a response also to the uninhibited fondness with which Mbuti fathers treat their children. There is no shame or embarrassment on the part of a man fondling a child, male or female, and the children expect and desire it. To both child and man, such an expression of love is entirely natural, and the fact that they are virtually naked is of no consequence whatsoever, for to the Mbuti, this too is natural.

Kevin Duffy, anthropologist

We do not have to go back to such a long-lived tribe as the Mbuti to discover examples of taboo-free interactions between father and child. But the more 'civilised' a culture feels itself to be, the greater the likelihood that it has developed prohibitions to do with infant modesty. In fact, innocent touch from earliest infancy onwards is the best way to guarantee that a child grows up free from sexual neurosis. Child abuse is simply not an issue among highly tactile groups like the Mbuti, or the !Kung San people of the Kalahari Desert: '!Kung parents are gentle, protective and permissive with all their children and express their affection especially with babies. It is a most common sight to see fathers fondly kissing them with pursed lips and smacks' (Lorna Marshall, anthropologist).

Many fathers enjoy the innocent pleasure of holding their children and are highly skilled in matters of babycare. In Bali society, for instance, men and women are said to be two halves of a complementary whole and there is little division of labour. Both sexes toil in the rice fields, perform religious ceremonies and share in the role of bringing up baby. After she has breastfed her infant, a Bali mother frequently hands him on to someone else – and that someone is often the baby's father: 'Fathers also share in child-rearing and are often more demonstrative than their wives, carrying their babies everywhere and talking to them as equals' (Gayle Brandeis-McGunigle, American writer).

A little drool may not be as dangerous as some dads believe.

Some Like It Hot

An ugly baby is a very nasty object – the prettiest is frightful when undressed.

Queen Victoria (1819–1901)

Babies of the world wake up to find themselves in a wide range of climates and cultural situations. Those whose parents live near the equator have no need to cover up, of course, and many of them stay in their birthday suits for many birthdays to come. But some nomadic populations found it necessary to cover up, wrapping baby either next to their bodies under communal animal skins, or in their very own primitive baby clothes. Clothes were just another aspect of the ingenuity which enabled humans to adapt to a harsh world: 'The human animal does not, like a bear, grow himself a polar coat in order to adapt himself, after many generations, to the Arctic. He learns to sew himself a coat and put up a snow house' (Ruth Benedict, anthropologist).

Babies must be constantly protected against cold air. They cannot shiver at all when tiny; their bald heads lose heat quickly; their sweat glands are immature and their skin is paper thin. They are at a massive disadvantage compared with adults, easily becoming chilled or over-heated.

Zoologist Desmond Morris suggests that many babies died as a result of human movement towards the earth's poles. However, it is unlikely that tribes would have put their babies in the way of unnecessary risk. If large numbers of babies were unable to withstand the cold, it is probable that the first travelling groups would simply have changed direction. Since survival of the young is vital for the future of the race, babies' comfort and adapt-ability would have been the barometer for human migration. If a baby could survive a given climate, then so could the rest of the group.

In fact, the earliest pioneers had one major trump card which protected their babies against the ravages of bitter winds and long winters. They had their skin.

Babies benefit so greatly from skin-to-skin contact that they may not even need clothing of their own. Experts tell us that the quickest way to warm a dangerously chilled infant is to hold him naked against the skin and wrap both of you up together. This is far more effective that bundling baby in blankets by himself. Even in the chilliest of climates, infants survived because they were carried and cuddled right next to their mothers' and others' bodies.

Netsilik women of the Canadian Arctic traditionally carry their bare babies on their backs, wrapping fur around their two intertwined frames. Babies have no chance alone in temperatures as low as −20°C (although Arctic winters have become several degrees warmer over the past thirty years). Cutaneously bonded to their care-givers, however, human babies survive just fine: 'The Netsilik infant is placed in the back of the mother's 'attiggi' (fur parka) . . . it snuggles naked against its mother's skin. Most of the infant's ventral anatomy is in close tactile and cutaneous contact with its mother and its dorsal body is completely encased in fur, protecting it from the fierce Arctic cold' (Richard James de Boer, researcher, living in a Netsilik snow house, 1960s).

Cuddling remains the body-warming device of choice in many cold climates and millions of people manage without electricity, gas or running hot water, simply by living in close quarters. Extra clothing only becomes absolutely necessary for children once they are moving independently, out of their parents' protective arms.

SKIN AND SKY

Throughout Europe, the accepted baby colours are blue and pink, for boys and girls respectively. Midwives in Italy hang pink or blue ribbons on the front door to announce the baby's arrival to passers-by. Elsewhere, babies are dressed in pink or blue clothes to identify and reinforce their gender.

The reasons for the choice of colour date back to the ancient preference for baby boys. Blue, the colour of the heavens, was selected for dressing male infants, so giving them the best possible protection against the evil eye. In some parts of the Middle East, the front door itself is painted bright blue after a baby boy has been born.

There seems to be a common human need to identify gender in order to slip into a comfortable relationship with even the smallest child. Like it or not, most of us react in gender-typical ways, even with babies. Not to know the baby's sex can make adults feel ill at ease. To differentiate their girls, European mothers chose pink, the colour of the European baby's skin, thus emphasising the girl-child's overall human (rather than heavenly) appeal.

Swaddling Stories

How now, how does the child? . . . Unswaddle him, undo his swaddling bands . . . wash him, before me . . . Pull off his shirt, thou art pretty and fat my little darling . . . Now swaddle him again, But first put on his biggin [cap] and his little band [collar] with an edge, where is his little petticoat? Give him his coat of changeable [shot] taffeta and his satin sleeves.

Where is his bib? Let him have his gathered apron with strings, and hang a Muckinder [handkerchief] to it.

You need not yet to give him his coral with the small golden chain, for I believe it is better to let him sleep until the afternoon.

A mother instructs her child's nurse, 1568

The practice of binding babies may not be universal, but it forms a sizeable chapter in child care history. It seems to have emerged around 4,000 years ago, when Early Bronze Age humans in cold climates were looking for ways to warm and soothe their babies.

While equatorial infants were carried naked on their mothers' hips, parents in dodgier climates bound babies up in tight little parcels. European and Asian mothers tied them up like miniature mummies and Native American mothers bound their infants to portable 'cradleboards' (see Chapter 1). They had invented the original carry cot.

Psychoanalytical historian Lloyd deMause claims that 'almost all nations' swaddled their babies, but this was clearly never the case. Although the medieval English took to swaddling with gusto, their Irish counterparts did not. Gerald of Wales, writing his *Topography of Ireland* at the turn of the twelfth century, comments that Irish parents do not 'put their babies in cradles or swathe them'. African babies are not usually swaddled, but strapped to their minders' hips. Ancient Peruvian mothers bound their babies loosely, so their babies' limbs could be free (which rather defeated the point).

While the ancient Egyptians and Romans swaddled, the Spartans and the Celts of Scotland did not (they had other ways of 'hardening' babies). Even in imperial Russia, where mothers were famous for prolonged swaddling, practice varied dramatically. Many rural Russians simply carried their babies in a large, loose cloth. However, others sewed together scraps of cotton to make the three necessary layers: a head band ('*izgolovnik*') loin cloth ('*podguznik*') and over-cloth ('*pelenka*'). And while English babies were only swaddled for the first four to six weeks, Russian babies kept their swaddling bands for up to a year. Russian state hospitals today continue to swaddle with a vengeance: 'Inside the nursery, we saw a sea of screaming infants, swaddled like papooses. A nurse wearing a mask . . . changed a tiny baby in front of us. She whipped the white cloth between his legs, fixed his arms down at his sides and wrapped him again and again, until he was a tight, motionless bundle' (Whitney Taylor, American journalist, visits Moscow's Birth Clinic No 25). Childbirth campaigner Sheila Kitzinger remarked, after a visit to a Moscow state hospital in 1989, that the newborn infant only seemed to become human once it was properly swaddled. 'Till then,' she said, 'it's handled very much like a hunk of meat.'

Jewish mothers swaddled their babies, as we know from many biblical references to swaddling clothes. In some communities, the elaborate swaddling cloth worn by a baby boy at his eight-day '*brit*' (circumcision), is kept until the boy reaches thirteen. It is then cut into a strip called a 'wimpel' and used to tie around the Torah, the sacred, handwritten scroll of the Old Testament which is kept in the synagogue. Now the child is old enough to read from the Torah at his Bar Mitzvah. This symbolic use of the swaddling cloth emphasises the importance which Jewish communities place on religious learning, from infancy to adulthood.

Swaddling refers to all kinds of baby binding. In medieval to mid-eighteenth-century Europe, it could take the nurse up to two hours to swaddle a baby. In fifteenth-century England, splints were actually bound to the baby's limbs to keep them straight. In the wealthiest sixteenth- or seventeenth-century homes, swaddling began with a fine linen shirt and a 'bellyband' to support the stomach and hold the healing navel down. The nappy or 'tailclout' was a square of linen, in 'diaper' weave. One or two compresses or linen caps would cover the baby's head. The caps were often trimmed with lace and a decorative triangle adorned the forehead.

Then came the real swaddling clothes. A large rectangle called the 'bed' was used to straitjacket the baby's arms against his sides. This was turned up over his feet and held in place by 'swaddling bands', strips of linen two inches wide. The whole was topped off with another 'bed' to make a nice, fat sausage. To keep the baby's head from turning, a 'stayband' was fixed from his cap to his shoulders. Bibs and collars could then be tied around the immobile infant neck.

Once swaddled, there was a reluctance to undo all one's careful work. Although all the child care authorities pleaded with women to change their babies three times a day, the extreme passivity of the child and the trouble it took to get him that way militated against his being frequently unwrapped. Some people even argued that babies were best stewed in their own 'nourishing juices'. This tiny scrap of humanity might be laid behind the warm oven or hung from a nail out of harm's way in the kitchen, so that mother or maid could get on with domestic tasks. In this way, the infant was kept for some weeks or even months, although the arms were generally allowed to poke through after a few weeks had passed.

From classical civilisations to medieval Europe, swaddling caught the imagination of the child care experts, who dreamt up a dozen reasons why no newborn baby should be left unfettered. Greek philosophers Plato and Aristotle were both great fans of swaddling. So was Eucharius Rösslin, a sixteenth-century German doctor whose babycare book, translated into English by Richard Jones, was a British bestseller. Rösslin likened the baby to a sapling plant, and his mother or nurse to a firm but gentle gardener:

The nurse must give all diligence and heed that she bind every part right and in his due place and order, and that with all tenderness and gentle entreating and not crookedly and confusedly, the which also must be done oftentimes in the day: for in this it is as it is in young and tender imps, plants and twigs, the which even as you bow them in their youth so will they evermore remain unto age.

Richard Jones, *The Byrth of Mankinde*, 1540

Pruning and training were not the only justifications for infant swaddling. Here is a quick survey of some of the most prevalent reasons given:

* prevents babies kicking and so distorting their bones
* protects the child from draughts
* stops the baby becoming crooked and taking 'evil' shapes; restores 'natural heat' to the interior of the body; aids digestion of food (Bartholomew of England, thirteenth-century encyclopaedist)

* inhibits the startle reaction (modern-day Malaysia – being startled can deplete a person's vital spirit)
* suppresses baby's crying
* reduces stiffness (sixteenth-century France)
* prevents child getting knock-knees and bow legs (rickets were a medieval fear)
* imitates the comforting conditions of the womb

Some of these arguments make sense, in a strictly limited way. Tight binding is reassuring for a baby after his enclosure in the womb: studies in the 1960s showed that it slows down baby's heartbeat, steadies his breathing and induces hours of artificially deep sleep. According to psycho-historian Lloyd deMause, these ultra-passive babies were also less likely to be beaten.

But the dangers and the downsides were greater than the short-term gains. Swaddled babies suffered dreadfully from body sores unless their bands were changed with great regularity. They could hardly be cuddled while they were trussed up and as a result their development was delayed compared with unshackled infants.

The bundled human infant was so unresponsive, so unable to communicate his own needs, that he was treated like a foreign object. Apparently, it was customary in some families to throw the swaddled bundle around as if it were a ball. French servants apparently played 'catch' with their aristocratic swaddled charges, resulting in the untimely deaths of both the brother of Henry IV and the infant Comte de Marle: 'One of the gentlemen-in-waiting and the nurse who was taking care of him amused themselves by tossing him back and forth across the sill of an open window . . . Sometimes they would pretend not to catch him . . . the little Comte de Marle fell and hit a stone step below' (Nancy Lyman Roelker, historian).

Even though babies, once unswaddled, soon caught up with the body skills of their peers, there was a gradual resistance to the binding, moulding and shaping of young limbs. Led by eighteenth-century philosopher Jean Jacques Rousseau, the 'freedom of movement' school eventually won the day. Although swaddling is still practised in eastern countries, only Russian and Iraqi babies are still tightly swaddled for up to the first year of life. This description of half-hearted swaddling from north Yemen shows how ordinary parents are often unwilling to impose strict child care practices which their babies don't like:

While all [Yemeni] infants are swaddled, it is not uncommon for a mother to discontinue the practice if her baby appears to dislike the tight confinement. Boys are more likely than girls to be perceived as highly active and chafing against restraints, and so are unswaddled sooner. Whether or not they are objectively more active and wilful or just perceived as such is unknown.

Susan Dorsky and Thomas B. Stevenson, anthropologists

NEW BABIES OR OLD?

Baby clothes have many forms and functions: sometimes to beautify and enhance the infant, sometimes to make him look dull or older than he really is, and so confuse the evil spirits. Two very different traditions from East and West demonstrate the same impulse to disguise.

In oriental tradition, the baby's first clothes must be used, not new. In India and Japan, they must be borrowed from an older sibling or cousin. In Vietnam, the father is only allowed to see his baby once the infant has been dressed in old clothes. Meanwhile, in Christian custom, when the baby first ventured out for his christening, he was wrapped in a heavy silk 'bearing cloth' up to nine feet square. By the mid-eighteenth century, this had became a long white dress that stretched way beyond his toes. White was the colour of purity and innocence. It is in just such a long white gown that thousands of western babies are still transported to their christenings today.

Both costumes are devices to fool the malicious spirits into thinking that the infant is either nothing special, (for who would dress their darling baby in old rags?), or not a newborn at all, but a much older — or at any rate, longer — child, well past the vulnerable stage.

Calls of Nature

It is . . . unusual for an Eskimo baby to urinate or defecate while in the pouch or amauti of her parka. When Dr Otto Schaeffer asked an Eskimo mother how she knew when her baby needed to urinate and always got the message in time, she was astonished by the implication of his question that any mother could be so 'dumb' as not to know. She assured him that any capable mother knew when her child needed to void by the movements of his legs and always attended to him immediately.

Ashley Montagu, social scientist

First, there is the meconium. The word means 'like opium juice' and refers to the sticky, dark green stuff that fills the baby's intestines before birth and passes through his system in the first twenty-four hours. Breastfeeding frequently from birth helps meconium to pass and to protect the baby against jaundice; the bilirubin it contains can become reabsorbed by the newborn body if it is not expelled quickly. Colostrum, the baby's first milk, is also nature's first laxative. It is all he needs.

Societies which traditionally did not trust colostrum sometimes resorted to purging and enemas to move the meconium through the newborn system. In South Africa, Zulu parents would insert the stem of a castor oil plant into the baby's anus, a dangerous practice which can prove fatal. The Swazi of Swaziland, who forbid the mother to breastfeed for four or five days after birth, administer daily enemas to the newborn. In sixteenth-century Germany and England, mothers were advised to handle the baby's 'sitting place' with the aim of purging the belly. They were also told to stroke his stomach, 'to provoke the child to the making of water'. None of this would have been necessary had the baby been allowed to nurse frequently from the beginning.

In sharp contrast to these purging practices, most cultures make little or no fuss about babies' bottoms. Nappies are non-existent in many warm climates — in fact, they would be an impossibility in the heat and humidity of the rainforest: 'Except for mongongo leaves, the Mbuti do not have waterproof materials, and diapers, even if available, would probably be unhealthy in the humid rainforest, where harmful bacteria and fungus spores are ever-present and waiting for a host' (Kevin Duffy, anthropologist in central Africa).

The Mbuti pygmy mother, carrying her naked baby against her body all day, bathes as often as she can. Jamaican mothers, meanwhile, are as relaxed about babies' mess as they are about everything else:

If a baby started to empty its bladder when sitting on the mother's lap, she casually parted her legs and let the urine stream to the ground. Her dress would soon dry out in the sun. When the baby grunted and made little noises that told her that it was having a bowel motion, she strolled outside her hut and held her baby out over the dried mud a little way from the homestead.

Sheila Kitzinger, anthropologist

For the Netsilik mother of the Bootha Peninsula in the Canadian Arctic, there is no question of not responding instantly to the baby's needs, usually before he wets or soils her body. How does she anticipate his calls of nature? Scientists have discovered that, with the baby jammed against her back, his legs spread wide, the mother feels his involuntary thigh spasms. These tell her as soon as the bladder is full and — just before the sphincter opens

– she whips him out of her fur parka. The same intuition once applied to mothers everywhere:

Puzzled by [the undiapered babies of Uganda], Jean [MacKellar, a doctor's wife] finally asked some of the women how they managed to keep their babies so clean without diapers and such. 'Oh,' the women answered, 'we just go to the bushes.' Well, Jean countered, how did they know when the infant needed to go to the bushes? The women were astonished at her question. 'How do you know when you have to go?' they exclaimed.

Joseph Chilton Pearce, *Magical Child* author and lecturer

We might let our babies run around 'butt-naked', as the Americans say, if only we didn't have carpets and furniture and germ-free environments to worry about. In the highlands of Laos, south-east Asia, the dirt floor is sprinkled with water and swept every morning and evening with a grass and bark broom. A homemade bamboo dustpan is used to collect the faeces of young children and is emptied in the forest. Here, as in many other places, small babies are not allowed to touch the ground.

Families in parts of rural Malaysia live in wooden stilt houses, built between two and seven feet off the ground to protect against the monsoon floods. The floors are designed for easy cleaning and parents can afford to be relaxed about the occasional puddle: 'The floorboards are not flush. Space is deliberately left between them, not only for ventilation, but for the disposal of sweepings and other debris . . . Accidents of children who have not yet mastered toilet training are easy to clean with a bucket of water and a coconut husk' (Carol Laderman, social anthropologist).

Throughout history, and until quite recently even in Europe, children's bottoms were left unhampered by any kind of covering. In fact, knickers were considered unhygienic until the eighteenth century. In England at the end of the nineteenth century, at least one old-fashioned family doctor disapproved of children's underwear and some of his patients duly left their children knickerless. This caused some embarrassment for an unfortunate young schoolgirl:

At the age of 12, this young lady was sent to boarding school at Brighton; and, in her first letter home, she begged her mama to send her some drawers. The other girls were laughing at her because she had never worn any! The family doctor disapproved of such things and had said: 'Let the good air of Heaven get to their little limbs.' Chill counsel!

F. Gordon Roe, historian

Changing Baby

> . . . we must help him out
> in changing him frequently:
> when he's wet, we must dry him
> and wash him with a little wine . . .
> We change three times a day
> the wool and linen cloths and white bands,
> and we never get tired or cross
> being with him so he won't cry . . .
>
> Song of the 'balia', medieval Italian wet nurses

Anticipation of the infant bladder is no longer necessary in the age of the disposable, ultra-slim nappy. Twenty-first century western mothers can relax completely about toilet training since their babies are clad in perfectly leak-proof pants. Most British parents are prepared to spend around £1,000 over two and a half years (at 2002 prices) to swathe their babies' behinds in a super-absorbent layer which soaks up twenty times its own weight in liquid. The estimated cost for American babies is around $2,000.

Disposable nappies are also supposed to reduce the incidence of urinary tract infection in babies and make diaper rash a rarity. They certainly make life easier for the person who does the laundry. In 1998, disposable nappies were named one of the most valuable inventions of the twentieth century by the Female Millennium conference, USA.

If only disposables were really disposable. Thirty million trees a year are chopped down to cover the bottoms of British and American babies (that's five trees a year for each baby). Every *day* British parents dump another nine million nappies, creating a pile of methane-emitting waste which adds to greenhouse gases and may not decompose for half a millennium. If only ancient woodlands in North America and Scandinavia were not being destroyed to meet our demand; if only animals were not used to test the toxicity of the super-absorbent gel that lines the nappy fluff pulp.

The history of the nappy is intimately connected to the story of baby clothes and that – of course – means swaddling. In the days before either the safety-pin or straight pin, swaddling bands were wound around the child to keep his napkin in place. Linen was used for all underclothes in Europe until the nineteenth century, as it absorbs body fluids well and can be boiled in the wash. For boys, however, the simplest expedient was to allow the penis to poke through the swaddling bands, making a very odd-looking bundle indeed. The Nootkan Native Americans of Vancouver Island's west coast had a similar idea, though the baby was strapped in a canoe-shaped cradleboard: 'The baby was bound into this cradle, which was carried vertically. A girl baby's cradle had three holes bored in the footboard for urine to leak through, but a boy baby's cradle did not; he was left with his penis exposed' (Carleton S. Coon, anthropologist).

Worldwide, all sorts of natural materials have been used to mop up babies' backsides. Here are a few examples:

* !Kung San babies are carried in a non-restrictive hip sling, or '*kaross*'. This is lined with grass, which can be quickly and easily changed.
* In the Punjab, a baby under six months might be wrapped

in a '*potra*', a square piece of home-spun cotton. Although there is a bigger nappy, the '*langot*', for toddlers, many mothers do not like the nappy habit, and prefer to hold their babies out and let them run free.

- Sphagnum moss pads were used by many Native Americans – sphagnum is a herb that can absorb up to twenty-two times its own weight in liquid (compared with six times for a cotton diaper) and has disinfectant properties.
- The Anasazi baby of the American Four Corners wore soft rabbit fur, or deerskin, with milkweed pads. These early diapers were fixed with deerskin bandages.
- An Inuit baby wears a caribou skin nappy inside his mother's parka.
- Arab babies lie on a soft, woolly bed of sheepskin, which is easily washed and dried.
- Aboriginal mothers from south-west Australia diapered their babies using the light brown fluff that grows between the fronds of macro zamia, an ancient fern-like plant dating back 250 million years.

In seventeenth-century Belgium, a young woman would make a collection of strong sticks in anticipation of getting married. These were her 'nappy drying' sticks, a bottom-drawer item that signified her desire for children. By this time, nappies were firmly embedded as part of the cultural baby kit.

The first European nappies were 'tailclouts', so called because they were made from the tails of father's old shirt. The finest nappies were made from linen, and the most practical ones from terry towelling – Turkish towelling was used in Britain in the 1920s. When the first disposables were developed in Scandinavia in the 1950s, they met with little interest. But now that technology has improved, they are used by ninety-five per cent of western mothers. Even some well-to-do families on the Indian sub-continent are being tempted to buy them, although sourcing disposables can be difficult in some countries: 'Can I afford the time, with London screaming deadlines, to go on a Pampers hunt: a magical mystery tour which can take up to a full day or more to yield results' (Miranda Ingram, mother and newspaper correspondent based in Moscow).

Nappies are catching on all over the world. Most American, European, Asian and Australian baby bottoms are well and truly diapered. What impact will this invention have on our already polluted planet? Diapers now make up nearly ten per cent of household waste, and many generations of babies will come and go before they have decomposed. The very latest disposables are supposed to decompose in five years, although they are also more expensive to buy. Either manufacturers must meet an increasingly urgent list of environmental concerns (including their own claims to reforest ancient woodlands which took thousands of years to grow) or the future will look as bleak as a landfill site full of plastic and poo.

HOME TRUTHS

When babies are born, they don't know what century it is, nor do they know on which continent they were born, nor the standards or rules of conduct imposed by outside influences. They do know what they need.

Jody McLaughlin, editor of *Compleat Mother Magazine*, America

A baby may be born into a tropical climate, or temperatures well below freezing; he may have parents who bathe him daily or never; he may be swaddled like an Egyptian mummy, or held skin-to-skin next to his parents' heartbeat. All these possibilities make us realise that, rather than worry about getting things forever 'wrong', we might do better to experiment until we find what works.

Is bathing your baby, for instance, a mutually enjoyable experience? Does it enhance your relationship or make you both more stressed than you started out? It took me a week of struggling with my first baby to realise that I was just not skilled enough to balance her in a baby bath, wash her hair, keep the water out of her eyes and all the time keep her happy. I resorted instead to communal bathing, a sublimely simple remedy which involved my husband handing her carefully over to me in a not-too-hot hot tub. Here, with my baby resting on my raised knees, I gradually gained in confidence. A daily chore had been transformed into ten minutes of fun and games. If only I had realised that I was not alone with this creative solution: humans have been bathing with their babies for thousands of years.

When our predecessors moved to the far north and south thousands of years ago, they never guessed that one day homes would be centrally heated and thermostatically controlled. This modern tool gives us an added refinement to our parenting which we often take for granted. By simply turning a dial on a radiator, we can simulate temperatures which take the baby right back to his evolutionary roots.

A naked newborn baby is perfectly at home in an ambient temperature of 90°F, or 32°C. This replicates his prehistoric expectation of being born in an equatorial climate. Now, as never before, it is possible for us to experiment with the body freedom of our African cousins. We have the chance to give our babies some skin-to-skin contact and even brief freedom from their nappies, if we can stand the consequences (a terry square can be laid under the baby, rather than wrapped around him).

The needs of babies are few, but they are fundamental. When we look at the vast range of ways to meet these needs, we begin to realise just how adaptable humans can be. And in the newborn baby's resilience, we see the reason for the survival of the human race.

11. Tiny Tears

A baby cries – and all the world has an opinion as to what he means. Some cultures see crying as the bane of babyhood, an irritating sideshow to be conquered or ignored. Others treat each cry as a signal, an alarm which requires a serious and swift response. Wherever he cries, the baby is using the universal language of infancy.

Crying Out Loud

If the child does not cry the mother knows not its wants.

Russian proverb

Rhesus monkeys coo. Ape babies scream. And human infants cry. The distress signals of young animals are designed for maximum reaction from their own species parents and that – traditionally, at any rate – is what a human baby could expect.

Crying represents the highest state of arousal in an infant, and it elicits some pretty strong responses in his carers, too. A mother's heartbeat races when she hears any infant cry, from pregnancy onwards. More specifically, studies show that a newly-delivered mother is attuned to her own baby's cries, even when she cannot see him. And as time goes on, she learns to interpret his crying as clearly as her own language.

But why do so many babies seem programmed to switch straight into alarm mode at the slightest hitch? And why did humans evolve such an upsetting mode of communication? Swiftly attended to, the baby's cry may be no more than a squeak or a whine; a wake-up call for his dozing attendant. But not all crying is easy to eliminate and parents soon flag when they find their baby is capable of howling without cease for hours every day. This is the paradox which many western parents struggle with until they snap.

The answer is that crying did not evolve as a solitary activity. It is part of a call-and-response mechanism, designed to alert care-givers to an immediate need. Following the precept that 'It is precisely as serious as it sounds' (Jean Liedloff, continuum therapist), hunter-gatherer families attended to babies' cries as swiftly as they could. This, after all, was the evolved function of crying: to elicit a response. Cuddle the baby, feed the baby, rock the baby and (more or less) the crying goes away. It was no more refined than that. Because the hunter-gatherers held their babies from birth and carried them everywhere; because they had an active lifestyle and lived outdoors; because mothers nursed on demand at frequent intervals, there was very little for babies to cry for. A short wail to indicate a need and – hey presto! – the need was met. A call-and-response system in perfect motion.

The problem comes when lifestyles shift and carrying becomes incompatible with work, child-rearing fashion and other social norms. Cultures start to impose new meanings on infant crying: meanings which encourage parents to engage in a head-on battle with the baby. Instead of being an unsophisticated alarm, crying now has emotional intent; it is – for instance – the infant's attempt to master you or make you work for him, to keep you attached to him and to 'wrap you around his little finger'.

Before long, the child is being left to cry by himself, and his distress signal has the opposite effect from that of its evolutionary origins. It is a major cause of parental stress and hostility. Because the child practises his crying skills on a daily basis, he no longer expects his demands to be met by giving out subtle signals, like body movements or squeaking. He learns to go almost immediately into a full-blown yell. Crying is something he does well. I recently met a mother who told me how the baby's grand-mother *would* keep picking the infant up, even though her five-month-old daughter was 'perfectly happy' to cry in her room. This revealing comment shows how parents, through cultural conditioning, can inure themselves to a state of chronic indifference about crying.

The mother's contradiction-in-terms ('happy to cry') is the rationalisation she needs to convince herself that her strategy does not harm. But, make no mistake, it is a strategy – one provided by many sources in western child-rearing belief. Each culture has its own set of crying theories, although most translate their theory into compassionate action. They do not try to rationalise it away. After all, infant crying is the same signal it has always been – a cry for help. Newborn babies can cry as well as three-year-olds, and they have nothing more manipulative on their minds than eliciting some kind of human response.

Western parents have earned themselves rather a bad press in the crying department. Although the fashion for leaving baby to cry has diminished over the past forty years, western babies' crying potential has achieved worldwide fame. In India, Africa and South America, people express their amazement at the white mother's strategy of ignoring her crying baby and the white baby's ability to scream. Older generations of the Sioux tribe of Dakota, for instance, regret recent changes in child-rearing practices, because their grandchildren learn to cry 'like a white baby'.

Whites, they thought, want to estrange their children from this world so as to make them pass through to the next world with utmost dispatch. 'They teach their children to cry!' was the indignant remark of an Indian woman when confronted with the sanitary separation of mother and child in the government hospital, and especially with the edict of government nurses and doctors that is was good for babies to cry until blue in the face.

Erik Erikson, psychoanalyst, among Native American Sioux

When researchers played videos of an American mother and baby to Gusii mothers of Kenya, it was the American baby's crying which most alarmed the African women. It seemed to them that either the mother was wilfully ignoring her baby's distress, or that she did not have the skills to soothe him. In Gusii culture, crying is a signal that the baby wants to be soothed.

When we showed a group of our sample mothers a videotape of an American mother changing the diaper of her baby of a few weeks old, they became upset at the point where the baby was screaming on the changing table as the mother reached for and folded a clean diaper. From the Gusii point of view, a mother should know enough to clean her baby without that amount of unattended crying; they saw the American mother as incompetent. They were also startled by the sight of the same baby's grandmother holding the squalling infant for a while without being able to quiet it. One Gusii woman thought the grandmother was strangling the baby, but the others were simply amazed that a woman would not or could not soothe an infant immediately. This illustrates the Gusii assumption that the infant's cry demands a response intended to alleviate it and that a mother should be capable of doing so.

Robert LeVine, anthropologist in Kenya

In western society, there is an expectation that babies will cry a lot and that there is no need to indulge their constant demands. More important than being responsive is staying in control. American parents admit they learn about what is 'normal' for babies firstly from their paediatricians, secondly from child care books and only thirdly from their families. British parents are also reassured that babies' crying is 'normal' by scientists who have counted the number of hours a day a baby is likely to cry.

A team from London University found that English babies usually cry for two hours in twenty-four. Fifty minutes of the crying is concentrated into the early evening. An unlucky fourteen per cent of study parents had to endure four or more hours' crying daily, but researchers said there was no evidence for classifying this as colic, or any kind of 'gastro-intestinal disturbance'. A companion article in the *Nursing Times* expressed relief; now mothers could be reassured that their infants' excessive crying was 'a normal phenomenon and absolutely not a sign of failure'.

The article failed to mention the fact that babies in some cultures hardly cry at all, while babies in the west seem altogether prone to it. 'Babies' relentless crying in early evening "natural"', ran a newspaper headline describing the London University findings, a statement which few African mothers would be able to comprehend.

Of course parents feel a sense of failure when their babies cry excessively, and the principal duty of all good child care authors is to reassure them that self-blame is unnecessary. So here I am to reassure you: the reason for all this crying is not personal – it is culture-specific. Many of our difficulties are induced by the traditions and attitudes of western society and the reason one parent struggles will hold true for many other parents in the same society.

CRY-BABIES OF THE WORLD

If prolonged crying really were 'normal' for human babies, then we might expect all babies of the world to exhibit the same tendency. Of course, the reality is that culture makes a massive difference to the quantity and quality of the cry.

* Research on Zincanteco babies in southern Mexico found they spent no time at all crying intensively.
* A comparison of American, Dutch and !Kung San babies from Africa found that all babies initiated the same amount of crying,

but while the San babies were quickly soothed, the American and Dutch babies cried longer per bout and each day.
* At three to four months old, Gusii babies of Kenya cry less than half as much as American babies.
* A study of Korean babies found no signs of colic, evening crying, or crying peaks in two-month-olds.

The Meaning of a Baby's Cries

Darling, why are you crying?
Darling, is it for bathing you are crying?
Child, what are you crying for?
Child, is it for sleep?
Darling, Ro-ro-ro.

Veddas lullaby, Sri Lanka

We know our babies are trying to communicate with us. If only we knew what they wanted to say. Here are some causes you may or may not have considered:

* Tibetan parents believe that children, through their innocent actions, are capable of predicting the future. If a child cries incessantly for no apparent reason, it means a distant visitor will arrive soon.
* The old Celtic belief in the 'changeling' seems to originate in babies who cried a lot. In Scotland, it was said the Fey Folk could steal a human child and replace him with one of their own. The Irish said that while human babies were happy and easy to care for, a changeling would scream and cry through the day, and the sound of his crying would transcend the limits of mortal endurance. Changelings were also said to have unnaturally large appetites. A fifteenth-century text on witch-hunting declared that changeling babies 'always howl most piteously and even if four or five mothers are set on to suckle them, they never grow' (James Sprenger and Heinrich

Krämer, *Malleus Maleficarum, The Witch Hammer,* medieval handbook for the persecution of witches, 1486).

* In Malaysia, a baby's incessant crying can be caused by the 'Hantu Meroyan', the spirits of the placenta, blood and amniotic fluid. These birth siblings are said to be unsatisfied that they receive less attention than their human brother or sister, and so may seize the chance to upset the baby. Postnatal rituals are directed at keeping the 'Hantu Meroyan' away.

* The Ibo people of West Africa say that when a newborn baby cries, he is calling to the spirit world. His friends, the unborn spirit children he has left behind, are calling to him to return to them and he wails in response.

* For centuries, European mothers were told that the baby's crying was a form of exercise that was good for his lungs. 'A little crying empties the brain and enlargeth the lungs,' said herbalist Nicholas Culpeper in 1651. 'Instead of being feared, the practice of crying in children in want of muscular exercise is most beneficial in its effects,' said nineteenth-century doctor and social reformer Samuel Smiles. The belief that crying was good for babies persisted into the twentieth century, with advice like this:

The lungs do not expand to their full extent unless they are exercised every day. The infant cannot sing or shout and therefore he has to cry. If Nature is regularly thwarted by some well-meaning person who picks up the baby and distracts his attention after the first squeak, there is a risk of the lungs remaining almost unexpanded.

Mrs Charis Ursula Frankenburg, *Common Sense in the Nursery*, 1922

There is a grain of truth in the exercise idea. Crying does exercise the lung capacity. And as the whole body tenses and jerks about, it generates heat and uses up calories. However, this pent-up state is 'crying out' for the relief of human contact. Babies take their exercise through contact with another person's body, not through stiffening and tensing as they cry alone.

By the late twentieth century, reasons for baby's cries ranged from boredom to over-stimulation, severe pain to the slightest discomfort. But we do not need to agree on universal causes in order to meet the needs of each individual baby at a certain moment in time. Each child is learning to communicate with his own mother or father, and each response is their way of communicating with him. All-purpose meanings will never suit every occasion. The baby, undoubtedly, is crying to make his needs known. His crying is not a rebuke, not a judgment on your parenting, just a ringing tone calling for some kind of human response.

There, There

Leafy walls do little to impede sounds between huts in a camp of nomadic Mbuti pygmies, especially during the still hours between dusk and dawn.

I rolled over on the rough, earthen floor and peered out the open doorway at the dim shapes of the other huts. The bubbling noise had stopped, and from another direction an infant began to cry and was soon soothed by an attentive mother.

Kevin Duffy, anthropologist among the Mbuti pygmies in Zaire

Just how swiftly do mothers and others soothe their babies' cries? Here are some examples from around the globe:

* Hausa mothers of north-western Nigeria are helped by a variety of other women to care for their babies. In a study of 173 crying episodes, ninety-two per cent of baby cries brought a response, in all but two cases within thirty seconds.
* Okinawan parents regard infant crying as a bad habit. As soon as the baby makes a peep, he is taken to his mother, who nurses him.
* Maya babies of Yucatan, Mexico, are put to the breast at any sign of discomfort.
* In Africa's Kalahari Desert, when !Kung San babies cry, they

receive a response within ten seconds more than ninety-two per cent of the time. Every cry is answered with the breast. Fathers tend to hand baby back to mother at any hint of infant distress.

* In India, babies are rarely left to cry. They are picked up immediately and either put to the breast, jiggled around or distracted. Of course, within this pattern, individual responses vary. In Uttar Pradesh, south of the Himalayas, Rajput mothers were asked how swiftly they responded to their babies' cries. Out of twenty-four mothers, twenty-one said they would pick up a crying baby and pacify him – of these, nine said they would respond at once, nine said as soon as possible and two said they would wait a while.

* Among the Tiriki people of western Kenya, no baby is allowed to cry unattended. Mother usually breastfeeds in response to crying and if she is at work farming or gathering firewood, the baby is brought to her by the child nurse.

* Some peoples create strong taboos around crying. The Yanomama of the Amazonian rainforest in South America say that if a child is left to cry, his soul might escape and wander around the jungle. In Jamaica, it is said that if you leave a baby crying, the duppies (or ghosts) will come and find him and spirit him away.

IT'S GOOD TO CRY

A child who cries long will live long

European proverb

A study of Jamaican mothers and their new babies showed that the babies who cried before breastfeeding put on more weight than those babies who did not cry first. This seems to imply that the mothers responded to crying to prompt nursing. It might also mean that hungry babies cry more. It might even show that the louder baby gets his needs met more readily than the passive or 'good' one. In scientific terms, we know that babies' crying has an effect on the mother's mammary gland, making it pulsate. This in turn stimulates milk release, a physical prompt for breastfeeding, as any nursing mother can testify.

So crying invites nurture. In critical conditions, this adaptive mechanism may be crucial to a baby's survival. In the 1970s, Dutch researcher Marten de Vries was observing Maasai babies in Kenya during a period of severe drought. Infants were labelled 'difficult' or 'easy' according to western concepts of these terms: if a baby cried intensely and required skilful management, he was 'difficult'. Babies who were more passive and apparently less needy were termed 'easy'.

Returning to his research after three months, de Vries could not find all of his nomadic mother and baby pairs. Of the thirteen he located, seven babies had died during the famine. Amazingly, six of these were the infants he had previously labelled 'easy' to care for. Only one of the supposedly 'difficult' babies was dead. In evolutionary terms, at least, it seems that crying may be a better strategy than passive acceptance.

Though some western parents rationalise that crying is not harmful for babies and that it may even be good for them, crying appears only to be good for those babies who receive an appropriate response. Crying expresses the human baby's almost insatiable need for comfort, warmth and food and it prompts parents to communicate at the simplest of levels. Nursing, rocking, soothing and lulling are one side of a vital conversation and most cultures see no danger in an inordinate amount of baby-holding, breastfeeding and loving care.

Crying for a Cure

It is worth thinking about differences in culture and parenting as this shows how we have moved away from what a baby finds most natural. When travelling around Asia I noticed that I did not hear babies cry. This was because they were always carried by their mothers or attached in a sling (no pushchairs or prams) and could be easily fed as soon as needed. They would also sleep with their mothers and this would be the normal way of caring for a baby.

Mary Knott, British health visitor

If there were a catch-all 'cure' for crying, no doubt someone would have bottled it and made their fortune long ago. All babies in all cultures cry, because that is their defence mechanism in an unpredictable world. But parents in most cultures try to pre-empt crying by anticipating the baby's needs.

Scientists studying babies in Kenya found it almost impossible to tell whether 'maternal holding' helped to reduce crying, because mothers held their babies so much of the time – three- to four-month-old babies were carried around for most of their waking hours. So they looked instead at data from American mothers in Boston and found that crying was 'significantly less frequent' when mothers held their babies. This dampening effect might, they said, explain why the mean frequency of crying in Kenyan babies was less than half that of the Boston babies.

Since the 1970s, many studies have come to similar conclusions: the best way to soothe a crying baby is to pick him up. Holding and carrying are repeatedly shown to work better than pacifying with a dummy or changing the formula feed. In a 1990s study of 201 mothers from Manchester, England, the babies who cried least were those who were breastfed longest (13 weeks or more) and picked up immediately.

Another cross-cultural comparison helps to clarify precisely what it is that babies seek when they cry. A study of two-month-old Korean babies found no signs of colic, evening crying, or crying peaks – just the age when western babies are reaching the height of their crying powers. Although many Korean families share the socio-economic status of western families, the child-rearing styles are starkly different.

At one month old, Korean babies spend 8.3 per cent of their time (around two hours a day) on their own. American babies spend 67.5 per cent of their time alone. Korean babies are carried around twice as much as American babies. And Korean mothers respond instantly to their babies' cries, while American mothers often ignore crying or wait before responding (one study found that American mothers deliberately did not answer 46 per cent of their babies' cries in the first three months of life).

The Korean childcaring pattern is a total package which seems to eliminate serious crying (including colic) on a culture-wide basis. It involves a lot of carrying, a lot of company and a *swift response*. A study of American La Leche League (breastfeeding group) mothers confirms this final element. Babies who were fed frequently but received a slow maternal response cried just as much as babies who were fed at long intervals. Babies are looking for a mother who is engaged and responsive; they need parents who answer their crying readily, as if it were a question, not an accusation or an attempt at emotional manipulation.

In the 1960s, a period when western babies were routinely left to cry, American researcher Peter Wolff tried to discover exactly what methods were best for pacifying unsettled infants. He found that just picking up and holding the baby soothed him even though he might be waiting to feed. Changing the baby's nappy also worked, even if a wet nappy was used to replace the old one! In other words, it was the personal contact babies craved − they were not complaining about a damp nappy and were prepared to delay their need for nurture.

What simply did not work was filling the baby's stomach with milk via a tube: babies with full stomachs continued to cry, because they were still deprived of any sensual experience and physical contact. Touch is the factor which seems to normalise babies.

When carrying is not enough, a little magic can relieve the tension. Spiritual healing in many cultures extends to every aspect of human disease, including discomforted cries of an unhappy baby. Here are some crying cures and rituals around the world:

* If a baby cries during conversation, the Yequana mother of Venezuela hisses softly in his ear. Studies have shown that a crying baby stops immediately when someone confronts him with 'baby talk', because he feels compelled to copy the babble of sound.
* The Samals, an Islamic people of Tawitawi Island in the Philippines, say the prophet Mohammed cried non-stop for seven days when he was three months old. Nothing his mother did would appease him, until she trimmed a lock of hair from the infant's forehead. This hair-cutting ritual is incorporated into a ritual called '*paggunting*', the Samal version of a welcome-to-the-world ceremony. Candles and incense are burned, the imam (priest) reads from the Qur'an and the baby's forelock is perfumed before being cut.
* The Mansi people of Siberia believe that night-time crying is caused by the soul of an ancestor who has entered the baby's body. Once they have discovered, through ritual, the name of the unsettled spirit, he is appeased and the crying will cease.
* In Tanzania, the Barabaig mother knows how to calm her crying baby when they are at home. She pretends to be at work. She straps him to her body, bends and straightens her torso in a rhythmical fashion and makes the sound of grinding maize.

ABSOLUTE SILENCE

We are used to hearing babies crying in supermarkets and other public places. We are not worried that the noise they make will alert predators to our whereabouts. But for people who share their habitat with wild animals, a baby's cries might give the game away. Not only is it crucial that cries are answered instantly, there are times when crying must be stopped in its tracks. The anxiety created around a baby's wailing is partly to do with this ancient fear of detection, as described in a lullaby from Tanzania, East Africa:

> Do not cry, my child!
> What are you crying for?
> If you wail, the leopard will devour your mother.
>
> **Chagga mother's lullaby**

In the rainforest, as in the desert, hunter-gatherer babies are taken along on hunting trips, where absolute silence is essential. It is the role of Mbuti pygmy women to participate in the elephant hunt just as much as men, and any noise from the baby would give away the position of the human hunting party. In an emergency, mothers pinch their babies' noses, a mechanism which forces the infant to mouth-breathe and stifles his cry. The method is used by some child care-takers in Africa – the Tiv of Nigeria, for instance – who tell their charges unceremoniously to 'Shut up!'

Colic – A Cry Too Far

[Gusii] Mothers recognise a kind of crying during the first three months which cannot be satisfied by nursing, and they call it *enyancha*, which means 'the lake'. Some view it as a disturbing stimulation of the child's genitals caused by the wind from Lake Victoria; others think it is a kind of stomach trouble and have potions to feed the crying infant during the night. Most often at night, however, the mother puts on a light, binds the infant to her back and walks about in the house, shaking him up and down.

Robert and Barbara LeVine, anthropologists in Kenya

You may think 'the lake' sounds like a fictitious crying disease concocted by parents to explain the inexplicable crying of their babies. Well, many modern doctors would say the same about colic. Colic is one of those shadowy conditions identified by some cultures but not others, which afflicts between 10 and 40 per cent of western babies (according to definition) without apparent reason.

Most babies struggle at one time or another with what is called colic – that umbrella phrase used to describe the way he draws up his knees and plunges into parox-ysms of screaming, the reasons for which nobody has ever been able to deter-mine. Baby books will tell you that it is gas in the intestines as a result of fermentation. The truth is nobody knows what causes it. Nobody has even come up with proof that it exists.

Leslie Kenton, health writer

Colicky babies appear to be in pain. The face is scrunched, the mouth is set in a rectangle, the cry is rhythmic and desperate. The knees draw upwards, as if in agony (which is why many parents believe the problem to be digestive) and the baby goes red in the face. Yet the colicky cry is not a typical pain reaction. Most infant pain is characterised by a sudden cry (no prelimi-nary whining, just a sharp intake of breath and a yell), by an initial long cry (older children exhibit this pattern, too – there is a long gap after the injury, followed by an even longer scream) and by subsequent breath-holding.

In contrast, colic is associated with repetitive cries, like an alarm which cannot be disconnected. The baby seems unable to stop himself and – after hours of yelling – is unlikely to remember the origin of his distress. Clinically, the label of colic is given only if crying sustains for more than three hours and continues for more than three days in a week.

Colic may or may not be connected with infant diet. Some studies suggest that bottle-fed and breastfed babies are equally likely to cry excessively – others tell us that formula-fed babies have significantly more colic symptoms at two weeks than do breastfed infants. A change in formula milk has been shown to have, at best, a placebo effect in reducing colic symptoms. Yet the origin of the word seems to be the Greek '*kolikos*', relating to the colon, so linking the condition to digestive origins. Whatever the truth, the root of babies' evident distress probably reaches beyond nutrition.

We do have a few mysterious clues to the causes of colic. For instance, established colic does not respond to the carry-and-respond treatment which works so well with ordinary crying. Mothers who carry their babies around a lot and respond to them swiftly are usually able to reduce the length of crying bouts in their children. But when the same methods are tried on babies already labelled as 'colicky', they do not work. By four weeks of age, babies' colicky behaviours are entrenched. Carrying them around for an extra two hours or more each day does not, according to studies, relieve their symptoms.

Another clue is the way that babies take in air. As we saw earlier (Chapter 6: Burping Baby) infants who lie on their backs to feed are liable to take in more wind. And the biggest cause of a bloated stomach and gas in babies is prolonged crying. Babies who feed on their backs, or are carried that way, and who are left to cry for a long time, are more likely to accumulate the gas which may be giving them colicky pain.

Perhaps colic is a vicious circle: an intense crying habit learnt early on and not easily broken. Perhaps the cure is a pre-emptive strike: like the hunter-gatherer parents of the past, we could carry our babies around from the beginning, as a matter of course. We might also nurse our babies in a more upright position, which seems to improve digestion. On the other hand, colic might be a disturbing stimulation of the child's genitals caused by the wind from Lake Victoria, in which case, there's very little we can do . . .

The Gob-Stopper

[The dummy is] an invention of the devil to tempt mothers to harm their children. If the Lord had intended little babies to be always sucking something, He'd have sent them with dummies round their necks already.

Helen Hodgson, Durham health visitor, 1909

Babies are born with their sucking reflex fully intact and already tested. Without waiting for instructions as to whether or not his culture approves, an unborn baby will often suck his own thumb, or the back of the hand. The desire to suck is powerful and – at birth – instinctively directed towards the breast, via rooting reflexes and an ability to identify and reach the areola. If allowed, the baby will suck frequently over twenty-four hours, both for food and to gain inner peace. Most babies like to suckle themselves to sleep.

There is no doubt that sucking calms a baby. Tests have shown that rubber pacifiers soothe crying infants – and indirectly, they soothe distressed parents, too. The soother has become an instrument of peace for the western family, a means of temporarily switching off the baby's alarm signal.

The history of the artificial teat goes back to before the days of plastic and rubber. In eighteenth-century Russia, for instance, babies were left to suck on a 'saska', a long poultice or bag filled with milk-and-bread pap, for hours at a time. But this practice had a perilous history. Unnoticed, the bags sometimes broke open and babies could choke on the coarse mixtures which had been stuffed inside.

Many babies around the world are raised without artificial

gob-stoppers. Early humans managed by allowing their babies to suckle as often as they wanted. And still today . . .

* The Rajput baby of northern India has no dummy – he is soothed by grandmother or another woman if his own mother is not available.
* The Okinawan child in the Pacific sucks neither his thumb nor a pacifier.
* Babies in New Zealand are far less likely to be given a pacifier than European babies.
* In modern-day Japan, only two per cent of one-month-old babies are given a dummy.

Dummies seem more popular in cultures where, for reasons of modesty, most nursing is done in private. Visiting north-east Brazil, this British mother comments on the use of pacifiers in a small fishing village:

Although babies in the village are generally [breast-]fed for many years, in the time I was there, I didn't often see any being fed. I rarely saw any bottles, which was a good sign, but also I rarely saw any at the breast. What I did see were lots of dummies so I came to the conclusion that babies were mainly fed in the home.

Rennie Loewenthal, La Leche League breastfeeding support group leader, London, spends five months in Canoa Quebrada, Brazil

The problem with pacifiers – and any non-human substitutes – is that they can only be used symptomatically. Soothers satisfy one aspect of a baby's needs (the need to suck) without stimulating the breast, helping to promote lactation, honing the infant's sucking ability, or adding to the daily quota of human touch.

A study of Swedish mothers showed that use of a dummy for more than two hours a day interfered with breastfeeding. A group of mothers intending to nurse for six months or more were discharged from hospital with their babies assessed as 'correctly' breastfeeding. After four months, ninety-six per cent of babies who had not been given a dummy were still breast-feeding. But those babies who used a dummy experienced more breastfeeding problems. Just fifty-six per cent were still nursing at four months.

In Austria, most babies are given a dummy without stigma – even those who are fully breastfed. A recent study showed that more than eighty per cent of Austrian babies are given a dummy soon after birth, to keep them peaceful and prevent them thumb-sucking. Many Austrian mothers believe babies cannot manage without a pacifier – on a trip there with my six-month-old baby, I was frequently approached and asked why she did not have one.

Doctors are now warning Austrian parents that dummies delay babies' talking and listening skills. The pacifier renders the baby's world quieter, as he cannot hear himself babbling and his care-takers are less likely to chat and stimulate him. It also prevents the infant from putting everything in his mouth: his evolved way for exploring the world.

Alone Again – Naturally?

I was put in my crib and left to cry it out, more or less . . . I developed into a head-banger – I'd get on all fours and bash the top of my head against the head-board. It was comforting, like listening to punk rock sixteen years later.

John Seabrook, author and journalist

There are many western training programmes which leave babies to cry, in order to learn how to be alone. Some operate like a sharp shock, ignoring every whimper, while others proffer a more gentle approach, encouraging parents gradually to taper off their responses. Either way, the child eventually learns that his alarm signals are unheeded. He stops expecting comfort from his parents and begins, instead, to learn the lifelong cultural lesson of self-reliance.

Generations of babies have been put out of earshot precisely so that mothers did not have to listen to their main distress signal, crying. Some babies keep on crying until they receive the comfort they seek. Others sublimate their deep needs into acts of self-comfort. One survey of babies at bedtime found that infants who were laid in their cots when already asleep were more likely to become 'signallers' – crying for their parents – while those babies who were laid down whilst awake became 'self-soothers', finding their own methods of comforting themselves to sleep.

In the recent past, western society has preferred the self-soothing baby to the crying baby. Frequent criers are viewed (understandably) as the height of annoyance, interrupting their parents' sleep and gradually destroying their sanity. Children are encouraged to suck their thumbs or pacifiers, twirl their hair or adopt a blanket: habits which keep them quiet and are moderately unembarrassing when practised in public. However, chronic self-soothing can be a sign of emotional withdrawal. It's the tactic all animals use to try to escape from an unbearably solitary environment.

To understand the mechanisms of self-comforting, we might begin in the average zoo. Unable to interact sufficiently with members of their own species, animals interact with themselves:

We are all familiar with the repetitive pacing to-and-fro of the caged animal, but this is only one of the many strange patterns that arise. Stylised masturbation may occur. Sometimes this no longer involves manipulation of the penis. The animal (usually a monkey) simply makes the back and forth masturbatory movements of its arm and hand, but without actually touching the penis. Some female monkeys repeatedly suck their own nipples. Young animals suck their paws. Chimpanzees may prod pieces of straw into their (previously healthy) ears. Elephants nod their heads for hours on end . . .

Desmond Morris, zoologist

Western children are not animals and very few are abandoned to this degree. But many are kept in their cots for long periods, and their self-comforting behaviours reflect, albeit in milder form, the behaviours of other lone creatures. Self-rocking, for instance, is viewed by Desmond Morris as an indication that babies need more loving contact, and it 'should be taken seriously as a sign that all is not well'. America's favourite sleep-training expert Dr Richard Ferber devotes a whole chapter to 'Headbanging, body rocking and head rolling', in which he speaks entirely from western clinical experience:

Most young children rock back and forth occasionally and about 20 per cent of children do so more consistently, rocking back and forth on all fours at least once a day . . . On the *average*, body rocking starts at six months of age, headbanging and head rolling at nine months . . . Parents usually find headbanging most frustrating . . .

In the infant and young toddler, rhythmic patterns are of little significance and you will not need to intervene. If the rocking or headbanging is especially severe, as with Timothy [a case history child aged two], then for the sake of more quiet at night, less damage to the furniture and fewer complaints from the neighbours, you may want to consider several approaches, though these are only occasionally successful.

Dr Richard Ferber, American paediatrician

Note the repeatedly expressed frustrations of parents, a feature of many parent-centred child care manuals. Ferber is sorry for the neighbours and even finds a word of sympathy for the furniture, but he does not mention the child's needs, physical or emotional. At least, from the comfort of his clinical office in the Boston Center for Pediatric Sleep Disorders, Ferber can be sure of one thing: headbanging, rolling and body rocking are all perfectly normal. 'If your child does any of these things, you may be comforted to know that headbanging, body rocking and head rolling are very common in early childhood and, at least at this age, are usually normal' he says.

Ferber's headbanging chapter is not the only one to deal with the fall-out of solitary infant sleep training. He has a section on night-time fears, one on bedwetting, another on nightmares and a cheery chapter entitled 'Sleeptalking, sleepwalking, thrashing and terrors – a spectrum of sudden partial wakenings'. Only in the West could we create such a catalogue of disasters in the pursuit of parental privacy.

From birth, babies cling to their parents like comfort-seeking missiles. And most cultures consider that to be perfectly all right.

Drugged Babies

I buy a bottle of Godfrey's Cordial for making children sleep, since Geordy keeps all the house awake, also almost kills his poor mother.

John Stedman, lieutenant-colonel, writes in his journal about
his 19-month-old son, George, England, 1785

For thousands of years, mothers and nurses fed opium to babies to make them sleep. The Ebers Papyrus, an ancient Egyptian medical manual which dates back to 1500 BC, recommends feeding babies a mixture of poppy seeds and fly dung, because 'It acts at once'! In medieval Europe, a fretful baby might receive a mouthful of poppy seed tea. But by the eighteenth century, chemists had taken over where the herbalists used to hold sway. It was a time of great deprivation for many and opiates were often cheaper than food. People knew it could kill them, but still they sedated themselves and – not surprisingly – their babies.

In colonial America, mothers fed their infants 'soothing syrups' which contained an astonishing mixture of opium, morphine, chloroform and cannabis. In Britain, pharmacists reported that customers were buying opium or laudanum for themselves ('laudanum' is just a tincture of opium) and Godfrey's Cordial or Quietness for the babies. Godfrey's was a mixture of opium, treacle, water and spices. At the height of its popularity, the good people of Coventry, in the English Midlands, bought twelve gallons of Godfrey's a week – enough for 12,000 paediatric doses. In Nottingham, one druggist (a town councillor) personally sold 400 gallons of laudanum a year. Of course, not all of this was going down infant throats: some adults were partial to a sip of Godfrey's themselves.

Godfrey's Cordial was the most popular, but other preparations aimed specifically at babies also contained opium: Grove's Baby Bowel Formula, for instance, Green's Syrup of Tar and Steedman's Powder for 'teething' (teething was a broad diagnosis in the eighteenth century: the serious symptoms doctors describe sound more like infantile scurvy caused by vitamin deficiency). An American advert for Cocaine Toothache Drops showed two cute children crossing a stream. Its slogan was 'Instantaneous Cure!'

Even Coca-Cola contained cocaine until 1903. Around this time, the manufacturer Bayer was selling a product called 'Heroin', claimed to be 'highly effective against coughs'. Colic was treated, right up to the twentieth century, with 'paregoric', a camphorated tincture of opium spiced with benzoic acid and aniseed. Those babies who were spared a drugged infancy might be rocked to sleep with alcohol. In eighteenth-century France, sleepless babies were given eau-de-vie, while one American doctor wrote in 1904 that he had treated a baby who was addicted to crème de menthe.

These preparations did nothing to preserve the babies, unless by 'preserve' a certain amount of pickling is implied. In East Anglia, where opium could be bought over the counter in penny sticks and opium was added to infants' 'poppy tea', babies were reported to shrink up like little old men and become 'wizened like little monkeys'. Both in America and Britain, there was a flourishing trade in patented sleep-inducers. Wet nurses even rubbed laudanum on their nipples to send babies to sleep – and for some, the sleep was permanent. In the opinion of one doctor, thousands of babies were killed annually by mother and nurses, '. . . forever pouring Godfrey's Cordial down their little throats, which is a strong opiate and in the end as fatal as arsenic. This they pretend they do to quiet the child – thus indeed many are forever quieted . . .' (Dr Hume, 1799).

Godfrey's was still popular in American as late as 1910. Not until the formulation of food and drug laws did it become illegal to feed babies narcotics to force them to sleep. But after opium came another range of sedatives for desperate parents. Gripe Water, the mainstay of the twentieth-century family medicine cabinet, was (until recently) a combination of dill syrup and five per cent alcohol. Colic drops and paracetamol syrups, antihistamines and teething gels all contain sedatives.

A quarter of western babies take sedative drugs by the time they are eighteen months old. Ostensibly, this is to relieve pain, but it is almost always, incidentally, to induce sleep. Used sparingly, they may ease acute symptoms swiftly. But some babies are daily spoonfed on sedatives for months at a time, which does them no good at all. Over-use of paracetamol, for instance, can deactivate the body's natural pain killers.

Western parents are not the only ones to resort to dosing their babies to sleep. During the 1950s, researchers in northern India found mothers occasionally gave their babies opium, as white mothers had done for centuries during the British Raj. The researchers imply that drug use becomes more prevalent when the mother is placed under undue stress:

If the mother is very busy and has no one to help carry the baby, she may resort to the use of opium to put the baby to sleep. The women agreed that this was not good for babies and should be used only as a last resort. One busy mother administered two grains of opium a day to a baby who was a few months old. When under the influence of the drug, it was impossible to awaken the baby even by vigorous shaking.

Leigh Minturn and John Hitchcock, anthropologists in the Rajput region of India

In modern-day Afghanistan, many thousands of people have been living in crisis ever since the 1979 invasion by Russia and the subsequent take-over by the fundamentalist Muslim Taliban regime. Decades of drought and war have taken their toll and some 600,000 people have been displaced – at the time of writing, around 40,000 are living as refugees in the mountains to the east of the country. Increasingly, Afghan mothers have resorted to feeding opium to their babies and young children to make them sleep. It is believed by Afghans that babies are happy when they stop crying – however they stop crying.

Afghanistan is the only country in the world where all television is banned. However, radio is tolerated by the Taliban regime (which does not permit women to work or otherwise transmit female voices on national radio). The opium issue was recently tackled by a popular BBC radio soap called 'New Home, New Life'. Through the story line, Afghan listeners learn about current affairs and health questions, such as the dangers of opium dosing their babies. Ironically, Afghan's exiled president Burhanuddin Rabbani has accused Taliban of financing its war through poppy cultivation, drug production and sales.

Of course, for most parents, deliberately drugging the baby is a last resort, a coping strategy for use in a crisis. As birth campaigner Sheila Kitzinger points out, when a lonely, inexperienced mother turns to her doctor in desperation, what she really needs for her long-term sanity is the support of a caring community. But doctors don't have armies of willing volunteers at their disposal. What they can do is choose from a squadron of sedatives, each licensed for babies and young children, to ease whatever ails them:

A 20-year-old first-time mother was prescribed six different drugs for her baby by her doctor: Infacol, Merbentyl, Piptal, Dentinox, Eastrop and phenobarbitone, and when the baby continued to be restless, she gave her gripe water and whisky as well. The problem, the woman explained to me, was that her baby cried for about one hour every day and she couldn't stand it. This mother needed help with her loneliness, anxiety and depression, and her resulting panic when the baby cried. But she never got that. Instead her baby was drugged to the eyeballs.

Sheila Kitzinger, anthropologist

HOME TRUTHS

We are not like the Goras (whites) who after feeding the baby leave her in the upstairs bedroom – cry or no cry ... In my family, if a baby is slightly ill the whole family is awake to comfort and support the young mother. A completely different Tarika [method] of raising children – by the whole family.

Punjabi grandmother, from a farming household

The western interpretation of infant crying sets us apart from most of the world. For some reason, we persist in judging the miserable baby as 'bad'. Observe people's reactions when they meet a passive, a quiet, a sleeping or an unusually docile infant. Someone will say, 'Isn't he good?', or 'He's no trouble', or 'Aren't you lucky?' to the hapless mother, who (though momentarily proud) is aware that her temporarily silent baby may become troublesome again at any moment. 'Oh you should have heard him last night!' she might reply. 'He was up for two hours – you wouldn't have thought he was so good then.'

The association of passivity with goodness in western culture makes it difficult for us to empathise with the distressed baby. In fact, empathy is severely discouraged, as it is thought to get in the way of parental control. Crying is not a signal we seek to attend, but an irritation we try to avoid.

So entrenched are we in our cultural response to infant distress that we forget that other species and societies still operate on the old-fashioned alarm-response system. Over many hundreds of years, our irritation at the crying of babies has turned into an aversion. The sound repels us. If a stranger's baby cries in a supermarket or train, we move as far away as possible. When our own babies cry and we cannot stop the noise, we put the vacuum cleaner on or leave the baby where we cannot hear him. We treat the crying as we treat medical symptoms: with suppressive or averting tactics.

This is the opposite of the view in many other places – Kenya, for instance, where prolonged infant crying is a sign that a parent is not responding swiftly or empathetically enough: 'No virtue is seen in letting a baby cry; on the contrary, it is regarded as a disgrace. Gusii women have little tolerance for a crying baby, particularly a very young one; they feel something must be done immediately to calm it' (Robert A. LeVine, anthropologist in Kenya).

Somewhere between these two extremes is a vast range of possible responses to the distressed baby. Only one principle seems to hold true for babies everywhere. Crying babies may be more annoying than the culturally 'good' passive ones – but the criers are the ones most likely to get their fundamental needs met.

12. The Big Sleep

Is your baby sleeping through the night yet? In a culture already deprived of sleep, parents come off badly. But not all families are exhausted by their attempts to train babies into adult sleep habits. In some cultures, babies are given the sleep treatment they expect. Welcome to a world without bedtime routines, transitional objects, or chronic insomnia . . .

Sleep Like a Baby

The notion of a zestful awake phase during the day followed by a smooth unbroken sleep time in the night is probably more of a cultural fantasy than a biological imperative.

Meredith Small, ethno-paediatrician

Infant sleep is a topic of serious concern for western parents. Our 'monophasic' sleep pattern (one long sleep every night) clashes instantly and disastrously with the baby's 'polyphasic' style of snoozing (six or seven bouts of sleep in twenty-four hours, without any noticeable distinction between night and day). It's not the baby's fitful sleep we object to, but his wakeful neediness during the night, when he demands to be nursed and cuddled, rocked and amused to a timetable of his own making.

Our own cultural sleep experiences leave us unable to fall asleep easily once woken out of deep sleep. Parents swiftly become sleep-deprived as they take it in turns to soothe the baby and return him to the nursery they decorated especially for him. Before long, the infant is on a sleep-training programme, where he learns that crying brings little or no attention. 'Be prepared for a battle of wills!' says CRY-SIS, the British parents' support group. 'He is not going to give in without a fight.'

Once war is declared, there are likely to be winners and losers. Parents may or may not triumph in the first battle, persuading their babies into long phases of sleep during the night. Some children refused to be 'Ferberized' (the new verb from the famous American sleep-training author, Richard Ferber). Even those babies who give in now are liable to come back later for nocturnal comfort – perhaps when they can walk and talk and make their way into their parents' bedrooms.

Any behaviour that challenges the deep, monophasic sleep which our culture prefers is considered more or less pathological. But one culture's pathology is another culture's sign of good health. Sleep, the casualty of new parenthood in the western world, is not a topic of concern for most other cultures, because babies are not expected to sleep through the night without waking. Traditional cultures, especially, know the value of light healthy sleep, and would be concerned about any baby who was so passive or ill that he slept for eight hours without rooting for the breast or seeking the comfort of human touch.

Young children [in two low-income neighbourhoods of Cairo] always sleep with their mothers and no special provision is made for infants to sleep more often in the daytime. Some mothers think that when infants sleep less it means they are healthier. If a baby sleeps a lot, the mother is sometimes advised to wake the infant and give him or her exercise to make the baby's body strong.

Homa Hoodfar, anthropologist, on sleep attitudes in Egypt

A cross-cultural comparison of attitudes to infant sleep makes it clear just how obsessed we have become with this topic. In Boston, America, a 1995 study found that more parents seek advice on training their children to sleep than on any other infant health issue or behavioural problem. In America and

Britain, a good baby is one who sleeps through the night, a view reinforced by health professionals. Parental competence is implicated in the label of a 'sleepless child'. The context for sleep in our society is one of emotional intensity and private pain.

Not so in Italy, however. In 1996, researchers interviewed Italian mothers on their babies' sleep patterns, but the mothers were unable to answer many of the questions. Sleep was not a big deal and they did not keep track of how their children slept. Since their babies slept with them, disturbance in the night was minimal – in fact, the Italian mothers were puzzled at so many queries on so straightforward a subject.

American mothers, approached by the same research team, were, by contrast, highly aware of their children's wakenings and sleep phases. They knew where the babies had slept, how much sleep they had taken, how many times they were forced to get up out of bed, how long it took them to get back to sleep – in short, just how sleep-deprived they really were. They understood exactly why the sleep research team were so interested in their nocturnal habits.

SLEEP: YOUR CULTURE EXPECTS IT

It is hard to imagine how such vastly different cultural approaches could *not* affect the infant, and of course they do. When we look at infant sleep around the world, we find babies responding strongly to the early messages their culture gives them. Broadly speaking, babies can be trained to take more sleep; to sleep more deeply and to adapt to the patterns which their culture demands of them.

* In Holland, babies are strictly regulated so that they will sleep according to parental ideals. This is a culture which regards

adaptation to routine as a marker of emotional maturity and so every day brings the same, unchanging treatment. The Dutch baby, once tucked up early at night, is expected to amuse himself should he wake up. As a result, Dutch babies sleep two hours longer every night than American babies.

* Yurok babies of California are not traditionally allowed to fall asleep in the late afternoon or early evening. Each mother must prevent her baby from dozing off around twilight, 'lest dusk close his eyes for ever'.

* Kipsigis parents in Kenya encourage their children towards early motor development, but place little emphasis on long periods of sleep. Consequently, a four-month-old Kipsigis baby sleeps for around twelve hours a day, with the longest sleep episode lasting for around four and a half hours. This would be considered problematic, if not pathological, by American or British families whose four-month-olds may sleep for fifteen hours out of twenty-four, with a long eight-hour sleep at night.

Of course, none of these statistics tell us about the heartache or methods involved in shaping babies' sleep habits. They don't hint at the importance of light sleep for humans, nor do they explain how the majority of the world's parents manage without sleep-training programmes, clinics and sleep-inducing mechanisms. They don't tell us about the world's best-kept sleep secrets . . .

The Human Cradle

Sleep sweet in my arms,
Which are surrounding you like soft silk.
Greek lullaby

The Ganda of Uganda, Maori of New Zealand, Guayaki of Paraguay, Walmadjeri Aborigines of Australia, Katab of Nigeria and Tzeltal of Mexico all sleep with their babies. Ache babies of the Paraguayan jungle receive one hundred per cent bodily contact at night. Balinese babies are kept close to their mothers' bodies by night as well as by day. Eskimos traditionally sleep naked together in their igloos. Mothers and infants throughout Africa and Asia do it, and some fathers, too. In hammocks and futons, on straw and bamboo benches, inside mud huts, igloos and Mongolian gurs, peoples of the world sleep with their babies and small children. They call it co-sleeping – the ancient, once universal, art of sleeping near, or right next to, your baby or small child.

This is the way almost everyone slept until nineteenth-century Europeans decided to break the habit of millennia. Before humans had secure homes, and long before they had separate bedrooms with central heating, co-sleeping was the only way of successfully nurturing a baby through the night. While eighteenth-century children slept with their parents (or siblings, or servants, depending on their age and class), sleep was not an issue for child care writers. 'The bosom of the mother is the natural pillow of her offspring,' wrote Dr John Ticker Conquest, early nineteenth-century author of *Advice to Mothers*.

The baby's inability to generate sufficient body heat was reason enough to keep him close to his mother at night – all the authorities agreed. At this time, it was routine for small babies to sleep next to their mothers for the first eight weeks of life. But by the seventh edition of his book, Conquest had apparently changed his mind: babies were to sleep alone. The consensus had shifted and babies should now fit in around their mothers' schedules, not vice versa.

While the parents of northern Europe were about to embark on a Two Hundred Year War with their babies, the rest of the world carried on obliviously co-sleeping. The model of mother and infant sleeping in close proximity, with or without other family members, is still the most prevalent pattern on the planet today. In one survey of ninety different societies, seventy-one expected mother and baby to sleep together at night. In another study of 186 non-industrial societies, all under-ones slept with their parents. And a third survey of 172 different cultures showed that all young children were routinely sleeping with parents for some part of the night, even if only for a few hours. It's an evolutionary thing:

According to Ferber [Dr Richard Ferber, author of *Solve Your Child's Sleep Problems*], the trouble with letting a child who fears sleeping alone into your bed is that 'you are not really solving the problem. There must be a reason why he is so fearful.' Yes, there must. Here's one candidate. Maybe your child's brain was selected by natural selection over millions of years during which mothers slept with their babies. Maybe back then if babies found themselves alone at night it often meant bad news (that the mother had been eaten by a beast, say). Maybe the young brain is designed to respond to this situation by screaming so that any relatives within earshot will discover the child. Maybe, in short, the reason that kids left alone sound terrified is that kids left alone naturally get terrified. Just a theory.

Robert Wright, author and co-sleeping father

THE RULES OF CUDDLING

Cultural rules tell us whether we should welcome or exclude our babies in the night. Whether we are heading for harmony or havoc depends on the clash between the rules and reality. For instance, a study of American urban sleep habits showed that the main difference between black and white families lay not in children's behaviour, but in parental attitude.

Co-sleeping occurred in both black and white homes, but black families were far more likely to sleep with their babies from the very beginning, and to share the bed all night, every night. White families tended not to sleep with babies under one, but began co-sleeping after this. They also tended to let the child into the bed halfway through the night, rather than start off co-sleeping. And in the white families (but not the black) co-sleeping was associated with family stress, such as illness, the arrival of a sibling, or recent separation.

In other words, black families co-slept as a matter of routine or tradition, while white families did so as a response to their children's expressed needs, especially once children were old enough to wander into their parents' room. Since they felt that answering their children's pleadings was 'giving in', white parents were more likely to feel bad about co-sleeping and to view it as a symptom of a wider sleep problem. Black families merely accepted that their children needed them at night. White parents were failing according to their own set of rules, while black parents were thriving on theirs.

Sleep Bonding

It makes me laugh, the amount of us who lived in our house – two full families, with grandparents, the odd aunt or uncle, all the kids and the parents. All sharing beds and sleeping top to toe.

Gilda O'Neill, author, remembers a childhood in London's East End

The East End of London was a tough place to be in the first half of the twentieth century: people had few belongings and barely scraped a living; disease was rife and living conditions in the back-to-back slums were unsanitary. But the vibrancy of community life and the strength of the East End character were both legendary.

Sleeping patterns are a strong indicator of cultural values. Western babies learn to sleep alone in order to foster self-reliance, and traditional societies sleep in family groups to encourage community values. The irony is that self-reliance is best learned from a position of security. Co-sleeping in particular provides a source of strength for individuals who find themselves struggling for survival, a situation which was true for all the hunter-gatherer tribes of our human past, but which could also be applied to the urban poor today.

If sleep is part of our cultural education, then co-sleeping teaches us about community. It also allows the baby to forge unconscious emotional bonds with his family. The strongest communities sleep communally – as though bonding were an involuntary activity, something that happens when we are not looking.

When we considered trends in breastfeeding (Chapter 8: Feelings and Fashions), we saw that many non-western mothers were attracted by the idea of bottle-feeding. Formula milks, an expensive and difficult-to-obtain commodity, quickly gain social status in countries where breastfeeding used to be universal. But night-time separation does not, it seems, have the same allure. In India, for instance, co-sleeping has nothing to do with social class:

One of our first discoveries was that Indian families sleep together at night. At first, we thought this might be due to the cramped living conditions among the poorer families; but over the years, we observed this sleeping arrangement across all the socioeconomic levels of society. We learned that it is simply the age-old Indian way. Even wealthy families who have adopted such Western accoutrements as TVs, cars, fashion, and houses filled with fancy furniture cling to this ancient custom.

Leslie Jacobs, American mother who lived and
worked in south India for sixteen years

Co-sleeping is a tradition which Asian and African families have happily imported to Britain and America. Despite awareness of the western ideal and warnings from white health professionals, most immigrant families persist in sleeping together. A recent study of two generations of Punjabi families in Britain showed that, while many new mothers were keen to bottle-feed, they still preferred to keep their babies near them at night: 'He had a cot but he never slept in it. He used to wake up every hour and it was too painful. I had to come down and feed him.

Eventually I just picked him up and put him in my bed'
(Graduate Muslim mother living in Britain).

Co-sleeping continues among Asian immigrant families in
Britain, and not purely because of lack of space. Sleeping together
seems to be a fundamental way of expressing the ancient community ethic, and Punjabi children may be allowed to sleep with
another family member up to the age of eight or nine. In a 1993
study, ninety-four per cent of British Asian babies slept in their
parents' bedrooms compared with sixty-one per cent of whites.
The same trend has been observed among Hispanic immigrant
families in East Harlem, New York, where eighty per cent of
children share a room with their parents.

Where we sleep changes our feeling of belonging.

Reasons to Snuggle Up

Co-sleeping is like the fine print at the bottom of the breastfeeding contract.

John Scabrook, American author and journalist

Sleeping with a baby allows the mother to nurse without being
unduly disturbed; to respond immediately should he become ill
or stop breathing; to reassure him with the unconditional acceptance of human touch; and to sleep while he sleeps, without the
need to wake fully, or soothe him after the stress of periodic abandonment. Here are some of the benefits as the world sees them.

In the Gusii culture of Kenya, where all mothers and babies
co-sleep, there is an explicit rule that a nursing mother should
never stay away from her baby overnight. Co-sleeping promotes
breastfeeding. A study from America recently demonstrated that
babies who share their mother's bed nurse three times as much
during the night as babies who sleep alone (night feeds are particularly beneficial for keeping the milk supply flowing and
ensuring contraceptive protection).

Younger babies consume around half of their milk intake at

night. Since the breasts produce milk just as much at night as they do during waking hours, the baby's frequent suckling eases congestion in the milk ducts and helps to prevent engorgement or mastitis.

A breastfeeding mother does not enter the fourth, or deepest, stage of sleep, but sleeps lightly throughout the night, never having to wake fully in order to feed. This is in harmony with her evolutionary role as the baby's protector and source of all his comfort and nurture.

Indian parents say that family sleeping strengthens the nerves and calms the baby. Indian children associate going to bed with warmth and security, not isolation or punishment – and they show no resistance to going to sleep.

Co-sleeping allows busy parents more loving contact with their babies. For the Maori of New Zealand, co-sleeping is a '*taonga*', a treasure, or much-prized ancient practice which literally puts parents and children in touch. It also greatly adds to self-confidence, so long as parents are happy and not resentful about the arrangement.

Fathers can do a tremendous amount of baby-bonding while they sleep. Even dads who are absent during the day may get their fill of child-contact at night. Japanese children traditionally sleep between both parents, to symbolise their role as a river which flows between two riverbanks. The baby is intimately connected to his parents, as a river is to its bed. A slightly different arrangement is described here in this domestic scene from south-east Asia, but the father is just as involved:

Our house is all one room but it is very nice. The floor is earth. If you want to sleep, you take some bamboo, you cut it open and split it into small pieces that are springy and make it into a bed. We sleep next to the fireplace where it is warm because we don't have any blankets. My husband sleeps on one side holding a baby. I sleep on the other side holding another baby, and the older children keep each other warm.

Foua, Hmong mother from Laos

Ache mothers of the Paraguayan forest do not lie beside their babies to co-sleep, but – astonishingly – sleep in a hunched sitting position, their babies carefully cradled in their laps. This arrangement is to protect the babies from the dangers of the forest. Co-sleeping is indeed protective of babies, as it allows parents to respond instantly to infants' needs, whether they are cold or overheated, sick, in pain or prone to attack from wild animals.

Co-sleeping parents quickly develop a sixth sense about their babies in the night, and new sleep laboratory footage from Britain and America shows how mothers care for their babies in many ways while still half-asleep. Sleeping lightly is a skill most cultures value highly. It allows people to be awake enough for personal safety, to care for babies and to be woken occasionally without the misery of being unable to return to sleep:

At night his mother sleeps beside him, her skin next to his, as always, while she breathes and moves and sometimes snores a little. She wakens often during the night to tend the fire, holding him close as she rolls out of her hammock and slips to the floor, where he is sandwiched between her thigh and ribs as she rearranges the logs. If he awakens hungry in the night he signals with a soft grunt if he cannot find her breast; she will then give it to him, and again his well-being will be re-established.

Jean Liedloff, continuum therapist, observes the Yequana of Venezuela

Western society's love of deep sleep is bizarre in any context. Most people wake at night – it's the ones who are unable to doze off again who have the problem. For babies, light sleep is a blessing which may even save their lives (see 'A Sudden Death', later in this chapter).

Babies are born with a flexible sleeping skill, which co-sleeping allows them to hone and retain. It makes them easy sleepers for the rest of their lives. Co-sleeping with a baby re-educates most parents into a lighter style of sleep. If willing, they learn to sleep lightly and well in the living environment of the family bed.

Small babies have poor temperature control when they lose touch with other humans. Skin-to-skin contact and co-sleeping make babies' temperature control more efficient. A recent study from Bristol, England, showed that even though the external temperature of a co-sleeping baby may soar, his core temperature remains stable, or even lower than when he sleeps alone. The researchers speculate that either the lone baby is more stressed than the co-sleeping baby, or that the baby becomes, through human contact, better able to regulate his own temperature.

Co-sleeping matches the evolutionary expectations of babies. The modern sleep police are unlikely to call round, and the ancient needs of our 'stone-age' babies may be met in peace: 'It is a primitive need of the child to have close and warm contact with another person's body while falling asleep, but this runs counter to all the rules of hygiene which demand that children sleep by themselves and not share the parental bed' (Anna Freud, psychoanalyst).

Co-sleeping babies cry less and sleep more. Observation of Hispanic and other co-sleeping mothers in America has shown that they respond more swiftly to babies' needs when sleeping nearby. Biological anthropologist Professor James McKenna, who runs the Mother-and-Baby Behavioural Sleep Lab in Indiana, says the co-sleeping pair perform a synchronised dance throughout the night, their movements and breathing patterns stimulating and harmonising with each other.

Research from Bristol, England, likewise shows how co-sleeping mothers repeatedly touch, kiss and reposition their babies throughout the night, without even gaining consciousness. These slight arousals are extremely healthy for the immature, and therefore vulnerable, human infant.

BACK TO THE WOMB

The picture which appeared in the papers perfectly captured the story. Here are two tiny babies – wired up in the manner of most babies in intensive care – and they are sleeping together in an incubator built for one. One of the twins has her arm protectively around the other. They are Kyrie and Brielle Jackson of Westminster, Massachusetts, whose story may have saved a life and changed the lives of many twin babies in America.

Kyrie and Brielle, identical twins who had shared the same placenta, were born twelve weeks premature in October 1995. In her incubator, the larger twin, Kyrie started to gain weight and improve rapidly. Her two-pound sister, however, was failing. Brielle's heart rate soared, her oxygen levels plummeted and she became increasingly stressed. Although her mother, Heidi, held her for a while, Brielle's condition did not improve. The staff nurse, having heard about a European practice of bedding twins together, suggested that the girls might like to be reunited:

> 'We moved Kyrie way over to the other side [of her crib] and put Brielle next to her' [said Heidi]. 'It was really quite amazing . . . Brielle just snuggled right up against her and fell asleep.'
>
> Almost immediately, Brielle's heart rate and breathing improved. 'My husband and I looked at each other and at Gayle [the nurse] and she said, "I can't believe it!" We stared at her for 10 minutes to see if she was going to stay like that or whether it was just a fluke. She stayed like that.'
>
> **Liz Corcoran, reporter, interviews Heidi Jackson**

Within minutes, Brielle's blood oxygen readings had stabilised. Weight gain soon followed. The twins were discharged with no more crises in their recovery. A number of American hospitals are now bedding twins together and studies are underway to confirm the positive effects, which are thought to include improvements to heart rate, breathing, weight gain, motor development and parent-infant bonding. There is also a mysterious effect called 'co-regulation', which is where the twins balance and support one another towards a swifter recovery. The twin family bed is, for the newly born, a kind of home-from-home.

Practical Pillow Talk

> Go to sleep upon my breast,
> All the world is sleeping.
> Till the morning's light you'll rest,
> Mother watch is keeping.
>
> Traditional Welsh lullaby

To sleep with baby is an ancient practice which needs explaining and re-inventing to meet the needs and queries of modern parents. Unlike cot-training programmes, there are few rules, but it is worth approaching the family bed with the same awareness and common sense with which we tackle other parenting issues. The two main concerns of western parents are sex (getting some) and smothering (will we roll over on the baby?)

Sex

At four months, does the baby really care if you have sex while he's in the bed? Chances are he'll sleep through it, but even if he doesn't he'll probably think it's funny. And it is funny. (Thank you for reminding us.) But then, at a certain point you definitely want to knock it off, right? At what point is that? Six months? Ten months?

John Seabrook, American author and journalist

Privacy is a commodity which has allowed us to shape our morality, and this involves keeping children in the dark about love-making and sexual activity for as long as possible. Sex, after all, is the sub-text for most bedroom arrangements. It is the reason why little Jamie must sleep alone, but mother and father are allowed to share the comfort of each others' bodies. Small wonder that children are confused and hurt by our refusal to let them into our comfort zone at night.

Sex is not hidden from children in traditional societies. How could it be? Where people share huts and one-roomed houses, gurs and igloos, sex can rarely be practised in complete privacy. And so, despite the warnings of Freudian analysts and modern moralists, many children are raised with a subliminal awareness of sex from the start. This, throughout thousands of years of human evolution, is how children received their first sex education:

At night, when a child lies beside her mother, in front, and her father lies down behind and her mother and father make love, the child watches. Her parents don't worry about her, a small child, and her father just has sex with her mother. Because, even if the child sees, even if she hears her parents doing their work at night, she is unaware of what it is her parents are doing; she is still young, without sense. She just watches and doesn't have any thoughts about it.

Nisa, !Kung San woman of the Kalahari Desert

!Kung San parents, like many other couples living in communal groups, do try to find private places and times to make love. They also wait until their young children are asleep before having sex in their company. But there is a consensus in most traditional societies that small children do not have much sense and that any love-making they witness will be taken at face value and not frighten them. By the time they are five to seven years old, most children have moved into peer-group sleeping huts, partly to avoid increasing curiosity.

The taboo is much stronger in western society, where labels

of child abuse are easily applied to any fudging of sexual mores. Although some western children do, inadvertently, stumble in upon the sex act, rarely do they receive an honest explanation of what they have seen. Few parents would wish their children to start their sexual education this way, as it might cause alarm among their peers, if not the social welfare agencies. Furthermore, some parents find it hard to relax for sex with a baby or toddler in the bed, or even in the room. No, if we are to co-sleep with our children, we must become a little more inventive with our sex lives.

Most parents find sexual activity diminished after the arrival of a baby, wherever he sleeps, and most could use a few new ideas for rekindling romance. Rendezvous in different rooms; evening encounters when the children first doze off; lots of reassuring touching and holding without necessarily expecting intercourse – these are some of the solutions which keep love on the back-burner while babies' needs are still on the boil. If co-sleeping meant the end of your sex life, the human race would simply not be here today.

The good news is that co-sleeping parents get more sleep, because they do not have to stay awake for hours at night soothing the baby. And good sleep is the prerequisite for a healthy libido.

Smothering

If anyone overlays an unbaptized baby, she shall do penance for three years; if unintentionally, two years.

St Hubert, Penitential, c. 850 AD

Another major fear for new co-sleepers is that they might roll over on the baby at night. Smothering (or 'overlaying') was a subject of moral concern for European preachers in the Middle Ages, because mothers might be suspected or accused of infanticide – many such deaths were highly suspicious, as might be expected in a culture which featured intense poverty and no

contraception. Penitentials of the period designate greater punishments for mothers who deliberately overlaid their babies, than
for mothers who 'accidentally' did so.

In the seventeenth century, the Italians even invented a
wooden contraption called the '*arcuccio*' to protect babies from
being smothered in bed. The *arcuccio* had a headboard, side panels
and a hoop around the baby's body, so he could be 'safely laid
entirely under the Bed Cloathes in the Winter without Danger
of smothering'. Into each side panel was cut a semi-circle,
through which the mother or wet nurse might present her breast
for nursing. Florentine wet nurses were obliged to use them or
risk excommunication from the Catholic Church. But many
historians suspect that talk of overlaying was, in any case, a diver-
sion from a less palatable truth:

The euphemistic catchall term *overlaying* used to be involved when infants were
'accidentally' smothered by their caretakers . . . Then as now, one suspects, it was
rare for co-sleeping to result in smothered babies. (Harder mattresses, or forbid-
ding caretakers to drink or take opium, would have been more effective at preventing *true* accidents than prescribing this cumbersome contraption.)

Sarah Blaffer Hrdy, professor of anthropology

Perhaps the *arcuccio* would be useful for the Rajput mothers of
northern India, who tend to cover their babies from head to
toe for the afternoon nap: 'During the day, when the baby is
not in need of food or some other attention, it is placed on a
cot with a quilt or sheet entirely covering it, to protect it from
insects and envious glances. Babies are often so well hidden by
piles of quilts that one cannot detect their presence' (Leigh
Minturn and John Hitchcock, anthropologists).

Safe family sleeping is now seriously explored by scientists
around the world, under the umbrella of cot death research.
Mechanical suffocation of babies under the duvets or pillows is
possible whether the baby is in bed or a cot, but records show
this to be a rare form of infant death.

In 1999, an American study resulted in advice from the United States Consumer Product Safety Commission not to co-sleep, and yet the evidence it was based on clearly demonstrated that overlaying was highly unlikely – much less likely, for instance, than cot death in a cot. Of 3.9 million babies born annually in North America, around a million are estimated to share their parents' beds at night. Over the course of the eight-year study, 120 babies were apparently 'overlaid' in bed. During the same period, around 400 babies were mechanically suffocated by bedding alone in their cots and at least 44,000 died from Sudden Infant Death Syndrome. Every year, in the whole of Britain, there are around half a dozen cases of mechanical suffocation of babies, whether sleeping in a bed or a cot.

However, there are conditions which make bedsharing a dangerous activity for the vulnerable infant. Swaddled or drugged, medieval European babies would have been at risk, since they could not free their limbs or struggle for breath. Drunk, drugged or smoking cigarettes, modern parents may pose an equal danger to the child – and recent research indicates smoking and co-sleeping may be a particularly lethal combination.

Many hours of co-sleeping video evidence from laboratories in America and the UK demonstrate just how responsive mothers are when they sleep by their babies, and how they continue to meet their infants' needs even while asleep. Co-sleeping seems to be a protective activity when it is done with caution. In homes without soft mattresses, drug abuse or alcoholism, and where parents do not smoke, co-sleeping allows parents to respond to their babies' needs instantly in the night, and also provides the human nest which babies have evolved to expect. The house rules for co-sleepers are these:

> Do not smoke
> Do not drink or take drugs
> Use a firm mattress
> Avoid water beds and sofas

Do not co-sleep if you or baby are very ill or
    movement is impaired
Keep pillows away from baby's head
Do not cover baby with bedding
Do not dress baby too warmly
Oh, and Do enjoy a very tactile and healthy
    night's sleep

Weaning

I bless God all my dear children are well. My daughter Nanny is grown almost as tall as I, Susanna breeds her teeth apace. My affection is very equal to them all ... My daughter Nanny is a very good bedfellow and I would by no means part with her.

Frances Hatton writes to her husband Christopher, the governor of Guernsey, England 1678

A third western objection to co-sleeping is the issue of weaning. If we 'give in' to our babies' nightly demands for bodily contact, say detractors, we will pay the price with children who never leave the marital bed. Fear of weaning does not prevent parents from putting their babies in nappies or wheeling them everywhere in a buggy – they know, from personal experience, that most babies one day get toilet trained and start to walk. Children move out of the family bed in much the same way.

Of course, the moment of transition is up to each family (or culture, if there is a parenting consensus). In the past, when people were less afraid that their children would fail to grow up, co-sleeping sometimes continued for as long as the children lived at home.

Each culture has its own ideas about the appropriate length of time for co-sleeping. While Tibetan children sleep with their parents for five to seven years, the time-span for western children is more variable. Since the whole idea is still fairly taboo in America and northern Europe anyway, parents make up their own rules. Some babies are moved out at around six months old, others stay until breastfeeding is over, and yet another subset continues until the child has made the transition to school.

The key is not to be afraid of setting rules and sticking to them. Babies who have their fill of close-contact nurture turn into resilient children, who are perfectly able to adapt.

You're Feeling Very Sleepy

Because sleep is associated with warmth and security, both [Indian] parents are willing to stop whatever they are doing when their children become sleepy, and to lie down with them to put them to sleep. In the families I visited, fathers and mothers took turns doing this each night, depending on who was most available. In lieu of stories or doll play, the bedtime ritual was simply this: the parent would lie down next to the child until the child fell asleep.

Leslie Jacobs, American mother who lived in south India for 16 years

Bedtime routines are given a positive gloss in western society. They are a way of expressing our intense concern for children's sleep. Most families cannot imagine parenting without these rituals, which are anticipated as 'quality time', a chance for intimate one-to-one parent and child interactions at the end of the day. And yet, when viewed by outsiders, our routines are seen merely as elaborate distractions aimed at preparing babies to sleep alone.

In one cross-cultural study of American and Guatemalan (Mayan) parents, Mayan parents were unimpressed by the sophisticated games played by American parents every night. The bath, the teddy bear, the lullabies, the stories, even the cute pyjamas seemed to them poor substitutes for the warmth of the mother's body at night. Equally, the American mothers disapproved of Mayan practice. They felt the close nocturnal bonds created by Guatemalan mothers were emotionally unhealthy; that the trauma of separation was best completed when the baby was still young; and that they themselves would lose their own privacy at night.

Bedtime rituals are neither inherently good nor bad. Babies grow fondly attached to their bath–story–lullaby routine as they would to any special attention. And parents also enjoy the quiet intimacy of a winding-down period. It's the separation which follows which causes the disagreement between cultures.

As we administer these nightly soothers, it may interest us to know that co-sleeping parents engage in far less ritual. Studies indicate that babies who sleep alone are given more complex sleep routines each evening, a compensatory behaviour which parents develop without, perhaps, being aware of it.

SLEEP STROKES

Bedtimes are an excuse for many tactile contacts after a busy day. Many western parents bathe their children before bed, a ritual which calms, cleans and allows for lots of cuddling and patting dry. Babies also enjoy being stroked to sleep and kissed goodnight.

Massage is an excellent way to relax babies before they go to sleep. Parents in Fiji use massage as their bedtime ritual, and so do parents in Nepal:

> We stopped one night at a tea house in the Himalayas ... After the meal, when everything was cleared and put away, the parents began what was obviously a nightly ritual. The baby was lovingly massaged with oil and it was evident that both the parents and the baby thoroughly enjoyed this procedure. The baby was gurgling, the parents were smiling and sharing the task, one doing between the toes while the other concentrated on another area. Eventually the baby fell into a profound and peaceful sleep and the whole family retired contentedly to bed.
>
> **Malcolm and Marjorie Jack, travellers to Nepal**

Lulla Lulla Lullaby

OM TARE TUTTARE TURE SOHA

Green Tara mantra, sung to Tibetan
babies for spiritual protection

Musicologists and anthropologists consider the lullaby to be the single most important early music lesson for humans. This intimate, one-to-one communication between singer and baby has a universal quality which connects mothers, fathers and children of every nationality. We do not need to understand the words to feel calmed by the hypnotic rhymes and repetitive note sequences. Even the tiniest baby stops to listen to the marriage of mother-tongue and tune, in a melody that is only a step away from baby talk.

The traditional lullaby uses syllables that soothe, often at the expense of serious meaning. It is, perhaps, the simplest form of song, an art form which requires almost no art. However, birth researcher Michel Odent suggests that traditional lullabies are easily forgotten. On a trip to meet Berber families in Algeria, he encountered an eighty-year-old woman and her granddaughters in their twenties. The young mothers were unable to sing the lullabies which the old grandmother had remembered all her life. But new lullabies are soon created: singing to a baby is an invitation to improvise.

In fact, the only essential part of the lullaby is the 'lull'. Lulling a baby to sleep implies a literal 'lull-lulling' of the tongue, in sympathetic harmonies designed to catch the baby's ear and calm his nerves. In Tibetan families, the lullaby may be a mantra, a protective incantation, repeated over and over in soothing tones. Among families in the Herat region of Afghanistan (before the 1979 Soviet invasion), researchers found a web of musical taboos which meant that few songs were sung to children by their parents. Lullabies were the exception: and at their most basic, these consisted of many repetitions of the phrase

'Allah Hu'. 'Closely associated with the rhythm of the rocking cradle and the trancelike state before sleep, the lullaby was undoubtedly an important early musical experience common to virtually all Herati children' (Veronica Doubleday, researcher and John Baily, ethno-musicologist in Afghanistan). Perhaps there is even an ancient linguistic connection between primitive lulling and the Arabic word for Allah, or God.

Lullabies, instinctual communications which make loving music to our babies' ears, seem somehow fundamental to early human learning. No society yet recorded, from the remotest pygmy tribe to the most sophisticated urban western elite, has tried to rear its babies without these simple songs. Perhaps all this mother-and-baby music will, one day, become worthy of scientific exploration:

In a futuristic encyclopaedia 'lullaby' might cover pages, with numerous sub-headings. The topic will become so vast that the editor will need the cooperation of a multi-disciplinary team – experts in human development will evaluate the role of sensory stimulation associated with lullabies; experts in brain asymmetry will explain why most mothers cradle their babies on the left-hand side when singing lullabies; physiologists will explore the transition from a waking state to a sleeping state; anthropologists . . . etc.

Michel Odent, obstetrician and primal health researcher

We cannot leave the subject of lullabies without a mention of the most common reason for all this lulling: the desire to ease a baby into sleep. This seems to be the primary function of the restful songs which are hummed and whispered from America to Africa every evening as the sun goes down.

A WORLD OF SLEEP SONGS

A trawl through the lyrics of the world's lullabies is like wading through an unconscious mind. It is clear (from the mention of distant fathers) that the mother is the usual purveyor of infant lullabies, and that though the tune may be gentle and the tone soft, the words sometimes betray women's deepest desires and fears for their tiny babes. We have . . .

* *the hypnotic* – simple repetitions of lulling syllables, gently exhorting the baby to sleep. Korean mothers repeat the word 'sleep' over and over again; one Jewish lullaby just says 'sleep my child . . .'
* *the promise of reward* – one Greek cradle song pledges that the child will receive the city of Alexandria filled with sugar, all of Cairo filled with rice and finally, a three-year reign over Constantinople. A Mexican lullaby offers 'pretty toys', while the traditional American song 'Mocking Bird' gives a long list of gifts from Daddy, including a diamond ring, a billy goat and – of course – a mocking bird. In Surinam, South America, the stakes are not so high: the baby will receive a cucumber.
* *the ambitious* – a Jewish lullaby for a boy talks, for instance, of his future as a rabbi, or spiritual leader. Some songs imagine baby girls getting married and baby boys becoming successful hunters.
* *the religious* – lullabies from Spain, Germany and throughout Europe compare the baby's sleep to the slumber of the infant Jesus. Such songs often invoke spiritual protection for the child – from angels, for instance – or, in the case of the Muslim lullaby, from the prophets of Islam.
* *the weather report* – lullabies often give a brief local geography and climate lesson. Swiss mothers sing of mountains and shepherds, Hebridean mothers off the north coast of Scotland sing of the

moaning sea-mew (seagull), while mothers on the coast of Ireland tell their babies to sleep on despite the roar of the rolling waves.

* *the vague threat* – 'Rock-a-Bye Baby', the English favourite, is also sung to an old Native American tune by parents in America. The threat of the bough breaking and cradle falling is not so very sinister when you compare it with all the falling and catching lap songs that babies delight in. Nevertheless, some lullabies do have a less protective feel to them. One American rhyme promises to wrap the baby up in calico and send her off to daddy-o if she won't fall asleep.

* *the song of the absent father* – from the English: 'Bye Baby Bunting, Daddy's gone a-hunting', to '*Ferme tes yeux*' (Close your eyes), a traditional Breton lullaby which reassures the baby that mother is here, even though father is '*là haut*' (off and away) and the modern Zulu: 'Your father's on the train, It will take him into town, And we must wait'.

Can't Sleep, Won't Sleep

The best sleeping tablet may be the one that is never taken but placed by the bedside. Knowing that it is there, ready for use just in case, can be very reassuring.

Dr Jim Horne, sleep researcher

Dr Horne is talking about sleeping drugs for adults, but there is also a long and unfortunate history of sleep-inducing drugs for babies. Infant sleeplessness – a rare condition in some cultures, but commonplace in others – can wreak havoc on family life. Depending on the medicine available in any given society, children are often treated with whatever is to hand. For some, that means a spiritual cure; for others, it implies something even stronger . . .

A little sleep magic
If a baby refuses to sleep, Seri parents in New Mexico attempt

a magical cure. The traditional healer collects twigs from the nest of 'the bird who sleeps in the afternoon'. These are burned in four little piles on four mounds of sand around the baby. The healer sings to the spirit of the bird, calling on her to cure the baby's crying and help him sleep.

In America, the Pennsylvania German mother places an open Holy Bible under the pillow of a child who has difficulty falling asleep:

> . . . and there is treasure kept,
> While one short, fervent prayer she said,
> And lo! her darling sweetly slept!
>
> Amish poem

Peaceful sleep is ensured for all babies of the Pacific island of Okinawa, through a birth ritual known as '*mansang*'. Six days after the birth, celebrations are held to thank the deities for the health of mother and baby. A female elder (priestess) on the father's side says a prayer over a tray of rice, rice wine and incense. She offers thanks to the ancestors and nature gods for the health of mother and baby – and prays that the child will sleep peacefully and not be troubled in the night.

A herbal remedy

Dill is the supreme sleep-inducing herb. Its name comes from the Old Norse 'dilla', meaning to lull, and Scandinavian mothers would feed their babies a weak dill tea to help them sleep. Breastfeeding mothers prefer to sip the tea themselves, or stuff the child's pillow with dill seeds.

Essential oil of lavender was used in medieval Germany and France to sweeten and sterilise the atmosphere of a room. It is a calming herb, and a few drops of lavender oil on a handkerchief near the baby are said to encourage sleep.

* Herbs which induce calm include limeflower, lavender and chamomile. Make a strong infusion of fresh herbs and add to

the child's bedtime bath. Chamomile tea was given to rest-less children by mothers in medieval Europe.

* Honey warmed in milk is used in many countries as a sedative combination.
* Neroli oil is made from the freshly-picked flowers of the Seville bitter orange tree which grows in the Mediterranean. One or two drops in a light carrier oil can be used to massage a child who has trouble falling to sleep.
* In Sweden, mothers traditionally place a sprig of Lady's Mantle (Alchemilla vulgaris) under the pillow of their children to promote calm slumber.
* Children who suffer from nightmares may be given a weak tea made with thyme – just two to six teaspoons before bed. Or place a fresh cutting of the herb inside the child's pillow.

A Sudden Death

In the evolutionary and cross-cultural view, light sleep is normal and a deep six hours is pathological.

Meredith Small, ethno-paediatrician

Sudden Infant Death Syndrome accounts for around ten per cent of infant deaths in America, the UK and other parts of Europe. It is the leading cause of baby deaths, annually killing five times more children than leukaemia and thirteen times more than meningitis. It is not a disease, but, as its name suggests, a collection of symptoms and conditions or rather, a lack of symptoms and conditions. In Britain, approximately eight apparently healthy babies a week die in their sleep. When found, they seem to have simply stopped breathing and post-mortems reveal no other reasons as to why they died.

While the West struggles to understand the ongoing, mysterious deaths of so many babies between one and nine months, other cultures watch with interest. For cot death is not a universal phenomenon. SIDS is so rare in some countries and among certain ethnic groups that it does not qualify as a syndrome at all.

Travelling through China in the 1970s – when cot death was at its height in Britain – Dr Michel Odent tried to ask doctors about their SIDS rates. Neither the doctors nor the more westernised translators knew what he was talking about:

Nobody understood my questions; the concept of sudden infant death or cot death was apparently unknown among professionals and lay people in such different places as Peking, Hsian, Loyang, Nanking, Shanghai, and Canton. Furthermore I learned that Chinese babies sleep with their mothers, even in the most westernized families, such as the families of interpreters. Ever since then I have held the view that, even if it happens during the day, cot death is a disease of babies who spend their nights in an atmosphere of loneliness and that cot death is a disease of societies where the nuclear family has taken over.

Michel Odent, obstetrician and primal health researcher

Odent's hunch proved increasingly accurate over the next thirty years, as SIDS research gathered pace. Meanwhile, other medically-trained ex-pats were noticing a similar lack of SIDS phenomena around the world. British paediatrician Dr David Davies noted only fifteen cases of cot death diagnosed and recorded during a five-year residency In Hong Kong. At home, up to 1,200 deaths would have been expected for this size of population. Of the fifteen cases reported, eleven were ethnic Chinese babies, three British and one Japanese – a higher proportion of western babies than would be expected from the racial mix on the island.

British doctors in Africa were also beginning to report on the lack of cot death cases arriving at their A&E departments. And back in the West, researchers investigating the lifestyles of immigrant Asian populations found they, too, had lower cot death rates than the surrounding white population. In Yorkshire, a twenty-two-month study of Pakistani and white families found that white babies were three times more likely to die of SIDS than Pakistani babies. Dr Davies, who was by now studying Bangladeshi babies in Cardiff as professor of paediatrics at the University of Wales, was able to corroborate his earlier speculations from Hong Kong:

Bangladeshi babies are thought to be vulnerable, and they sleep close to other people both day and night; at night they are either in the mother's bed or in a cot next to it . . . It is not simply a question of space, but of a belief that, as one mother put it, 'I like to wake up in the night and see all my family around me.' . . .

Long periods of lone quiet sleep may be one factor that contributes to a higher rate of sudden deaths in white than in Asian infants.

D.P. Davies, professor of paediatrics

Those cultures which appear to be immune to the ravages of cot death are also cultures without cots. Exactly what is going on here? Why should Asian and African babies have some of the lowest risks of cot death in the world? Why is the cot-death rate in Hong Kong, even today, twenty-three times lower than in Britain? For the answers, we need to look more closely at the baby's sleep environment.

First, we should remember just how neurologically immature the human infant really is. At birth, he is more undeveloped and helpless than babies of any other species. One of the most important developmental changes a human baby must endure is the shift in breathing patterns, as he prepares for speech. Between two and four months, when babies are most susceptible to SIDS, he goes from around eighty-seven to forty-seven breaths per minute. At this age, too, he is particularly responsive to human touch.

By keeping a baby next to his mother at night – the place where his sleep evolved over millennia – his sleep environment comes alive. Here is the breastmilk, which he is designed to drink on and off throughout the twenty-four hours. Here is movement and warmth, touch, heat and gas exchange, all of which have been shown to stimulate regular, healthy breathing.

Here is a swift response to any signs of distress, as witnessed by the research team at the Anne Diamond Sleep Lab in Bristol, England.

Sleeping (typically) 20 to 30 cm apart, facing each other, mother and baby are practising the art of healthy, light sleep which was known to all humans before they became too civilised. Babies, far from being encouraged to sleep as deeply and for as long as possible (according to the western ideal) spend less time in sleep stages three and four. Breastfeeding episodes double, although they don't last so long, and mothers are often seen to fall asleep on the job. In cramped homes, where the baby is never alone or in hunter-gatherer nomadic lifestyles, where babies are slept with and carried everywhere, the baby is surrounded day and night by human stimulation. This stimulation may help him to stay alive.

'Busy homes make babies less liable to cot death' says one newspaper headline. While western parents painstakingly create hushed, laboratory-style conditions for their infants to sleep in, babies in traditional cultures must muddle along with the rest of the family and are almost never alone. Modern Tibetan families raise their babies in much the same lively environment which was once common in medieval England, in a bed in the centre of the house: 'Lhamo settled on a bed in the main room, which would serve as a focal point for the activities of the house during the day. Here Lhamo could easily pick up, nurse and play with her new daughter. The baby lay next to her, sleeping when she liked' (Anne Hubbell Maiden, psychologist, and Edie Farwell, anthropologist, observe postnatal practices among Tibetan families).

Even noise vibrations are known to be helpful in protecting children against breathing irregularities. The uncommon quietness of the modern nursery bears no resemblance to the busy community life of the traditional community, and acoustics specialists are now looking at the possibility that a certain amount of sound and vibration is necessary to stimulate key functions in the baby. Babies need a human context in order to thrive – and for some, the context may be more crucial than others.

HOME TRUTHS

Things have really changed for us, it's not like it was . . . except unfortunately for one thing – we keep on giving birth to stone-age babies. These little twenty-first-century creatures want to be held, all the time if possible, against our bodies, close to our hearts to hear that familiar beat . . . These babies . . . even go so far as to vomit up . . . expensive [bottle] formulas, soiling the 100% cotton sheets, the allergy-free mattress, staining the natural woodwork, alone in their designer cot with every safety device. No, it's not just during the day they follow their ancient instincts, but it goes on into the night, when they need to be snuggled down between the two bodies who first gave them life.

We have come a long way. Let's go back to our babies.

Julie Whitfield, member of La Leche League GB, breastfeeding support group

In Turkey, they have a saying: 'If you want to learn something, listen to the children.' And that is what many western parents do. Despite the cultural taboo against cuddling each other in the night, lots of parents respond to their crying toddlers and children by taking them into the family bed. They may not mean to, they may not find it easy, but when resistance is low, they'll do anything for a good night's sleep.

The only difference between this pattern and most of the rest of the world is that other parents co-sleep from the beginning. They do it all night, every night, without waiting to be prompted by a baby's cries or a toddler toddling in. Of course, they don't call it anything as technical as co-sleeping. It's just sleeping. Holding your baby at night doesn't require a technical name when it is the unquestioned practice of millennia.

The point is not that we should all immediately sleep with our babies – although the babies certainly wouldn't argue. While constant night nurture is the perfect solution for some, it is disruptive for others, whose own sleep training has left them with a preference for privacy. But no parent should feel guilty because her baby struggles to sleep alone, or straight through the night. It helps to realise that it's not the babies' fault – they were designed that way – and that cultural rules sometimes make things harder than they need to be.

We don't need more rules, we just need to listen to our own children's individual needs. We might treat them with sympathy when they beg for our company at night. We should not feel bad about cuddling our babies to sleep, rocking them in our arms, or in a cradle next to our bed, nursing them as often as they desire or lavishing them with human touch.

We might make a point of singing the old lullabies, because – like a chain letter through time – these connect us to our grandparents and the generations before them. Cuddles and songs are pleasures which will one day light up our great-great-great grandchildren's eyes. They are a lifeline from the far distant past to the unimaginable future.

Night nurture is not a hard-line concept, but a question of degrees. If we want to help raise easy, flexible sleepers for the future, we might begin by being easy and flexible with our babies.

13. Mind Over Matter

When a baby falls ill, parents can feel powerless as never before. At least, this is often true in the West, where mothers and fathers have a limited framework for explaining disease. While western doctors use powerful medicines to help in the fight against infection, other parents must rely to some extent on spiritual support. Here are some magical attitudes to childhood illness, its diagnosis and treatment – and infant death . . .

The Roots of Illness

Although the Hmong believe that illness can be caused by a variety of sources – including eating the wrong food, drinking contaminated water, being affected by a change in the weather, failing to ejaculate completely during sexual intercourse, neglecting to make offerings to one's ancestors, being punished for one's ancestors' transgressions, being cursed, being hit by a whirlwind, having a stone implanted in one's body by an evil spirit master, having one's blood sucked by a *dab* [fairy], bumping into a *dab* who lives in a tree or a stream, digging a well in a *dab*'s living place, catching sight of a dwarf female *dab* who eats earthworms, having a *dab* sit on one's chest while one is sleeping, doing one's laundry in a lake inhabited by a dragon, pointing one's finger at the full moon, touching a newborn mouse, killing a large snake, urinating on a rock that looks like a tiger, urinating on or kicking a benevolent house spirit, or having bird droppings fall on one's head – by far the most common cause of illness is soul loss.

Anne Fadiman, journalist and author,
among the Hmong people of south-east Asia

Our systems of medicine divide us almost as completely as our religions. Beliefs about illness and health, including the cause, interpretation and treatment of disease, are as diverse as humanity itself. In this field, western parents have good reason to give thanks for their place of birth. We only have to compare our infant mortality statistics with those from traditional societies, or those of our own recent past, to realise how lucky we are. More of our babies will be born with a good chance of a long and healthy life than any babies throughout history.

Most of us are pretty sure we understand the roots of illness and how to avoid it. We know that the real causes begin with social deprivation and poverty, inadequate diet and stress – we also believe that germs and bad luck play a significant part. We no longer see fairies lurking in every corner of the natural landscape waiting to trip us up as we go about our daily business. We do not see the danger in 'doing the laundry in a lake inhabited by a dragon' (apart from the chill one might expect to catch). We do not believe in dragons, we rarely venture into lakes and we do our laundry without even getting our hands wet.

While the Hmong system of medicine is based on that culture's unique lifestyle and ancient beliefs, ours is based on our own unique western lifestyle and a relative lack of faith in anything. When we are ill, we take a pill. But when you believe that the world is full of magical and mysterious forces, of which you are a part, the causes of infant illness expand enormously. Tibetan parents believe in twenty-four spirit disorders which may possess a small child: these may be aggressive or passive, male or female, animal or ghost-like, hot or cold. Symptoms of spirit possession include sudden fear, crying, refusing to breastfeed and fever.

The !Kung San of Africa's Kalahari Desert believe, like most traditional peoples, in benign and malicious spirits which inhabit their natural world. Here a mother describes the bird which caused the death of her second child:

Bau was growing. She'd crawl around and play . . . The sickness came from her little chest and it killed her. The medicine men tried to cure her, but they said the sickness was coming from a bird, one that hovers in the air, one that comes from the heavens and is sent by God. The spirit of the bird entered her and killed her.

Nisa, !Kung San woman

Fontanelles of Wisdom

It is believed that placing a dab of butter on the soft spot on top of the baby's head for the first seven to ten days of his or her life will make the baby strong bodily and spiritually.

Anne Hubbell Maiden, psychologist and Edie Farwell, anthropologist

Around 1.5 million years ago, human brains suddenly expanded to about double their previous size. One million years later, they doubled again to reach the proportions with which we are familiar today, all of which made giving birth a much more arduous process for females of the Homo Erectus genus. The conundrum which evolution had created was that the enlarged infant head was now simply too big to squeeze though the bipedal pelvis of his mother. If the pelvis became any wider, women would not be able to walk on two legs. If the infant's head became smaller, humans would have been forced to regress in intelligence and adaptability.

Nature's compromise was the unfinished infant skull, a phenomenon which zoologist Desmond Morris calls 'a remarkable piece of human engineering'. At birth, babies' heads may look irregular or elongated, and shortly afterwards, one or two soft spots are noticeable on the top of the head. These are the fontanelles, the 'little fountains', which look as if they are holding in water, rather like the cover on a swimming pool.

There are six fontanelles, in fact, of various sizes, spaces in the unfused skull which allow the newborn head to mould its way through the narrow birth passage during labour. Nature's plan works reasonably well, provided the baby is not simply too big overall for his mother's pelvis. But as a consequence of this evolutionary compromise, the baby's brain arrives unfinished and, unlike many other animals, he is unable to do anything for himself.

After birth, the fontanelles take a long time to fuse – from four months to four years, depending on the child. Perhaps there is a reason for this – the fontanelles have their uses in the early weeks and months. They are known by parents all over the world as a gauge to their baby's health. When he is well, the baby's anterior fontanelle pulses visibly. This may look alarming, but it is a good sign – after all, the soft spots are not delicate, but protected with strong membranes. When the fontanelle sags or bulges, or stops pulsating, then parents know something is wrong.

Most cultures have wisdoms which help to protect the fontanelles and promote their use as a kind of health oracle.

* The Wana of Sulawesi say that the major fontanelle is actually the seat of the baby's soul. They believe each person has a dreaming soul, which looks like the individual in embryo and lives in the fontanelle. When the skin is visibly pulsating on a baby, it is a sign that his dreaming soul is alive and well.
* In some African traditions, a weakened fontanelle is called '*chiponde*', and is believed to be the root of a baby's illness.
* The people of Cuba, Mexico and Puerto Rico have a disease known as '*caida de la mollera*' (fallen fontanelle) in babies under one. They say this condition, which is accompanied by vomiting and diarrhoea, is caused by removing the breast too rapidly from the suckling baby's mouth, so 'displacing' his internal organs. This theory evidently safeguards breastfeeding, which is highly protective against the menace of vomiting and diarrhoea. '*Caida de la mollera*' is a perfect circle of diagnosis and appropriate treatment.

Whatever your background or beliefs, the fontanelle can be used to give you a clearer idea of you baby's health. A sunken soft spot is not, in itself, the cause of disease, but it may be one of various signs that the baby is dehydrated. This is an acute condition which should be treated immediately, especially when accompanied by other symptoms like vomiting or fever. When your baby cries, you may notice that his fontanelle bulges slightly, and as he calms down, it may sink a little. If bulging persists or becomes extreme, it may be a sign of pressure on the baby's brain – a doctor should be consulted straight away.

Fontanelle wisdom is an excellent example of wildly different cross-cultural beliefs which point to a similar conclusion. Sometimes we need to look beyond cultural theories to their practical effects.

Fairy-Tales

> Baloo, balili, baloo, balili,
> Baloo, balili, baloo, ba.
> Gae awa' peerie fairies, gae awa' peerie fairies,
> Gae awa' peerie faeries, Frae oor bairn noo.
>
> The Bressay Lullaby, Shetland traditional

Anthropologists love to tell us how much parents in other cultures dote on their offspring. Children are ardently desired, say western writers. Small children are 'much-loved', 'over-indulged', 'pampered', 'treasured'. ('The phrase "spoilt to death" goes through one's mind,' wrote journalist Peter Popham in 1997 on the reincarnation and inauguration of a new Tibetan lama, four-year-old Ugyen Tendzin Jigme Lyundrup, 'though as all children in the east are indulged it probably does not apply.')

In biological terms, human babies are K-selected. This means that we have a few infants, each of whom requires an enormous investment of our effort and time. (We may be compared with r-selected species, such as insects, who produce a large number of offspring at a rapid rate and invest little time in nurturing each baby.) Add to this the fact that in some places more than half of children die before their first birthday and emotion is understandably heightened around the time of birth. This is a passionate story of global proportions, the need to make babies and to keep them safe, healthy and happy. It is the story of 1.5 million years of the human genus, of longing and perseverance in the face of frequent tragedy.

So it is not surprising that many societies came to believe in magical powers which were jealous of the bonny newborn baby. Small wonder that the new arrival, so anticipated, so desired, should be the potential object of malicious sorcery. How else could people explain the sudden deterioration of a previously healthy infant? Why else should so many coveted children fall ill or die despite the best efforts of a loving family and supportive community?

BABY SNATCHERS

In folk belief, there is a wide cast of characters waiting in the wings to cast a spell and make a small baby fall ill. Norwegian parents used to fear the nocturnal activities of malevolent trolls, while the Balinese believe in a whole cast of baby-threatening characters, from witches to fearsome beasts, bad-spirited rivers and unkind trees. The Scots said it was fairies you had to beware of, mischievous Fey Folk who liked nothing better than to steal a baby's soul. The ritual to counter this involved fire: a flaming torch was carried sunwise around the mother and newborn, creating an invincible barrier against spiritual intrusion. Once a naming ceremony had also taken place, the baby was thought to be safe from fairy magic.

In some societies, the danger is thought to stem from other humans, who – wittingly or unwittingly – carry the curse of the evil eye. Evil eye is so common a phenomenon throughout the world that we can only assume people found it a very persuasive explanation for ill-health. In a culture where babies are as vulnerable as they are desirable, it must be easy to scape-goat other members of the community – especially women without children, a potent source of jealousy. It is usually other women whose ill-wishing is said to be the cause of trouble. Here, a mother describes her beliefs and actions whenever her baby sickens:

He was victim of the evil eye on several occasions. Whenever I gave him a bath and put nice clothes on him, he felt unwell. This happened many times in Pakistan, but not in this country. Whenever it happened I touched the child with chillies and threw them into the fire, and sometimes I took a little sand or dust from underneath the feet of the child and threw that in the fire.

Muslim mother living in Britain

But evil eye is not merely a cycle of blame and recrimination. It is a complete healing system, with diagnosis and treatment, a catalogue of herbs, charms and rituals to offset any ill-effects.

Gusii mothers of Kenya call the belief in evil eye magic '*oko-biriria*'. Small, pale-skinned babies are vulnerable to other women's bewitching stares and, once affected, small 'particles' – a feather, fibres, flower pollen or grain – may adhere to the baby's skin. These become absorbed by the body and may eventually kill the infant. Avoidance of particles (or what western parents might call 'germs') requires daily washing and oiling of the baby, constant carrying and keeping him off the ground.

Among Hispanic immigrants to America, '*mal ojo*' is believed to inflict babies when someone admires them without touching. The symptoms may start with wakefulness and extended crying. A folk healer ('*curandero*') can be called in, but the easiest cure is for the admirer to touch, hold and care for the baby. This unexpectedly simple remedy ensures that babies are passed around, stroked and patted as much as possible.

In old Europe, as in India today, it was commonly believed that a baby's hair or nail clippings could be used in black magic. Only the mother was allowed to bite the baby's nails (biting still being preferred by many parents to the use of sharp scissors).

Similarly in Morocco, a new baby is not to be left alone in the first week after birth, in case a '*jinni*' or evil spirit snatches him, substituting one of her own children. So babies are carried everywhere. These are just a few of many examples where belief in sorcery promotes more solicitous infant care.

And according to one child-health researcher in Egypt, evil eye is more often used to explain tragic events than to over-protect children: 'No mother prevents her child from socializing or appearing in front of others . . . In fact, if others are envious of a child, it is considered a compliment to the mother, especially the young mother' (Homa Hoodfar, anthropologist).

Spiritual Intervention

If this child thrives under your devoted care, may its face shine. May it uproot the nightshade bushes with its brushing thigh. May it not become ill.

Chagga prayer to protect newborn, Tanzania, East Africa

Prayers come in many different guises. Some people dance and trance, some lay on hands, some simply raise their palms to the sky. But the intent is the same – to summon up super-human forces in the cause of healing.

Yesterday, my younger sister gave birth to her baby, but when it was born, its eyes wouldn't open and it wasn't breathing. Only the slightest pulse was in his heart. I tried to revive him in every way I could, but nothing seemed to work. That's when I started to pray to the spirits of my father and grandfather, asking them to let the child live. I kept rubbing his face, head, and back with water. Eventually, he opened his eyes and started to cry. He's been fine ever since.

!Kung San woman of the Kalahari desert, Africa

This story, from a nomadic hunter-gatherer, is a tale of empowerment. Not only did the aunt feel she had magically healed her sick nephew, but her healing was later confirmed after a medicine dance, in which a trancing shaman 'saw' what had happened. Some ancestral spirits had wanted to take the baby's life, said the shaman, but the grandfather spirit shouted out and saved the child. He confirmed that it was the aunt's intervention which had saved the baby.

It is very hard for western adults to see any magic in the world about them, and most would prefer not to look. But in !Kung San society, as in other traditional groups, ordinary mortals are able to access the powers of the spirit world to help them heal. This gives them an enormous sense of solace and personal strength, even though their efforts and prayers cannot always be successful. When it comes to infant illness, parents tend to use every means at their disposal, from natural medicines to magic.

Sometimes, the place of healing is important. In pre-Roman Italy, women went to specially-constructed sanctuaries, bringing votive offerings to the gods to beg them to reprieve their sick babies. In rural Australia, women would take their babies 'out bush', to sacred sites where powerful rituals may be performed. Away from ordinary life, and despite desperate situations, people summon up a supernatural optimism. 'A sense of hope and empowerment, either through the use of medicinal remedies or through spiritual encouragement, would often in itself bring healing or a change of behaviour or attitude' (Margaret Stewart, midwife, in Western Australia).

There are untold examples of magical healing used by mothers and fathers around the globe:

* People of southern Africa see the moon as a symbol of growth and healing. The Venda and other tribes hold the baby upside down to the full moon and call on its power to protect against illness.

* When a Yurok baby of California is ill, his grandmother takes responsibility for healing his pain. She goes to the garden after dark, and cries to the spirits, 'This is our child; do not harm it.' If this does not work, the grandmother next door comes in to sing the baby her song. Every Yurok grandmother has her own special healing song for such occasions.

* Tibetan babies who have crying fits or other unexplained illness may be treated with a dough-ball rub. Tsampa (barley flour) or wheat dough are rolled all over the baby's body by the mother, to pick up any negative influences. The baby is finally made to squeeze the dough between his fists. The 'bad' dough, containing the impression of the baby's tiny hands, is taken away by a lama and thrown out, together with dough models of the invading spirits which made the baby cry. The tsampa dough is said to be food for the spirits, who will not bother the baby again.

* Malay parents use simple magic to treat '*lekat kenan*', the disease of pre-natal influence. If a baby is prone to vomiting, it may be because his mother saw a cat vomit during pregnancy. The cure is to burn the fur, claws and whiskers from a cat and mark the child with the ashes. Chicken feathers may be burnt to cure a baby who thrashes about with his limbs, a sign that the pregnant mother saw a chicken being slaughtered.

* In south-west North America, pubescent Apache girls were considered to have supernatural healing powers. Everyone, from babies to the very old, as well as Apache priests themselves, would appear before the newly-menstruating girl to receive the blessing of her touch.

* Fire was used by many ancient peoples in their healing rituals for babies. In Native North American tribes, 'smudging' may be performed. A piece of sage, lavender or cedar is placed in an abalone shell and set alight briefly. This must be softly blown out so that it smoulders, and a feather is used to waft the smoke over the baby, as the prelude to any healing ritual. All the implements are symbolic:

The shell gives respect to water – the life blood of Mother Earth. The plants that you burn honour the people that grow from the body of Mother Earth and fulfil many of our needs. The feather respects the air and the other two-legged creatures of creation, and the fire is symbolic of the cleansing fire of life itself.

Grey Wolf, Lakota tribe

THE MAGIC KISS

A mother's kiss or/and affectionate embrace has much healing power, and such utter trust and faith are often strong enough to suppress pain.

Norman Autton, hospital chaplain and author

Western adults use magic to heal their children, too. The 'utter trust and faith' is that of the small child, who does not question his mother's ability to heal. His faith is well founded. Parents 'heal' their babies daily by patting, stroking, kissing, nursing and making better. When in crisis, the growing baby retreats to his parents' arms for comfort, instantly restoring his sense of well-being. It takes years for a child to realise that his parents' healing is not as all-powerful as he might once have believed. And in some cultures, where fathers and mothers possess the gift of shamanic healing, children's early faith is confirmed. They learn that their parents do indeed have the power to heal.

Meanwhile, the act of offering a 'magic kiss' does very well. Kissing the injured spot is based on the ancient practice of sucking out evil, in an attempt to take away the pain. In a typical Yurok healing session, the traditional doctor of this native Californian tribe 'sucks' a number of pains from an ill child before spitting them out again. She then dances, to make the pains disappear. '. . . Over the years the true meaning of 'kiss and make it better' has been forgotten and a simple, loving kiss now replaces the witchdoctor's sucking action' (Desmond Morris, zoologist).

A Charmed Life

> You are not on this earth; you are within this stone.
> No wind may reach you; no iceberg may crush you,
> but it will break in pieces against the edges of this
> stone.

Spell of the Inuit shaman in Canada, as he gives parents
and baby protective necklaces of red stone

The baby charm is a little bit of magic to protect the infant through his early years. Charms are considered 'apotropaic' by many societies, in other words, capable of averting evil. Such amulets are a fixture of human tradition in every continent. Perhaps the most famous amulet is the '*bulla*' of ancient Rome, a necklace given to freeborn babies on the ninth or tenth day after their birth. This was the '*dies lustricus*', or Purification Day. Friends would bring presents and an animal was sacrificed.

Most charms are chosen because they have a powerful resonance for their society. Among the Ainu, an ancient tribe of Japan, a stick of willow was the most potent charm a family could bestow. Their creation story says that people were made from the willow tree, the supple branch being the template for the human backbone and the seat of the soul. The baby's grandfather would fetch a green branch of willow from the riverbank and whittle it into a stick or '*inau*'. It was decorated with shavings and set into a pillow of reeds. The grandfather was permitted to enter the birth room, where he would present the baby with the inau and whisper: 'We call upon thee, oh willow *inau*, to watch over this child while he is growing up. Guard him and give him strength, together with long life' (Prayer of the Ainu grandfather).

A WATCHFUL EYE

An Ocho de Dios, or 'Eye of God', is an ancient charm used by the Huichol people of Jalisco, Mexico. It is a woven ornament, traditionally crafted by the baby's father at birth – Pueblo men were renowned for their spinning and weaving skills. (Pueblo refers to the people as well as the villages they lived in.) The Huichol name for Ocho de Dios is '*sikuli*', which means 'the power to see and understand the unknown'.

At the baby's arrival, his father would take two sticks and weave them into a cross with dyed cottons – rabbit-brush flowers gave a brilliant yellow, while cactus fruits produced a faded lilac. This cross, pointing out the four elements of earth, fire, water and air, formed the central 'eye'. Every year, the weaver would add more colours in diamond formation between the sticks, until the child was five. When the charm was done, it might be hung on the wall or even in the child's hair.

In the sixteenth century, following the Spanish conquests of America, Pueblo people started to work with wool and a wider range of dyes: indigo blue, brazil-wood brown and their favourite, cochineal red. Even to this day, the vivid colours of the Ocho de Dios remind Mexican children that they are magically woven into their parents' protection.

Umbilical cords – readily available and brimming with birth magic – were used as charms throughout the world. Children of the Sioux tribes, who roamed the wide American plains of Dakota with their parents, carried ornate, beaded purses, each with the supernatural umbilicus inside. Some cultures used rope-like imitations to weave their cord magic. Women of Okinawa island near Japan would hang an irregularly left-woven rope in the delivery room, to keep out spirits who might harm the baby.

Later, civilisations who could afford to trade with travelling merchants began to opt for the opulence of gemstone charms. Sparkling, deep-hued gems and crystals were easily invested with magical properties. Coral was a favourite from Roman times to the Middle Ages, when beads of red were hung over cradles. Coral was considered an all-purpose safeguard against illness and witchcraft, lightning, whirlwind and fire. It could also, apparently, be used to gauge infant health: 'Coral is good to be hanged about the neck of children . . . to preserve them from the falling sickness. It has also some sympathy with nature, for the best coral . . . will turn pale and wan if the party that wears it be sick, and it comes to its former colour again as they recover' (Sir Hugh Platt, *Jewel House of Art and Nature*, 1594).

This medieval thermometer stayed in fashion for many hundreds of years. In Tudor England, babies were often given coral rattles. It was a Roman Catholic idea to add bells to the coral amulet, to ward off evil spirits. In Italy to this day, a coral-red ribbon is tied to the baby's cradle as a protective charm.

One of the most poignant charms is bestowed by Mbuti pygmy parents of the Ituri rainforest in central Africa. The newborn baby (un-named as yet, for fear he will not stay) is bathed in water mixed with juice from the forest vine. His amulets are circles of vine around his waist and wrists. Wooden ornaments are added, partly for decoration, but specifically to place the child in physical contact with the forest. It is the spirit of the forest which, the Mbuti believe, brings humans into existence and sustains them on life's journey.

Scratching the Surface

The small-pox, so fatal, and so general amongst us, is here entirely harmless, by the invention of engrafting, which is the term they give it . . . they make parties for this purpose, and when they are met (commonly fifteen or sixteen together) the old woman comes with a nut-shell full of the matter of the best sort of small-pox, and asks what vein you please to have opened . . . The children or young patients play together all the rest of the day and are in perfect health to the eighth. Then the fever begins to seize them, and they keep their beds two days, very seldom three . . .

. . . you may believe I am well satisfied of the safety of this experiment, since I intend to try it on my dear little son.

Lady Mary Wortley Montagu, wife to the British ambassador at the court of the Ottoman Empire, Turkey, letter to England 1717

Infant vaccination is a topic which creates strong feelings in many parents. But this is not merely a debate of modern times. Vaccination has a long, cross-cultural history; some ancient peoples understood the art, while others feared and shunned it. It is a system which requires the absolute faith of those who offer up their children for its apparently magical protection.

Immunisation – the introduction of diseased cells, dead or alive, into the bloodstream – is the most popular modern method of warding off disease, particularly the common diseases of childhood. Where once the immature immune system was boosted by intermittent battles with fever (protected, to a large extent, by the immunological properties of breastmilk), now babies are sent for a series of vaccinations at increasingly early ages. Common childhood illnesses such as measles, rubella and mumps, are now disappearing from populations subjected to the 'herd immunisation' principle.

The debate continues to rage as to whether vaccinations against minor childhood diseases are really necessary and whether or not they work. Some suspect that they contribute to the growing spectrum of chronic illnesses (asthma, eczema, allergy) which affect so many children today. What we do know is that ancient cultures pursued the idea of immunising their children, using a variety of spiritual theories and an almost universal desire to scratch the surface of their babies' skin:

- Ancient Egyptians tattooed cat silhouettes on their baby's arms, to enlist the protection of Bastet, the cat-goddess of maternity, breastfeeding and child care.
- The Batangueño people of the Philippines prick each new-born baby on the cheek, to allow impure blood to spill out. 'It is the Batangueño way of immunising the infant from future illness,' says birth researcher Nid Amina.
- The Bhaca of southern Africa scarify their babies' cheeks at full moon, hoping for a spiritual protection against illness.
- Druid priests of ancient Britain and Germany attempted to vaccinate against smallpox using pus taken from smallpox victims.
- Immunisation was known to Chinese mystics before the tenth century AD. The technique, practised by Taoist hermits from Szechuan, was used to fight smallpox for centuries, only becoming widely practised in the sixteenth century.
- Medieval doctors developed a method called 'isopathy', introducing diseased matter into the bloodstream of a healthy person.

Smallpox, a vicious and deadly disease which claimed many lives, was a constant worry for parents. Desperate to protect their children against at least one of many threats to their health, aristocratic mothers led the way in trying the 'Chinese' method, which had made its way to Turkey by the eighteenth century. Lady Mary Wortley Montagu had her six-year-old son 'engrafted' in 1718, a highly controversial experiment which nevertheless helped to popularise the vaccine in Britain.

The legend of Edward Jenner, the eighteenth-century physician and his pioneering crusade against smallpox, is one of lone heroism. Jenner was preceded not only by centuries of eastern wisdom, but by a Dorset farmer who inoculated his family with cowpox in 1774. Benjamin Jesty of Yetminster was himself following age-old folk medicine when he deliberately infected his wife, Elizabeth, and their two sons with pus from a diseased cow. Elizabeth nearly died as a result, but all three survived, and word of his success soon spread. Jenner was instrumental in persuading many nations to immunise their babies as Jesty had done.

Although smallpox did eventually decline in Europe, it did so even in populations which were unprotected by inoculation. Improved hygiene, better measures for quarantine and the natural life cycle of the disease were all factors which helped in its destruction. Other killers of the time – typhoid, cholera, TB and dysentery, for instance – diminished at a similar rate. Deaths from diphtheria had already declined by ninety per cent before antibiotics and mass immunisation were introduced.

THE SMALLPOX GODDESS

In northern India, newborn Rajput babies are protected against disease by a special ceremony called Chotili. The rite involves tying a sacred scarlet thread around the leg of the mother's bed and invoking the names of goddesses who guard against disease. Mata, the smallpox goddess, is one of 101 sister goddesses on hand to protect the baby.

Up to nine deities may be addressed during the ceremony, including Bahamata, the maker of children, whose image is carved out of cow dung. Gifts of grain are given to the new mother and the Bahamata figurine is hidden in the house for good luck.

Early attempts by white doctors to immunise the babies of indigenous populations met with great resistance: Native Americans refused to take jabs from well-wishing Jesuits and parents on the Isle of Man (off England's north-west coast) were equally dubious. Manx islanders were quoted as saying that 'If they had twenty children they would not put the cow-pock on

one of them.' Anti-vaccination rebellions flared up from India
to Brazil.

After a hundred years of scientific development, immunisation programmes are now instituted worldwide, with unforeseen effects on a new generation of children. Mothers in
traditional cultures today treat vaccination sessions as they would
any stressful occasion, counteracting the distress of their babies
with the comfort of the breast. '. . . All the babies in the village
[of Taira] were being given a series of inoculations for diphtheria and typhoid. As the injections were given in one large,
open room, the cries of the infant being inoculated prompted
others to cry. Invariably the mother offered the breast to the
baby' (Thomas and Hatsumi Maretzki, anthropologists in
Okinawa, Japan).

For some babies in high-risk populations, vaccination is clearly
not the answer. A shocking story of unchecked medical fervour
comes from Alice Springs, Australia, in the early 1970s. In a flash
of protective enthusiasm, state doctors were rounding up
Aboriginal babies for jabs of many kinds – and the babies were
dying in ever-increasing numbers. In some parts of the Northern
Territory in 1971, 500 out of every 1,000 babies died.

Research doctor Archie Kalokerinos interviewed the area's
Minister of the Interior, who described his dawning realisation
that vaccination was killing the Aboriginal babies:

Suddenly it clicked. 'We have stepped up immunisation campaigns . . . There was
no need to go to Alice Springs, I knew. A health team would sweep into an area,
line up the aboriginal babies and infants and immunize them. There would be no
examination, no taking of case history, no checking on dietary deficiencies. Most
infants would have colds. No wonder they died . . . If some babies and infants survived, they would be lined up again in a month, for another immunization. If some
managed to survive even this, they would be lined up again. Then there would be
booster shots, shots for measles, polio and even TB. Little wonder they died. The
wonder is that any survived.

'Ralph', Minister of the Interior for Alice Springs, Australia

The orthodox view is that herd immunisation protects the majority and that the occasional casualty is acceptable. But cross-cultural catastrophes of this kind should tell us that immunisation is not a route to be followed blindly. What works in one culture may create havoc in another.

Furthermore, it is unclear whether immunisation is having the effects which doctors always anticipate. Despite insisting on the benefits of vaccination, the World Health Organisation recently reported that disease and mortality rates in the developing world do not correlate directly with immunisation programmes. Levels of hygiene and the standard of a community's diet are, they say, better predictors of resistance to disease.

Nevertheless, modern health campaigners are keen to claim victory over polio. A global drive to eliminate the disease saw eighty-five per cent of the world's under-fives immunised during 2000. That represents a staggering 550 million children in eighty-two countries. If the push is successful, polio will be the second recorded disease to be sent to history's 'recycle bin'.

In the West, we continue to be faithful to the cause of exterminating an ever-increasing range of childhood diseases. But mothers in other cultures do not necessarily share our medical beliefs, any more than we share theirs. In Cairo, Egypt, women interviewed by health researchers showed little faith in vaccination, merely using it to hedge their bets in the battle against infantine disease. 'Despite this, many mothers do make partial attempts to have their children vaccinated. As one mother put it, "Who knows, perhaps it does work"' (Homa Hoodfar, anthropologist).

Spirit Baby

The life-souls of newborn babies are especially prone to disappearance, since they are so small, so vulnerable, and so precariously poised between the realm of the unseen, from which they have just traveled, and the realm of the living. Babies' souls may wander away, drawn by bright colors, sweet sounds, or fragrant smells; they may leave if a baby is sad, lonely, or insufficiently loved by its parents; they may be frightened away by a sudden loud noise; or they may be stolen by a *dab* [fairy].

Anne Fadiman, American journalist and author,

on the souls of Hmong babies from south-east Asia

Imagine – if you can – that a baby is a spirit come to earth. Not just a human being on the cusp of creation, but a reincarnated thing, fragile and closely connected to unseen forces. This is how much of the ancient world viewed the state of infancy, and how many traditional cultures still consider the baby to be. He is an elusive soul, who may at any time, and at whim, decide to return to the other world.

The idea of the spirit baby is not merely a way of explaining infant death, although it helps to ease the pain in cultures where many babies die in the days and weeks after birth. It is an understandable way of perceiving new life, when you also believe that the world is imbued with living spirits. Tribes who converse with the spirits of trees and animals, make pacts with the landscape and honour the souls of their ancestors have no difficulty in identifying the spiritual dimension of the new infant.

There are many manifestations of the human spirit, both abstract and concrete, in world religion. In Aboriginal Australian culture, a baby is given his spiritual identification with an ancestral being – usually an animal or a plant – around the time of birth. The mother receives a sign during pregnancy. Perhaps a magpie flies into her path on the very day she feels her baby first move inside her: from now on, she knows her child is spiritually linked to the Magpie Dreaming or totem. These spiritual links connect Aborigines to the land. Each spirit belongs to a safe haven, a sacred site to which it will one day return.

For many peoples, a newborn baby is simply out of this world. Rural Mexicans sometimes refer to their babies as angels. In Japanese tradition, infants are seen as godlike. Until the age of six or seven, a child is said to be a 'gift from the gods', a free spirit who must be tamed and brought into the family unit. This explains the ancient Japanese desire to enfold each precious new infant within the close protection of the family.

To the Balinese, newborns are 'celestial creatures entering a more humdrum existence'. (Margaret Mead, anthropologist.) A new arrival is so close to the spirit world, he is not allowed to enter the sacred temple – it is just too close to home.

Underlying all these beliefs is, of course, the fear that the baby will die in infancy – 'before he has shared his first bowl of rice', in the words of the Balinese. In Guatemala, for instance, children are seen as gifts from the Place in the Sky, and will return there immediately should they die young. The Afikpo people of eastern Nigeria, who consider each soul to be a reincarnation of one or more of their ancestors, say a baby's spirit is apt to change its mind and simply 'go back'.

As a precaution, the Wodaabe, a Nigerian Fulani tribe, refer to the newborn as 'it' for the first week of life – until the naming ceremony, the infant is not a person. The Swazi of south-east Africa go even further, refusing to name the baby before three months. Until the moment when the child is named and ritually presented to the natural world, he is a 'thing', a vulnerable, weak creature, liable to depart at any time. And for the Afikpo, there is no reassurance until the child starts to walk and talk. Then, they say, the spirit baby has decided to stay and become a fully-fledged human child.

ARE WE BORING YOU?

Newborn babies usually take big gulps of air soon after birth. These are reflexive 'birth yawns' which help to fill the lungs with oxygen. But in ancient times, a baby who yawned too much was thought to be at risk of letting his soul escape. Roman mothers were advised to cover babies' mouths when the infants yawned, and children were taught to do the same for themselves. It is a gesture which has remained in the European repertoire of good manners for many centuries.

When a Baby Dies

I have been the mother of seven children, the most beautiful and the most loved of whom lies buried near my Cincinnati residence. It was at his dying bed and at his grave that I learned what a poor slave a mother may feel when her child is torn away from her. In those depths of sorrow which seemed to me immeasurable, it was my only prayer to God that such anguish might not be suffered in vain.

Harriet Beecher Stow, author of *Uncle Tom's Cabin*, to the English writer Mrs Follen, America, 16 February 1853

Babies die before and after birth in every culture. In traditional societies, where each mother may have many babies in difficult conditions, the possibility of death is never far away. Some historians have claimed that, living so close to death, parents became inured to the pain of losing their young. But close inspection of ancient literature, graves and gravestones reveals no lack of grief. The death of a baby remains with parents for as long as they live.

Many traditional societies do not consider the unborn or newborn baby to be fully human, or to possess a human soul. Rather, they see the baby as a delicate spirit, hovering between this world and another. So even stillborn babies have a history and a destiny. In old Gaelic belief, the stillborn spirit was called '*mac talla*', which means 'echo' or 'rock child'. The tiny body would be buried after dark in a sacred spot, so its spirit could return to the rocks.

The echo in a cave was just one elusive force of nature which reminded people of their departed infants. Some Mexican peoples say that every star is a miscarried baby. French parents once believed that unbaptised babies turned into birds, flying aimlessly about until they received the blessing of John the Baptist. Baptism was, to Catholic minds, the only blessing which could save infant souls from an eternity spent wandering in limbo, never to meet their parents in paradise.

To avoid this fate for their children, some mothers in France, Switzerland, Germany, Austria, the southern Netherlands and Italy had recourse to attempts to resuscitate the baby by miraculous means.

If the little corpse could be made by a miracle to show some signs of life, the merest fluttering of an eyelid, a change of colour from waxen blue to white, a drop of urine, then the child could be pronounced to have shown signs of life, could be quickly baptized, and was spared limbo.

Olwen Hufton, social historian

For many early humans, the belief was in neither heaven nor hell, but in reincarnation – and, more specifically, a recycling of infant spirits within the same family. The Karenni people, who live as refugees in Thailand, are just one traditional society who believe that the spirit of a dead baby reappears with the birth of the next sibling. The Karenni are famous for their long-necked women, who wear a series of uncomfortable-looking neck rings and make a little money by posing for the cameras of tourists who arrive by the coach-load. Here, the pre-Christian belief in reincarnation is married with Catholic observance:

One photograph shows a long-neck woman, Moo Paw, who has just given birth, sitting in a makeshift sauna, to cleanse herself after labour . . . The year before they had had a stillborn child whom the wife believed was a spirit child, who would be reborn as their next baby. The stillborn baby's remains were kept in a cardboard box on a bed of cotton wool, next to a Catholic shrine and a small bowl of rice and water. The spirit child, which its parents said talked to them in their dream, had finally come.

Mary Braid, journalist

A belief in reincarnation permeates many cultures today. If a baby dies among the Andaman Islanders of the Bay of Bengal, the mother's next baby will be given the same name, for this is the older brother or sister, returned to earth. Infant spirits were handed down from sibling to sibling, according also to the ancient Anasazi Native American people of Arizona and New Mexico. The infant body was sometimes buried under the floorboards of the house, to encourage this miracle of rebirth.

Here, a Kwakiutl mother of Vancouver Island implores the spirit of her dead baby to return to her womb to be born again:

Ah, ah, ah, why have you done this to me, child? You chose me as your mother, and I tried to do everything for you. Look at all your toys and all the things I have had made for you. Why do you desert me, child? Is it because of something I did to you? I will try to do better when you come back to me, child. Only do this for me: get well right away in the place where you go, and as soon as you are strong come back to me. Please do not stay away. Have mercy on me who am your mother, child.

Kwakiutl mother's lament at the death of her baby

The simple sentiments of this lament are, in fact, part of an ancient ritual. All the women of the community join the mother and wail as she addresses her child. All about her, dolls, toys and miniature carvings are laid out, many of which the mother would have commissioned for the occasion, to help her woo her baby's spirit back to life. Her next pregnancy will be regarded as proof that her prayer has been heard.

GUARDIANS OF THE SPIRIT

Her maid told me she'd left a half hour earlier 'to worship'. I knew exactly what this meant: Mameha had gone to a little temple just at the eastern edge of Gion to pray before the three tiny *jizo* statues she'd paid to have erected there. A *jizo*, you see, honors the soul of a departed child.

Arthur Golden, *Memoirs of a Geisha*

They can be seen all over Japan. Along the sides of the roads, in temples, in gardens: small, upright stone statues with baby faces, red bonnets and matching bibs, surrounded by flowers, food offerings and gaudy windmills. These are the '*jizo*', the guardian beings who banish fear and lead people out of trouble into peace and understanding. In particular, the statuettes guard the souls of children who have died, including those who are aborted, miscarry or do not survive birth. The windmills are their playthings; the flowers and food keep their spirits calm. Their eyes are usually closed and the palms folded upwards in an eternal greeting of 'Namaste'.

HOME TRUTHS

The Kamajors take more than rice and ammunition to the battlefield. Famously, they take magical protection . . . 'You see,' Mr Hinga Norman said in his mellifluous English, 'you call them medicine men, but you have your own armour in western armies and sometimes it does not work, which is the same with us. Sometimes we get hurt and sometimes we get killed, but that doesn't mean it doesn't work.'

Martin Wollacott, journalist, describes the Kamajor [hunter] militia, fighting alongside the Sierra Leone army in West Africa

Magical armour (whether used in war or against disease) receives the brunt of our western scepticism. Few of us see the point of pursuing apparently useless rituals in the treatment of our children. Yet there are still many aspects of health, especially infant health, which are yet to be brought under our control.

When a western baby falls ill, his parents usually hand over their power to doctors and other medical experts. Just when our babies need us absolutely, we feel at our most vulnerable and helpless. But health crises often bring out the best in parents of traditional cultures. They are able to display great courage and resourcefulness, for they have access to a supernatural repertoire of diagnoses and cures.

The French have a saying: 'There are no miracles to the man who does not believe in them.' Miracles, many of us assume, are things which belong in the Bible and in fairy-tales. We manage our everyday lives without miracles to ease the pain. But there are times when nothing else will do.

Faith has always played a great part in healing and diagnosis. In terms of infant health, faith gives a framework for parents seeking to understand their babies' sickness, disability and even death. Medical know-how and local plant lore are supplemented by complex belief systems, which help parents towards appropriate action and – if necessary – acceptance of their lot. It requires a step of faith to hand your baby over to a nurse for vaccinations which work invisibly, under the skin. It requires a certain magic to 'heal' your baby with a kiss, a healing transaction which the young child soon learns to accept as real.

The world of our ancestors was a place populated by natural spirits. They imagined a spiritual life in all living things: the earth beneath their bare feet, the trees, in running water and in the animals they hunted for food. So the death of a baby was cat-astrophic, but not absolutely final. The infant spirit pre-existed its time on earth and it often survived its short life. It might even be reborn as a sibling or other family member. Beliefs like these take over where comprehension falters. Miracles are all around us – if only we know where to look.

14. Human Healing

Parents – those who enjoy the greatest possible intimacy with their babies – are likely to be the first to notice when things go wrong. They also have a vital part to play in their infants' healing. Most parents want to know how to keep their babies healthy and how to take practical care of an ill baby. They are following a nursing tradition which can be traced to the beginnings of humanity.

Vital Signs

We were impressed with the level of maternal vigilance for disease in the community and the willingness of Gusii mothers to take time off from agricultural work to seek treatment for sick children and to nurse sick infants on their own bodies for many hours on end.

Robert LeVine, anthropologist

Parents in every culture must stay vigilant in case their babies fall ill. One strong argument for allowing each baby to have a primary carer is that intimacy brings more subtle awareness. Mothers and fathers are attuned to their babies' 'normal' appearance and behaviour. They are on the look-out for changes which might indicate infection or failure to thrive.

There are many clues they might use. In India, Hindu mothers know their children by smell and have, for thousands of years, used this ability to detect when their babies are ill. According to Hindu folk belief, if a baby smells good, he must be good.

Diagnosis by smell was common practice in former times: typhus patients, apparently, smell like freshly-baked bread, while a child with measles smells like 'plucked feathers'. Females are far more adept at detecting subtle smells than are men. There are some substances – hormones, for instance – which mothers can smell 1,000 times more effectively than fathers (or male doctors). It is essential, therefore, that experts listen to mothers who insist that their babies are seriously sick. They may be sicker than primary symptoms alone suggest.

Meanwhile, a national survey of Mexican mothers found that they looked into their babies' eyes to discover their state of health. 'Even when considering the worsening or improvement of diarrhoea (a common and potentially life-threatening illness in third world countries) whilst the [Mexican] mothers rely on obvious symptoms related to changes in the child's well-being . . . *the more important signs that they recognize are focused on the child's eyes*' (Adam Jackson, iridologist).

Besides the most pressing symptoms of disease, there are other vital clues like body temperature, behavioural changes and the child's facial complexion. I was upset recently to see my six-year-old son walking into the room; although he did not speak and was not crying, his eyes were glazed and his face completely ashen. 'Joe,' I said, 'you've had a fall!' And he had.

Intensive Care

It is simply that Duncan became ill – nothing major, just a tummy upset, but it meant that all he wanted to do was to be held – and nursed. So of course, any theories . . . went completely out the window!

Alison Parker, breastfeeding mother, England

When a child becomes ill, all he needs is to be a baby again. Regression is normal for all humans when they are feeling weak and vulnerable. Even adults curl into a ball and wrap themselves up tightly when feeling rotten.

Babies and small children often require intensive care: rocking, cuddling, breastfeeding and a thousand small attentions are the ways they like to be nursed back to health. Even in western society, they have a mysterious way of appearing in their parents' bed on nights when they are feeling weak and vulnerable. Cultural theories and training programmes seem unimportant when faced with a needy child.

Nursing is what used to happen when mothers had time. We live in a culture with less and less patience for the process of ordinary illness: a baby's sickness is not even considered a legitimate reason for a parent to take a day off work. Painkillers and antibiotics serve to suppress and shift symptoms which once would have received prolonged maternal attention. 'I have just spent a whole day simply being with my daughter. That was absolutely all I did. I feel frazzled, restless, yet under these currents, calm and centered. It is a spiritual experience to serve your child in sickness, to let fly all your important tasks, to coax her small system back to health' (Valerie Schultz, writer and mother, California).

All this extra carrying and nursing makes the baby feel comforted, of course, but it offers much more than the immediate psychological benefits. Skin-to-skin contact helps the ailing body to stabilise; it promotes steady breathing and calms the nerves. Increased breastfeeding helps to centre the baby, nourishing him with a perfect invalid diet (at a time when he may be unable to stomach anything else). And being tenderly cared for also has long-term benefits, forming an important part of the childhood experience. Days spent cocooned from the world in mother's arms are among the most precious memories many of us possess.

Fresh-Air Therapy

Gross and thick air makes
1 Fat unweildy bodies.
2 Dull wits.

> An air near the Fens or near the sea, makes
>   sickly bodies. Pure and clear air makes
> 1 Nimble bodies.
> 2 Quick wits.
> The breathing in of ill air, and the eating of
>   ill diet is the cause of most infirmities.
>
> Nicholas Culpeper, herbalist, 1651

Shivering at my desk on a cold May morning, I can see why fresh air fell out of fashion – in the British Isles, at least. But in times gone by, the Great Outdoors was the place to be, if you wanted to stay in optimum health.

Modern central heating, air conditioning and cavity walls conspire to keep us from the fresh air we were designed to breathe. Throughout history, humans have spent far more time outdoors than those in the industrialised nations do today. During the eighteenth and nineteenth centuries, people began to retreat indoors for work, play and child-rearing. As babies were increasingly likely to be cooped up with nanny in a self-sufficient, equipped nursery, child care experts remonstrated: 'Babies,' they proclaimed, 'need fresh air' – and plenty of it.

The rigours of the daily constitutional applied just as much to Victorian babies as to their older brothers and sisters. In the days before perambulators, babies were carried about, in arms, in all weathers. 'Besides, in very cold weather, or in a very young infant, the warmth of the nurse's body, while he is being carried, helps to keep him warm, he himself being naturally cold. In point of fact, the child, while being borne in the nurse's arms, reposes on the nurse, warm and supported, as though he were in a nest!' (Dr Pye Henry Chavasse, obstetrician and healthcare author, 1880). Indoors, babies were placed on cushions and paraded near open windows (not too near, of course).

By the 1920s, fans of fresh air were able to implement the ideas of child care expert Frederick Truby King, who advised that babies spend almost the entire day *al fresco*, lying in a pram at the bottom of the garden during the day and sleeping at night in the 'airiest bedroom'. By now, of course, the infant was rarely held and so could not benefit from the warmth of an adult body. 'It was a little hard on British babies that fresh-air fetishism in its ultimate form should be introduced by a New Zealander, whose home country offered a considerably more attractive climate for open-air life' (Christina Hardyment, social historian, on Truby King).

Another late Victorian preoccupation was the avoidance of germs. This was the generation which insisted on separate bedrooms and separate beds, even for married couples. In the 1890s, the twin bed was recommended on health grounds, as it prevented either spouse having to breathe the breath of the other. For babies, this was disastrous thinking, as the breath of his co-sleeping parents was an important evolutionary trigger, reminding him to keep breathing at all.

Germ-prevention was just another excuse for separating the baby from his community; strangers were not even supposed to kiss babies any more. If we want to know what happened to the baby-friendly society, we have only to consult turn-of-the-century child care experts, who were deeply concerned about such evils as unregulated baby-kissing: 'Many a horrible case of disease has arisen through the indiscriminate kissing of babies by men in the park' (Ada Ballin, *From Cradle to School, a Book for Mothers*, London 1902).

GERM WARFARE

The idea that baby must only touch his mother is found in a range of cultures. It is a proscription practised by a number of tribes, including the Dusun people who live in the mountains of North Borneo. For the first eight to ten days, the neonate must not be touched by anyone else and an incantation assures the child that 'no stranger will be allowed to touch you to bring you harm'. As it happens, this mother-only rule is in harmony with modern wisdom on bacterial protection:

> At birth, a baby is germ-free. Some hours later there are billions of germs covering his mucous membranes. The question is — which germs will be first to colonise the baby's body? Bacteriologists know that the winners of the race will be the rulers of the territory. The germ environment of the mother is already familiar and friendly from the perspective of the newborn because mother and baby share the same antibodies (IgG). In other words, from a bacteriological point of view, the newborn human urgently needs to be in contact with only one person — the mother.
>
> **Michel Odent, obstetrician and primal health researcher**

The Akkha people of northern Thailand create an invisible boundary around the new mother and baby. It is customary for the whole family to stay inside the village compound for two days after a baby is born, in case 'evil spirits' (germs?) from the jungle should cling to them and so reach the infant.

> When I visited a very new mother in an Akkha village, I didn't realize their feelings about outsiders and touched the baby. The mother was very concerned that I might have inadvertently brought evil spirits with me so ... I tied a piece of white cotton around the baby's wrist. I then gave the baby a silver coin which he grasped, showing that everything was probably all right.
>
> **Jacqueline Vincent Priya, birth researcher**

Along with germ-awareness came the importance of nose breathing for babies: early twentieth-century mothers were advised to close the infant's open mouth while he slept to encourage him to use his nostrils. In fact, all babies nose-breathe by preference, only breathing through their mouths when nursing or if they have a cold.

Over the course of the twentieth century, the fresh-air fad was gradually forgotten. It faded into insignificance besides more pressing healthcare issues, such as vaccination and diet. Without wishing to condemn our babies to a life spent wailing in the back garden, we might usefully include more 'fresh-air therapy' in our daily lives. Many a colicky baby is calmed by a simple evening walk, hanging over the shoulder of a devoted parent. Sometimes, babies like a change of air.

Skin Deep

And as for thy nativity, in the day thou wast born thy navel was not cut, neither wast thou washed in water to supple thee; thou wast not salted at all, nor swaddled at all.

Ezekiel, Old Testament prophet, likens Jerusalem to
a neglected and unwanted baby

Salting babies is only one of many ancient practices which we in the West have long forgotten. The point was not to preserve the infant like a piece of meat, but to bestow on him all the magical properties of salt, a highly-valued commodity with strong spiritual overtones. The ancient Greeks, Egyptians, Jews, Buddhists and Christians all used salt in their rituals and in south-west America, Pueblo Indians even worshipped the revered Salt Mother.

Salt was rubbed lightly into the newborn baby's skin because it was believed this would help to keep his spirit intact. In medieval times, salting was done 'to comfort its limbs and free them of mucus', as the thirteenth-century encyclopaedist Bartholomew of England put it. ('Mucus' was a reference to the amniotic grease, or vernix.) Salt was sustenance for the skin and an offering to the new infant soul, to help it strengthen its hold on the body.

Although we may prefer not to salt our babies today, there are other naturally-occuring skin treatments with a long and interesting history. Some have a spiritual dimension, too. At the very least, they give people the chance to touch their babies, just as their babies crave to be touched:

* Hopi Native Americans from Arizona used to soften their babies' skin with volcanic ash, rather like an early talcum powder. The baby's father would collect the powder from Baby Ashes Mountain and the mother would apply it to the baby for three days after birth. (Ashes were also boiled in animal fat by the Babylonians to make soap as far back as 2,800 BC.)

* Many Filipino parents rub their babies' skin with ash, for its healing properties. Among the Aetas, people of the north-western Zambales region, the newborn baby is rolled over and over in a banana leaf tray of ashes. The baby must lie here for two days and nights, to immunise him against disease.

* In England, medieval midwives rubbed the newborn baby's limbs with crushed rose leaves or with honey.

* In Siberia, the baby's skin is rubbed with fermented tamarind, considered to be an exotic and valuable spice.

* The ancient Pueblo Indian grandmother would wash the newborn with soap made from the roots of the yucca plant. The root was pounded and stirred into a bowl of water, creating a rich natural lather. Yucca suds are used by some Native American women today in preference to commercial shampoo.

* Immediately after birth, the Rajput Indian midwife rubs the baby's body with flour.

* Rice paste, made from powdered rice, is painted on the forehead of a newborn Malay baby. Rice paste and lime juice are also added to the baby's first bath. Rice, the staple of the East and fruit of the earth, is said to repel bad spirits.

* In parts of Germany, the baby was given his own special treatment to ensure he would have a good skin. On the first Thursday after his birth, when the moon was waxing, the midwife rubbed his body with fat, sprinkled him with flour and massaged the whole lot in, before giving him a bath.
* Butter and milk symbolise purity and spirituality to the Pon people of the Himalayas. The newborn is given a sheep carved out of butter and his skin is ceremoniously washed in milk.

Cradle cap

It is hard to tell whether or not cradle cap is a universal phenomenon. It is apparently more common on boys than in girls. The yellow crusts which form on the scalp of many western babies' heads may be unsightly, but they are only a problem if they start to itch. Cradle cap is caused by over-productive sebum glands, a condition which may be related to eczema, and thus possibly to a cow's milk allergy, either through bottle-feeding or the diet of the breastfeeding mother. On the other hand, it may appear without provocation.

In past times, cradle cap was thought to be nature's own protection for the babies' vulnerable head bones and no attempt was made to remove it before the fontanelles (gaps in the skull) had closed over. In Holland and England, butter was rubbed into the child's head and in Spain, pure olive oil was used.

Cold-pressed olive oil remains the treatment of choice today. It should be massaged gently into the head at night and washed out in the morning. Baby oil, which is mineral in origin, is not recommended, as it can add to the irritation. (Modern baby shampoos may also be at the root of the problem, rather than its remedy; try not to wash the baby's hair too often.) In India, where the baby's head is ritually shaved, the scalp is treated afterwards with a 'mud pack' of oil, clean earth and turmeric.

Milk spots

Many babies develop white facial spots a week or two after

birth. In medical terms these are 'milia', blocked oil glands on the skin which disappear as the pores start to work normally. In England, they are sometimes known as 'milk spots', and are said to be caused by milk in the baby's or breastfeeding mother's diet. But '*milia*' is actually the Latin word for grains of millet, which is what baby spots look like. Coincidentally, the Hmong people of south-east Asia link baby pimples to rice grains:

Foua never shares her meals with anyone, because there is a postpartum taboo against spilling grains of rice accidentally into the chicken pot. If that occurs, the newborn is likely to break out across the nose and cheeks with little white pimples whose name in the Hmong language is the same as the word for 'rice'.

Anne Fadiman, journalist and author

Nappy rash

The biggest cause of nappy rash is the nappy. As soon as we cover up our babies' behinds, it becomes possible for soreness and infection to set in. Whatever kind of nappy is used, terry or disposable diaper, frequent changing is the key to keeping the bottom rash-free.

Mothers of Okinawa in Japan apparently find it hard work changing their swaddled babies. The older the baby, the less often he is changed, resulting in urine burns and diaper rash. Child nurses in medieval Europe were advised to change their babies three times a day, while modern mothers expect to change their babies around six times.

Nappy rash can be treated with many home remedies, depending on the plants and materials to hand:

* Olive oil was the favourite European treatment and was liberally coated on a baby's buttocks before the 'tailclout' was applied.
* Traditional herbal remedies include powdered orris root, cornflower and arrowroot.

- In Egypt, many mothers use no soap, cream or powder at all.
- Your kitchen cupboard is full of useful treatments, eg. live yoghurt (especially good for infant thrush); finely powdered oatmeal, egg white and diluted cider vinegar – use only one treatment at a time and allow to dry before changing the nappy.
- Lavender oil and Australian tea tree oil are excellent rash treatments – a few drops can be applied directly to the skin of older babies (check first for sensitivity).
- Allow your baby to go for as long as possible without a nappy!

Massage of Love

Every other culture massages their babies, sometimes three times a day until the children are a year or two old.

Anita Roddick, Body Shop founder

The benefits of massage are known to most of us by now. Although unlikely to be a daily feature in our busy lives, it has finally become accepted as a 'complementary' therapy. This tends to mean that massage is a luxurious option, a professional body treat for those who don't have an aversion to being touched by strangers. Other cultures do not view massage in this way. For most, it is an essential component of ordinary life, a daily health insurance, a reassurance of affection from other human beings and a cure for most minor ills.

Reasons for massaging baby vary from culture to culture.

- Hawaiian mothers believe massage makes the baby's face more beautiful, and they carefully work on the area around the head.
- The Balinese, the Mongolians and the Australian Aborigines use massage to relieve children's head- and stomach-aches.
- Tibetan parents are told that massage is essential for full infant development.

* Russian mothers say that massage helps develop the baby's central nervous system.
* Maori mothers pay special attention to the leg joints, to make their children supple and graceful.
* The Zinacanteco of Mexico believe that a baby must be massaged and embraced frequently, or he will lose his soul.

In any of these cultures, to deprive a baby of massage would be to close him off from a world of sensual enjoyment and personal interaction. Most cannot imagine relating to their babies without it.

The fundamental argument for baby massage relates to human biology. Human babies are born without the coating of warm, protective fur which characterises the other primates. This has the disadvantage of making it impossible for human babies to cling to their parents as monkey babies do. On the plus side, it makes them extremely touch-sensitive.

For thousands of years, people exploited the advantages of human skin from infancy to old age, using massage to restore a person's emotional and physical equilibrium. Yet western parents often ignore the potential of the skin for healing and human contact. We gradually teach our children to cope without much touching at all. 'Babies starved of touch show extreme distress. Yet from the moment of our birth our quota of touch is reduced: from the constant massage of the "in utero" baby to the less frequent cuddles and nappy changing; from the occasional kiss of a grazed knee to embarrassed adolescent encounters' (Gerry Pyves, therapeutic masseur).

TOUCH – DON'T TOUCH

Some cultures believe that no part of a baby's body should go untouched. From Bali to Liberia, mothers fondle their children's private parts as freely as their fingers or toes. They enjoy their infants' bodies and teach their babies to enjoy them, too:

- 'Mothers often fondle their small sons' penises, especially while nursing them, and boys are not punished for autoeroticism' (anthropologist James Gibbs describes the Kpelle people of Liberia).
- 'One day, while sitting on his mother's lap, he took his penis in his hand and said "penis" several times. His mother laughed and said, "He is showing you his penis." Some time later we saw this child's aunt playfully pull the child's penis while joking with him' (anthropologists Leigh Minturn and John Hitchcock observe an eighteen-month-old Rajput boy in Khalapur, India).
- 'In Jamaica peasant women play with their babies' lips, suck bubbles from their mouths and fondle a boy's penis' (anthropologist Sheila Kitzinger).
- 'Everyone joins in the mild titillating teasing of little babies, flipping their fingers, their toes, their genitals . . .' (anthropologist Margaret Mead watches the Balinese at play).

Many of the world's children grow up in an atmosphere of utterly uncomplicated body freedom, even if, at a later stage, they learn to be shy or even prudish. There is no hint of child abuse in these accounts. By many peoples it is clearly understood that babies are a species apart – they thrive on an innocent tactile contact which need not be limited by the usual sex taboos.

Peter Walker, author of baby massage books, advocates touch as a primary means of communication between adult and child.

He talks of 'getting the feel' of the baby and of remaining 'in touch'. Even our language is a clue to our evolutionary history, packed as it is with body-talk.

Massage is the original art of 'rubbing better', of creating ease through all and any parts of the body ... Massage stimulates the circulatory and immune systems and benefits the heart rate, breathing and digestion. It provides a perfect balance and support to the development of the baby as he or she co-ordinates and strengthens. It also cultivates the resilient elastic quality of the muscles and improves the ability to relax both in action and at rest.

Peter Walker, physical therapist

Perhaps that is why mothers from Fiji massage their babies just before they go to sleep. Yet Fiji mothers are unlikely to analyse their actions: they just know that it works. Only recently have humans started to seek proof that the evident pleasure our babies derive from tenderness is doing them some scientifically-measurable good.

Anthropologist Ruth Benedict once said that the only way we might tell how prehistoric humans once lived would be to look at the universal (or near-universal) behaviours which are still around today. Massage, despite its recent neglect in western society, is one of those universals. It has been a part of the baby-care repertoire for many thousands of years. Perhaps the best reason to massage your baby is the sheer delight it induces in both of you. Loving touch, the most primitive of all early-learning experiences, needs no other justification.

Stroking Better

A baby's belly is hungry. No doubt.
But its skin is just as hungry.
Its skin is craving, and so is its back, and so is
  its spine,

Craving for touch, craving for sensations.
Just as its belly craves for milk.

Frédérick Leboyer, French birth pioneer

Baby massage is a gentle art. The idea is to give pleasure to the baby's delicate skin, not to manipulate or mould him (although baby moulding was briefly fashionable in medieval Europe). We need to erase any image of the punitive adult massage and enter instead a world where the fingers dance lightly, responding to the needs of the baby.

The babies are laid on cotton mats, stripped of clothes and nappies and anointed with oil.

The technique, which is routine to mothers in the Soviet Union, India and China, is not the kneading and pummelling of the massage parlour but caressing strokes over the babies' faces, legs, backs, arms and stomachs.

Polly Samson, journalist

Stroking is a useful term, conveying the right intimation of pressure and tenderness. In India, the mother sits on the ground to massage her baby. She places him along her outstretched legs, with the infant's head cradled in her feet. According to touch expert Ashley Montagu, 'not a nook or cranny' of the baby's body is missed by the mother's loving hands:

Throughout the greater part of India children receive much tactile attention from their earliest days. Babies from about one month to six months are regularly bathed and massaged with such mixtures as turmeric paste and castor oil. As children they run around naked until six or seven; from the earliest days they are hugged and kissed by everyone.

Ashley Montagu, social scientist

If massage is done unresponsively, it can be a torture instead of a loving communication. This detailed description of a Gowda grandmother from Karnataka, South India, massaging her

newborn granddaughter demonstrates what happens when the
baby has had enough:

> The old lady took the baby and sat on the steps in the light of the open roof: its
> skin was deep pink, crinkled and wrinkled over the joints; its hands flapped feebly;
> its eyes were shut hard against the brightness. Taking a handful of castor oil she
> rubbed the skin with her coarse, stiff fingers poking between the limbs, smoothing
> it over and over. She coated its hair, wiped its mouth, wiped the eyelids and ears;
> the baby began to scream.
>
>   'Wah, wah,' cooed the old lady, bouncing it on her lap. 'Wah, wah, why are you
> crying like that?'
>
> Sarah Hobson, documentary film maker

The grandmother goes on to tickle and soothe the baby, talking
to her all the while. There is something disquieting in this
account, but it may merely be the author's choice of 'it' to refer
to the baby girl, whom she describes in rather detached, pathetic
terms. No doubt the grandmother herself would have described
the incident quite differently.

The fine art of baby massage lies in the interaction between
the masseur and the baby. This is not an intrusive therapy, a
treatment to be applied whether the infant likes it or not. It is
a subtle but powerful form of communication. And like any
good communication, messages are received as well as given.
Massage is a kind of metaphor for good mothering or fathering:
ideally you need to be firm, but gentle, relaxed and confident,
yet not over-imposing; open and receptive, yet in charge. All this
is learned with practice. If you are willing, your baby will be
the best teacher.

A quiet, darkened room, soft background music and skin-to-
skin contact are all you need to get going. Wait until your baby
is quiet and alert, unless you are wanting to ease his colic or
soothe him to sleep. The ambient temperature should be warm:
as the baby's body relaxes, it may become chilled. Heat your
hands up before you start. Make yourselves comfortable with

blankets and cushions. Perhaps the baby might sit facing you securely in your lap, stretched out Indian-style along your legs, or comfortably on a towel as you kneel over him. Oh, and you might like to use a little oil . . .

SMOOTH TALKING

All the baby books emphasise the sensitivity of a baby's skin. Only the gentlest of oils and lightest of powders are suitable for baby massage. Almond oil is ideal. Olive oil has been used for centuries as a tonic for delicate babies; it is classed as an 'inunction', a substance whose properties can be absorbed through the skin. It is also a natural sun filter. On newborns, use virgin olive oil without the 'extra' label, as this can be quite heavy.

However, almond or olive oils are not the only concoctions at your disposal. Tudor babies of England were smothered in acorn oil to protect them from smoke and cold. Other babies are also traditionally massaged in oils from native plants. Here is a selection of oils used worldwide in baby massage:

- butter (Gusii and Rwanda of East Africa)
- fish oil (Inuit, Canada)
- olive oil and buttermilk (Bedouins, Israeli desert)
- snake fat (Badjao tribe, Philippines)
- oil of myrtle or rose (England, early thirteenth century)
- coconut oil (Malaysia)
- palm oil (Bagam of the central Cameroons, Africa)
- a healing mixture of oil and red ochre, or antpit mud (Warmun, Australia)

> Most aromatherapy oils are too strong for babies and may irritate the skin. If your baby's skin is not over-reactive, you could try adding one drop of either Roman chamomile or lavender in 50ml of almond oil. To be on the safe side, leave aromatherapy until the child is older. Children aged six and over may be massaged with essential oils in half doses.

Born Too Soon

Another woman I know gave birth to a very small baby . . .

The old people said, 'Can it possibly live?' No, even if people take care of it well, it will die. Because this little thing was born too soon. If it lives, it will only be because God wants it to.

Nisa, !Kung San woman of the Kalahari Desert, Africa

Once upon a time, the fate of the premature baby was very much in God's hands. An infant born long before his time needed a miracle if he was going to live. The story of this premature San baby ends with sadness: his mother died soon after giving birth and although he was nursed by his father's lover and raised as her own, he eventually died, too. In societies where life is a constant struggle, every baby needs the strongest possible start in order to have a hope of surviving to adulthood.

Modern miracles happen all the time in western society. The intensive medical approach is equipped to keep younger and younger babies alive, assisting them to breathe and feed until they can manage by themselves. Babies born at (or even before) twenty-four weeks are known as 'micro-prems'. Since the heart, brain, gut and lungs are not fully formed at this point in gestation, such babies can only hope to survive with massive medical intervention. The dilemma facing doctors is how and whether to treat the extremely 'unready' babies, knowing that their chance of physical disability and brain damage is between ten and ninety-eight per cent.

Traditional cultures had fewer ethical dilemmas, but they do have their own special ways of giving premature babies the best possible chance. Roughly summarised, their strategies mirror everything that is done for full-term infants, but with greater intensity. Here are some examples from around the world:

- The Ga baby of Ghana is protected 'like an egg' after the birth. His aunt is dispatched to a medium who in turn consults an oracle to discover any special needs the newborn might have. Until she returns, the mother must sit holding her unwashed baby in her arms. After a bathing and a blessing, the baby is 'incubated' next to his mother's body indoors for at least seven days. If after that he is still alive and well, he has survived the 'seven dangers' of birth and becomes a human being.
- Inuit mothers wrap their premature babies in the soft skin of a seabird and hang him over a small oil lamp for up to a month. The baby is fed with oil and expressed breastmilk until he learns to suckle.
- The Gusii mother of Kenya makes herself completely available to her ill or premature baby. She remains in her house near her cooking fire, and next to the placenta, which is placed in a metal bowl and covered with special leaves called 'emesabakwa' – the placenta offers protection to the newborn against anyone who may wish him harm. The father (who usually works away from home), is summoned. At his arrival, the placenta may be buried and from now on the only permitted visitors are those who have already 'greeted' the infant (in a ritual courtesy called 'ogokwania omwana'.) Now the mother and baby must stay indoors, the fire must be kept going and the mother must be fed good food. She holds her baby constantly and breastfeeds frequently in a seclusion which may last up to six weeks. This is the original form of incubation: the warmth and nurture provided by a mother's own body.

In ancient practice, the special care provided for a premature baby is channelled entirely through his primary resource: his mother. Rather than separating the baby as in the western medical model, taboos force mother and infant into close contact: mother is fed the best food and the baby receives as much breastmilk as he needs. The baby is kept warm in his mother's arms, and she must stay secluded and quiet, near a constantly flickering fire (whatever the local climate).

INCUBATOR BABIES

Intensive, close-contact nurture is the result of an instinctual desire to keep weak babies safe and close to every maternal comfort. It is, of course, the way that most mothers reared their ailing newborns before the invention of the incubator in the 1890s.

Two doctors, Alexandre Lion and Martin Couney, are separately credited with the invention of the modern incubator. Lion's 'couveuses' were a series of metal ovens into which wrapped premature babies could be deposited for feeding and cleaning. Of course, he advocated the separation of mother and baby in order for medical procedures to be monitored in a scientific way. The babies in boxes visited many French cities and visitors were charged fifty centimes a head to peek inside. Meanwhile, Couney's sideshow toured the fairs and expositions of Europe and America for twenty years, displaying more than 5,000 premature infants. Babies were only returned to their mothers when they reached five pounds in weight.

Before long, every self-respecting American hospital used the incubator as a standard piece of neonatal equipment. Couney had not allowed mothers to visit their babies during treatment, and hospitals instituted a similar practice, bringing babies to the ward only at feeding times. The incubator (and its companion, the nursery cot) were the primary instrument of separation between the newborn and the mother whose body he craved.

Traditional care of premature babies continues in many rural areas. Incubator care is expensive and requires not only an electrical supply, but a system of hospital routine. Working in Mozambique, East Africa, during the 1990s, one London doctor commented:

We don't have any special facilities for premature babies. However tiny the baby, he is simply wrapped in a kanga [an African woman's wrap] and given to the mother to hold and keep warm against her own body and give him breastmilk, maybe expressed and with a spoon if he is too weak to suck.

I pick up these little scraps that I can hold in the palm of one hand and weigh them; often they are alert and sturdy, and soon start to suck.

Once they are gaining weight they go home, even if they are still only a couple of pounds, because they are not having any particular treatment here and it is much easier for mother and child to be looked after by the extended family in their own village.

Dr Eleanor Clark, British GP

In 1983, doctors in Colombia, South America, decided to replicate folk medicine in their treatment of premature babies. At the Juan de Dios Hospital in Bogotá, doctors encouraged mothers to hold their babies skin-to-skin next to their bodies instead of placing them alone in heated cots. They also sent babies home much sooner than is the accepted practice in developed countries. The doctors soon estimated that they were saving hundreds of lives.

Previously, fifty per cent of prematures under 4.4 lbs were dying: now ninety-five per cent survived, they claimed, even those in the 'micro-prem' category.

There are many suggested benefits of this kind of 'Kangaroo Care'.

- Skin-to-skin contact with another body keeps the baby at a perfect temperature and does this more reliably than an electronic incubator, rising and falling in response to the baby's needs.

- Body movement is a constant stimulation reminding the baby to breathe.
- Mother contact gives the baby a human context: smell; colostrum and breastmilk on tap (to the perfect consistency and quality for the individual infant); the sound of the heart-beat and the sweet reassurance of a familiar voice.
- The upright position on a parent's chest helps to clear the baby's airways for breathing.
- Studies show that 'Kangaroo' babies cry less each day than their premature counterparts and that their mothers go on to nurse for four weeks longer.

Although Kangaroo Care has its limits (it should not be used as a substitute for intensive medical treatment, but rather as a supplementary benefit), it reintroduces a human element to pre-mature babycare which has been missing in the West for a hun-dred years. In the words of the paediatrician who pioneered the Kangaroo project: 'In an incubator the baby is too quiet. It is not stimulated in any way. No voice, no sound, no touch – just glass. We came to look upon the mother as the best incubator. We encourage free feeding, and stimulation through the mother's singing and talking' (Dr Edgar Rey, Kangaroo Care pioneer).

There were also some unexpected benefits to the method. Nurses noticed that it gave confidence to anxious mothers and fathers who had previously been unable to bond with their babies. The bonding problem has long been documented: in the West, premature babies are more likely to cry a lot after birth, to display behavioural problems later on and to be physically abused. Could the lack of early intimacy be interfering with parents' primeval protective instincts? After a trip to Colombia, one medical team was determined to find out.

. . . What struck Andrew Whitelaw [British paediatrician] and Kathy Sleath [neonatal sister] was that the mothers in Bogotá looked so happy. 'There was such a contrast

between their happy faces and the worried faces of the mothers in the premature baby ward back in London.' . . .

Kathy Sleath finds the effect on their mothers most significant of all: 'Women
feel so totally different about their baby after they have tried skin-to-skin contact,'
she says. 'Some burst into tears; some say they feel their child has been born again.
One father who tried it said, 'I feel pregnant now.'

Emily Smyth, journalist

A Special Need

In a sense, the community considers these children blessed, or surrounded by a
light of holiness.

Homa Hoodfar, anthropologist in Egypt, on disabled
children in a poor urban area

The special requirements of disabled children inevitably make
extra demands on their parents, carers and immediate community. In early human cultures, where life was a constant struggle
for every member, a baby born with severe deformity was
unlikely to be kept. There might be a suspicion of black magic
and a fear that the child would not be able to survive into independent adulthood, a prerequisite for the nomadic lifestyle.

In the earliest societies – as today, in the western climate of
pre-natal testing and abortion – few children with disabilities
were to be found. The Spartans of ancient Greece were notoriously strict in weaning out weak infants. Elders of the state
would examine each newborn to determine whether or not it
was healthy and might be kept. '. . . If it was puny and deformed,
[the Spartans] dispatched it to what was called "the place of
rejection" (Apothetae), a precipitous spot by Mount Taygetus,
considering it better both for itself and the state that the child
should die if right from birth it was poorly endowed for health
or strength' (Plutarch, essayist and biographer, first century,
Greece). Even surviving babies were 'tested' for strength by
bathing them in wine, rather than water. The Spartans believed

that the wine would cause an epileptic or ailing child to stiffen and lose his senses, but that a healthy baby would be strengthened by the treatment.

Throughout early human history, each culture had its own criteria for infanticide. In some, breech-birth babies were not allowed to live. Among the Ache of Paraguay, where most babies are born with a full head of hair, a baby was not considered human if he was born bald. In former days, he would have been buried at birth.

The most common folk view of disability is that it is caused by events during pregnancy. Shocking experiences and broken taboos are believed to affect the well-being of the foetus. Medieval mothers were told to avoid shocks and not to let their imagination run wild, as even bad thoughts might affect the baby. 'The experts recommended that women should avoid fixing their gaze on the abnormal in whatever form it came – dwarfs, cripples (beggars with sores and deformities followed pregnant women, knowing that they would be bought off), ugly crones, hags and cretins, toads and nasty creatures' (Olwen Hufton, social historian). Although bizarre to us today, these warnings have their equivalents in modern pregnancy taboos. Western doctors associate a number of disabilities with pregnancy problems, such as dietary inadequacies (or vitamin overload), smoking, drinking, infection and severe stress.

In medieval Europe, it was the midwife's job to check the newborn baby for signs of abnormality – and by all accounts, these were fairly common at the time. In Christian society, as elsewhere, it was often assumed that the parents had sinned in the eyes of God. Both parents had to pay penance for their 'errors', since the father's seed was understood to contribute equally to the creation of the child. Some African peoples also subscribe to this view, requiring parents, or even the entire community, to perform penance and renewal ceremonies after the birth of a disabled baby.

In rural Malaysia, Islamic law places the emphasis less on sin than on humility in the face of divine will: 'Serious defects, such as missing joints, cannot be cured and must be accepted as lessons (not punishments) from God. The lesson is twofold and clear: remember your wife and child when they are most vulnerable; and be careful not to inflict unnecessary cruelty on animals' (Carol Laderman, social anthropologist).

So what must parents do, when gifted a baby with special needs? The traditional response is to supply those needs without question, treating the child with an intensive loving care. In Tibet, for instance, the baby with Down's syndrome is nurtured using as much physical contact as possible. When parents accept each baby as an important part of the family, the rest of the community swiftly follows suit.

In Kenya, Gusii mothers apply a 'squeaky wheel strategy' to babycare, according to anthropologists. So a baby who is small for his age will be fed more; a baby who is developing slowly is carried more and his weaning delayed.

Extreme cases support this rule: A hydrocephalic child observed in the 1950s and a child with a serious metabolic deficiency observed in the 1970s, both of whom never became capable of standing or walking, were constantly held and fed (when they would take food) long after the normal age of weaning . . .

Gusii mothers made heroic efforts to save deformed, disabled and vulnerable infants, often successfully.

Robert LeVine, anthropologist in Africa

None of this intensive maternal care would be possible without the equally intensive support of the surrounding community, whose positive attitudes and practical assistance help families cope with disabilities of every kind. In the poorest quarters of Cairo, Egypt, where families have little in the way of social security or clinical help, the entire community pulls together.

The mothers of these children often receive help and sympathy from their neighbors. On occasions when the mothers are tired and frustrated, they are advised not to curse the children or their fate, but to remember that God will reward them with tranquillity. These supportive talks often change the mother's mood and she resumes her responsibilities with a lighter spirit.

Homa Hoodfar, anthropologist in Cairo, Egypt

HOME TRUTHS

For minor ailments the mistress of a household was expected to know the proper remedies and how to make them. In most cookery-books there was a section on home-made medicinal brews and salves, some of them age-old. A great many of these recipes contained herbs, which were grown in most gardens.

Janet Dunbar, historian of Victorian England

Parents are increasingly looking for ways to empower themselves in the healthcare of their babies. Although we have a wealth of drugs and modern diagnoses at our disposal, there is still plenty we can do to strengthen our own healing capabilities before we rush to the doctor. We may, for instance, use our senses to tell us whether or not a baby is really ill – look into his eyes or smell his skin: his body is a casebook packed with evidence pointing to his state of health.

And when it comes to healing, we have many home-grown techniques and tools at our fingertips. Minor conditions like nappy rash can be dealt with using benign ingredients from the kitchen cupboard; gentle touching techniques help to soothe an unsettled baby; a day's intensive nursing can do wonders to see a cold or a tummy bug run its course.

In all questions of babycare, the baby carries the clues. He will tell you without hesitation the minute you reach his level of tolerance. His body language tells you when he is feeling out of sorts. His relaxed manner during a massage session reveals his inner contentment. He will display his evident pleasure at being soothed, changed or rubbed better by your hands – and if he starts to squirm or cry, then he has had enough.

We are, of course, lucky to live in a culture where scientific understanding helps us to give our babies the best possible start in life. We benefit from healthcare systems which serve our babies' needs with consistency and give us access to some of the most effective treatments in history. But we should beware any complacency that western medical methods are the only way. Symptomatic treatment with powerful drugs undoubtedly raises questions which future generations must answer. Mass vaccination programmes, the routine use of antibiotics, water laced with fluoride, vegetables coated with pesticides – these are just a few interventions which affect our children in ways we may not yet fully understand.

For too long, mothers' hunches and fathers' intuition were ignored by medical experts with a pre-set programme to follow. Today's doctors are far more likely to listen to parents' own assessments, based on the wisdom which comes from intimacy. Optimum infant health draws on every perspective, a lesson which most of us are happy to concede.

15. Happy Talk

The variety of human language is first-hand evidence of the difference that culture makes. Babies have no problem picking up the ambiguities and accents of their mother tongue – it's the grown-ups who struggle to learn the merest smattering of holiday French. But talking is only one of many ways that people speak to their babies . . .

A Quiet Start

From the moment of birth every society has evolved its own unique ways of dealing with the child. It is on the basis of repeated sensory experiences of the culturally prescribed stimulations that the child learns how to behave according to the requirements of the culture.

Ashley Montagu, social scientist

What are our culturally-prescribed stimulations for a newborn baby? Lots of eye contact, communicating from a distance, proto-conversations, early learning – these are all encouraged in western culture. Experts presume that parents want to encourage their children towards early, fluent speech in order to increase their chances of academic success. As British BabyTalk consultant Dr Sally Ward puts it:

Language is what distinguishes human beings from the rest of creation, and there can be little doubt as to its importance to our society and culture . . . It is clear, therefore, that there can be few things more important than ensuring that our children acquire the very best communication skills that we can give them. Delay in language development, however, is recognised as the most common childhood disability.

But one culture's 'disability' may be another culture's norm. Despite the western fixation on language acquisition as a desirable goal, there are many societies where speech is mistrusted and little or no emphasis is placed on teaching it to babies.

Some cultures take the emphasis away from words when they interact with babies and small children. They place a high value on body language and non-verbal exchanges. By contrast, holding, handling, stroking and fondling are all considered essential aspects of communication with infants in many pre-literate and non-industrialised societies. And since all babies are born pre-literate and non-industrialised, they probably appreciate the conversation.

- Among the Amish people of Pennsylvania, north-east America, there is a long tradition of non-speaking and symbolic communication. Their personal relationships are characterised by intimacy and simplicity – they shun higher education and (persuasive) missionary work.

- Japanese people traditionally distrust verbal skills. Although they talk to their babies as much as American mothers do, their conversation is more soothing than stimulating. They also carry their babies more and, in consequence, the babies tend to be more subdued than their American peers.

- Sioux parents of Dakota are in no hurry to communicate with their babies through language. They carry their babies on cradleboards and nurse them at will – and this, it seems, is communication enough. Baby talk is minimal and, consequently, language learning may be delayed. However, children become bilingual in the end: 'The early development of the child is watched by adults with amusement and patience. There is no hurrying along the path of walking and talking. On the other hand, there is no baby talk. The language usually taught first is the old Indian one: English is still a problem to many children when they enter school' (Erik Erikson, psychoanalyst, among the Sioux people of South Dakota, 1950).

* Gusii mothers of Kenya see no need to talk to their babies, and they think it is 'silly' to do so. In normal, domestic situations, conversation is slow and restrained – people do not feel a need to fill the silences. Gusii mothers talk to their babies half as much as American mothers during the first ten months and do not expect the infants to respond or interact in any way. Since Gusii babies are held all the time, and their needs met through non-verbal cues, there is less opportunity for eye contact, one of the prerequisites for promoting speech: '"Talking to" means "looking at". "Look at me when I'm talking to you," Eric Morecambe used to say to Ernie Wise. To get real communication going with the baby, you have to keep in eye contact' (David Crystal, professor of linguistic science).

* Tibetan mothers carry their children for up to four years and communications are exchanged via body rhythm and intuition. Since words are not always necessary, Tibetan children tend to be slower than western children in learning to speak.

Members of many traditional families often appear happy to coexist without constant conversation, a phenomenon surprising to western observers:

The old lady was still talking to herself. 'There's no milk in anybody's house. He went and asked in everyone's house. Hey, Saroji . . . no, it's Sudhammi, hey, child, run and see next door whether they've got some milk. She's curdled it. See, I'd kept it aside for coffee.'

But the child did not move, and the old lady forgot to remind her. It was strange how the women and children, through working so closely together, barely seemed to communicate; or if they spoke, it was to tell one another what to do.

Sarah Hobson, documentary film maker,
among the Gowda women of south India

Show Me a Sign

> Just watch someone accidentally swallow something boiling hot, and you see how eloquently he speaks – and how wordlessly. He leaps up, hops from foot to foot, frantically waving his hands as though to rid himself of the excess heat. His face is contorted, his eyes are watering. Whether he is Eskimo, Turk or Japanese he has managed to say 'I've burned myself' – and to say it without using a single word.
>
> Frédérick Leboyer, natural birth pioneer

Long before they can talk, babies communicate with us. Neonates are capable of imitating facial expressions, sounds and hand gestures within minutes of birth. They are also equipped to convey their happiness and distress, the desire for 'more' or 'less'. But do we always read the signs? In our highly verbal culture, we may be more receptive to babbling and early speech, the obvious signs of intellect. Meanwhile, some of our babies' earliest communications may be missed.

Many parents longingly anticipate the day when their babies will be able to describe their needs with words. As babies get older, although they continue to express themselves through body language, we continue to insist that they construct fully-formed sentences. We interrupt the crying child to make him tell us what is the matter. But there is little need to ask how children feel when they are jumping for joy, stretching from boredom, or red in the face with anger. It might be more useful to be aware of our culture's tendency to lean on words when there are so many other ways of communicating:

Impatiently, we wait for our children to be able to express themselves verbally; we congratulate them for speaking like adults and being able at last to protect us from the raw truth that they had been continually trying to express through their body. We're reassured when, like us, they can use verbal language as a screen to hide their true desires, to modify their natural tendencies, to master their sensations. 'Talk to me. Tell me what's on your mind. If you don't talk to me, how do you expect me to know what's wrong,' say parents to children emitting corporal distress signals that they don't see.

Thérèse Bertherat, Mézières body therapist

During the first year of life, babies develop increasingly subtle means of communication, mostly without words. An elaborate repertoire of gestures – some automatic, others less so – are there for anyone to read. Even the tiniest baby will brush the back of his hand against his mouth to indicate a desire to feed. And anyone can tell at a distance when their child needs the toilet. Some analysts say these signals constitute an early stage in the development of speech. Certainly, babies continue to make them even when no one appears to be in the room.

A growing number of parents in America and Britain are learning to use a system of signs to communicate with their preverbal babies. Using a programme devised by early childhood development researcher Joseph Garcia, based on the American sign language, parents begin to teach their babies signs for simple words from the age of six months. By the eighth or ninth month, babies begin signing back, learning up to seventy-five words to communicate their needs and frustrations. (Although these are hearing babies, the system may be used with deaf babies, too. Garcia was originally inspired by the superior language ability of a ten-month-old child who had been taught to sign by his deaf family.) Studies show that seven years later, children who were first taught to sign have a mean IQ of 114 compared with 102 in non-signing babies.

More importantly, signing may increase the subtlety of interaction between parent and child, so creating a greater repertoire of communication. Some cultures and sub-cultures have made use of these early signalling abilities in unusual ways. Actions, not words, are the basis for learning manners and other required behaviours in a diverse range of human cultures:

* Mothers of Okinawa, Japan, instruct their babies in the signs

of politeness from a very early age. They may teach them 'thank you', which is performed at the end of a meal by raising the empty bowl with a nod of the head and the words 'Gochiso-sama' (it was a feast). After nursing their babies, they lay their tiny hands one over the other, palms up, bend their bodies into a small bow, and say 'Gochiso-sama' for them.

- Western parents encourage their small babies to wave 'goodbye' to a departing guest and to clap their hands in appreciation of a job well done.

- Balinese babies are taught to move their fingers, hands and limbs in all directions, to develop their youthful dexterity for dancing. Later on, the children will have their limbs moulded and twisted into the required positions by dance teachers to form graceful shapes. 'This suppleness is not only the pre-requisite of professional dancers, it is part of everybody's life, and the movements are valued by all Balinese' (Anthony Forge, social anthropologist in Bali).

- Maori babies of New Zealand learn to rub noses with friends and family — this is the traditional way of greeting.

- Quite small children in African culture are taught to shake hands when they meet relatives and friends. A number of different hand-clasps are used (two chiefs of Nigeria will place the backs of the hands together to show high status). Gusii mothers of Kenya hold out the hands of small babies for visitors to shake.

- Tibetan babies are shown how to pray. For instance, when visiting the statue of a god, the child will be made to bow, hold his hands together and touch his head to the object of reverence. This might even apply to the religious icons in a museum:

The grandmother lifted the baby toward each statue, gently touching her head to the glass case so the baby could also receive the blessing of each statue. The baby seemed to enjoy the process, eyes wide as she came close to the glass, blinking once or twice as she made contact. Even at this young age, the baby was brought up to pray in this way.

Anne Hubbell Maiden, social psychologist and Edie Farwell, anthropologist

By the time they are toddling around, Tibetan children can already identify the deities and will bow to them respectfully. 'It is,' say Anne Hubbell Maiden and Edie Farwell, 'one of the first acknowledgments of their culture that Tibetans learn.'

* In Nepal and India, mothers place their babies' palms together in the traditional and spiritual greeting of 'Namaste', which means 'I bow to you'.

Talking It Over

The number of sounds that can be produced by our vocal cords and our oral and nasal cavities are practically unlimited. The three or four dozen of the English language are a selection which coincides not even with those of such closely related dialects as German and French. The total that are used in different languages of the world no one has even dared to estimate. But each language must make its selection and abide by it on pain of not being intelligible at all. A language that used even a few hundred of the possible – and actually recorded – phonetic elements could not be used for communication.

Ruth Benedict, anthropologist

To talk is to be human. Chimps can't do it (despite the laborious efforts of research scientists) and even the most loquacious budgerigar isn't really talking, since he has about as much brain as a tape-recorder. But the average five-year-old human child uses 2,000 words, understands 2,000 more and is already fluent in 1,000 grammatical rules (or as many as he needs for his own language). If necessary, he will effortlessly pick up two or three extra languages along the way, like the Amish child of Pennsylvania, who speaks Pennsylvania German at home, English in school and uses High German for Bible study.

Language acquisition remains one of the most amazing feats of the natural world. All languages have nouns and verbs and grammatical rules. In fact, the oldest known languages in the world also have the most complex grammar – there is no such thing as a grammatically 'primitive' language. No wonder so many cultures consider the arrival of infant speech to be a matter of utmost importance. Talking helps us to convey cultural traditions from the past, survival techniques for the present and plans for the future. If we all spoke one language, it would require us to enter each other's thought patterns and begin to embrace each other's values.

However, it is likely that any attempt at imposing a universal language like Esperanto or 'Wol Wantok' (World One-Talk, the noble campaign by British actor Ken Campbell to teach everyone pidgin English) would merely result in a splintering into dialects which would be barely intelligible from one side of the globe to the other. Cultural and linguistic diversity are flip-sides of the same coin.

While languages are the bonding glue for every culture, they also help to keep intruders out. The older, more elaborate languages in particular seem designed for exclusivity, acting as defence barriers against intrusion from the neighbours. Where there is competition for resources, many languages may develop in a small area – there were once several hundred different dialects to be found in the highlands of Papua New Guinea. Today, a hundred of these are threatened with extinction.

Talking also has a social function within each community: other primates groom each other to cement their relationships; humans chat about the weather. Talking feeds our imagination and consoles us; it excites and subdues us; it can empower and disempower, cherish and destroy, depending on how it is used.

BRAIN TALK

When a baby learns his mother tongue, he is shaping the structure of his brain. He is becoming a member of his own community. Mark Pagel, a biomathematician from Oxford University, has studied the effect language learning has on the infant brain.

All babies are born with the ability to tell all sounds apart from each other and to utter any of the sounds necessary for their own language. Yet within a few years, a Japanese child is unable to hear the difference between an 'l' and an 'r', much less pronounce them accurately. 'The brains of Japanese-speaking adults differ from those of non-Japanese-speaking adults,' says Pagel, 'and do so at a physiological level.'

> One's own experience as a language learner is to become another person. Who among those who have learned to speak French moderately well has not had the sensation of discovering a new personality, one to whom shrugs, hand gestures, and an urge towards precision come naturally?
>
> **Peter Popham, journalist**

This is just one of the many reasons why it is so difficult to talk about genetic programming with reference to the human species. Whatever our genetic predisposition, our early learning experiences help to change us fundamentally. Within a few weeks of being held or put down, breast or bottle-fed, massaged daily or left to cry nightly and exposed to a particular language, we are different people. It is impossible to say which aspects of our behaviour are due to nature and which have been shaped by nurture. We are all moulded, from conception onwards, by the overwhelming environment.

An Ear for Language

The day your baby is about to be born, that day your heart is miserable. But once it is lying on the sand, a baby is a wonderful thing. Your heart is very happy because you love children. You and your child talk together, even if it is just tiny.

Nisa, a !Kung San woman of the Kalahari Desert, Africa

Intimate conversation between a mother and baby begins at birth, and even before the baby is born. Thai mothers believe that the foetus reacts to all his mother's sensual experiences and so pregnant women deliberately seek out positive sensations. Mothers from many cultures sing and speak softly to the baby they are carrying. 'Oh my darling,' sings the Indian mother in her Song of the Fifth Month, 'I can hear your heartbeats.' From the sixth month of gestation, foetuses start responding to external sounds, jumping at loud noises and even moving in rhythm to their mother's speech. Cultural conditioning has begun.

After birth, even the tiniest of infants can tell the difference between one language and another. Week-old French babies were tested to see how they responded to French and other languages. Simply hearing their mother tongue excited the babies' sucking reflex. Dr Jacques Mehler of Paris believes babies respond to the melody of language rather than to individual words, and this is precisely what is going on when parents all over the world coo and sing to their newly-born babies. Cradle-songs soothe, even when you don't understand a thing:

> Nina bobo, oho ninana bobo.
> Kalau tidak bobo di gigit nyamuk.
> Tidurlah sayang adikky manis.
> Kalau tidak bobo di gigit nyamuk.
> Indonesian mother's song to her baby

Lullabies are an obvious form of aural comfort – but how essential are they for language development? In the thirteenth century, the German King and Roman Emperor Frederick II conducted an experiment to find out which language children would speak if they were reared without ever hearing the human voice. Would it be Hebrew, Greek, Arabic, Latin, or their mother tongue, he wondered. But the experiment was a disaster. Without exposure to human speech or lullabies, the babies all died, 'because they could not live without the petting and the joyful faces and loving words of their foster mothers, or without those "swaddling songs" which a woman sings to put a child to sleep and without which "it sleeps badly and has no rest"' (Salimbene de Adam, thirteenth-century Italian Franciscan Friar).

Ancient peoples placed enormous weight on the ability to speak, and to speak well. The art of oratory was considered essential for political and personal power. The Romans actually defined babyhood as the inability to converse: '*infans*' or infant meant 'he who does not speak'. (The word 'infant' applied to all children under seven, as it was reasoned they took seven years to learn to speak eloquently.)

However, the ancients did realise that babies had an ear for language and so they deliberately tried to surround them with well-spoken nurses and servants. If the baby was destined to become an orator, he should be influenced by good speech models in his infancy: 'Literature on rhetorical training sometimes invoked the idea that significant learning might occur in the early years and that it might therefore be hazardous to hand over young children to servants of dubious morality and syntax' (Suzanne Dixon, lecturer in classics and ancient history).

When choosing a wet nurse, a mother was advised to consider the musicality of the woman's tongue as well as the milk in her breasts. The nurse should be 'Not ill-tempered: since by nature the nursling becomes similar to the nurse and accordingly grows sullen if the nurse is ill-tempered, but of mild disposition if she is even-tempered . . . And she should be a Greek so that the infant nursed by her may become accustomed to the best speech' (Soranus of Ephesus, Greek physician, *Gynaecology, c.* 500 AD).

The ancients were right to believe in babies' receptivity to language. Modern studies suggest that infants as young as seven months are able to understand the rudiments of grammar, recognising patterns in speech even if they don't always understand the words. By nine months old, three per cent of children have already uttered their first word, and by eighteen months, ninety per cent have started speaking.

WHISPER WORDS OF WISDOM

In Muslim tradition, the first words a newborn baby hears must be uttered by a man, bringing a message of spiritual purity. The custom of Azan dictates that words of God must be the first to pass the newborn's ear. The baby's father or grandfather whispers 'Allahu Akbar', 'Allah is the greatest', into the baby's right ear. Although, of course, the baby is not yet able to understand the meaning, he most probably appreciates the intimacy and melody of this already-familiar voice.

Going Ga-Ga

> Dance, baby, diddy;
> What shall Daddy do widdy?
> Sit on his lap,
> Give it some pap;
> Dance, baby diddy.
>
> **English dandling rhyme**

We all do it. We may not realise we're doing it and if we are caught in the act, we might feel a little foolish, but when we speak to babies, we instinctively enter the zone of 'baby talk'. Men baby-talk as well as women; people in quiet cultures do it and so do people in societies which value sophisticated language.

When we baby-talk, we amplify the pitch and timing of our words until they sound more like song than speech, and we use exaggerated facial expressions. We throw in lots of endearments and short phrases, especially questions, and we invent new words. With our voices, we are gently wooing the receptive baby: 'No matter the language, no matter the culture, "baby talk" is the same the world over because all human parents are adapted to engage their babies vocally in the same way, and all babies are ready to hear what their parents have to say' (Meredith Small, ethno-paediatrician).

Baby talk is a sweet condescension. Children do not use it to each other and many adults find it highly irritating when directed at them. It is speech reserved exclusively for babies – although it is occasionally used by western couples who equate the intimacy of the love relationship with babyhood. By the time they are around three or four, children are able to use this special language themselves, to communicate with even younger children and dolls.

Here are some global soundbites to chew on . . .

* In thirteenth-century Europe, wet nurses were delegated the role of teaching the baby to speak in upper-class homes. 'Hers was the hand that rocked his cradle and hers the voice that soothed him with lullabies; it was she who began teaching him to speak, "lisping and repeating the same words"' (Mary Martin McLaughlin, historian, describes the job of medieval wet nurse).

* American baby talk is perhaps the most highly-honed in the world. Parents repeatedly question their babies, lavishing them with praise for every tiny response and use 'gyrating' expressions to obtain the baby's attention. Looking at baby is also very much a part of American maternal behaviour. Since they are less likely to carry their babies around than mothers in traditional cultures, American mothers tend to interact with

their babies from a distance. A study of mothers from Boston showed that they gazed at their babies during twenty-eight per cent of research time, while the babies looked at their mothers only eight per cent of the time (the ratio applies to western European mothers, too).

* Research on French mothers in the 1940s concluded that they were more likely to baby-talk with babies than to chatter with older children. 'While mothers and nurses direct a good deal of affectionate talk to a baby in a carriage, they tend to ignore the three-year-old squatting at their feet or sitting on the bench beside them,' said anthropologist Martha Wolfenstein.

* According to the Wodaabe, a Fulani tribe of north-east Nigeria, it is the mother who must take on the responsibility of teaching the child to speak, using baby talk in a playful way. She makes games out of basic words, passing over difficult terms, until, gradually, the child begins to repeat them back to her.

* Tibetan parents use names to teach their babies to talk. They patiently point out the infant's many relatives, naming each one according to their relationship with the child: Grandma, Grandpa, Brother, Sister and so on. Likewise, small children are taught the names of deities kept in the family shrine.

EARLY LEARNING

Mothers in some cultures put their baby talk to good use. They do not chatter thoughtlessly to their infants, but use the time to impart early moral, religious and cultural lessons. The babies may not understand the words, but they are delighted and soothed by this intimate interaction and their mothers' tone of voice.

> Orthodox Jewish mothers whisper blessings to their babies. Australian Aboriginal mothers and grandmothers also teach their babies simple lessons from birth. Touching the baby's forehead with her hand, the mother says, 'You must give, you must share always', touching the mouth, she says, 'Use only fine words', and touching the eyes, 'Keep your eyes away from others' belongings'.
>
> In this picture the mother is doing healing to her baby. Touching her baby everywhere with smoking leaves. Telling the baby not to use bad language, how to behave themselves, having respect for older people, especially about what foods to eat, listening to her mother, father and grandmother, telling her baby not to just walk in into someone's home but to knock first, not to steal anything either. The mother puts the smoking leaves over the baby on her baby's mouth, hands and head. She is telling her young baby that when she grows up they will have to learn to go bush, and look for fish, kangaroo, and bush tucker, bush orange, bush berry, blackfella bush honey. She's got to learn the Aboriginal way.
>
> Polly Widaldji, woman of Warmun, Western Australia

Babbling Babies

Whatever the baby is doing at the time is taken as a basis for communication, whether the baby intends it to be communicative or not.

Bronwen Burford, movement therapist

One of the amazing aspects of human language is our ability to make conversation with babies – even though the babies are not, strictly speaking, talking back. We do this by reading multiple meanings into any squeaks and signs the infant might make.

Research has shown that adults treat babies as social, conversational beings long before speech emerges. Every sneeze, every hiccup is treated as the baby's part in a dynamic exchange.

Parents even leave gaps in their baby talk, graphically demonstrating where the baby's turn might come. Eventually, the baby learns to fill those gaps.

Adults do sometimes play games with a baby's babble – imitating it, and trying to elicit more of it. They also hear 'words' in it, and try to persuade the baby to speak. An English mother, for example, may think her baby has named her when she hears [mamamama]; but, alas, this is not so. The real word for mummy will not appear for some time yet.

David Crystal, professor of linguistic science

As we have already seen, parents in some cultures respond more eagerly to babies' burbles than others. While American parents answer twenty per cent of any vocalisation their baby makes, the particularly taciturn Gusii mothers respond to only five per cent. It is likely the American figure would be even higher if many babies were not being deliberately ignored as part of their sleep-training programmes. Interestingly, American mothers become even more engaged with their babies once the babies start to speak. Maternal attention increases as the child starts to babble and talk.

YOU TALKING TO ME?

The Bantu peoples of South Africa celebrate the first time a baby answers to his own name. Many cultures consider using a person's name to be akin to summoning up his soul.

When babies start babbling, at between twenty-five and fifty weeks, they are making a serious attempt to practise the consonants they will need for their first words. In some cultures, this babbling is considered to be a serious attempt at talking. When British researchers asked mothers from Calcutta, India, when they expected their babies to start 'saying words', the Calcutta mothers said, 'Before nine months.' The researchers were understandably surprised by this response, since only the most precocious baby manages real words at this age:

However, discussion with our colleagues in Calcutta suggests there may be a conceptual difference between other Indian parents, in particular, and Western parents. It was suggested that, traditionally, the intonated babble strings that children produce in the months before they use single words have the status attributed in the West . . . to use of single words.

J. Goldbart, psychologist and S. Mukherjee, Spastics Society of Eastern India

Any movement or signs the baby makes may be interpreted and rewarded with further interaction from his carers. Early vocal play and long strings of babble will do; the melodic utterances which develop after babbling will certainly do.

In response to the babble of a child aged nine to eighteen months, parents start to sound like the Park Ranger in *Skippy*, the Australian children's TV drama. 'Hey!' says the Park Ranger, confronted by an agitated bush kangaroo. 'Skip seems to be trying to tell us something . . .'

Quite suddenly, a 'chunk' of babble stands out, with a more definite shape. It gives you a clear impression that the baby is trying to say something. It's impossible to say what, but parents quickly feel that their child is trying to be more communicative. They say things like 'He's definitely trying to tell us something,' and they associate different melodies with different associations. 'She's asking for her panda again', 'I think he wants to go back in his bouncer.'

David Crystal, professor of linguistic science

All babies in all cultures babble. It's a universal language, even for deaf babies. While the babbling of a deaf infant starts to diminish after six months or so, the babbling of the hearing child increases and starts to sound more meaningful. The baby is approaching his first words.

MY SON, THE GENIUS

Anthropologists studying East European Jewish families just before the Second World War noticed that everyone was on the look-out for first signs of intelligence in the baby. Smiles, vocalisations and imitations were seized on by parents as examples of the baby's advancing progress. While mother taught the baby a few early words, the baby could often hear his father's melodic prayers in the distance:

> As soon as the baby starts to talk, his mother teaches him religious blessings and sometimes a few simple Hebrew words. More important, however, the child is steeped in the atmosphere and the spirit of learning . . . The child becomes used to the melody of learning – the chant always uttered as the scholar reads – to the father's continual swaying as he studies.
>
> **Mark Zborowski, cultural researcher of East European Jewish origin**

Games Parents Play

> Teeta, Teeta, Teeta
> Papa brought a little fish,
> We're going to eat it in olive oil.
> My frying pan is sputtering.
> My cat's already nibbling the bones,
> Papa washed his hands, but found
> The Asaida prayer was finished.
> So he clapped his hands to his face.
> Teeta, oh Aneba
> What did Papa bring us?

He brought us lots of henna
So I'm going to put on henna
And give the rest to Shoosbena.

Tunisian pat-a-cake song for parent and child

All over the world, parents play with their children. The gentle, whispered conversations we have with our newborn infants gradually make way for a more robust kind of exchange as the baby grows older. With very few exceptions, parents use songs and games to extend their intimate conversations with their very young children. Nursery and 'dandling' rhymes use hand movements, bouncing, tickles and repetitions to elicit responses of delight. Why do parents do this? Because they love it.

Human adults enjoy invoking laughter in their tiny children, and this is done with remarkable consistency across the world. They make mock attacks on their children, tickling them, menacing them, or mock-biting them. They sometimes lift and shake them, or even throw them in the air and catch them again. Like the exaggerated contours of baby talk, this activity is directly evoked as a consequence of the parents' interest in the child, and has no conscious motivation.

Terence Dixon and Martin Lucas, authors in evolutionary science

It is hard to find a culture where parents do not play with their babies. One exception is the relationship of the Gusii mother and baby in Kenya. Gusii mothers keep stimulation of babies to a minimum, and if they do play with them, the interaction is usually brief and non-verbal. Although older siblings, aunts and grandmothers are more likely to make eye contact with the baby, excitable games are just not their style.

But baby games are a key part of the western parent's repertoire. Desmond Morris identifies four main strands of interactive play between an adult and a child under one – 'funny face', 'peek-a-boo', 'gentle tickle' and 'vertigo'. We know that mothers played hide and seek (or peek-a-boo) with their children as far back as the early thirteenth century. (One German painting of this period portrays a small child 'hiding' by clamping his palms over his own eyes — he believes, as all small children believe, that no one can see him.) Meanwhile, the medieval encyclopaedist Vincent of Beauvais recommended that babies be given two baths a day and lots of play.

Baby games emerged much earlier than this, of course. They are a part of the ancient evolved pattern of oral education, from first baby talk to adult conversation. We have only to look at hunter-gatherer groups to see the antiquity of baby games. !Kung San babies in the Kalahari Desert, Botswana, for instance, are constantly held, played with and talked to by all members of the band. Baby talk includes addressing the baby at length in 'conversational tones'. It is part of a package of babycare which seems highly pleasurable for all involved:

The !Kung never seem to tire of their babies. They dandle them, kiss them, dance with them, and sing to them. The older children make playthings of the babies. The girls carry them around, not as a task set by their parents (though they might carry babies around for that reason also), but because they play 'mother'. The boys also carry babies around, give them rides, and drag them on karosses [a cloak or baby sling] (a favorite game) . . . Altogether the babies appear to be as serene and contented as well-fed puppies.

Lorna Marshall, anthropologist

Parents sing to their babies, they clap with them and teach them hand movements (the purpose of the Tunisian song quoted above), and they gradually increase the excitement level as the baby's tolerance for tickling turns into a desire for ever-increasing thrills. Lap games turn into carefully calculated forms of catch-the-baby.

These games of approach and retreat prepare the baby for his inevitable forays into the real world: a world where his parents are not always in sight and where he will not always be held in arms. It may not be the mother who initiates this riskier kind of play. In studies, fathers from all cultures have been shown to indulge in more boisterous games, believing that their babies need more active stimulation than their mothers give them. Here, a British father records his evident delight in setting his daughter's heart racing:

The first time your baby roars with laughter is a memorable moment, up there with the first 'dada'. For Lola, it was a hint of danger that set her off. To disapproving looks from some mothers and right-on dads I used to take her buggy racing, running along park pathways, steering the buggy one-handed or shouting 'Look, no hands!' as I allowed it to freewheel downhill.

Pete May, journalist

Studies have yet to be done on the role of the visiting uncle, who (with a twinkle in his eye) is predisposed to wind the children up into a state of frenzy just before bed.

First Words

Everyone knows that most children spend more time with their mothers than with their fathers, in the first year or so of life. So it may come as a surprise to learn that most children use the word for 'father' earlier and much more often than the word for 'mother'.

David Crystal, professor of linguistic science

The original baby talker is, of course, the baby himself. The simple words which parents repeat all over the world are those very same sounds which the infant starts to utter around three to four months. After the open-mouthed cooing come the consonants – daa, taa, baa, maa, paa and gaa are some of the favourites. It is no coincidence that, in many languages, these simple sounds form the basis for the key figures in the baby's life: himself, his mother, father and grandparents. Consonants such as 'r', 'f' and 'z', which are harder for babies to say, are much less likely to appear in pivotal relationship terms.

But why should the baby – in carefully recorded cross-cultural studies – have an early preference for the word 'dad'? Linguists tell us that, in every culture, children are five times more likely to repeat the consonants 't' and 'd', 'b' and 'p', which are easier to say. It also happens that simple 't', 'd', 'b' and 'p' syllables feature widely in the word for father. 'Which leaves the $64,000 question. Why have words for 'father', over the course of human history, come to be more pronounceable than the words for mother?' (David Crystal).

Perhaps we should look at it the other way around. The most pronounceable syllables for human babies have been attributed to dads throughout history, in order to include dads in the family equation. Mother gives birth and traditionally carries the baby around, so the baby is like an extension of her body. Father's connection has to be pointed out and reiterated. Dads feature in lullabies and stories; they are remembered in their absence and anticipated when they come home from work. Just as mothers are keen to insist on paternal resemblance (Chapter 3: From Here to Paternity), so they reinforce the baby's linguistic relationship with Daddy: 'Billy asked for you again today . . .' It all helps to bond the father to his offspring. So when the baby starts to babble, 'daddy' is the first word most cultures choose to hear.

Here are some of the world's mummies and daddies by name:

* The Indo-European word for mother is 'mamma', pronounced 'mammee' by the ancient Greeks. It was based on the baby's spontaneous cry for his mother, and for her milk. The Greek verb 'mamman' meant to cry for the breast. The Romans used the noun 'mamma' and the adjective 'mammalis' to refer to the breasts. This, of course, is where the word 'mammal' comes from – she who suckles her young.
* Tembé mothers and fathers in the Amazonian rainforest of Brazil are known as 'Mamãe' and 'Pai' respectively.
* In Indonesia, Sulawesi children call mother 'Ma' and father 'Bapa'.

* A Jordanian child calls his father 'Ya-ba' and his mother 'Ya-ma'.
* Chinese and Egyptian children alike call mother 'Mama' and father 'Baba'.
* Nomadic children of Mongolia call their mother 'Aav' and their father 'Eej'.
* A Japanese mother is 'Otohsan' and the father is 'Okahsan'.
* On the Philippine island of Panay, children call their parents 'Papang' and 'Mamang'.
* Argentinean (Spanish-speaking) children call their parents 'Papi' and 'Mami'.
* In Greek homes, mother is called 'Mama', father is 'Baba' and grandmother is 'Yaya'.
* In Tanzania, East Africa, Maasai children say 'Mama' to all their father's wives.
* In Korea, mothers are called 'Omma' and fathers are 'Aboji'.

SEPARATE IDENTITIES

Tibetan parents have a superstition that if baby's first word is 'A-ma' (mother), the child will be separated from his mother first. If he says 'A-pa', he will be parted from his father. The most auspicious first word is 'A-ni' or aunt.

In many cultures, learning to talk is more than just a question of grasping grammar. Speaking is a magical skill, which binds the child to his community, and it comes with a wide range of beliefs and taboos:

* On the hundredth day after the baby is born, some Chinese families conduct a ceremony to encourage the baby to speak.

Friends and family arrive with gifts of fish and chicken, which are cooked for a celebratory feast. When the chicken is cooked, its tongue is rubbed over the baby's lips – this will make him a good talker.

* The Amish people of Pennsylvania say you should not tickle a child under one year old, or it will make him stammer.

* Among the Ganda of Uganda, a child who cannot speak is deemed to 'have no sense'. This is a protective philosophy, designed to give the baby the chance to make mistakes – born without common sense, he does not deserve to be disciplined or punished. Indian and other cultures also believe it is futile to try to correct the pre-verbal child.

* Just as they manipulate their babies' bodies into desired positions, so Balinese parents presume to speak for their infants before they can speak for themselves: 'I'm very happy to meet you' says the mother on behalf of her baby-in-arms. We can observe a twist on this theme in western families today, as grandmothers – afraid to address their daughters personally – speak through the child: 'You want a nice warm blanket, don't you? Why didn't Mummy give you a nice warm blanket?'

* Salt is used in a Malay ritual for newborns, for the 'opening of the mouth'. The quality of salt known as '*masin*' is also used in Malaysia to describe effective speech. By ritually touching the newborn's mouth with this magical substance at birth, the midwife is ensuring that he will grow up to be a persuasive speaker.

* In Germany, it was traditional for neighbours to bring the six-week-old baby a '*Schwatzei*', or chatting egg. They would tap the baby's mouth three times with the egg to encourage him to talk.

* Kpelle parents of Liberia are anxious that their children should learn to speak well and use language properly. Children are prompted and corrected in their speech from the earliest age.

* For the !Kung San people of Africa's Kalahari Desert, sharing

is the most important community ethic. It is no surprise, then, that two of the first words !Kung San children learn are '*na*', give and '*ihn*', take.

HOME TRUTHS

The life-history of the individual is first and foremost an accommodation to the patterns and standards traditionally handed down in his community. From the moment of his birth the customs into which he is born shape his experience and behaviour. By the time he can talk, he is the little creature of his culture, and by the time he is grown and able to take part in its activities, its habits are his habits, its beliefs his beliefs, its impossibilities his impossibilities. Every child that is born into his group will share them with him, and no child born into one on the opposite side of the globe can ever achieve the thousandth part.

Ruth Benedict, anthropologist

Language helps to make us who we are. No wonder people place so much emphasis on the spoken word. Bound up in our mother-tongue are a myriad ancient assumptions, beliefs, prejudices and survival strategies which help us to belong to our tribe. For some cultures – the Afikpo, an Ibo people of eastern Nigeria, for instance – the child who walks and talks is finally considered fully human. His spirit has decided to remain on earth.

Parents in western cultures work hard to encourage infant speech. Using a potent combination of ritual, eye contact and baby talk, they coax the infant into verbal responses, fondly believing they hear 'first words' where none were uttered. There is no apparent harm in this: children love positive interactions of all kinds. At the very least, they are learning that their parents appreciate the art of conversation. And in a society which places so much value on verbal fluency, children who speak early are likely to flourish in all sorts of ways.

Babies' first words tell us where their focus lies: in the people around them. Father, mother grandparents, siblings and the family cat – these are usually the first objects to be named by a speaking baby. In many hundreds of different languages, human babies are all saying the same thing: 'Hello everyone, I'm here.'

But there is no hurry. When babies' listening skills are intact, they will learn to speak. Whether the process is swift or slow depends on many factors: cultural conditioning, parents' verbosity and place in the family, to name a few. By the time they utter their first words, babies have already done much of the hard work. Their brains are imbued with the intonation and meaning of life in their own culture. And when, eventually, they are fluent, they will have absorbed many of the broad assumptions of their people. Later, they will mould the language to suit their own needs – to question or conserve cultural assumptions; to wage wars or broker peace; to create barriers, or – if they choose – build tolerance and understanding.

16. The Baby Grows

Living with a small child is like watching one of those time-lapse movies, where a flower unfolds before your eyes. The strides a human baby makes are more amazing than those of any other young animal, as his brain development makes up for lost time. These are months of great excitement and discovery – for both of you.

Testing, Testing

His mother weighs him regularly, proud of his progress.

Jean Liedloff, continuum therapist

Healthy infant development is the goal of all cultures, but each of us has a different definition of what this might mean. Some societies encourage their babies to crawl; others consider crawling unnecessary or 'impure'. Some train their babies into long bouts of sleep; others consider light sleep, broken by breast-feeding, to be the healthy ideal. In the West, equipped as we are with scales and machines for measuring a wide variety of vital statistics, we have a penchant for testing babies. But how mean-ingful are our tests, and what do they tell us about babies from wildly different backgrounds?

The study of childhood has developed enormously over the past fifty years, with almost every feature of infant life put under the microscope. This, of course, ought to give us a better under-standing of infancy and so improve our care of babies and, in many ways, western parents lead the world in awareness of health issues. We know about the value of colostrum and breastfeeding; we know about the importance of variety and purity in infant diets; we understand the dangers of cruelty to children and have well-formed ideas on early education. But at the same time, we might not realise that the standards we are working to are culturally biased.

When scientists developed the major developmental tests for babies, they were mostly working with white babies in hospital clinics and laboratory conditions. The tests themselves, designed by western researchers and doctors in the 1950s and 1960s, were based on western clinical assumptions of the period. The results they produced went on to become the gold standard for measuring all other babies.

Although nobody mentioned it at the time, this was a very narrow way of defining 'normality'. Developmental test results, while true of the white babies tested in specific conditions, may have little or no value when taken out of context. And for context, we need to look to the rest of the world.

Here are some examples of culture-specific baby testing and its dubious uses:

Infant personality tests

American psychologist Dr Jerome Kagan conducted a number of experiments to discover the limits of personality. How much is due to inborn nature, and how much to nurture? To settle this relentless debate, he followed children for the first few years of their lives, confronting them with new objects, unfamiliar voices and faces. When small, the baby sits in a plastic car seat in front of a video screen; later an unknown female researcher presents the baby with each new object. Around 30 per cent of the babies show a stress reaction – in other words, says Kagan, they are showing a predisposition to shyness or unsociability. Although Kagan believes that upbringing does affect the personality, he also says that inborn temperament is hard to shift.

Babies labelled as 'sociable' or 'cautious' tend to stay that way as they grow up. But with her ethno-paediatric view of these experiments, Meredith Small has her doubts as to their validity for all babies:

One can only imagine attempting to perform this same test on !Kung San infants [of the Kalahari desert]. First of all, a San mother probably would not allow a strange white researcher to take her baby out of her sight and [be] put in a stiff plastic seat in the first place. And the notion of offering novel objects or unfamiliar people is ludicrous for a hunter and gatherer who grows up in the same social group handling the same objects over time. A Gusii baby [from Kenya], on the other hand, has been molded from infancy to be quiet and affable. More than likely, there will be little reaction from a Gusii baby. And a Japanese child might be more disturbed by being separated from its mother than by any toy dangling in its face. In other words, the test setup . . . is a white, Western, middle-class scenario.

Meredith Small, ethno-paediatrician

Baby weighing

Infant growth charts are a cause of controversy among breast-feeding mums. All western babies have their weight plotted against the 'normal growth curve' which is supposed to show whether or not they are thriving. On the basis of a baby's position on the curve, health professionals may offer advice on infant diet. The growth charts are based on data collected in Yellow Springs, Ohio, America, between 1929 and 1975, using babies who were bottle-fed or breastfed only up to three months. Many of these babies were also already on solids, according to the child care practices of the period. But breastfed babies do not add weight at the same rate as bottle-fed, or early-weaned babies. They tend to grow rapidly in the first two or three months, but then slow down in comparison with babies on artificial milks.

Because of the slower growth velocity of breastfed infants, they often appear to be 'faltering' after the first two to three months when their growth is plotted on current growth charts, even if they are healthy and thriving. Their mothers may be counselled that their breast milk production is inadequate and that complementary formula or foods should be added.

Kathryn Dewey, professor of nutrition,
and M. Jane Heinig, postgraduate researcher

Reassessing the norms for breastfed babies could change the way we look at babies both here and abroad. For instance, children in so-called Third World populations are known to 'grow well' in the first three months of life (when they are breastfed frequently) but this spurt is typically followed by a much slower gain as they start to rely on other foods. These children usually end up on or below the fifth percentile according to western weight charts, the lowest curve within 'normal' range.

Sometimes such a pattern reflects an inadequate diet and malnutrition. But it may also have a lot to do with lifestyle, breastfeeding and a diet that is not stuffed with animal proteins. Studies of middle-class American breastfeeding mothers show that their babies, too, gain weight more slowly after three months than bottle-fed babies. Growth in babies' length and head circumference does not slow down, so the breastfed infants tend to be leaner than their formula-fed counterparts.

The slower growth rates and lower energy intake of breastfed infants in our population were not associated with any deleterious consequences in terms of illness, activity level or behavioural development. Breastfed infants with lower intakes or slower weight gain were no less active or healthy than those with higher intakes. Thus, it seems reasonable to conclude that it is normal for breastfed infants to gain weight less rapidly than current reference data suggest.

Kathryn Dewey and M. Jane Heinig

As the racial complexion of western society shifts towards a multi-cultural palette, we need to reassess our assumptions at home, too. For some immigrant populations, there may be a disparity between birth weight and chart averages at the outset, since white babies are born bigger than babies in many other ethnic groups. And when it comes to nutrition, only white, bottle-fed babies could possibly hope to achieve the label of 'normal', according to current growth charts.

For breastfeeding mothers of all cultures, the old growth charts can be disempowering, creating unnecessary anxiety and leading to poor nutritional advice. The task for health workers is to devise charts which have meaning for a particular community and even for individual families, taking into account personal history, physiology and methods of nurture.

Sleep standard tests

Sleep standards for western babies are based on data obtained from cot-bound, bottle-fed, white infants who have been trained to a schedule of long periods of solitary slumber. Since formula milk contains more fat, it induces a deeper kind of sleep. And with long intervals in their feeding schedule, many western babies learn not to ask for milk before their time is 'up'. Parents are told to expect 16 1/2 hours of sleep a day from their new-borns, 15 1/2 hours from babies at one month old and 14 1/4 hours at six months.* But real babies rarely perform to schedule. A study of seventy-five babies found that some slept as little as 10.5 hours a day, while others slept an astonishing 22 hours out of 24! Over-estimated sleep routines not only undermine parental confidence, they also give out unhelpful health messages.

Developmental tests

When anthropologists arrive in strange cultures, they are usually armed with developmental tests and interviews designed for use with their own populations. If the target children perform poorly according to these questionnaires, the researchers may presume that the children, not the tests, are lacking. But of course, the tests may be the limiting factor.

---

*According to one guide to 'The Newborn Baby', 'On average, in the first three months babies sleep about 18 hours a day.'

For instance, Kipsigis children of Kenya are raised to a high level of comprehension of language before the age of three. However, they are not encouraged to respond verbally to their parents, but merely to obey commands and listen attentively. This is entirely in keeping with Kipsigis goals in child-rearing, which demand that a child should be passive and helpful, not demanding or full of questions. However, this makes it devilishly hard for western researchers to quantify the intelligence of the Kipsigis child. Once again, the tests have been shaped to suit the temperaments of western babies and the expectations of western researchers, themselves children of their own culture.

Perhaps these examples will make us think twice before we pore over charts of infant development, checking off our children's achievements and anxiously anticipating any items they appear to have missed out. Some children never roll; others never crawl; some say their first words before they can walk; others go to school before they learn to sleep through the night; and thousands of children are perfectly healthy without following the precise rules of outmoded infant growth charts.

We have to remember that each child is an individual, that each individual belongs to a family, and each family to its own culture, with its own set of rules and biological differences. Test results are only a small part in the picture of a child's overall health. There may be more things in heaven and earth than are dreamt of in the testers' philosophy.

Stages of Life

> The first six years of life on earth
> We to January would compare,
> For in that month strength is as rare
> As in a child six years from birth.

French fourteenth-century poem, reprinted many times until the sixteenth century, representing childhood as 'January' and each month as another phase of growing old.

It always used to puzzle me. When I walked down the street with one of my babies, older women would stop to admire the child before saying, 'Make the most of it. This is such a precious time. And it's over so quickly.' As far as I was concerned, time seemed to be standing still.

When you are right in the middle of mothering or fathering, it is often hard to feel the months changing, or feel that you are making progress. If you are struggling – as so many of us do with the challenges of parenthood – it can seem as though each stage will last for ever. And yet now, with all my children in school and no babies to pull me into the present, I am beginning to understand what the women meant. Infancy may be something parents only really appreciate when it is done.

Each culture has its own way of describing babyhood:

- For the Romany (Gypsy) people of California, on America's west coast, babyhood is associated with innocence, a state which protects infants from the pollution taboos associated with puberty and adulthood. A 'sha' (boy) and 'shey' (girl) are considered intrinsically pure, a state which returns in old age.
- Among the Quechua communities of Peru, South America, the life stages are mapped out according to developmental progress. The first phase is the time between birth and the appearance of the first teeth; the second is the time spent crawling and walking around the house; another is the period when a child 'wanders' around his own village with his own social group.
- In Malaysia, life stages are explained in terms of the 'hot' and 'cold' humoral system. The bodies of babies and young children are considered to be fairly cold, which is why they tend to suffer from stomach-aches (which are a 'cold' condition).

First Things First

When the baby smiles for the first time, celebrate it. When the baby walks for the first time, this is significant. Write it down. Capture the magic and celebration of each new development in an infant's life.

Gyatso, Tibetan Buddhist lama

The birth of a baby is, in all societies, a joyful event, and his healthy growth is equally important. Parents in some cultures enjoy the developmental stages with quiet pride, while others are ritually bound to take notice of each 'first' and make a fuss of it.

It has often been pointed out that childhood was a concept unknown to medieval Europeans; that the child, once weaned, simply joined in adult games and pastimes. Yet there is also proof – in parents' letters and elsewhere – that childhood was observed, objectified and discussed by doting mothers and fathers:

Even in the sixteenth century, when times were violent, there surfaces a great deal of evidence of joy at the spectacle of the child's development, the babbling, the first words, the initial independent steps, 'their stammering, their little angers, their innocence, their imperfections, their necessities, are so many little emanations of joy and comfort'.

Olwen Hufton, social historian, quotes Jeremy Taylor, a father, 1600

In Tibetan culture, small incidents – such as the baby's first suckle at the breast, the first time he claps his hands, or the moment he first rises to his feet – are noticed and celebrated as part of the mosaic of childhood. Each accomplishment is a sign that the child is engaging with the human world, and the physical is always celebrated in spiritual ways:

When a child does something for the first time, the family acknowledges the event, recognizing its uniqueness and valuing the feeling that accompanies it. Unobtrusively, they create a special quality in the situation so that the child can sense that something different is happening. If a parent, other adult, or older sibling is around, it is considered important that they notice the event, express their joy, and celebrate the event with an appropriate ritual. These are moments that can never be repeated. Children and parents can never return to the moment when a child smiles or walks for the first time.

Anne Hubbell Maiden, social psychologist and Edie Farwell, anthropologist

All Smiles

Pretty Joy!
Sweet Joy, but two days old.
Sweet Joy I call thee.
Thou dost smile,
I sing the while, Sweet joy befall thee!

William Blake, English poet, 1789

A baby's first smile is like a ray of sunshine in the lives of his parents. Whether he is destined to struggle for survival, or live a life of pampered luxury, the baby is unconcerned. He is programmed, like Bottom in *A Midsummer Night's Dream*, to fall in love with the first human he sets eyes on. And his parents, like butter, are programmed to melt whenever he smiles.

The baby's smile is not a random thing. It develops, between birth and six months, into a beam of delight, focused specifically on one or two very special people in the baby's life. Some people dismiss early smiles as the result of wind or reflexes, but natural birth pioneer Frédérick Leboyer wonders if there is more to it. He photographed newborn babies in a state of ecstasy, not merely smiling, but chuckling to themselves.

Sometimes, when the baby is born it wears a mask which hides it, disfigures it, makes it ugly . . . The mask of tragedy – brows knitted, corners of the mouth turned down . . . But there is another mask. A mask of gaiety, of joy – a comic mask. With a wide mouth lifted into a smile. With eyebrows relaxed, and eyes crinkled with pleasure.

Frédérick Leboyer, French obstetrician and author

He also identified a mask-less newborn face: a peaceful, Buddha-like, beatified baby in a state of utter contentment. This serenity, these smiles, are noticed early on by parents who hold their babies close. While western paediatricians tell us that the baby's 'general smile' does not appear for four weeks, many intimate observers know better.

Of course some early smiles are no more than fleeting facial tweaks, but the real smile develops swiftly and surely in babies who are often smiled at. The smile is the baby's trump card, his personal gift of persuasion, reminding parents to pick him up and care for him. But the smile is not merely a one-way currency. It is an expression of mutual joy which deepens and helps to cement the relationship between the infant and his circle of carers. It is a very subtle and powerful form of early communication.

Monkeys smack their lips at each other to tighten the bonds of friendship; babies and parents smile and coo. Scientists tell us that babies know how to smile, even if no one ever smiles at them. 'It is a deeply ingrained, inborn facial expression of our species and even babies born blind, who have never encountered a smile, will perform one when they reach the age of four weeks' (Desmond Morris, zoologist).

Many cultures attach special significance to a baby's smiles:

- The Ganda people of Uganda consider sociability a very important aspect of personality. Parents encourage their babies to smile from the first, and train them to use their smiles to greet everyone they meet.
- Some cultures give magical meaning to their babies' early smiles and laughs. In Welsh tradition, a baby who laughs in his sleep is being kissed by the fairies. Tibetan parents also believe that babies' smiles mean fairy mischief.
- Malays parents say that a baby who smiles and gurgles for no apparent reason is playing with his spiritual sibling, the placenta.

Babies not only smile from a very early age, they laugh, too. In fact, laughter is closely related to crying: if measured on a spectrograph (an instrument for mapping the human voice) the infant chuckle looks suspiciously like a cry. Responsive laughing does not happen until four or five months after birth, when the baby is aware enough to take delight in a surprise encounter with someone who makes him feel safe.

The meaning of human laughter has a lot to do with fear and safety. When parents play 'hide and seek' with their babies, or pretend to drop them during a lap-bouncing game, they are creating an environment of mild excitement. The child, uncertain whether to cry at first, learns that he is not in any real danger. He relaxes; his fearful out-breaths (which could so easily have led to tears) become a chuckle of relief. Laughter is a joyful release of tension, which humans seek from a very early age. For babies, it is an invitation to 'come, play with me'.

Two Front Teeth

> Now the child is complete.
>
> **Chagga saying, at the arrival of baby's first tooth**

When a Chagga baby of Uganda cuts his first tooth, there is an immediate celebration. Grandmother arrives, with special herbs to massage the baby's gums. She also offers a blessing, in hope of a good, strong set of molars. At last, the baby will be given a name and a taste of solid food.

Baby's first tooth is an obvious landmark of development. It stands out like a clear, white milestone from his pink gum, the result of months of minor symptoms and premature diagnoses. A very few babies are born with 'natal teeth'. These were often thought to be a bad omen and were treated with suspicion in many societies. However, legend has it that many powerful people were born this way: Julius Caesar, King Louis XIV of France,

Napoleon Bonaparte and even William Shakespeare are some of the most famous candidates.

Despite all this dental precocity, most babies teethe slowly. There is no hurry for teeth in an animal that survives on mother's milk. Teeth take energy to produce and this energy can be expended at leisure. Some babies are still toothless at fourteen months of age.

Since children's teeth appear and disappear in mysterious ways, many beliefs have grown up around them. In European folklore, if a child teethes early, it means his mother will have another baby soon. Might there be a vague physiological connection between frequent breastfeeding, its contraceptive effect and the late arrival of baby teeth? Another (old English) superstition says that the number of teeth a baby has by his first birthday indicates the number of brothers and sisters he will have.

In Punjabi families, an important rite is performed as soon as the first tooth shines through. It's a rather strange affair, involving all the women of the community. Someone with particularly healthy teeth chews a morsel of coconut and spits it over the baby's face. A meal of coconut is then shared by all the women and even distributed around the village. Researchers say the occasion is a chance for women of the community to meet and give the mother support and recognition, but the custom is dying out among middle-class families: 'It is only in remote small villages that people still engage in such ceremonies . . . My eldest son was about seven to eight months old when his grandmother, who knew a lot about these things, threw masticated coconut on his face' (Sikh mother).

In medieval Europe, mothers were warned not to wean their babies until the milk teeth were through, as this would create all sorts of teething problems. Of course, early weaning was liable to damage the baby's overall health. 'Wean it not until the teeth are bred, least when the eye-teeth come forth, it cause feavers, and ache of gums and other symptoms' (Nicholas Culpeper, herbalist, 1651). Once again, 'teething' was a catch–all diagnosis for a wide range of infant crises.

The first milk teeth to appear are usually the 'lower central incisors', the two bottom front teeth. Some cultures consider it unlucky if a baby cuts his upper central incisors first. For the Afikpo Ibo people of eastern Nigeria, the premature arrival of lower teeth is an offence against '*ale*', the ground, requiring punishment in the form of a sacrifice to the guardian spirits.

Punjabi families hold that a baby whose top teeth appear first is a very bad omen. They must perform a healing ritual, including both sides of the family and the toothy baby, who meet in silence outside the village boundary. Mustard oil is poured into a bronze container and once the maternal relations have seen the baby's reflection in the oil, all will be well. Here is the ritual enacted by a Punjabi family living in England:

If a child cuts upper teeth first this is 'bad' for all the relations on the maternal side . . . My husband's sister's baby daughter was in Bradford. She cut her upper teeth first, and we went to M1 [Motorway to London] to do the ceremony. The meeting was arranged by phone . . . though I don't believe in it, we had to do it to satisfy the maternal relatives.

Sikh mother

TEETHING TROUBLES

Teething was a considerable problem for babies in the past. At least, their doctors thought so, and blamed a whole casebook of symptoms on this mysterious condition. Here is a short-list: 'irritation of the tender nervous parts of the jaw, occasioning inflammation, fevers, convulsions, gangrene, etc' (John Arbuthnot, English physician, 1731).

In modern day Cairo, Egypt, children living in the poorer parts of the city are prone to a long list of teething troubles, many of which have more to do with diet and hygiene than with cutting teeth. Mothers assume that symptoms as diverse as diarrhoea, fever, loss of weight and sleeplessness are down to teething; they treat them all with a vitamin boost, or 'teething injection'.

Since over half the children in the sample had this injection, I accompanied one mother to the pharmacist when she went to buy it. She was given a box containing ten ampules, each with a one-milliliter solution of calcium and vitamins D and B. She was instructed to take the child to a nurse for an injection every other day. Though injections are more costly [than tablets], they are often preferred to other types of medication because they are thought to enter the child's blood directly and thus make him or her strong.

Homa Hoodfar, anthropologist in Cairo

So what's the best way to treat a teething baby? Each culture has its own ideas:

- Honey used to be rubbed into babies' gums, to promote appetite and soothe teething pains. Eighteenth-century French children were prescribed Narbonne honey in particular. Pure honey has antibacterial properties and can help sore gums to heal.
- Eighteenth-century English babies were given a piece of coral to chew on while teething.
- In Australian Aboriginal culture, a solution made from parts of the Whistling Tree is used to cure toothache.
- Old herbal remedies for teething include chamomile or fennel tea. A few teaspoons of syrup made from marshmallow root can be added to baby's food to soothe inflammation. Oil of cloves may be rubbed directly on the gums.

Creepy-Crawlies

Throughout the world children of all cultures follow an identical pattern of development . . . Every child sits before crawling properly and crawls before standing and walking . . . The order of development is a natural instinctive pattern, and you have no influence on its sequence; nor should you hurry a child through a sequence.

Peter Walker, physical therapist

The pattern of infant development may be set, but it is set in jelly, not stone. For instance, not all babies crawl. How, when and whether a baby achieves a particular skill depends not merely on biology (nature), but also very much on child-rearing (nurture). As if to prove this, many societies rear their babies in defiance of nature's plan.

Each culture has its own way of emphasising the essential human qualities, those aspects which make us different from other animals. Myths and legends are used to reinforce the ideals of human nature: the Kayapó of central Brazil, for instance, believe that mastery of fire and the ability to cook food makes us superior to members of the animal kingdom.

To the Balinese, crawling is an impure and bestial act, even for babies. Animals crawl on all fours and have fang-like teeth; walking upright and having flat teeth are both features which, the Balinese say, make us human. To emphasise these differences, Balinese babies are prevented from crawling, and everyone must, at some stage in their lives, have their teeth filed flat. Teeth may be filed in childhood, at puberty or marriage, or even after death, since the human soul may not enter the spirit world until this is done.

As far as crawling is concerned, the Balinese baby spends so much time in his parents' arms – their feet must not touch the ground at all before they are six months old – that the transition from carrying to standing is remarkably quick:

There is a horror of appearing in any way animal-like, and babies are in no way exempt. When a baby shows signs of wanting to crawl, an older child is assigned to watch it and lift it to its feet when it tries to move: if the baby crawls, the child gets into trouble. Fathers often build little sets of hand rails at baby height in their courtyards, so that the infant can hang on as it sways precariously around. Some babies use a sitting bottom shuffle for a time, which seems to be allowed, but most simply develop walking skills quickly.

Anthony Forge, social anthropologist

A few babies in all cultures bottom-shuffle in preference to crawling. But babies in some cultures seem to make a virtue of it. Maya babies of Mexico simply skip the crawling stage according to western researchers, who speculate that this might be because the Maya baby is never allowed to lie prone on a flat surface.

There are some obvious practical problems with allowing a baby to crawl around. A room with expensive furniture and delicate knick-knacks is not conducive to the free movement of an intensely curious baby. Western parents usually prepare their rooms for the crawling stage, moving plants and precious items up high, guarding fires and sealing electric sockets with safety covers.

Dislike of crawling goes back many centuries in European homes:

In rooms with open fires, the child needed protection from accidents. Cooking pots and trivets surrounded the fireplace and could be dangerous if the mother's back was turned unless the child's mobility was restricted. Even in upper-class nurseries, crawling was held to delay the time when the child would walk. To allow the child to crawl was to allow mankind to adopt animal practices by going on all fours.

Olwen Hufton, social historian, on sixteenth- to eighteenth-century attitudes

In William Shakespeare's birthplace, a Tudor house in the centre of Stratford-upon-Avon, visitors may see the place where a pole was once set in the kitchen floor. To this pole, the crawling baby might be chained, so restricting his movement to a small circle and keeping him just out of the way of the open hearth. This probably saved a lot of nagging.

Keeping an eye on a crawling child can be stressful and time-consuming, which is why the babies of Okinawa, Japan, are rarely allowed to do it: 'There is no crawling stage in Taira. Older siblings are too involved in play to sit and patiently watch a crawler . . . The only children who were allowed to crawl about were the sons of two fishermen. Fishermen's wives, compared to the farmer-woodsmen's wives, have a great deal more leisure time' (Thomas and Hatsumi Maretzki, anthropologists).

Anyone wishing to prevent their baby from crawling must be prepared to carry the child or restrain him. Ache babies of Paraguay, South America, are carried by their parents right through the crawling phase and well into the time when they could be walking for themselves. It would never occur to an Ache adult to allow a baby to crawl around the forest floor for random encounters with poisonous plants, snakes and other wild animals. Even today, living in the less perilous environment of a settlement, old child care patterns die hard: 'On the reservation, [Ache] parents continue to pull babies back from attempts at exploration; and the babies echo this pattern, exploring with hesitation and easily jumping back into their mothers' laps' (Meredith Small, ethno-paediatrician).

Does it matter if children miss the crawling phase? Crawling, though inconvenient to the parent or caretaker, is an opportunity for the baby to explore his boundaries in ever-increasing circles. Like the Tudor baby strung to his pole, the crawler is emotionally connected to his mother, returning to her frequently for reassurance: a quick suckle, a moment of eye contact, a chance to be scooped back in familiar arms should the wider world appear suddenly alarming. This is also a chance for parents to radiate their confidence (or otherwise) in the pioneering child. If we can demonstrate a certain amount of trust during the creeping phase, we can start to empower baby into using his innate powers of self-preservation.

Some cultures deliberately encourage crawling. African babies, for instance, reach the milestones of motor coordination faster than do most western babies and once they are crawling, many are given immense freedoms. The Mbuti pygmy baby of central Africa, is encouraged to imitate adult activities from the moment he starts to become mobile.

Rural East African parents actively encourage all developmental stages, from sitting, through creeping on all fours, to walking, just as many western parents do. This encouragement, coupled with much carrying, results in early achievement of the required goals.

NO SEX PLEASE, WE'RE STATIONARY

In the traditions of the Yurok, a Native American people who once inhabited an area around the mouth of the Klamath River, California, we find an interesting twist on the crawling theme. According to ancient taboo, Yurok parents may only resume sex once the baby has started to crawl. This results in a concerted community effort to get that baby crawling as soon as possible.

The baby's legs are left uncovered in the Yurok version of the cradleboard, and from the twentieth day on they are massaged by the grandmother to encourage early creeping. The parents' cooperation in this matter is assured by the rule that they may resume intercourse when the baby makes vigorous strides in creeping.

Erik Erikson, psychoanalyst

Standing Room Only

> Toddler, toddler
> Oh my son! Look how he's growing;
> He brought a basket of apricots;
> He gave them all to his mother;
> And none to us.
>
> Tunisian song to sing to a child who is learning to walk

As the child rises uncertainly to his feet for the first time, he re-enacts the evolutionary moment which must once have occurred to our earliest ancestors. Just as they emerged hesitantly from the rainforests to a bipedal life on the open plains, so the child steps warily into the wider world. Unsteady at first, he will soon leave his infancy, forgotten, behind him.

Tibetan parents believe that once the child can stand, he loses his innocence and spiritual knowing. While in arms, or crawling, the infant is in a state of purity. He has a direct line to the spirit world and the ability to remember previous incarnations on earth. But standing and walking change all this – they connect the child to the human community. Every time he falls over and gets up again, another past-life is shed from the child's memory.

Gusii mothers of Kenya rarely coax their children into speedy development, but they do teach them to stand and walk. Standing is practised by holding the child's hands as he rises to his feet, and saying 'person-pole, person-pole' over and over to him in a good-humoured way. As for walking, the Gusii mother or older sister may take the baby out to toddle in the early morning dew. This method is designed to cool the 'hot blood' of the child's feet, giving him a firm and confident foot-hold on the earth. 'The [child] nurse sets the child on his feet in the grass and says "Ta, ta," encouraging him to walk toward her. Although most children are taught to walk in this fashion and are able to walk well before they are 2 years old, there is no emphasis on early walking as an accomplishment' (Robert and Barbara LeVine, anthropologists in Kenya).

On the Pacific islands of Samoa, traditional feasts were held for the 'sitting of the child', the 'crawling of the child' and the 'standing of the child'. But the greatest celebration was reserved for the first steps, which marked the end of complete dependency. There would be a grand feast, with singing and dancing that went on all night.

CUTTING THE CORD

The Mbuti pygmies of the Ituri rainforest in Africa, known for their uncomplicated approach to birth, have a ritual to celebrate the new independence of the toddling child. At birth, one of the father's arrow blades is used to cut the baby's umbilical cord. The blade and the cord stump are kept wrapped in leaves until the baby is old enough to walk. He then celebrates his independence by walking to the nearest stream, proudly carrying his precious cord and blade. These are ritually buried in a shallow hole in the river bank, ready for the next high tide. From now on, the baby will be as independent as the free-flowing water which runs downstream.

Walking is a great moment for all children, whether they are American or Tibetan, African or Australian, although each culture has its own feelings on this important stage of development.

● Hildegard of Bingen, the twelfth-century German ascetic, wrote at length about human infant development. She explained that humans walk later than other animals because their flesh and bones are fragile, and their greatest power is in the head (the seat of reason). Other medieval writers agreed:

slow development was a sign of human superiority compared with the animals.

* !Kung San babies of the Kalahari Desert in Africa are encouraged in all their motor skills – they sit, crawl and walk earlier than most western babies. Adults spend their leisure time teaching babies to stand and walk, holding their arms outstretched to receive babies making their first steps. Gross motor development has always been extremely important for their nomadic lifestyle, although now their work and child care patterns are changing.

* After the christening service was over, it was a tradition in Schwabia, Germany, for the youngest godfather to pick up the baby and run home with him. This, it was said, would make the baby walk early.

* Some Egyptian mothers regard a baby who walks early as 'difficult'. Mothers of such children are given a lot of sympathy from their friends.

* In past times, Chinese mothers, keen that their children should have a strong step, bound their babies' ankles and feet loosely with a wide ribbon, to hold the feet at a right-angle, ready for walking.

* Just as they were discouraged from crawling, Balinese babies are also constantly discouraged from walking – until they can do so gracefully. The upright position is often supported and guided by the expert hands of their parents, to help them glide along elegantly.

* The Athenians of ancient Greece had a ritual to make their children fleet of foot. Soon after birth, the new baby would be 'snatched' by a naked man, who then ran once or twice around the hearth with the baby in his arms.

* Babies who are strapped to a cradleboard for most of their infancy do not develop normal muscular agility. They are unable to crawl, let alone walk, when they are finally released from a year of bondage. However, muscle tone swiftly returns and Native American and other swaddled babies quickly catch

up with their unfettered peers. It is yet another example of the amazing ability of children to adapt to a variety of child-rearing methods.

When does a child take his first steps? Each individual child will, of course, develop on his own personal schedule. The current western average seems to be between ten and sixteen months, but most of us know children who have walked earlier and later than this, without any cause for alarm. There are also cultural differences, which can be explained by swaddling, massage, parental attitude and a range of other factors. While San babies of the Kalahari Desert may walk at eight months and American or British children start to walk at around one year, Ache children of Paraguay rarely walk before twenty-one months – because their parents insist on carrying them everywhere. They all catch up in the end.

Baby Extreme

Her son, as he began to crawl, was free to wander, unimpeded by playpens or gates, and tied to a human back only when it was time to go out. He, too, seemed relaxed and happy, despite a conspicuous lack of toys, rockers and mobiles. Best of all, he never had to spend a moment with people too tired to give him their full attention.

Pamela Crimmins, photographer in Morocco

The shift from the passive, sitting-up baby to the independent model takes many parents by surprise. Suddenly the child bombs around as if he's just joined the dangerous sports club. Once toddling, his vision reaches new heights, and his hands are into everything (one of the main reasons that children are motivated to move on two feet is to free up their ever-exploring fingers). Marmite sandwiches posted through the video flap; charcoal dust prints on the carpet; tea parties with the fine china – these are just some of the joys awaiting the mobile baby and his increasingly mobile parents.

Caring for a crawler or toddler on the go takes time and vigilance. Mothers in all communities are aware of the dangers which await their precious offspring. The Gusii of Kenya have a saying, 'lameness is up', which, roughly translated, means that a walking (or upstanding) child is more likely to get injured. The most common injury observed by anthropologists around the world is burning. In some cultures, knives are not considered a problem for dextrous young fingers, but fire is not so easily tamed:

Although a watchful surveillance is always kept, [!Kung San] adults rarely interfere in children's play, nor do they offer frequent suggestions . . . The greatest danger in an otherwise fairly harmless village environment is fire, and burns – minor and severe – occur with an unsettling frequency. Despite parental admonishments, children are often seen picking up coals (and quickly dropping them again) or running from one fire to the next with burning branches or weeds. They also handle knives (double-edged, long and sharp) with what appears a casual abandon; yet cuts are rare. Poisoned arrows and spears, the most dangerous of the ordinary objects in the village, are carefully hung out of children's reach.

Marjorie Shostak, anthropologist in the Kalahari Desert, Africa

In inner cities, cramped living conditions can make the fire risk much worse. In Jordanian and Egyptian homes, kerosene heaters are usually placed in the middle of the room and most houses have an exposed gas tube. And in the poorest quarters of Cairo, parents' protective instincts have not caught up with the evident perils associated with the domestic oven:

Accidents are a frequent form of morbidity in the community. Attempts to keep dangerous items out of a child's reach are rare. This is partly due to material conditions and limited space and partly due to lack of knowledge about the possibilities of, and ways to prevent, such accidents. Children play around their mother as she cooks, cleans and washes. Often, children upset hot water or gas burners onto themselves or others, sometimes with very regrettable and long-lasting consequences.

Homa Hoodfar, anthropologist in Cairo, Egypt

The living conditions in developing communities seem, paradoxically, more dangerous for children than those among the technologically 'primitive' groups. While the urban poor struggle to store drugs and chemicals safely, or protect their children from gas fires, hunter-gatherers use the instinct of millennia to protect themselves from the natural dangers of the jungle or the desert.

Yequana mothers in remote Venezuela also manage to arrange their lives so that the children play safely around them. While they work and chat, they exude vibes of trust in the baby's instincts for self-preservation. Few children in the world are raised with a complete sense of their own survival mechanisms, but you can't set up stair gates all around the jungle:

When he goes about on hands and knees, a baby can travel at a fair speed. Among the Yequana, I watched uneasily as one creeper rushed up and stopped at the edge of a pit five feet deep that had been dug for mud to make walls. In his progress about the compound, he did this several times a day. With the inattentiveness of an animal grazing at the edge of a cliff, he would tumble to a sitting position, as often as not facing away from the pit. Occupied with a stick or stone or his fingers or toes, he played and rolled about in every direction, seemingly heedless of the pit, until one realized he landed everywhere but in the danger zone. The non-intellect-directed mechanisms of self preservation worked unfailingly.

Jean Liedloff, continuum therapist in Venezuela

The key to safety is not always through the angst-ridden eyes of adults who live as if the worst were always about to happen. Babies are born with a strong sense of spatial awareness, although many adults find this unbelievable. We live in a culture which does not allow babies to practise self-protection and therefore our babies display little aptitude for it.

Babies, like animals, are perfectly equipped to assess visible physical dangers, to anticipate and to avoid them. Of course, they have no defences against invisible hazards, like electricity or bleach, and they cannot be expected to comprehend the perils posed by modern roads, where traffic moves at speeds unimagined by the evolutionary plan. But they quickly learn to deal with flights of stairs and slippery floors, to keep their fingers away from sharp edges and to negotiate their way superbly through tight spaces. However, to hone these skills, they need practice. They also need a sense that their parents trust them in their first exploratory endeavours.

Strategies for safety are not entirely absent in traditional communities, however. The most placid parent may nevertheless have a watchful eye over her children. And we have already seen how many cultures carry their babies through the crawling stage, precisely to protect them from environmental dangers. The Ache people of the Paraguayan forest, for instance, make safety their overriding child-rearing concern. Mothers hunch over their babies at night and parents carry their children for years − two strategies designed specifically to protect the young from danger.

Some parents even tie their young children by a leash to a tree to keep them from wandering into harm's way. Here, a mother from Okinawa, in the Pacific, puts her crawling baby out of the way of a sharp knife, without fuss or conveying any sense of alarm. The mother is weaving a bamboo basket on the floor of her front room:

The floor was littered with bamboo shavings and slats. As the mother worked, she was relaxed. She turned and twisted the sharp ends of the bamboo slats, leaving pointed ends swinging in the air, and dropping the huge knife in a careless fashion on the floor near her. Suddenly there was the sound of a crying baby and her eldest girl appeared with the 8-month-old on her back. Unstrapping the baby, the girl plopped her onto her mother's lap. Instinctively the mother pushed the basket, bamboo slats, and knife away as she unbuttoned her blouse to nurse the baby.

Thomas and Hatsumi Maretzki, anthropologists

All parents are equipped to use their instincts to protect their babies in ways which do not hinder the child's own sense of competence.

SAFETY IN NUMBERS

In ancient Gaelic tradition, mothers would protect their babies with five magical circles at birth. Each concentric circle represented a danger: one for wounding (in battle), one for drowning at sea, one circle for fire, another for enchantment (evil spells) and the last for wolves (the danger of predators.)

These five concentric circles can be seen in Celtic iconography and are referred to in old Irish legends. They also appear on prehistoric Scottish stones, in early Tibetan mandalas, and on the mystical designs of didgeridoos in Northern Territory, Australia. The five bands of protection around the newborn infant connected him to some extremely powerful worldwide magic.

HOME TRUTHS

Because the mother loves to nourish her little one, she does not on that account want him to remain little. She holds him with caresses, feeds him with her milk, does everything for the little one; but she wants him to grow, so that she may not always have to do these things.

Saint Augustine, fifth-century sermon

Bringing up babies is a bitter-sweet occupation, as most parents will testify. The immense joy and pride which come with the child's advancing body skills also bring challenges. Unless we live in a culture protected by a child-rearing consensus and a framework of taboos, we have a lot of difficult decisions ahead of us. We may worry whether our children are developing normally, we may be concerned for their safety, and we sometimes find it hard to enjoy each stage until they have moved out of it.

The mixed delights of looking after a crawling baby are a metaphor for what parents go through at every stage of their children's development . Some societies regard crawling as a perilous and unnecessary stage, and they do away with it altogether. Others invent equipment to curtail the child's movements. But both reactions merely postpone the day when we must give freedom to the increasingly independent child. In contrast, the Tibetan mother just clears the decks and make herself available to the emboldened baby: 'When the baby starts crawling, the mother will create a space and sit nearby. The baby begins to crawl away, look back at her, and then crawl back. The mother welcomes the child back, holding out her arms, ready with a hug and a pat' (Anne Hubbell Maiden, social psychologist and Edie Farwell, anthropologist).

This image of the baby creeping tentatively away from his mother before retreating into her arms is a useful metaphor for all stages of child-rearing. As the baby grows, the parent must learn to risk the child in the wider environment. And yet, paradoxically, each developmental shift requires parents to stay earthed, to be available (emotionally, if not physically) because the child's need for security does not entirely disappear.

Children may grow up, but they never really go away. Their attempts at independence are often matched by their need for support. So, from a very early stage, the emotions of parenthood are suspended in dynamic equilibrium. There is pride and there is protection; there is letting go and there is constant availability. Hope and fear are equal partners in the parenting contract.

Not that we need to convey all this to the children, of course. As we lead them out with language and example, sharing with them the rules and expectations of our culture, we do our best to keep our ambitions and our anxieties to ourselves. Parents' demands tend to get in the way of a child's own dreams. But in our hearts, we may keep a little prayer for their well-being, just like this prayer from the ancient Pueblos of New Mexico:

> May all the little boys
> And all the little girls
> And those whose roads are ahead
> May they have powerful hearts
> Strong spirits;
> On roads reaching to Dawn Lake
> May you grow old;
> May your roads be fulfilled;
> May you be blessed with life.
>
> **Prayer for the Zuñi children**

Notes

PREFACE

Margaret St John, 'Around the world in 3 pregnancies', *The Independent on Sunday*, 23 November 1997

Maureen Freely, *The Parent Trap*, pp. 11–12

Philippe Ariès, *Centuries of Childhood*, introduction

Jane Austen, *Persuasion*, 1815

Marjorie Shostak, *Nisa*, pp. 37–38

1. THE KIT LIST

Chapter 1: **Baby's Essential Shopping List**

Marjorie Shostak, *Nisa*, p. 45

Meredith F. Small, *Our Babies, Ourselves*, p. 79

James Bruce Ross, 'The Middle-Class Child in Urban Italy, Fourteenth to Early Sixteenth Century' in *The History of Childhood*, ed. Lloyd deMause, p. 191

Modern British Baby kit list supplied by mother and baby massage group, Bath, January 2001

Chapter 1: **Slings and Things**

Inuit lullaby quoted in *Mamatoto*, p. 162, and Sheila Kitzinger in *The Crying Baby*, p. 225

Terence Dixon and Martin Lucas, *The Human Race*, p. 21

Chapter 1: **The Carry Cot**

Jacqueline Vincent Priya, 'Birth Traditions', pp. 110–11

The Body Shop Team, *Mamatoto*, p. 145

Alice Marriott, *Indians of the Four Corners*, pp. 52, 114–16

Sheila Kitzinger, *The Crying Baby*, p. 226

David Levinson and David Sherwood, *The Tribal Living Book*, p. 58

Ashley Montagu, *Touching*, p. 323

Annette Hamilton, *Nature and Nurture: Aboriginal Childrearing*, p. 29

Polly Widaldjil quoted by Margaret Stewart in *Mother and Child*, p. 49

Margaret Stewart, *Mother and Child*, pp. 16, 54

Chapter 1: **The Cradleboard**
Zuñi prayer quoted by Ruth Benedict, *Patterns of Culture*, p. 65
Sheila Kitzinger, *The Crying Baby*, pp. 222–4
Ashley Montagu, *Touching*, pp. 158–9, 322–3, 368–70
Desmond Morris, *Babywatching*, pp. 120, 127
Carleton S. Coon, *The Hunting Peoples*, p. 116
Fiona Macdonald, *A Child's Eye View of History*, p. 44
Colin Taylor, *North American Indians*, p. 58
Erik H. Erikson, *Childhood and Society*, p. 123
Norman Bancroft Hunt, *Native American Tribes*, p. 99

Chapter 1: **The Hammock**
Brigitte Jordan, *Birth in Four Cultures*, p. 43
Ashley Montagu, *Touching*, p. 322
Sheila Kitzinger, *The Crying Baby*, p. 226
Alice Marriott, *Indians of the Four Corners*, pp. 115–16

Chapter 1: **The Rocking Chair**
Tricia Schleifer, 'The Joy of Rocking', *Mothering*, Summer 1989, pp. 17–19

Chapter 1: **The Cradle**
Brock Chisholm, 'Prescription for Survival', pp. 37–38
Mary Martin McLaughlin, 'Survivors and Surrogates: Children and Parents from
   the Ninth to the Thirteenth Centuries' in *The History of Childhood*, ed. Lloyd
   de Mause pp. 114, 117
F. Gordon Roe, *The Georgian Child*, pp. 6–7
Jean Jacques Rousseau, *Emile, ou de l'éducation* quoted by Christina Hardyment in
   Dream Babies p. 24

Chapter 1: **The Cot**
Albrecht Peiper, 'Cerebral Function in Infancy and Childhood', Consultants Bureau,
   New York, 1963, pp. 570–71
Anna M. Galbraith, *The Four Epochs of Woman's Life*, Chapter XIII, 'The New-
   Born Infant'

Chapter 1: **The Pram**
Dr Pye Henry Chavasse, *Advice to a mother on the management of her children and on
   the treatment of some of their more pressing illnesses and accidents*, Willing and
   Williamson, Toronto, Canada, 1880, p. 131 (full text at www.canadiana.org)
Desmond Morris, *Babywatching*, p. 127
Christina Hardyment, *Dream Babies*, pp. 7, 66–8, 97, 191, 256

Chapter 1: **The High Chair**
The Motherhood Book, plate 21
Philippe Ariès, *Centuries of Childhood*, pp. 50, 61
F. Gordon Roe, *The Georgian Child*, pp. 7–8, 13

Chapter 1: **The Baby Walker**

Nicholas Culpeper, 'A Directory for Midwives' in *Culpeper's Book of Birth*, ed. Ian Thomas, p. 123

Felix Würtz quoted by Lloyd deMause in *The History of Childhood*, p. 39

Olwen Hufton, *The Prospect Before Her*, p. 203

James Bruce Ross, 'The Middle-Class Child in Urban Italy, Fourteenth to Early Sixteenth Century' in *The History of Childhood*, ed. Lloyd deMause, p. 202, 223, Notes 121, 122

Leigh Minturn and John T. Hitchcock, 'The Rajputs of Khalapur, India', in *Six Cultures: Studies of Childrearing*, ed. Beatrice B. Whiting, p. 319

Sarah Boseley, 'Doctors urge ban on babywalkers', *The Guardian*, 2 December 1998

'Baby Walkers – A Mixed Blessing', *Early Days* 12, Summer 1988

Chapter 1: **The Playpen**

Luther Emmett Holt quoted by Christina Hardyment in *Dream Babies*, p. 139

Jean Liedloff, *The Continuum Concept*, p. 83

Chapter 1: **Reins and Leading Strings**

Charlotte Papendiek quoted by Linda Pollock in *A Lasting Relationship*, p. 74

Margaret Willes, *Memories of Childhood*, p. 24

Catherine Verney quoted by Linda Pollock in 'A Lasting Relationship', p. 73

Olwen Hufton, 'The Prospect Before Her', p. 203

Lady Anne Clifford quoted by Linda Pollock in *A Lasting Relationship*, p. 72

Chapter 1: **The Teddy Bear**

Dorothy Canfield, *The Homemaker*, London, 1924

D.W. Winnicott, *The Child, the Family and the Outside World*, Penguin, Harmondsworth, 1964

Dr Richard Ferber, *Solve Your Child's Sleep Problems*, p. 40

Sigmund Freud, 'Totem und Tabu' (1913), Fischer Taschenbuch Verlag, Frankfurt, 1991, part iii, 'Animismus, Magie und Allmacht der Gedanken'

Desmond Morris, *Babywatching*, p. 95

Michel Odent quoted by Deborah Jackson in *Three in a Bed*, p. 206

Judy H. Brink, 'Changing Child-Rearing Patterns in an Egyptian Village' in *Children in the Muslim Middle East*, ed. Elizabeth Warnock Fernea, p. 85

Sheila Kitzinger, *The Crying Baby*, p. 224

Meredith F. Small, *Our Babies, Ourselves*, p. 81

Chapter 1: **Electric Dreams**

Baby Link advertisement in *Practical Parenting* magazine (no date)

Michel Odent, *Primal Health*, p. 147

David Derbyshire, 'Can nightlights leave a child short-sighted?' *The Daily Mail*, 13 May 1999

Chapter 1: **The Artificial Heartbeat**
Heartbeat advert in *Practical Parenting*, September 1991
SmartSleep with Classical, Press Release, 2 May 2000

Chapter 1: **Home Truths**
Good Housekeeping's Mothercraft, p. 30
Judy H. Brink, 'Changing Child-Rearing Patterns in an Egyptian Village' in *Children in the Muslim Middle East*, ed. Elizabeth Warnock Fernea, pp. 85, 86

2. BABY BORN

Chapter 2: **Hello Baby**
Frédérick Leboyer, *Birth Without Violence*, p. 98
Meredith F. Small, *Our Babies, Ourselves*, p. 87
Annette Hamilton, *Nature and Nurture – Aboriginal Childrearing*, p. 29
Leigh Minturn and John T. Hitchcock, 'The Rajputs of Khalapur, India' in *Six Cultures: Studies of Childrearing*, ed. Beatrice B. Whiting, p. 311
Anne Hubbell Maiden and Edie Farwell, *The Tibetan Art of Parenting*, p. 100
Fiona Macdonald, *A Child's View of History*, p. 6

Chapter 2: **The First Cry**
Jenny Goodman, 'A Long Time Coming' in *Every Birth is Different*, ed. Pat Thomas, p. 192
Nid Amina, *Childbirth and Burial Practices among Philippine Tribes*, pp. 2, 33
Carol Laderman, *Wives and Midwives*, p. 144
The Body Shop Team, *Mamatoto*, p. 106
Frédérick Leboyer, *Birth Without Violence*, p. 96
The Osage Tribe's Official Website, www.osagetribe.com
Jacqueline Vincent Priya, *Birth Traditions*, p. 109
Michel Odent, *Water and Sexuality*, pp. 10-11
Margaret Mead, 'Children and Ritual in Bali' from *Childhood in Contemporary Cultures*, p. 49
Robert de Laroche, *The Secret Life of Cats*, p. 38

Chapter 2: **Big, Fat, Beautiful Baby**
'What is My Name?' quoted by Nikki Siegen in *Welcome to the World*, p. 17
Michel Odent, *Entering the World*, p. 113
Ushanda io Elima, 'Living With the Pygmies', *Mothering*, Summer 1988, p. 90
'Predicting unborn babies' weight', *Living*, October 1992
Judy Jones, 'Parents reward nurses by the pound in chocolate', *The Independent*, 14 September 1993
Olwen Hufton, *The Prospect Before Her*, p. 202
Philippa Waring, *Omens and Superstitions*, p. 76

Thomas W. and Hatsumi Maretzki, 'Taira: An Okinawan Village' in *Six Cultures: Studies of Child Rearing*, ed. Beatrice B. Whiting, p. 457

Anne Fadiman, *The Spirit Catches You and You Fall Down*, p. 7

Russell A. Judkins and Ann B. Judkins, 'Commentary: Cultural Dimensions of Hmong Birth', *Birth* 19:3, September 1992, p. 5

Carol Laderman, *Wives and Midwives*, p. 196

Robert A. LeVine et al., *Child Care and Culture*, p. 172

Dr Pamela Feldman, quoted in 'The friendly way to a healthy baby', *The Daily Mail*, 23 September 2000

Chapter 2: I Only Have Eyes for You ...

Kuki Gallmann, *I Dreamed of Africa*, p. 138

Michel Odent, *The Scientification of Love*, pp. 10, 11, 58

Desmond Morris, *Illustrated Babywatching*, p. 28

Meredith F. Small, *Our Babies, Ourselves*, p. 16

The Body Shop Team, *Mamatoto*, p. 105

Grey Wolf, *Native American Wisdom*, p. 30

Efé pygmy song quoted by Ushando io Elima in 'Living With the Pygmies', *Mothering*, Summer 1988, p. 90

Chapter 2: Don't I Know You?

Desmond Morris, *Babywatching*, p. 14

The Body Shop Team, *Mamatoto*, pp. 31, 105

M. Kaitz et al., 'Parturient women can recognize their infants by touch', *Developmental Psychology* 28, 1992, pp. 35–9

Meredith F. Small, *Our Babies, Ourselves*, p. 27

Jan Reynolds, *Mother and Child*, p. 24

Michel Odent, *Entering the World*, pp. 111–12

Richard H. Porter et al., 'The Importance of Odors in Mother-Infant Interactions', *Maternal-Child Nursing Journal*, 12:3, 1983, pp. 147–54

M.G. Smith, 'The Hausa of Northern Nigeria' in *Peoples of Africa*, ed. James L. Gibbs, pp. 148–9

Lennart Righard, Malmö, Sweden, 'How Do Newborns Find Their Mother's Breast?', *Birth*, 22:3, pp. 174–5

Chapter 2: Enter the Placenta

Placenta recipe from *New Generation*, September 1998, p. 23

The Body Shop Team, *Mamatoto*, p. 109

Robert A. LeVine et al., *Childcare and Culture*, p. 106

Anne Fadiman, *The Spirit Catches You and You Fall Down*, p. 5

Pat Thomas quoted from personal correspondence, 31 January 2001

Jacqueline Vincent Priya, *Birth Traditions*, pp. 98, 108

Meredith F. Small, *Our Babies, Ourselves*, p. 7

Mona Ramsay (Aboriginal name Wirritjil) talking to Margaret Stewart, *Mother and Child*, p. 19

Thomas and Hatsumi Maretzki, 'Taira: An Okinawan Village' in *Six Cultures: Studies of Child Rearing*, ed. Beatrice B. Whiting, p. 458

Carleton S. Coon, *The Hunting Peoples*, p. 316

Michel Odent, *Water and Sexuality*, pp. 77–8

Nikki Bradford and Jean Williams, 'What They Don't Tell You About Being a Mother and Looking After Babies', Press Release from HarperCollins, August 1997

Chapter 2: **The Navel String**

John Agard, 'Moonbelly', quoted by Nikki Siegen-Smith in *Welcome to the World*, p. 10

Desmond Morris, *Illustrated Babywatching*, p. 19

Maasai midwife quoted by the Body Shop Team in *Mamatoto*, pp. 108–9

Richard Jones, *The Byrth of Mankinde*, 1540: M.J. Tucker, 'The Child as Beginning and End: Fifteenth and Sixteenth Century English Childhood', *The History of Childhood*, ed. Lloyd de Mause, pp. 239, 241

Jacqueline Vincent Priya, *Birth Traditions*, pp. 13, 100, 101

Margaret Stewart, *Mother and Child*, pp. 7–9, 19

Nikki Siegen-Smith, *Welcome to the World*, p. 46

Carleton S. Coon, *The Hunting Peoples*, pp. 313, 316

I.M. Lewis, *Peoples of the Horn of Africa*, p. 134

Brigitte Jordan, *Birth in Four Cultures'*, p. 40

Amanda Hopkinson, 'Midwifery and Rural Health in Guatemala' in *The Midwife Challenge*, ed. Sheila Kitzinger, p. 165

Jean Robinson, 'Medical Uses from the Umbilical Cord', *AIMS Journal*, 5:3, 1993, p. 17

Prof. Naomi Pfeiffer, 'Blood Money', *AIMS Journal*, 12:4, January 2001, pp. 21–22

Chapter 2: **Cheers!**

Natania Jansz, 'Aravinda – Man of the Match' in *Every Birth is Different*, ed. Pat Thomas, pp. 18–19

Carol Laderman, *Wives and Midwives*, p. 41

Meredith Mann Taylor, *Transcultural Aspects of Breastfeeding*, p. 15

Robert A. Levine et al, *Childcare and Culture*, p. 131

Nicholas Culpeper, *A Directory for Midwives*, quoted by Ian Thomas, ed., *Culpeper's Book of Birth*, p. 81

Deborah Bee, 'What's really in the pot?', *The Guardian*, 20 October 2000

Chapter 2: **The Twin Set**

Nisa quoted by Marjorie Shostak in *Nisa*, p. 185

Aristotle quoted by Elaine Fantham et al in *Women in the Classical World*, p. 193

Maria Leach, ed., *Dictionary of Folklore, Mythology and Legend*, p. 1135

Anne Sutherland, 'Social Space' in *Face Values*, pp. 65–68

John P. Elliott, 'In the beginning . . . Pregnancy, Infancy and Beyond', Mothers of

Super Twins (MOST) Quarterly Internet Vol. 1, www.mostonline.org, March 2001

Colin M. Turnbull, 'The Mbuti Pygmies of the Congo' in *Peoples of Africa*, ed. James L. Gibbs, p. 305

Donna Launslauger, 'Incidences of Multiple Births' 1998, Parents of Multiple Births Association of Canada (POMBA), www.pomba.org

Desmond Morris, *Babywatching*, p. 141

Harold Courlander et al., 'Ibeji Link', www.culturalexpression.com, March 2001

Chapter 2: **A Grand Day Out**

Angot de Lespeyronnière, 1610, *La Lucine ou la femme en couches*, quoted by Olwen Hufton in *The Prospect Before Her*, p. 187

Nikki Siegen-Smith, *Welcome to the World*, p. 47

Anne Fadiman, *The Spirit Catches You and You Fall Down*, p. 11

Anne Hubbell Maiden and Edie Farwell, *The Tibetan Art of Parenting*, pp. 98, 119

M.G. Smith, 'The Hausa of Northern Nigeria' in *Peoples of Africa*, ed. James L. Gibbs, p. 149

Richard Emblin, 'Cable dancing', *The Independent on Sunday*, 16 April 2000

Chapter 2: **Home Truths**

Jacqueline Vincent Priya, *Birth Traditions*, p. 13

3. MOTHERCARE

Chapter 3: **Me and My Midwife**

Phyllis H. Klaus, book review of *Mothering the New Mother*, Birth 22:1, March 1995, p. 50

Lesley Page, 'The Midwife in Modern Health Care' in *The Midwife Challenge*, ed. Sheila Kitzinger, p. 254

'Herstory of Midwifery – The History of Midwives in Canada', http://getthe.net/pages/midwife

Vicki Iovine, *The Girlfriends' Guide to Pregnancy*, p. 71

Michel Odent, 'Creating a new world' in *Birth Matters*, ed. Ros Claxton, pp. 235–7

Carol Laderman, *Wives and Midwives*, pp. 111, 171

Nami quoted by Michel Odent in *The Scientification of Love*, p. 78

Sheila Kitzinger, *The Midwife Challenge*, pp. 40, 98, 230

Kate Gordon, *Baptism and Baby-Naming*, p. 33

Molly O'Brien, 'Every mother should have one', *You*, 9 February 1997

Michael Magenis, 'Mothering the mother eases labour pains', *The Daily Telegraph*, 10 January 1998

Chapter 3: **Visiting Time**

Ann Wallace and Gabrielle Taylor, *Royal Mothers*, p. 117

Thomas W. and Hatsumi Maretzki, 'Taira: An Okinawan Village' in *Six Cultures: Studies of Child Rearing*, ed. Beatrice B. Whiting, pp. 463, 466

Nikki Siegen-Smith, *Welcome to the World*, p. 47

Anne Hubbell Maiden and Edie Farwell, *The Tibetan Art of Parenting*, p. 97

Gitanjali Kolanad, *Culture Shock! India*, p. 84

Jennifer M. Russ, *German Festivals and Customs*, p. 131

Olwen Hufton, *The Prospect Before Her*, p. 188

M. J. Tucker, 'The Child as Beginning and End: Fifteenth and Sixteenth Century English Childhood' in *The History of Childhood*, ed. Lloyd de Mause, p. 237

Mary Martin McLaughlin, 'Survivors and Surrogates: Children and Parents from the Ninth to the Thirteenth Centuries' in *The History of Childhood*, ed. Lloyd de Mause, p. 148

Margaret Willes, *And So To Bed*, p. 42

Sheila Kitzinger, *The Midwife Challenge*, p. 5

Chapter 3: A Little Peace and Quiet

Guatemalan proverb quoted by Amanda Hopkinson in 'Midwifery and Rural Health Care in Guatemala' in *The Midwife Challenge*, ed. Sheila Kitzinger, p. 166

Russell A. Judkins and Ann B. Judkins, 'Commentary: Cultural Dimensions of Hmong Birth', *Birth*, 19:3, September 1992

Erik H. Erikson, *Childhood and Society*, p. 120

Marjorie Shostak, *Nisa*, p. 181

Frances McConville, 'The Birth Attendant in Bangladesh' in *The Midwife Challenge*, ed. Sheila Kitzinger, pp. 136–7

Carine Fabius, *Mehndi – The art of henna body painting*, p. 20

The Body Shop Book, ed. Tim Blanks, p. 138

Pamela Crimmins, 'Mothering in Morocco', *Mothering*, No. 68, Fall 1993, p. 110

J.S. Dosanjh and Paul A. S. Ghuman, *Child-Rearing in Ethnic Minorities*, p. 56

Michael Roman, 'Rusyn Customs, Traditions and Superstitions At the Birth and Baptism of Children', 1995 (previously on internet)

Walter H. Sangree, 'The Bantu Tiriki of Western Kenya' in *Peoples of Africa*, ed. James L. Gibbs, p. 59

Chapter 3: No Sex Please, We're Breastfeeding

Ian Thomas, ed., *Culpeper's Book of Birth*, p. 91

Phoebe Ottenberg, 'The Afikpo Ibo of Eastern Nigeria' in *Peoples of Africa*, ed. James L. Gibbs, p. 22

Gabrielle Palmer, *The Politics of Breastfeeding*, p. 98

George Monbiot, 'Of pigs and punners in the Stone Age', *The Independent*, 4 March 1989

Research from Minnesota quoted in 'Postnatal blues', *Independent*, 23 March 1993

Sarah Hobson, *Family Web – A Story of India*, p. 57

Carol Laderman, *Wives and Midwives*, p. 204

Chapter 3: **The Power of Touch**
Maggie Tisserand, *Aromatherapy for Women*, p. 107
The Body Shop Book, ed. Tim Blanks, pp. 35, 135, 138, 145
Robin Lin, 'Postpartum Practices Throughout the World', *Mothering* 66, Spring 1993, p. 87
Carol Laderman, *Wives and Midwives*, p. 178
The Body Shop Team, *Mamatoto*, p. 128
Amanda Hopkinson, 'Midwifery and Rural Health Care in Guatemala' in *The Midwife Challenge*, ed. Sheila Kitzinger, p. 165
Natural Home Remedies, ed. Karen Sullivan, p. 34, 37, 39, 41
Sheila Kitzinger, *The Crying Baby*, p. 230
Chrissie Wildwood, *Aromatherapy*, pp. 2–4, 201
Margaret Willes, *And So To Bed*, p. 42
Roger Highfield, *Can Reindeer Fly?*, pp. 29–31
Barbara Nieto, 'Aromatherapy and the Uses of Essential Oils', *Cahoots*, July–Sept 1988, p. 11

Chapter 3: **Bath Time**
Mona Ramsey quoted by Margaret Stewart in *Mother and Child*, p. 20
Mary Hoffman and Jane Ray, *Song of the Earth*, pp. 49, 53
J.S. Dosanjh and Paul A.S. Ghuman, *Child-Rearing in Ethnic Minorities*, p. 56
Amanda Hopkinson, 'Midwifery and Rural Health Care in Guatemala' in *The Midwife Challenge*, ed. Sheila Kitzinger, p. 165
M.G. Smith, 'The Hausa of Northern Nigeria' in *Peoples of Africa*, ed. James L. Gibbs, p. 149
The Body Shop Team, *Mamatoto*, p. 130
Maggie Tisserand, *Aromatherapy for Women*, pp. 103, 104, 144
Carleton S. Coon, *The Hunting Peoples*, p. 313

Chapter 3: **Brace Yourself . . .**
Brigitte Jordan, *Birth in Four Cultures*, p. 43
Nikki Siegen-Smith, *Welcome to the World*, p. 46
Nid Amina, *Childbirth and Burial Practices among Philippine Tribes*, p. 33
Brigitte Jordan, *Birth in Four Cultures*, p. 43
Ann Wallace and Gabrielle Taylor, *Royal Mothers*, p. 59
Philippa Waring, *Omens and Superstitions*, p. 114
The Body Shop Book, ed. Tim Blanks, p. 97

Chapter 3: **Warm as Toast**
Paschal Khoo-Thwe quoted by Jane Kelly in 'Heartache of a Bronze Age Boy', *The Daily Mail*, 13 June 1998
Sheila Kitzinger, *The Crying Baby*, p. 229–30
Carol Laderman, *Wives and Midwives*, pp. 174–76
Jacqueline Vincent Priya, *Birth Traditions*, pp. 114–15

Meredith Mann Taylor, *Transcultural Aspects of Breastfeeding*, p. 19

Margaret Stewart, *Mother and Child*, p. 4

Chapter 3: **Mother's Menu**

Robin Lin, 'Postpartum Practices Throughout the World', *Mothering* 66, Spring 1993, p. 87

Jacqueline Vincent Priya, *Birth Traditions*, p. 115

Nikki Siegen-Smith, *Welcome to the World*, p. 47

Carol Laderman, *Wives and Midwives*, pp. 36, 171, 187, 192, 212

Margaret Stewart, *Mother and Child*, pp. 31–36

Raquel Arias and Robert Small quoted by Anne Fadiman, *The Spirit Catches You and You Fall Down*, p. 9

Richard Pankhurst, *A Social History of Ethiopia*, p. 267

Carleton S. Coon, *The Hunting Peoples*, pp. 310, 313

Jennifer M. Russ, *German Festivals and Customs*, pp. 131, 133

Trefor M. Owen, *Welsh Folk Customs*, p. 146

Julia Roberts, *Horsemen of Mongolia*, Tigress Productions documentary for Channel 4, UK, shown September 2000

Mayeh Abu Omar and Maymuna Muhiddin Omar, 'Nomads in the Horn of Africa', *World Health* No. 6, Nov–Dec 1995

Philippa Waring, *Omens and Superstitions*, pp. 235–36

Chapter 3: **If You Take My Advice . . .**

Anita Roddick, quoted in 'Breastfeeding, bonding and big business' by Sharon Maxwell Magnus, *She*, September 1990, p. 38

Meredith F. Small, *Our Babies, Ourselves*, p. 224

Queenie McKenzie (1916–1998) quoted by Margaret Stewart in *Mother and Child*, p. ix

Carol Laderman, *Wives and Midwives*, p. 113

Jean Liedloff, *The Continuum Concept*, p. 103

Chapter 3: **Baby Blues**

Sheila Kitzinger, *The Year After Childbirth*, p. 132

Jane Ellen Panton, *The Way They Should Go*, London 1896, quoted by Christina Hardyment in *Dream Babies*, p. 291

Gabrielle Palmer, *The Politics of Breastfeeding*, p. 90

Staffan Janson, 'Life and Health of Jordanian Children' in *Children in the Muslim Middle East*, ed. Elizabeth Warnock Fernea, p. 195

Michel Odent, *The Scientification of Love*, p. 10

Deborah Jackson, *Three in a Bed*, pp. 96–7

Carol Laderman, *Wives and Midwives*, pp. 202–3

Anne Hubbell Maiden and Edie Farwell, *The Tibetan Art of Parenting*, p. 123

Chapter 3: Please Be Upsitting

Thomas and Hatsumi Maretzki, 'Taira: An Okinawan Village' in *Six Cultures: Studies of Child Rearing*, ed. Beatrice B. Whiting, pp. 459, 463

Leviticus XII, 6–7

Kate Gordon, *Baptism and Baby-Naming*, p. 41

Henrietta Leyser, *Medieval Women*, pp. 29–30

Donna Speer Ristenbatt, 'On the Trail of Our Ancestors: Birth and Baptismal Customs' at www.ristenbatt.com

J.S. Dosanjh and Paul A.S. Ghuman, *Child-Rearing in Ethnic Minorities*, pp. 56–7

Sarah Hobson, *Family Web – A Story of India*, pp. 204–5

Lady Mary Verney quoted by Margaret Willes in *And So To Bed*, p. 42

Chapter 3: Home Truths

Brahmin Indian priest quoted by Sarah Hobson in *Family Web – A Story of India*, p. 85

4. MEET THE TEAM

Chapter 4: It Takes a Village . . .

Fauziya Kassindja, *Do They Hear You When You Cry?*, p. 101

Rennie Loewenthal, 'Breastfeeding in Canoa, Brazil', *Feedback LLL GB*, Spring 2000, p. 31

Meredith F. Small, *Our Babies, Ourselves*, p. 25

Gitanjali Kolanad, *Culture Shock! India*, p. 178

Chapter 4: Baby – The Original Status Symbol

Paul Raffaele, 'Hunting with the world's smallest people', *Reader's Digest*, Sept 1998, p. 82

Elizabeth Warnock Fernea, *Children in the Muslim Middle East*, p. 5, 43

Tracy Chevalier, *Girl With a Pearl Earring*, HarperCollins, London 1999, p. 81

Terence S. Turner, 'The Kayapó of Central Brazil' in *Face Values*, ed. Anne Sutherland, pp. 260-62

Jennifer M. Russ, *German Festivals and Customs*, p. 101

Walter H. Sangree, 'The Bantu Tiriki of Western Kenya' in *Peoples of Africa*, ed. James L. Gibbs, p. 54

P.H. Gulliver, 'The Jie of Uganda' in *Peoples of Africa,* ed. James L. Gibbs. p. 176

Olwen Hufton, *The Prospect Before Her*, p. 173

Carol Laderman, *Wives and Midwives*, pp. 10, 63

Turkish proverb quoted by Elizabeth Warnock Fernea in *Children in the Muslim Middle East*, p. 43

Robert A. LeVine et al., *Childcare and Culture*, p. 32

Chapter 4: From Here to Paternity

Angot de Lespeyronnière, *La Lucine ou la femme en couches*, (Lucine, or The Woman in Labour) quoted by Olwen Hufton in *The Prospect Before Her*, p. 187

Meredith F. Small, *Our Babies, Ourselves*, pp. 33–34; 87–88

Polly Ghazi, 'Dad's the word', *The Guardian*, 25 October 2000

Suzanne Dixon, *The Roman Family*, p. 101

Philippa Waring, *Omens and Superstitions*, p. 166

The Body Shop Book, ed. Tim Blanks, p. 191

Marjorie Shostak, *Nisa*, p. 376

Robert A. LeVine et al., *Childcare and Culture*, pp. 31, 98

Sharon Maxwell Magnus, 'Breastfeeding, bonding and big business', *She*, Sept 1990, p. 38

Anita Roddick, *Body and Soul*, p. 207

Steve Connor, 'Amazon tribes believe a child can have more than one father', *The Independent on Sunday*, 24 January 1999

Chapter 4: **Birth Partners**

Hindu mother quoted by J.S. Dosanjh and P.A.S. Ghuman, 'Child-Rearing Practices of Two Generations of Punjabi Parents', *Children and Society*, II, 1997, p. 35

Jacqueline Vincent Priya, *Birth Traditions*, p. 108

The Body Shop Team, *Mamatoto*, p. 134

Chapter 4: **Anything You Can Do**

Warren R. Dawson, *The Custom of Couvade*, pp. 1, 9

Michel Odent, *Primal Health*, p. 141

'Couvade', Microsoft Encarta Online Encyclopedia 2000 http://encarta.msn.com

Diodorus Siculus quoted by Warren R. Dawson in *The Custom of Couvade*, p. 9

The Body Shop Team, *Mamatoto*, p. 134

Carleton S. Coon, *The Hunting Peoples*, pp. 310, 316

Meredith F. Small, *Our Babies, Ourselves*, pp. 31, 32

Erik H. Erikson, *Childhood and Society*, p. 156

Chapter 4: **Investment Bonding**

Sir Thomas More quoted by M.J. Tucker, 'The Child as Beginning and End: Fifteenth and Sixteenth Century English Childhood' in *The History of Childhood*, ed. Lloyd de Mause, p. 248

Meredith F. Small, *Our Babies, Ourselves*, pp. 26, 30-32

Michel Odent, *Primal Health*, p. 140

Erik H. Erikson, *Childhood and Society*, p. 141

Desmond Morris, *Babywatching*, pp. 17, 107

Adam J. Jackson, *Eye Signs*, p. 112–13

Anne Fadiman, *The Spirit Catches You and You Fall Down*, p. 3

Michel Odent, *The Scientification of Love*, pp. 40-41

Jennifer M. Russ, *German Festivals and Customs*, p. 132

Chapter 4: **A Grand Old Age**

Robert A. LeVine et al., *Childcare and Culture*, p. 83

Hindu parent quoted by J.S. Dosanjh and Paul A.S. Ghuman, *Child-Rearing in Ethnic Minorities*, pp. 69, 85

Stephen Vines, 'Honour parents, says nanny state', *The Independent on Sunday*, 9 June 1996

Kevin Duffy, *Children of the Forest*, pp. 128–9

Marjorie Shostak, *Nisa*, pp. 34, 50

Chapter 4: As for Everyone Else . . .

J. Holme, 'Growing up in Hinduism', *British Journal of Religious Education*, Summer 1884, pp. 116–20, quoted by J.S. Dosanjh and Paul A.S. Ghuman in *Child-Rearing in Ethnic Minorities*, p. 53

Colin M. Turnbull, 'The Mbuti Pygmy of the Congo' in *Peoples of Africa*, ed. James L. Gibbs, p. 292

AusInfo, *Australian Aboriginal Culture*, p. 16

Patricia Caplan, 'The Swahili of Chole Island, Tanzania' in *Face Values*, ed. Anne Sutherland, p. 167

The Body Shop Team, *Mamatoto*, pp. 160–61

Gitanjali Kolanad, *Culture Shock! India*, p. 178

Sheila Kitzinger, *The Crying Baby*, p. 219

Meredith Mann Taylor, *Transcultural Aspects of Breastfeeding – USA*, pp. 5, 6

Menachem Gerson, *Family, Women and Socialisation in the Kibbutz*, p. 71

J.S. Dosanjh and Paul A.S. Ghuman, *Child-Rearing in Ethnic Minorities*, p. 45

Chapter 4: The Circle of Life

Meredith F. Small, *Our Babies, Ourselves*, p. 58

Annette E. Weiner, 'The Trobrianders of Papua New Guinea', quoted by Deborah Jackson in *Three in a Bed*, p. 101

Clare Garner, 'Baby eases pain of last Christmas', *The Independent*, 26 December 1998

Deborah Jackson, *Eve's Wisdom*, p. 136

Lloyd de Mause, *The History of Childhood*, p. 18

Margaret Mead, 'Children and Ritual in Bali' in *Childhood in Contemporary Cultures*, p. 40

Gayle Brandeis-McGunigle, 'Childhood and Ritual in Bali', *Mothering*, No. 61, Fall 1991, p. 38

Marcel d'Hertefelt, 'The Rwanda of Rwanda' in *Peoples of Africa*, ed. James L. Gibbs, p. 420

Chapter 4: Home Truths

Joan Riviere, 'The unconscious fantasy of an inner world reflected in examples from literature' in *New Directions in Psychoanalysis*, ed. M. Klein, P. Heimann, R. Money-Kyrle, Hogarth, London 1955

Gayle Brandeis-McGunigle, 'Childhood and Ritual in Bali', *Mothering* 61, Fall 1991, p. 40

5. MAY WE PRESENT

Chapter 5: **A Small Announcement**
Luke II, 9–14
Ifeoma Onyefulu, *A is for Africa*
Gitanjali Kolanad, *Culture Shock! India*, p. 84
Leigh Minturn and John T. Hitchcock, 'The Rajputs of Khalapur, India' in *Six Cultures: Studies of Child Rearing*, ed. Beatrice B. Whiting, pp. 307, 308
The Body Shop Team, *Mamatoto*, p. 112
Olwen Hufton, *The Prospect Before Her*, pp. 187–8
Tradition China at www.babyzone.com, February 2001
Nid Amina, *Childbirth and Burial Rituals among Philippine Tribes*, p. 35
Jennifer M. Russ, *German Festivals and Customs*, p. 131

Chapter 5: **Back to My Roots**
Lucy Maud Montgomery, *The Story Girls*, chapter 2
Mary Hoffman and Jane Ray, *Song of the Earth*, pp. 26–7
The Body Shop Team, *Mamatoto*, pp. 112, 156
Philippa Waring, *Omens and Superstitions*, p. 237
Margaret Stewart, *Mother and Child*
Susan Milord, *Hands Around the World*, p. 71
Jennifer M. Russ, *German Festivals and Customs*, p. 131
Amanda Hopkinson in 'Midwifery and Rural Health in Guatemala', *The Midwife Challenge*, ed. Sheila Kitzinger, p. 164
David Pickering, *Dictionary of Superstitions*, p. 194
E. and M. A. Radford, *The Encyclopedia of Superstitions*, pp. 21–2
Kate Gordon, *Baptism and Baby-Naming*, p. 33

Chapter 5: **Soul Mate**
Oscar Wilde, *The Picture of Dorian Gray* (1891), Penguin, London 1985, p. 213
Piers Vitebsky, *The Shaman*, pp. 14, 19
The Body Shop Team, *Mamatoto*, p. 157
Carol Lee Johnson and Helen Petrie, 'On the Psychology of Personal Names: A boy named Sue?', paper presented at the British Psychology Conference, London, 17/18 December 1991
G. Jahoda, 'A Note on Ashanti Names and Their Relationship to Personality', *British Journal of Psychology*, 45, 1954, pp. 192–5
Philippa Waring, *Omens and Superstitions*, p. 162
Joules and Ken Taylor, *Scottish Folklore*, p. 143
Jacqueline Vincent Priya, *Birth Traditions*, p. 112
Tradition China at www.babyzone.com, February 2001

Chapter 5: **Pick a Name, Any Name**
Sarah Hobson, *Family Web – A Story of India*, pp. 204–5

The Body Shop Team, *Mamatoto*, pp. 157, 159
Kevin Duffy, *Children of the Forest*, p. 136
David Levinson, 'Birth and Childhood Rights' from *Religion: A Cross-Cultural Encyclopedia*, excerpt at http://berkshire-reference.com/bk/religion encyclopaedia2.html
M.A. Qazi, *What's in a Muslim Name?*, p. 1
Islamic names for boys and girls: Abdoulrahman at www.idleb.com
J.S. Dosanjh and Paul A.S. Ghuman, *Child-Rearing in Ethnic Minorities*, p. 74
Jacqueline Vincent Priya, *Birth Traditions*, p. 112
Thomas and Hatsumi Maretzki, 'Taira: An Okinawan Village' in *Six Cultures: Studies of Child Rearing*, ed. Beatrice B. Whiting, p. 459
Ruth Benedict, *Patterns of Culture*, p. 183
David Fontana, *Teach Yourself to Dream*, p. 14

Chapter 5: **What's in a Name?**
Jewish saying quoted by Kate Gordon in *Baptism and Baby-Naming*, p. 43
Anne Fadiman, *The Spirit Catches You and You Fall Down*, p. 9
Alicia T. Jewett, 'What's in a Name?: An Ibani Example', *Cambridge Anthropology* 10, No. 2, 1985, p. 60
Anglo Saxon names at www.babycenter.com
Modupe Odyoye, *Yoruba Names*, p. 84
Myra Vanderpool Gormley, 'Colonial Naming Customs' from *Colonial Homes*, 1996, p. 24, at www.intersurf.com
Norman Bancroft Hunt, *Native American Tribes*, p. 83
Erik H. Erikson, *Childhood and Society*, p. 115
Suzanne Dixon, *The Roman Family*, p. 127
'Carpatho-Rusyn Given Names' at www.rusyn.com (April 2001)
Nicolas Slonimsky, *A Biographical Dictionary of Composers and Musicians* (1900), Schirmer Books, London 1988
M.J. Tucker, 'The Child as Beginning and End: Fifteenth and Sixteenth Century English Childhood' in *The History of Childhood*, ed. Lloyd de Mause, p. 239
F. Gordon Roe, *The Georgian Child*, p. 4

Chapter 5: **Wetting the Baby's Head**
Olwen Hufton, *The Prospect Before Her*, pp. 186, 189
Jennifer M. Russ, *German Festivals and Customs*, pp. 134, 136
Mary Hoffman and Jane Ray, *Song of the Earth*, p. 49
Gaelic midwife's blessing quoted by Tara MacAnTsior and Branfionn MacGregor in 'Gaelic Celtic Culture 6: Birth Customs' at www. sundown.pair.com
Fiona MacLeod, *By Sundown Shores*, pp. 90-94
Kate Gordon, *Baptism and Baby-Naming*, pp. 31, 34
Richard Pankhurst, *A Social History of Ethiopia*, p. 195
M.J. Tucker, 'The Child as Beginning and End: Fifteenth and Sixteenth Century English Childhood' in *The History of Childhood*, ed. Lloyd dc Mause, pp. 239, 243

Marianne Elliott, 'Just Like A Woman', *The Independent on Sunday*, 26 November 1995

Lloyd deMause, *The History of Childhood*, p. 10

Philippa Waring, *Omens and Superstitions*, pp. 25–6

Desmond Morris, *Babywatching*, p. 131

Nid Amina, *Childbirth and Burial Practices among Philippine Tribes*, p. 3

Trefor M. Owen, *Welsh Folk Customs*, p. 145

H. Owen, *Life and Works of Lewis Morris*, p. 142, quoted by Trefor M. Owen in *Welsh Folk Customs*, pp. 145–6

John A. Hostetler, *Amish Life*, p. 29

Chapter 5: **Signed and Sealed**

Didinga mother quoted by the Body Shop Team in *Mamatoto*, p. 156

David Levinson, 'Birth and Childhood Rights' from *Religion: A Cross-Cultural Encyclopedia*, excerpt at http://berkshire-reference.com/bk/religion encyclopaedia2.html

Leigh Minturn and John T. Hitchcock 'The Rajputs of Khalapur, India' in *Six Cultures: Studies of Child Rearing*, ed. Beatrice B. Whiting, p. 310

Olwen Hufton, *The Prospect Before Her*, p. 188

J.S. Dosanjh and Paul A.S. Ghuman, *Child-Rearing in Ethnic Minorities*, p. 57

New Arrivals: Non-Religious Naming Ceremonies, leaflet from the British Humanist Association, 47 Theobald's Road, London WC1X 8SP

Civil naming ceremony quoted by Alan Travis in 'Labour's plan to save the family', *The Guardian*, 24 July 1998

Suzanne Dixon, *The Roman Family*, p. 134

Stella Nyinah, 'Cultural Practices in Ghana', *World Health* No. 2, March–April 1997, p. 23

Carine Fabius, *Mehndi*, p. 17

Alice Marriott, *Indians of the Four Corners*, p. 112

Fiona Macdonald, *A Child's Eye View of History*, p. 16

Amanda Hopkinson in 'Midwifery and Rural Health in Guatemala', *The Midwife Challenge*, ed. Sheila Kitzinger, p. 161

Chapter 5: **Blessing Baby**

Fiona MacLeod (aka William Sharp), *By Sundown Shores*, pp. 90–94

Mary Hoffman and Jane Ray, *Song of the Earth*, pp. 15, 31, 49

Jennifer M. Russ, *German Festivals and Customs*, p. 132

Robert A. LeVine et al., *Childcare and Culture*, p. 137

Zuñi prayer quoted by Alice Marriott, *Indians of the Four Corners*, pp. 112–13

Maria quoted by Amanda Hopkinson in 'Midwifery and Rural Health in Guatemala', *The Midwife Challenge*, ed. Sheila Kitzinger, pp. 163–4

Kate Gordon, *Baptism and Baby-Naming*, p. 26

Tara MacAnTsior and Branfionn MacGregor, 'Gaelic Celtic Culture 6: Birth Customs' at www.sundown.pair.com

Chapter 5: **Gossips and Grand Lunches**

Gay Firth quoted by Joanna Moorhead, 'In the name of the godfather', *The Guardian*, 5 January 1997

Henrietta Leyser, *Medieval Women*, pp. 133

F. Gordon Roe, *The Georgian Child*, pp. 4, 6

Philippa Waring, *Omens and Superstitions*, pp. 107–8

James Bruce Ross, 'The Middle-Class Child in Urban Italy, Fourteenth to Early Sixteenth Century' in Lloyd deMause, *The History of Childhood*, p. 189

Olwen Hufton, *The Prospect Before Her*, pp. 188–9, 207

Jennifer M. Russ, *German Festivals and Customs*, pp. 135

Trefor M. Owen, *Welsh Folk Customs*, p. 145

Carleton S. Coon, *The Hunting Peoples*, p. 313

Chapter 5: **The First Cut**

Brahmin housewife quoted by J.S. Dosanjh and Paul A.S. Ghuman in *Child-Rearing in Ethnic Minorities*, p. 59

The Body Shop Team, *Mamatoto*, p. 169

Nid Amina, *Childbirth and Burial Practices among Philippine Tribes*, pp. 29–30

David Levinson, 'Birth and Childhood Rights' in *Religion: A Cross-Cultural Encyclopedia*, excerpt at http://berkshire-reference.com/bk/religion encyclopaedia2.html

J.S. Dosanjh and Paul A.S. Ghuman, *Child-Rearing in Ethnic Minorities*, pp. 73, 170

Chapter 5: **Permanent Markers**

Philippe Ariès, *Centuries of Childhood*, p. 103

Brigitte Jordan, *Birth in Four Cultures*, p. 41

St Augustine and Procter and Gamble quoted by Doris K. Cope in 'Neonatal Pain – The Evolution of an Idea', American Society of Anaesthiologists, www.asahq.org, September 1998

Michel Odent, *The Scientification of Love*, p. 11

Norman Autton, *Pain*, pp. 81, 83

Ronald Rabinowitz, 'Newborn Circumcision Should Not Be Performed Without Anaesthesia', *Birth* 22:1, March 1995, pp. 45–6

Meredith O'Brien, 'Childbirth Traditions: American Jewish', www.babyzone.com

Carine Fabius, 'Mehndi', p. 17

Phoebe Ottenberg, 'The Afikpo Ibo of Eastern Nigeria' in *Peoples of Africa*, ed. James L. Gibbs, p. 23

Elizabeth Warnock Fernea, *Children in the Muslim Middle East*, pp. 8–9

Hilda Kuper, 'The Swazi of Swaziland' in *Peoples of Africa*, ed. James L. Gibbs, p. 490

Chapter 5: **Home Truths**

Si Kahn, 'Welcome to the World', © Joe Hill Music. Performed by Roy Bailey on *Why Does it Have to Be Me?*, CFED 396; Fuse Records, Sheffield

6. CLOSE FOR COMFORT

Chapter 6: **Constantly Carried**
Penelope Leach, *Children First*, p. 66
R.D. Martin, *Primate Origins and Evolution*, Princeton University Press, 1990
Meredith F. Small, *Our Babies, Ourselves*, p. 171
L. Salk, 'Role of the heartbeat in the relationship between mother and infant', *Scientific American*, May 1973, pp. 24–29
Collection of Isis statuettes displayed at 'Cleopatra of Egypt' exhibition, the British Museum, 12 April–26 August 2001
Chris Mihill, 'Why left is best for baby', *The Guardian*, 21 June 1996
Desmond Morris, *Babywatching*, pp. 59, 114–15, 132
Anne Hubbell Maiden and Edie Farwell, *The Tibetan Art of Parenting*, p. 108–9
M.D.S. Ainsworth, 'Infancy in Uganda', p. 451
T.B. Brazelton et al., 'Neonatal Behavior among Urban Zambians and Americans', *Journal of American Academy of Child Psychiatry* 1, 1976, pp. 97–107
Lorna Marshall, 'The !Kung Bushmen of the Kalahari Desert' in *Peoples of Africa*, ed. James L. Gibbs, p. 263
Marjorie Shostak, *Nisa*, p. 48
Hilda Kuper, 'The Swazi of Swaziland' in *Peoples of Africa*, ed. James L. Gibbs, p. 489
Seteney Shami and Lucine Taminian, 'Children of Amman: Childhood and child care in squatter areas of Amman, Jordan' in *Children in the Muslim Middle East*, ed. Elizabeth Warnock Fernea, p. 75
The Body Shop Team, *Mamatoto*, p. 169
Elizabeth Warnock Fernea, *Children in the Muslim Middle East*, p. 7
John H. Douglas, 'Pioneering a Non-Western Psychology', *Science News* 113 (1978), pp. 154–58
Tim Blanks, ed., *The Body Shop Book*, p. 138
Peggy Durdin, 'From the Space Age to the Tasaday Age', *New York Times Magazine*, 8 October 1972, p. 14

Chapter 6: **Busy Going Nowhere**
Jean Liedloff, *The Continuum Concept*, p. 157
Wilkinet Baby Carrier, PO Box 20, Cardigan, Ceredigion, SA43 1JB, Wales. Tel: 01239 841844
Meredith F. Small, *Our Babies, Ourselves*, pp. 105, 239–40
Anita Roddick quoted in 'Breastfeeding, bonding and big business' by Sharon Maxwell Magnus, *She*, September 1990, p. 38
Leigh Minturn and John T. Hitchcock, 'The Rajputs of Khalapur, India' in *Six Cultures: Studies of Child Rearing*, ed. Beatrice B. Whiting, p. 318
Robert A. LeVine et al., *Childcare and Culture*, p. 202
Sheila Kitzinger, *The Crying Baby*, pp. 227–8
Ruth Benedict, 'Continuities and Discontinuities in Cultural Conditioning' in *Childhood in Contemporary Cultures*, ed. Margaret Mead and Martha Wolfenstein, p. 23

Anne Hubbell Maiden and Edie Farwell, *The Tibetan Art of Parenting*, p. 109
Barbara Wishingrad, 'Photography Show Rental', www.rebozoway.org

Chapter 6: **Cache and Carry**
Kevin Duffy, *Children of the Forest*, pp. 6, 44, 141
Meredith F. Small, *Our Babies, Ourselves*, pp. 9, 95, 212
Peter Martin, 'A skull. A bone. A stone', *Sunday Times Magazine*, 12 September 1999, pp. 18–23
Anne Hubbell Maiden and Edie Farwell, *The Tibetan Art of Parenting*, p. 109
Desmond Morris, *Babywatching*, pp. 30, 46
Michel Odent, *Primal Health*, p. 14
B. Lozoff and G. Brittenham, 'Infant care: Cache or carry', *Pediatrics* 95, 1979, pp. 478–83
Thomas W. and Halsumi Moretzki, 'Taira: An Okinawan Village' in *Six Cultures: Studies of Child Rearing*, ed. Beatrice B. Whiting, p. 464

Chapter 6: **Inter-Continental Baby-Carrying**
Sheila Kitzinger, *The Crying Baby*, pp. 224–5
Marjorie Shostak, *Nisa*, p. 387
Richard Bushey Lee, *The !Kung San*, p. 310
Aliza Orbach, *Motherhood*, pp. 7, 9, 19, 51, 100, 103, 104
Louisa Young, 'Yours for a cute £210', *The Guardian*, 29 March 1999
Elizabeth Warnock Fernea, *Children in the Muslim Middle East*, p. 7
Australian InFo International, *Australian Aboriginal Culture*, p. 22
Brigitte Jordan, *Birth in Four Cultures*, p. 36
Colin Taylor, *North American Indians*, pp. 76, 82–3
'Annuraaq – Arctic Clothing from Igloolik', The British Museum, 15 February–27 May 2001
Gina Rozon, 'In the Canadian Arctic', *LLL GB News*, No. 102, Nov–Dec 1997, p. 7
Meredith F. Small, *Our Babies, Ourselves*, p. 88

Chapter 6: **Holding with Confidence**
Margaret Mead, 'Cultural Differences in the Bathing of Babies', in *Mental Health and Infant Development*, ed. K. Soddy, pp. 170–71
Margaret Mead, 'Children and Ritual in Bali' in *Childhood in Contemporary Cultures*, pp. 46–7
Sarah Hobson, *Family Web – A Story of India*, p. 112
Brigitte Jordan, *Birth in Four Cultures*, p. 40
Sherri B. Saines, 'Do we idolize the tribe?', letter to *Mothering* 52, Summer 1989, p. 15

Chapter 6: **Rock Around the Clock**
Frédérick Leboyer, *Birth Without Violence*, pp. 83–4
Sheila Kitzinger, *The Crying Baby*, pp. 198, 226

Desmond Morris, *Babywatching*, p. 124

Ashley Montagu, *Touching*, pp. 158 9

Aletha Jauch Solter, *The Aware Baby*, pp. 26–7

Lloyd deMause, *The History of Childhood*, p. 31

Erik H. Erikson, *Childhood and Society*, p. 142

Annette Hamilton, *Nature and Nurture – Aboriginal Childrearing*, p. 29

The Body Shop Team, *Mamatoto*, pp. 122, 143

Douglas Haring, 'Aspects of Personal Character in Japan' in *Personal Character and Cultural Milieu*, Syracuse University Press, New York, 1956, p. 461

Chapter 6: **Dances with Babies**

J.A.M. Meerloo, 'The Dance', pp. 13–14

Desmond Morris, *Naked Ape*, p. 92

Ashley Montagu, *Touching*, p. 175

D.H. Lawrence, *Mornings in Mexico*, New York 1928, pp. 109–10, quoted by Ruth Benedict in *Patterns of Culture*, p. 93

Gayle Brandeis-McGunigle, 'Childhood and Ritual in Bali', *Mothering,* Fall 1991, p. 40

Jean Liedloff, *The Continuum Concept*, p. 63

Kevin Duffy, *Children of the Forest*, pp. 55–6

Chapter 6: **Home Truths**

Hugh Downman, 'Infancy, or the Management of Children: A Didactic Poem', 1774–6, quoted by Christina Hardyment in *Dream Babies*, p. 17

Jewish proverb quoted in *The Little Book of Motherhood*, Penguin, London, 1997

7. SHALL WE BEGIN?

Chapter 7: **Misunderstandings: The Story of Colostrum**

Bartholomew of England, *De Proprietatibus Rerum*, quoted by Mary Martin McLaughlin in 'Survivors and Surrogates: Children and Parents from the Ninth to the Thirteenth Centuries' in *The History of Childhood*, ed. Lloyd deMause, p. 115

Marjorie Shostak, *Nisa*, pp. 3, 181

Meredith Mann Taylor, *Transcultural Aspects of Breastfeeding – USA*, p. 12

Beverly Chalmers, *African Birth*, p. 21

Nid Amina, *Childbirth and Burial Practices among Philippine Tribes*, p. 23

Michel Odent, *Water and Sexuality*, p. 115

Anne Hubbell Maiden and Edie Farwell, *The Tibetan Art of Parenting*, p. 99

Erik H. Erikson, *Childhood and Society*, pp. 121, 158

Thomas W. and Hatsumi Maretzki, 'Taira: An Okinawan Village' in *Six Cultures: Studies of Child Rearing*, ed. Beatrice B. Whiting, p. 458

Desmond Morris, *Babywatching*, p. 51

Henrietta Leyser, *Medieval Women*, p. 134

Meredith F. Small, *Our Babies, Ourselves*, pp. 204, 215

Mary Renfrew, Chloe Fisher, Suzanne Arms, *Bestfeeding*, p. 76

Kitty Campion, *Holistic Herbal for Mother and Baby*, p. 123

Nikki Siegen-Smith, *Welcome to the World*, p. 46

Derrick J. Stenning, 'The Pastoral Fulani of Northern Nigeria' in *Peoples of Africa*, ed. James L. Gibbs, p. 391

Frances McConville, 'The Birth Attendant in Bangladesh' in *The Midwife Challenge*, ed. Sheila Kitzinger, p. 138

Stella Nyinah, 'Cultural practices in Ghana', *World Health* No.2, March-April 1997, p. 23

'The Life of the Ainu', www.ainu-museum.or.jp

Homa Hoodfar, 'Child Care and Child Health in Low-Income Neighborhoods of Cairo' in *Children in the Muslim Middle East*, ed. Elizabeth Warnock Fernea, p. 151

Chapter 7: **And Now the Good News**

Sani Aliou, 'People on the move', *World Health* No. 6, Nov–Dec 1995, pp. 26, 27

Pamela Crimmins, 'Mothering in Morocco', *Mothering*, Fall 1993, p. 111

Ashley Montagu, *Touching*, pp. 74–5

Michel Odent, *The Scientification of Love*, p. 40

Meredith F. Small, *Our Babies, Ourselves*, pp. 192, 194–5

Michel Odent, 'Newborn Weight Loss', *Mothering* 50, Winter 1989, pp. 72–3

Michel Odent, *Water and Sexuality*, pp. 115–16

Michel Odent, *We Are All Water Babies*, p. 85

Brigitte Jordan, *Birth in Four Cultures*, p. 43

Anne Hubbell Maiden and Edie Farwell, *The Tibetan Art of Parenting*, p. 99

Gabrielle Palmer, *The Politics of Breastfeeding*, p. 25

Chapter 7: **When The Milk Comes In**

Gabrielle Palmer, *The Politics of Breastfeeding*, pp. 41, 129

Erik H. Erikson, *Childhood and Society*, p. 158

Desmond Morris, *The Naked Ape*, p. 71

Meredith F. Small, *Our Babies, Ourselves*, p. 178

Chapter 7: **All in the Mind?**

Jacqueline Vincent Priya, *Birth Traditions*, p. 116

L. Conton, 'Social, economic and ecological parameters of infant feeding in Usino, Papua New Guinea', *Ecology of Food and Nutrition* 16, 1985, pp. 39–54

Robert A. LeVine et al., *Childcare and Culture*, p. 57

Robert A. and Barbara B. LeVine, 'Nyansongo: A Gusii Community in Kenya' in *Six Cultures: Studies of Child Rearing*, ed. Beatrice B. Whiting, p. 138

Meredith Mann Taylor, *Transcultural Aspects of Breastfeeding – USA*, p. 4

Meredith F. Small, *Our Babies, Ourselves*, pp. 187–91, 203

Isaiah quoted by Beverley Haagensen in 'Encouragement from Ancient Israel', *LLL GB News*, No.103, Jan–Feb 1998, pp. 8–9

Kevin Duffy, *Children of the Forest*, pp. 126–7
Michel Odent, *The Scientification of Love*, pp. 97
Michel Odent, *Primal Health*, pp. 14–15, 22
Michel Odent, *We Are All Water Babies*, pp. 80-81
Desmond Morris, *Babywatching*, p. 69

Chapter 7: What's Good for Baby ...
Ashley Montagu, *Touching*, pp. 71, 79–80, 85
Michel Odent, *We Are All Water Babies*, pp. 80-81
M. Sachs, 'BFN: The Breastfeeding Network Newsletter' No. 2, Feb 1998, pp. 6–9
Baby Milk Action, 'One baby lived. The other died', leaflet (undated)
WHO, UNICEF, UNESCO, UNFPA, *Facts for Life*, pp. 17, 18, 22–24
Michael G. Schwab, 'Mechanical Milk – An essay on the social history of infant formula', *Childhood* 3:4, November 1996, p. 487
Meredith F. Small, *Our Babies, Ourselves*, pp. 195–8
'Women of 200 years ago had healthier bones', *The Independent*, 12 March 1993
Robert A. LeVine et al., *Childcare and Culture*, p. 26
Gabrielle Palmer, *The Politics of Breastfeeding*, pp. 72–3, 107, 141
Sheila Kitzinger, *The Crying Baby*, p. 221
Marjorie Shostak, *Nisa*, pp. 66–7

Chapter 7: Milk of Human Kindness
Song of the 'balie' quoted by James Bruce Ross, 'The Middle-Class Child in Urban Italy, Fourteenth to Early Sixteenth Century' in *The History of Childhood*, ed. Lloyd deMause, p. 192
Martha Wolfenstein, 'Some Variants in Moral Training of Children' in *Childhood in Contemporary Cultures*, pp. 351, 364
The Dalai Lama quoted by Anne Hubbell Maiden and Edie Farwell in *The Tibetan Art of Parenting*, p. 100
Gabrielle Palmer, *The Politics of Breastfeeding*, pp. 42–4, 134, 141
Ian Thomas, ed,. *Culpeper's Book of Birth*, pp. 95, 101, 105, 107
Anne Hubbell Maiden and Edie Farwell, *The Tibetan Art of Parenting*, pp. 108, 109
Michel Odent, *The Scientification of Love*, pp. 38, 99
'The Taste Test', *LLL GB News*, No. 89, Sept–Oct 1995, p. 4
Patrick Holford, *The Optimum Nutrition Bible*, pp. 29, 206, 208
Desmond Morris, *Babywatching*, p. 69
Marjorie Shostak, *Nisa*, p. 66
John Steinbeck, *The Grapes of Wrath* (Heinemann 1939), Mandarin Paperbacks, London 1995, p. 535

Chapter 7: Going with the Flow
Lacnunga, an Anglo-Saxon treatise, quoted by Henrietta Leyser in *Medieval Women*, p. 135
Robert de Laroche and Jean Michel Labat, *The Secret Life of Cats*, pp. 33–8

Jacqueline Vincent Priya, *Birth Traditions*, p. 109

The Body Shop Team, *Mamatoto*, pp. 130-31

Leigh Minturn and John T. Hitchcock, 'The Rajputs of Khalapur, India' in *Six Cultures: Studies of Child Rearing*, ed. Beatrice B. Whiting, p. 307

'Unwashed breast best for feeding' Update, *The Independent*, 11 October 1994

Lennart Righard, 'How Do Newborns Find Their Mother's Breast?', *Birth* 22:3, September 1995, pp. 174–5

Desmond Morris, *Babywatching*, p. 42

Nid Amina, *Childbirth and Burial Practices among Philippine Tribes*, p. 33

Meredith Mann Taylor, *Transcultural Aspects of Breastfeeding – USA*, pp. 3, 15

Robert A. LeVine et al., *Childcare and Culture*, pp. 123, 132

Thomas W. and Hatsumi Maretzki, 'Taira: An Okinawan Village' in *Six Cultures: Studies of Child Rearing*, ed. Beatrice B. Whiting, pp. 460

J.S. Dosanjh and Paul A.S. Ghuman, *Child-Rearing in Ethnic Minorities*, p. 43

Gabrielle Palmer, *The Politics of Breastfeeding*, pp. 87–8

'Evolution beats diet deficiency' Harsh World, *The Guardian*, 13 February 1996

Meredith F. Small, *Our Babies, Ourselves*, p. 192

Patrick Holford, *The Optimum Nutrition Bible*, pp. 11, 42–3

The Body Shop Team, *Mamatoto*, p. 131

Marie Miczak, 'Herbs and Healthy Lactation' and Sunny Pendleton Mavor, 'Herbs for Breastfeeding', *Mothering* 78, Spring 1996, pp. 60-63

Karen Sullivan, *Natural Home Remedies*, pp. 16, 136

David Hoffman, *Holistic Herbal*, p. 95

Sheila I. Humphrey, Dennis J. McKenna, 'Herbs and Breastfeeding', *Breastfeeding Abstracts* 17:2, November 1997, pp. 11–12

'Toxic Herb Teas and Breastmilk', *AIMS Journal* 7:1, Spring 95

Mona Ramsay quoted by Margaret Stewart in *Mother and Child*, p. 20

Carol Laderman, *Wives and Midwives*, p. 178

N.M. Hurst, C.J. Valentine, L. Renfro et al., 'Skin-to-skin holding in the neonatal intensive care unit influences maternal milk volume', *Journal of Perinatology* 1997, Vol. 17, pp. 213–17

Michel Odent, *We Are All Water Babies*, p. 82

Amanda Hopkinson, 'Midwifery and Rural Health Care in Guatemala' in *The Midwife Challenge*, ed. Sheila Kitzinger, p. 166

Chapter 7: Home Truths

Robert A. LeVine et al., *Childcare and Culture*, p. 144

8. TRICKS OF THE TRADE

Chapter 8: Free to Feed

Ushanda io Elima, 'Living With the Pygmies', *Mothering*, Summer 1988, p. 91

Christina Hardyment, *Dream Babies*, Plate 5

David Levinson and David Sherwood, *The Tribal Living Book*, p. 185

Robert A. and Barbara B. LeVine, 'Nyansongo: A Gusii Community in Kenya' in
 Six Cultures: Studies of Child Rearing, ed. Beatrice B. Whiting, pp. 63, 69 note,140
'Stop this breast feeding', *Daily Telegraph* editorial (anonymous), 18 May 1994
Katherine A. Dettwyler, Professor of Anthropology and Nutrition, Texas University,
 addressing the European La Leche League conference in Nottingham, England,
 6 August 2000
Elizabeth Brendefur, 'Breastfeeding in Public', *New Generation*, June 1994, p. 5
Thomas W. and Hatsumi Maretzki, 'Taira: An Okinawan Village' in *Six Cultures:
 Studies of Child Rearing*, ed. Beatrice B. Whiting, pp. 462, 463, 472
Homa Hoodfar, 'Child Care and Child Health in Low-income Neighborhoods of
 Cairo' in *Children in the Muslim Middle East*, ed. Elizabeth Warnock Fernea,
 p. 152

Chapter 8: **Breast is Dressed**
Madonna reported by *The Evening Standard*, London, and quoted in 'Talking Dirty',
 The Guardian, 12 December 1996
Sally Weale, 'The big squeeze', *The Guardian*, 31 October 2000
Gabrielle Palmer, *The Politics of Breastfeeding*, pp. 124–5
Erik H. Erikson, *Childhood and Society*, p. 122
Ann Wallace and Gabrielle Taylor, *Royal Mothers*, p. 15
Inuit *amauti* displayed in 'Annuraaq – Arctic Clothing from Igloolik' at the British
 Museum exhibition, 15 February–27 May 2001
The Body Shop Team, *Mamatoto*, p. 110

Chapter 8: **This Way, That Way**
Thomas W. and Hatsumi Maretzki, 'Taira: An Okinawan Village' in *Six Cultures:
 Studies of Child Rearing*, ed. Beatrice B. Whiting, p. 463
F. Gordon Roe, *The Georgian Child*, p. 7
Lorna Marshall, 'The !Kung Bushmen of the Kalahari Desert' in *Peoples of Africa*,
 ed. James L. Gibbs, p. 263
Meredith F. Small, *Our Babies, Ourselves*, pp. 81–2
Odd Andersen (photographer), 'A woman returning with her baby to flood-ravaged
 Chokwe in Mozambique as the waters subside', *The Guardian*, 15 March 2000
Ashley Montagu, *Touching*, pp. 79, 323
Martha Wolfenstein, 'Some Variants in Moral Training of Children' in *Childhood in
 Contemporary Cultures*, p. 351
Annette Hamilton, *Nature and Nurture: Aboriginal Childrearing*, p. 29
Jean Liedloff, *The Continuum Concept*, p. 66
Desmond Morris, *Babywatching*, p. 83
Kitty Campion, *Holistic Herbal for Mother and Baby*, pp. 124–5

Chapter 8: **Clocking On**
Pamela Crimmins, 'Mothering in Morocco', *Mothering* 68, July–Sept 1993,
 p. 110
Homa Hoodfar, 'Child Care and Child Health in Low-income Neighborhoods of

Cairo' in *Children in the Muslim Middle East*, ed. Elizabeth Warnock Fernea, p. 152

Michael G. Schwab, 'Mechanical Milk. An essay on the social history of infant formula', *Childhood* 3:4, November 1996, p. 480

Gitanjali Kolanad, *Culture Shock! India*, p. 190

Sarah Hobson, *Family Web – A Story of India*, p. 239

Pye Henry Chavasse, *Advice to a Wife On the Management of Her Own Health* (numerous editions, 19th to early 20th century), pp. 220-21

Christina Hardyment, *Dream Babies*, p. 42

Mary Truby King, *Mothercraft*, 1938, quoted by Christina Hardyment, *Dream Babies* pp. 177–8

Mary Renfrew, Chloe Fisher and Suzanne Arms, *Bestfeeding*, pp. 134–5

Melvin Konner and Carol Worthman, 'Nursing Frequency, Gonadal Function, and Birth Spacing Among !Kung Hunter-Gatherers', *Science* 207, 15 February 1980, pp. 788–91

Brigitte Jordan, *Birth in Four Cultures*, p. 43

Leigh Minturn and John T. Hitchcock, 'The Rajputs of Khalapur, India' in *Six Cultures: Studies of Child Rearing*, ed. Beatrice B. Whiting, p. 314

Erik H. Erikson, *Childhood and Society*, p. 121

Meredith F. Small, *Our Babies, Ourselves*, pp. 82, 190, 202

M.F. Zeitlin and N.U. Ahmed, 'Nutritional correlates of frequency and length of breastfeeds in rural Bangladesh', *Early Human Development* 41, 1995, pp. 97–110

Margaret Mead, 'Children and Ritual in Bali' in *Childhood in Contemporary Cultures*, p. 47

J.S. Dosanjh and Paul A.S. Ghuman, *Child-Rearing in Ethnic Minorities*, p. 43

Chapter 8: **Tricks of the Trade**

Shirley Purdie quoted by Margaret Stewart, *Mother and Baby*, p. 12

Pye Henry Chavasse, *Advice to a Wife*, pp. 237–89

Chrissie Wildwood, *Aromatherapy*, pp. 9, 131, 201

Meredith F. Small, *Our Babies, Ourselves*, pp. 187, 210

Harriet Sergeant, 'The Japanese Way', *AIMS Journal*, Vol. 5, No. 3, Autumn 1993

Alyson Christy, 'About Cabbage Leaves', *LLL GB News*, Nov–Dec 1994, p. 11

V.C. Nikodem, D. Danziger, N. Gebka et al., 'Do cabbage leaves prevent breast engorgement? A randomized, controlled study', *Birth* 20, 1993, pp. 61–4

Jacqueline Vincent Priya, *Birth Traditions and Modern Pregnancy Care*, p. 117

Tim Blanks, ed., *The Body Shop Book*, p. 33

Joan Hyde, 'A Cracked Nipple in Winter', *LLL GB News*, December 1994, p. 5

Davina Dabeare, 'A Sore Point!' *Mother and Baby*, November 1994

Gabrielle Palmer, *The Politics of Breastfeeding*, pp. 41–2

WHO, UNICEF, UNESCO, UNFPA, *Facts for Life*, p. 20

Robert A. LeVine et al., *Childcare and Culture*, p. 26

Anne Hubbell Maiden and Edie Farwell, *The Tibetan Art of Parenting*, pp. 141–2

Eliza Warren quoted by Christina Hardyment in *Dream Babies*, p. 49

Chapter 8: **Breastfeeding and AIDS**

Paolo G. Miotti et al., 'HIV Transmission Through Breastfeeding', *The Journal of the American Medical Association*, Vol. 282, 25 August 1999, pp. 744–749

Chapter 8: **Share and Share Alike**

Gabrielle Palmer, *The Politics of Breastfeeding*, pp. 122, 133

Carleton S. Coon, *The Hunting Peoples*, p. 312

Lorna Marshall, 'The !Kung Bushmen of the Kalahari Desert' in *Peoples of Africa*, ed. James L. Gibbs, p. 261

Colin M. Turnbull, 'The Mbuti Pygmies of the Congo' in *Peoples of Africa*, ed. James L. Gibbs, p. 292

Menachem Gerson, *Family, Women and Socialisation in the Kibbutz*, p. 68

Nid Amina, *Childbirth and Burial Practices among Philippine Tribes*, p. 33

Robert A. and Barbara B. LeVine, 'Nyansongo: A Gusii Community in Kenya' in *Six Cultures: Studies of Child Rearing*, ed. Beatrice B. Whiting, pp. 139, 141

Blanche of Castile cited by Gabrielle Palmer in *The Politics of Breastfeeding*, pp. 122–3

Richard Jones quoted by M.J. Tucker, 'The Child as Beginning and End: Fifteenth and Sixteenth Century English Childhood' in *The History of Childhood*, ed. Lloyd de Mause, p. 241

Chapter 8: **Home Truths**

H.E. Bates, *The Vanished World*, p. 17

Michael G. Schwab, 'Mechanical Milk. An essay on the social history of infant formula', *Childhood* 3:4, November 1996, p. 479

9. A LOT OF BOTTLE

Chapter 9: **Milk for Sale**

Ian Thomas, ed., *Culpeper's Book of Birth*, pp. 85, 91

Marcel d'Hertefelt, 'The Rwanda of Rwanda' in *Peoples of Africa*, ed. James L. Gibbs, p. 419

Suzanne Dixon, *The Roman Family*, pp. 118–19, 128

Michel Odent, *The Scientification of Love*, pp. 96–8

Gabrielle Palmer, *The Politics of Breastfeeding*, p. 123, 125–6

Pye Henry Chavasse, *Advice to a Wife on the Management of Her Own Health*, p. 230

Lady Anne Clifford quoted by Linda Pollock in *A Lasting Relationship*, p. 62

Tacitus quoted in 'In Roman Times', *LLL GB News*, No. 91, Jan–Feb, 1996, p. 20

Mary Martin McLaughlin, 'Survivors and Surrogates: Children and Parents from the Ninth to the Thirteenth Centuries' in *The History of Childhood*, ed. Lloyd deMause, p. 115

Philippe Ariès, *Centuries of Childhood*, pp. 83, 362

Song of the 'balie' quoted by James Bruce Ross in 'The Middle-Class Child in

Urban Italy, Fourteenth to Early Sixteenth Century', *The History of Childhood*, ed. Lloyd deMause, pp. 184–6, 188, 193

Olwen Hufton, *The Prospect Before Her*, pp. 193, 196–198

Meredith F. Small, *Our Babies, Ourselves*, p. 205

F. Gordon Roe, *The Georgian Child*, p. 12

Lloyd deMause, *The History of Childhood*, pp. 33–35

Ann Wallace and Gabrielle Taylor, *Royal Mothers*, pp. 151, 154

'Crazy name, crazy girl', *Junior*, March–April 1998, p. 12

Chapter 9: Animal Magic

Francesco da Barberino and Paolo da Certaldo quoted by James Bruce Ross in 'The Middle-Class Child in Urban Italy, Fourteenth to Early Sixteenth Century', *The History of Childhood*, ed. Lloyd deMause, pp. 186–7

Meredith F. Small, *Our Babies, Ourselves*, pp. 193, 201–2, 205–6

Ann Wallace and Gabrielle Taylor, *Royal Mothers*, p. 15

Patrick Holford, *The Optimum Nutrition Bible*, pp. 42–3

Philippe Ariès, *Centuries of Childhood*, p. 362

Olwen Hufton, *The Prospect Before Her*, pp. 194–7

Leigh Minturn and John T. Hitchcock, 'The Rajputs of Khalapur, India' in *Six Cultures: Studies of Child Rearing*, ed. Beatrice B. Whiting, p. 314–15

Robert A. and Barbara B. LeVine, 'Nyansongo: A Gusii Community in Kenya' in *Six Cultures: Studies of Child Rearing*, ed. Beatrice B. Whiting, p. 141

J.S. Dosanjh and Paul A.S. Ghuman, *Child-Rearing in Ethnic Minorities*, p. 44

Mary Martin McLaughlin, 'Survivors and Surrogates: Children and Parents from the Ninth to the Thirteenth Centuries' in *The History of Childhood*, ed. Lloyd deMause, pp. 117, 151 (note 75)

Robert A. LeVine et al., *Childcare and Culture*, p. 143

Rupert Fawdry quoted by Sarah Boseley in 'Giving birth by numbers', *The Guardian*, 26 January 1999

Patrick P. Dunn, '"That Enemy is the Baby": Childhood in Imperial Russia' in *The History of Childhood*, ed. Lloyd deMause, p. 388

Michel Odent, *The Scientification of Love*, p. 98.

Chapter 9: Finding the Formula

Baron von Liebig quoted by Michael G. Schwab in 'Mechanical Milk', *Childhood* 3:4, November 1996, p. 483

Michael G. Schwab, 'Mechanical Milk', *Childhood* 3:4, November 1996, p. 485

Lloyd deMause, *The History of Childhood*, p. 36

Alison Sim, *Food and Feast in Tudor England*, p. 75

Henri Nestlé quoted by Michael G. Schwab in 'Mechanical Milk', *Childhood* 3:4, November 1996, p. 484

Tessa Thomas, 'Making baby hit the bottle', *The Independent*, 29 December 1992

Glenda Cooper, 'Baby milk rules "being flouted"', *The Independent*, 10 April 1998

Nestlé boycott: contact Baby Milk Action at babymilkact@gn.apc.org

Hannah Hulme Hunter, 'Why should mothers, on top of everything else, have to shoulder the burden of society's failure to support breastfeeding?' *MIDIRS Midwifery Digest*, Vol. 9, No. 2, June 1999, pp. 217–18

Chapter 9: **Feelings and Fashions**
India Knight, 'Three cheers for the bottle', *The Guardian*, 11 April 1995
Michael G. Schwab, 'Mechanical Milk', *Childhood* 3:4, November 1996, pp. 484, 490
J.S. Dosanjh and Paul A.S. Ghuman, *Child-Rearing in Ethnic Minorities*, pp. 76–7
Meredith F. Small, *Our Babies, Ourselves*, pp 204, 208
Ashley Montagu, *Touching*, p. 71
Olwen Hufton, *The Prospect Before Her*, p. 194
'You can't get fitter than a breastfed nipper', *MIDIRS Midwifery Digest* Vol. 9:3, September 1999, p. 361
Michel Odent, *The Scientification of Love*, pp. 97, 101
James Erlichman, 'Formula for success', *The Guardian*, 15 March 1995
Elizabeth Brendefur, 'Breastfeeding in Public', *New Generation*, June 1994, p. 5
Gabrielle Palmer, *'The Politics of Breastfeeding'*, pp. 42, 230
Dr Jane Pryer et al., 'Fears for breastmilk policy', *The Guardian*, 1 March 1995
Michael G. Schwab, 'Mechanical Milk', *Childhood* 3:4, November 1996, p. 489

Chapter 9: **Like a Weaned Child**
Psalm 131, 'A Song of Degrees of David', verse 2
The Body Shop Team, *Mamatoto*, pp. 166–7
Robert A. LeVine et al., *Childcare and Culture*, pp. 23, 27, 151–2, 259–60
Elizabeth Warnock Fernea, *Children in the Muslim Middle East*, p. 7
Nisa quoted by Marjorie Shostak in *Nisa*, pp. 78
Lorna Marshall, *The !Kung Bushmen of the Kalahari Desert*, p. 263
Erik H. Erikson, *Childhood and Society*, p. 158
James L. Gibbs, Jr, 'The Kpelle of Liberia' from *Peoples of Africa*, p. 208
Hilda Kuper, 'The Swazi of Swaziland' in *Peoples of Africa*, ed. James L. Gibbs, p. 485

Chapter 9: **The Bitter Truth**
Desmond Morris, *Babywatching*, p. 45
Guy Riddihough, 'So why do some like it hot?', *The Independent*, 20 April 1992
Leigh Minturn and John T. Hitchcock, 'The Rajputs of Khalapur, India' in *Six Cultures: Studies of Child Rearing*, ed. Beatrice B. Whiting, pp. 311, 321–2
Patrick P. Dunn in '"That Enemy is the Baby": Childhood in Imperial Russia', *The History of Childhood*, ed. Lloyd deMause, p. 388
Thomas W. and Hatsumi Maretzki, 'Taira: An Okinawan Village' in *Six Cultures: Studies of Child Rearing*, ed. Beatrice B. Whiting, p. 474, 477
Marjorie Shostak, *Nisa*, pp. 31, 46–7, 386

Chapter 9: **A Taste of Life**
Richard Pankhurst, *A Social History of Ethiopia*, p. 121

Carol Laderman, *Wives and Midwives*, pp. 205–6

Anne Hubbell Maiden and Edie Farwell, *The Tibetan Art of Parenting*, p. 70

Jacqueline Vincent Priya, *Birth Traditions and Modern Pregnancy Care*, p. 177

The Body Shop Team, *Mamatoto*, p. 133

Jennifer M. Russ, *German Festivals and Customs*, p. 132

Chapter 9: May I Introduce . . . ?

Mary Badger quoted by Linda Pollock in *A Lasting Relationship*, p. 74

Igor Kopytoff, 'The Suku of Southwestern Congo' in *Peoples of Africa*, ed. James
    L. Gibbs, p. 455

Meredith F. Small, *Our Babies, Ourselves*, pp. 186, 204, 222

Leigh Minturn and John T. Hitchcock, 'The Rajputs of Khalapur, India' in *Six
    Cultures: Studies of Child Rearing*, ed. Beatrice B. Whiting, pp. 311, 321–2

Anne Hubbell Maiden and Edie Farwell, *The Tibetan Art of Parenting*, p. 135

Chapter 9: Menu d'Enfants

Patrick Holford, *The Optimum Nutrition Bible*, p. 206

The Body Shop Team, *Mamatoto*, pp. 133, 167

Erik H. Erikson, *Childhood and Society*, p. 138

'Bottle-fed on fish oil', *The Independent*, 28 June 1995

Anne Hubbell Maiden and Edie Farwell, *The Tibetan Art of Parenting*, pp. 100, 110

Phoebe Ottenberg, 'The Afikpo Ibo of Eastern Nigeria' in *Peoples of Africa*,
    ed. James L. Gibbs, p. 22

Alison Sim, *Food and Feast in Tudor England*, p. 76

Homa Hoodfar, 'Child Care and Child Health in Low-Income Neighborhoods
    of Cairo' in *Children in the Muslim Middle East*, ed. Elizabeth Warnock Fernea,
    p. 153

Staffan Janson, 'Life and Health of Jordanian Children' in *Children in the Muslim
    Middle East*, ed. Elizabeth Warnock Fernea, p. 186

Tim Blanks, ed., *The Body Shop Book*, pp. 189, 192

Desmond Morris, *Babywatching*, pp. 79, 84

Chapter 9: Kiss of Life

Le Grand Propriétaire de Toutes Choses, quoted by Philippe Ariès in *Centuries of
    Childhood*, p. 126

Kevin Duffy, *Children of the Forest*, p. 130

Martha Wolfenstein, 'Some Variants in Moral Training of Children' in *Childhood in
    Contemporary Cultures*, p. 364

Margaret Mead, 'Children and Ritual in Bali' in *Childhood in Contemporary Cultures*,
    p. 47

Gabrielle Palmer, *The Politics of Breastfeeding*, p. 110

Lloyd deMause, *The History of Childhood*, p. 37

Ann Wallace and Gabrielle Taylor, *Royal Mothers*, p. 15

Chapter 9: Home Truths
Meredith F. Small, *Our Babies, Ourselves*, p. 222

10. BABY CARING

Chapter 10: Bathing Beauties
Louis XIII's bathing diary quoted by Olwen Hufton in *The Prospect Before Her*,
    p. 200
Fiona Macdonald, *A Child's View of History*, p. 53
Ian Thomas, ed., *Culpeper's Book of Birth*, p. 112
Olwen Hufton, *The Prospect Before Her*, pp. 187, 200
Desmond Morris, *Babywatching*, p. 18
Gayle Brandeis-McGunigle, 'Childhood and Ritual in Bali', *Mothering* 61, Fall
    1991, p. 39
Nikki Siegen-Smith, *Welcome to the World*, p. 47
The Body Shop Team, *Mamatoto*, p. 136
Ashley Montagu, *Touching*, pp. 304–5
Michel Odent, *Entering the World*, p. 109
Carol Laderman, *Wives and Midwives*, p. 157
Meredith Mann Taylor, *Transcultural Aspects of Breastfeeding – USA*, Lactation
    Consultant Series LLLI, 1985, p. 18
Fauziya Kassindja, *Do They Hear You When You Cry?*, p. 95
Tradition China www.babyzone.com, February 2001
David Levinson, 'Birth and Childhood Rights' in *Religion: A Cross-
    Cultural Encyclopedia*, excerpt at http://berkshire-reference.com/bk/religion
    encyclopaedia2.html
Tara MacAnTsior and Branfionn MacGregor, *Gaelic Celtic Culture 6: Birth Customs*
Nine Waves trans. from Carmina Gadelica by Caitlin Matthews, *Celtic Blessings*,
    p. 28
Jennifer M. Russ, *German Festivals and Customs*, p. 132
Anne Fadiman, *The Spirit Catches You and You Fall Down*, p. 4

Chapter 10: All Scrubbed Up
Jean Liedloff, *The Continuum Concept*, p. 29
Homa Hoodfar, 'Child Care and Child Health in Low-Income Neighborhoods
    of Cairo' in *Children in the Muslim Middle East*, ed. Elizabeth Warnock Fernea,
    p. 154
Margaret Mead, 'Cultural Differences in the Bathing of Babies' in *Mental Health
    and Infant Development*, ed. K. Soddy, pp. 170–71
Leigh Minturn and John T. Hitchcock, 'The Rajputs of Khalapur, India' in *Six
    Cultures: Studies of Child Rearing*, ed. Beatrice B. Whiting, p. 316
The Soap and Detergent Association 'History', http://sdahq.org
Ashley Montagu, *Touching*, p. 350

Chapter 10: **The Dangers of Drool**
'The good wife's guide', *Housekeeping Monthly*, London, 13 May 1955
Walter H. Sangree, 'The Bantu Tiriki of Western Kenya' in *Peoples of Africa*, ed. James L. Gibbs, p. 60
Gabrielle Palmer, *The Politics of Breastfeeding*, p. 35
Miranda Ingram, 'Bringing Up Baby in Russia', *She*, July 1995
J.S. Dosanjh and P.A.S. Ghuman, *Child-Rearing in Ethnic Minorities*, p. 52
Hindu father quoted by Dosanjh and Ghuman in *Child-Rearing in Ethnic Minorities*, pp. 81–2
Adrienne Burgess, Institute for Public Policy Research, quoted in 'No Kidding', *The Guardian*, 31 January 1996
Queen Victoria quoted by Ann Wallace and Gabrielle Taylor in *Royal Mothers*, p. 154
The Body Shop Team, *Mamatoto*, p. 162
Russell A. Judkins and Ann B. Judkins, 'Commentary: Cultural Dimensions of Hmong Birth', *Birth* 19:3, September 1992, p. 149
Kevin Duffy, *Children of the Forest*, p. 131
Lorna Marshall, 'The !Kung Bushmen of the Kalahari Desert' in *Peoples of Africa*, ed. James L. Gibbs, p. 263
Anne Sutherland, *Face Values*, pp. 88–89
Gayle Brandeis-McGunigle, 'Childhood and Ritual in Bali', *Mothering*, Fall 1991, p. 40

Chapter 10: **Some Like It Hot**
Queen Victoria quoted by Ann Wallace and Gabrielle Taylor, *Royal Mothers*, p. 158
Ruth Benedict, *Patterns of Culture*, p. 14
Desmond Morris, *Babywatching*, pp. 48–51, 142
Richard James de Boer, 'The Netsilik Eskimo and the Origin of Human Behaviour', quoted by Ashley Montagu in *Touching*, p. 297

Chapter 10: **Swaddling Stories**
Sixteenth-century mother quoted by M.J. Tucker, 'The Child As Beginning and End: Fifteenth and Sixteenth Century English Childhood' in *The History of Childhood*, ed. Lloyd de Mause, p. 242
Meredith F. Small, *Our Babies, Ourselves*, p. 112
Desmond Morris, *Babywatching*, pp. 120, 122
Olwen Hufton, *The Prospect Before Her*, p. 199
Philippe Ariès, *Centuries of Childhood*, p. 126
Lloyd deMause, *The History of Childhood*, pp. 11, 37, 38, 41, 50
Carol Laderman, *Wives and Midwives*, pp. 127, 157
Gerald of Wales (1147–1223) quoted by Henrietta Leyser, *Medieval Women*, p. 135
Christina Hardyment, *Dream Babies*, pp. 3, 16
Mary Martin McLaughlin, 'Survivors and Surrogates: Children and Parents from the Ninth to the Thirteenth Centuries' in *The History of Childhood*, ed. Lloyd de Mause, p. 114

Richard J.A. Talbert, ed., *Plutarch on Sparta*, p. 27

Patrick P. Dunn, '"That Enemy is the Baby": Childhood in Imperial Russia' in *The History of Childhood*, ed. Lloyd de Mause, pp. 386–7

Richard Jones quoted by M.J. Tucker in *The History of Childhood*, p. 241

Whitney Taylor, 'Assembly Line Production – Giving birth, Soviet style', *She*, October 1988

Sheila Kitzinger quoted by William Millinship in 'Suffering Red baby blues', *The Observer*, 28 May 1989

Meredith O'Brien, 'Childbirth Traditions: American Jewish' www.babyzone.com, February 2001

Clare Rose, *Children's Clothes*, pp. 15–18

Ann Wallace and Gabrielle Taylor, *Royal Mothers*, p. 59

Nancy Lyman Roelker, *Queen of Navarre*, quoted by Lloyd deMause in *The History of Childhood*, p. 31

Susan Dorsky and Thomas B. Stevenson, 'Childhood and Education in Highland and North Yemen' in *Children in the Middle East*, ed. Elizabeth Warnock Fernea, pp. 312–13

Gitanjali Kolanad, *Culture Shock! India*, p. 84

Meredith Mann Taylor, *Transcultural Aspects of Breastfeeding – USA*, Lactation Consultant Series LLLI, 1985, p. 18

Clare Rose, *Children's Clothes*, p. 15

Chapter 10: **Calls of Nature**

Ashley Montagu, *Touching*, p. 299

Desmond Morris, *Babywatching*, p. 130

Mary Renfrew, Chloe Fisher and Suzanne Arms, *Bestfeeding*, pp. 76, 87, 145

Penelope Leach, *Baby and Child*, p. 50

Beverley Chalmers, *African Birth*, p. 21

Hilda Kuper, 'The Swazi of Swaziland' in *Peoples of Africa*, ed. James L. Gibbs, p. 489

M.J. Tucker, 'The Child As Beginning and End: Fifteenth and Sixteenth Century English Childhood' in *The History of Childhood*, ed. Lloyd de Mause, pp. 241–2

Kevin Duffy, *Children of the Forest*, pp. 122–3

Sheila Kitzinger, *The Crying Baby*, p. 17

Joseph Chilton Pearce, *Magical Child*, p. 58

Anne Fadiman, *The Spirit Catches You and You Fall Down*, p. 3

Carole Laderman, *Wives and Midwives*, p. 10

F. Gordon Roe, *The Georgian Child*, p. 68

Chapter 10: **Changing Baby**

Italian wet nurses quoted by James Bruce Ross, 'The Middle-Class in Urban Italy, Fourteenth to Early Sixteenth Century' in *The History of Childhood*, ed. Lloyd deMause, pp. 193–4

Stuart Robbens, 'Changing nappies for the future', 21 July 2000, www.integra.org.uk

Hana's Generation 2000-2001, www.hanasgeneration.com

Rosalind Sharpe, 'Pampered little dears', *Independent Magazine*, 11 May 1996

Philip Delves Broughton, 'Nappies and the Pill set women free', *The Daily Telegraph*, 2 May 1998

Nick Stolerman, 'Bare Necessities' article for MIDIRS *Midwifery Digest*, 1993 (original text)

The Body Shop Team, *Mamatoto*, pp. 144, 163

Clare Rose, *Children's Clothes*, p. 15

Carleton S. Coon, *The Hunting Peoples*, p. 316

Meredith F. Small, *Our Babies, Ourselves*, p. 81

J.S. Dosanjh and Paul A.S. Ghuman, *Child-Rearing in Ethnic Minorities*, p. 47

Kitty Campion, *Holistic Herbal for Mother and Baby*, pp. 140-41

Alice Marriott, *Indians of the Four Corners*, p. 115

Carol Rudd, *Flower Essences*, p. 80

Olwen Hufton, *The Prospect Before Her*, pp. 174, 190

Gitanjali Kolanad, *Culture Shock! India*, p. 82

Miranda Ingram, 'Bringing up baby in Russia', *She*, July 1995

Susan Watts, 'New nappy can be put down the drain', *The Independent*, 11 December 1993

Chapter 10: **Home Truths**

Jody McLaughlin, cover review of *Primal Mothering in a Modern World*, by Hygeia Halfmoon

Desmond Morris, *Babywatching*, p. 51

11. TINY TEARS

Chapter 11: **Crying Out Loud**

Russian proverb quoted by Norma Gleason in *Proverbs from Around the World*, p. 21

Meredith F. Small, *Our Babies, Ourselves*, pp. 27–9, 105–6, 142–3, 153–4, 157

Jean Liedloff, *The Continuum Concept*, p. 73

Erik H. Erikson, *Childhood and Society*, pp. 114, 121

Robert A. LeVine et al., *Childcare and Culture*, pp xii, 149–50

Tom Wilkie, 'Babies' relentless crying in early evening "natural"', *The Independent*, 15 September 1989

Joanna Lyall, 'Crying with Confidence', *Nursing Times*, 18 October 1989

Desmond Morris, *Babywatching*, p. 61

T. B. Brazelton et al., 'Infant Development in the Zincantecan Indians of Southern Mexico', *Pediatrics* 44, 1969, pp. 277–290

Chapter 11: **The Meaning of a Baby's Cries**

Veddas lullaby quoted by the Body Shop Team in *Mamatoto*, p. 141

Anne Hubbell Maiden and Edie Farwell, *The Tibetan Art of Parenting*, pp. 140-41

Joules and Ken Taylor, *Scottish Folklore*, pp. 143–6
Irish fairies: the changeling, on www.irelandseye.com
Sprenger and Krämer quoted by Lloyd deMause in *The History of Childhood*, p. 10
Wicasta Lovelace, *The Malleus Maleficarum* article and book online at www.malleus maleficarum.org
Carol Laderman, *Wives and Midwives*, p. 202
Sheila Kitzinger, *The Crying Baby*, pp. 220-21
Christina Hardyment, *Dream Babies*, pp. 57, 252–3
Ian Thomas, ed., *Culpeper's Book of Birth*, p. 111
Samuel Smiles, *Physical Education, or the Nurture and Management of Children*, Edinburgh 1838, quoted by Christina Hardyment in *Dream Babies*, p. 55
Charis Frankenburg quoted by Christina Hardyment in *Dream Babies*, pp. 188–9
Meredith F. Small, *Our Babies, Ourselves*, p. 144

Chapter 11: **There, There**
Kevin Duffy, *Children of the Forest*, p. 37
Robert A. LeVine et al., *Childcare and Culture*, pp. xii, 38, 149, 201, 208
Thomas W. and Hatsumi Maretzki, 'Taira: An Okinawan Village' in *Six Cultures: Studies of Child Rearing*, ed. Beatrice B. Whiting, p. 462
Brigitte Jordan, *Birth in Four Cultures*, p. 43
Meredith F. Small, *Our Babies, Ourselves*, pp. 81, 168–9, 215
Marjorie Shostak, *Nisa*, p. 45
Gitanjali Kolanad, *Culture Shock! India*, pp. 81, 197
Leigh Minturn and John T. Hitchcock, 'The Rajputs of Khalapur, India' in *Six Cultures: Studies of Child Rearing*, ed. Beatrice B. Whiting, p. 313
Walter H. Sangree, 'The Bantu Tiriki of Western Kenya' in *Peoples of Africa*, ed. James L. Gibbs, p. 59
The Body Shop Team, *Mamatoto*, p. 141
European proverb quoted by Philippa Waring in *Omens and Superstitions*, p. 70
P.E. Jolly et al., 'Breast-feeding and weight change in newborns in Jamaica' *Child: Care, Health and Development*, 26:1, 2000, pp. 17–27
Marten de Vries quoted by Meredith F. Small, in *Our Babies, Ourselves*, pp. 168–9

Chapter 11: **Crying for a Cure**
Mary Knott, 'Cry babies', *Baby* magazine, November 1998, pp. 57–60
Meredith F. Small, *Our Babies, Ourselves*, pp. 145–6, 151, 153–5
Dr Tony Smith, 'Second Opinion', *The Independent on Sunday*, 11 June 1995
Robert A. LeVine et al., *Childcare and Culture*, pp. 198–200
P.H. Wolff, 'The natural history of crying and other vocalizations in early infancy' in *Determinants of Infant Behaviour*, ed. B.M. Foss, pp. 81–109
Jean Liedloff, *The Continuum Concept*, p. 66
Nid Amina, *Childbirth and Burial Practices among Philippine Tribes*, pp. 29–30
The Body Shop Team, *Mamatoto*, pp. 140-41
Sheila Kitzinger, *The Crying Baby*, p. 226
Kevin Duffy, *Children of the Forest*, p. 44

Paul Bohannan, 'The Tiv of Nigeria' in *Peoples of Africa*, ed. James L. Gibbs, p. 530

Chapter 11: **Colic – A Cry Too Far**

Robert A. and Barbara B. LeVine, 'Nyansongo: a Gusii Community in Kenya' in *Six Cultures: Studies of Child Rearing*, ed. Beatrice B. Whiting, p. 142

Leslie Kenton, *Nature's Child*, p. 18

I. St James-Roberts, 'Persistent infant crying', *Archives of Disease in Childhood* 66, 1991; pp. 653–5

Meredith F. Small, *Our Babies, Ourselves*, pp. 148–9, 152

Norman Autton, *Pain – An Exploration*, p. 82

'Colic' Home Health Fact File BV/IMP, August 1993

A. Lucas and I. St James-Roberts, 'Crying, fussing and colic behaviour in breast- and bottle-fed infants', *Early Human Development* 53:1, November 1998, pp. 9–18 and abstract by Dr Jenny Ingram, *Midwifery Digest* 9:3, September 1999, p. 367

The Body Shop Team, *Mamatoto*, p. 139

Desmond Morris, *Babywatching*, p. 83

H. Chapel and Mansel Haeney, *Essentials of Clinical Immunology*, Oxford 1984, p. 287

Chapter 11: **The Gob-Stopper**

Helen Hodgson, *Mrs Blossom on Babies*, Scientific Press, London 1909, quoted by Christina Hardyment in *Dream Babies*, p. 113

Desmond Morris, *Babywatching*, p. 69

Meredith F. Small, *Our Babies, Ourselves*, p. 146

Patrick P. Dunn, '"That Enemy is the Baby": Childhood in Imperial Russia' in *The History of Childhood*, ed. Lloyd deMause, pp. 387–8

Leigh Minturn and John T. Hitchcock, 'The Rajputs of Khalapur, India' in *Six Cultures: Studies of Child Rearing*, ed. Beatrice B. Whiting, p. 321

Thomas W. and Hatsumi Maretzki, 'Taira: An Okinawan Village' in *Six Cultures: Studies of Child Rearing*, ed. Beatrice B. Whiting, p. 475

Rennie Loewenthal, 'Breastfeeding in Canoa, Brazil' in *Feedback, LLL GB*, Spring 2000, p. 31

Lennart Righard, 'Sudden Infant Death Syndrome and Pacifiers: A Proposed Connection Could Be a Bias', *Birth* 25:2, June 1998, p. 128

L. Righard and M.O. Alade, 'Breastfeeding and the use of pacifiers', *Birth* 24, 1997, pp. 116–20

'Kinder Ruhiggestellt' ('Pacifying Children') ORF on Salzburg, Austrian TV online report 8 April 2001, http://oesterreich.ort.at

Chapter 11: **Alone Again – Naturally?**

John Seabrook, *Sleeping with the Baby*, New Yorker, 8 November 1999, p. 59

Marie J. Hayes et al., 'Early Childhood Co-Sleeping: Parent-Child and Parent-Infant Nighttime Interactions', *Infant Mental Health Journal*, 17:4, 1996, p. 349

Desmond Morris, *The Naked Ape*, pp. 96–7 and *Babywatching*, p. 124

Dr Richard Ferber, *Solve Your Child's Sleep Problems*, pp. 183–5

Chapter 11: **Drugged Babies**

John Stedman quoted by Linda Pollock in *A Lasting Relationship*, p. 74

Lloyd deMause, 'The Evolution of Childhood' in *The History of Childhood*, p. 36

The Body Shop Team, *Mamatoto*, p. 146

Olwen Hufton, *The Prospect Before Her*, p. 203

Peter Carlson, 'Museum charts U.S. drug use', *The Detroit News*, 9 May 1999

Christina Hardyment, *Dream Babies*, pp. 6, 57

'The Poppy', www.sfheart.com

Ian J., 'Advertising, Victorian – social deprivation', 19 March 1998, www.mailbase. ac.uk

Anthony S. Wohl, 'Opium and Infant Mortality', The Victorian Web, http://landow.stg.brown.edu

Dr David Simon, consultant paediatrician Hartlepool General Hospital, interviewed on 'You and Yours', BBC Radio 4, 24 November 1997

Dr Hume quoted by Lloyd deMause in 'The Evolution of Childhood', *The History of Childhood*, p. 36

Leigh Minturn and John T. Hitchcock, 'The Rajputs of Khalapur, India' in *Six Cultures: Studies of Child Rearing*, ed. Beatrice B. Whiting, p. 314

'Tales of Everyday Folk', narrator Felicity Finch, BBC Radio 4, 31 March 2000

Afghan crisis reported on 'News At Ten', BBC 1, 15 February 2001

'South Asia Afghan president says Taliban promotes drugs', BBC Online, www.bbc.co.uk, 9 June 1998

Chapter 11: **Home Truths**

Punjabi grandmother quoted by J.S. Dosanjh and P.A.S. Ghuman, 'Child-Rearing Practices of Two Generations of Punjabi Parents', *Children and Society* 11, 1997, pp. 29–43

Seagull report: *Independent on Sunday*, 31 December 1995

Robert A. LeVine et al., *Childcare and Culture*, p. 149

12. THE BIG SLEEP

Chapter 12: **Sleep Like a Baby**

Meredith F. Small, *Our Babies, Ourselves*, pp. 106, 117–18, 120, 222

John Seabrook, 'Sleeping With the Baby', *The New Yorker*, 8 November 1999, pp. 57, 58

'Sleep Problems in Babies', CRY-SIS Support Group, London WC1N 3XX

'Vital Signs', *The Independent*, 20 January 1998

Homa Hoodfar, 'Child Care and Child Health in Low-Income Neighborhoods of Cairo' in *Children in the Muslim Middle East*, ed. Elizabeth Warnock Fernea, p. 154

R.S. New and A. L. Richman, 'Maternal beliefs and infant care practices in Italy and the United States' in *Parents' Cultural Belief Systems*, ed. S. Harkness and C.M. Super, Guildford Press, New York 1996, pp. 385–404

Erik H. Erikson, *Childhood and Society*, p. 159
Robert A. Levine et al., *Childcare and Culture*, p. 49

Chapter 12: **The Human Cradle**
Greek lullaby quoted by The Body Shop Team in *Mamatoto*, p. 145
Meredith F. Small, *Our Babies, Ourselves*, p. 88
Gayle Brandeis-McGunigle, 'Childhood and Ritual in Bali' *Mothering*, Fall 1991, p. 40
Tine Thevenin, *The Family Bed*, p. 68
Deborah Jackson, *Three in a Bed*, pp. 162–3
Dr Conquest quoted by Christina Hardyment in *Dream Babies*, p. 53
Robert Wright, 'Why Johnny Can't Sleep', *Time*, 14 April 1997, pp. 74, 76
Betsy Lozoff et al., 'Cosleeping in Urban Families with Young Children in the United States', *Pediatrics* 74:2, August 1984, pp. 171–82
Marjorie F. Elias et al., 'Sleep/Wake Patterns of Breast-Fed Infants in the First 2 Years of Life', *Pediatrics* 77:3, March 1986, pp. 327–8

Chapter 12: **Sleep Bonding**
Gilda O'Neill, *My East End*, Penguin, London 1999, quoted in 'The Original EastEnders', *Daily Mail*, 13 January 2001
Leslie Jacobs, 'The Family Bed in India', *Mothering* 53, Fall 1989, p. 96
Muslim mother quoted by J.S. Dosanjh and Paul A.S. Ghuman in *Child-Rearing in Ethnic Minorities*, p. 84
Meredith F. Small, *Our Babies, Ourselves*, p. 114

Chapter 12: **Reasons to Snuggle Up**
John Seabrook, 'Sleeping With the Baby', *The New Yorker*, 8 November 1999, pp. 56–7, 59
Robert A. LeVine et al., *Childcare and Culture*, pp. 144, 148
James J. McKenna et al., 'Bedsharing Promotes Breastfeeding', *Pediatrics* 100:2, August 1997, pp. 214–19
The Royal College of Midwives, *Successful Breastfeeding* (1988), 1989, pp. 34–5
Richard Pankhurst, *A Social History of Ethiopia*, p. 121
Leslie Jacobs, 'The Family Bed in India', *Mothering* 52, Fall 1989, p. 96
'Babies, Bedsharing and Safety', *Education for Change* leaflet, Christchurch, New Zealand, www.efc.co.nz (May 2001)
Meredith F. Small, *Our Babies, Ourselves*, pp. 88, 99, 122, 128–9
Foua quoted by Anne Fadiman in *The Spirit Catches You and You Fall Down*, p. 105
Jean Liedloff, *The Continuum Concept*, p. 63
Jeanine Young, 'Night-time behaviour and Interactions between Mothers and their Infants of Low Risk for SIDS: a Longitudinal Study of Room-sharing and Bed-sharing', dissertation submitted to University of Bristol, March 1999
Anna Freud, *Normality and Pathology in Childhood*, International Universities Press, New York 1965, p. 155

James J. McKenna, 'Babies Need Their Mothers Beside Them', *World Health*, March–April 1996

Linda Lutes, 'Bedding Twins/Multiples Together', *Neonatal Network* 15:7, October 1996, p. 61

Liz Corcoran, 'Double Exposure', *WHO*, 17 June 1996

Chapter 12: **Practical Pillow Talk**

Welsh lullaby quoted by Mathilde Polee and Petra Rosenberg in *The Lullaby Treasury*, p. 43

John Seabrook, 'Sleeping With the Baby', *The New Yorker*, 8 November 1999, pp. 56–7, 59

Marjorie Shostak, *Nisa*, pp. 105, 111

St Hubert quoted by Mary Martin McLaughlin in 'Survivors and Surrogates: Children and Parents from the Ninth to the Thirteenth Centuries' in *The History of Childhood*, ed. Lloyd deMause, pp. 156–7, note 102

Henrietta Leyser, *Medieval Women*, p. 137

Naomi Stadlen, 'The Arcutio', *LLL GB News*, No. 90, Nov–Dec 1995, p. 10

Sarah Blaffer Hrdy, *Mother Nature*, p. 291

Leigh Minturn and John T. Hitchcock. 'The Rajputs of Khalapur, India' in *Six Cultures: Studies of Child Rearing*, ed. Beatrice B. Whiting, p. 313

National SIDS Resource Center, http://sids-network.org

Deborah Jackson, 'Don't throw the baby out with the bedclothes', Press Release for Bloomsbury Publishing, New York, September 1999

Desmond Morris, *Babywatching*, p. 90

Frances Hatton quoted by Linda Pollock in *A Lasting Relationship*, pp. 56–7

Chapter 12: **You're Feeling Very Sleepy**

Leslie Jacobs, 'The Family Bed in India', *Mothering* 53, Fall 1989, p. 96

Meredith F. Small, *Our Babies, Ourselves*, pp. 113, 137

Terence Dixon and Martin Lucas, *The Human Race*, pp. 244–6

J.S. Dosanjh and P.A.S. Ghuman, 'Child-Rearing Practices of Two Generations of Punjabi Parents', *Children and Society* 11, 1997, p. 30

L. and R. Hackett, 'Child-rearing practices and psychiatric disorder in Gujarati and British children', *British Journal of Social Work* 24, 1994, pp. 191–202

Sally Morris, 'Do children need a set bedtime?', *Prima*, January 1997, p. 116

J.S. Dosanjh and Paul A.S. Ghuman, *Child-Rearing in Ethnic Minorities*, p. 54

Betsy Lozoff et al., 'Co-sleeping in Urban Families with Young Children in the United States', *Pediatrics* 74:2, August 1984, pp. 171–82

Kevin Duffy, *Children of the Forest*, pp. 68–9

Marie J. Hayes et al., 'Early Childhood Co-Sleeping: Parent-Child and Parent-Infant Nighttime Interactions', *Infant Mental Health Journal*, 17:4, 1996, p. 348

The Body Shop Team, *Mamatoto*, p. 146

Malcolm and Marjorie Jack quoted by Gabrielle Palmer in *The Politics of Breastfeeding*, pp. 90-91

Chapter 12: **Lulla Lulla Lullaby**

Green Tara mantra quoted by Anne Hubbell Maiden and Edie Farwell in *The Tibetan Art of Parenting*, p. 110

Veronica Doubleday and John Baily, 'Patterns of Musical Development among Children in Afghanistan' in *Children in the Muslim Middle East*, ed. Elizabeth Warnock Fernea, p. 436, 443

Michel Odent, *The Scientification of Love*, p. 99

Ashley Montagu, *Touching*, p. 146

The Body Shop Team, *Mamatoto*, p. 147

Chapter 12: **A World of Sleep Songs**

Susan Milord, *Hands Around the World*, p. 63

Mathilde Polee and Petra Rosenberg, *The Lullaby Treasury*, pp. 12, 15, 22, 24, 29, 38, 46, 50, 61, 66, 70, 72–4

Farha Ghannam, 'Kuwaiti Lullabies', *Children in the Muslim Middle East*, ed. Elizabeth Warnock Fernea, p. 77

Sheila Kitzinger, *The Crying Baby*, p. 196

Chapter 12: **Can't Sleep, Won't Sleep**

Jim Horne, 'Insomnia: some facts and fiction', *The Practitioner* 229, 1985, p. 916

Sheila Kitzinger, *The Crying Baby*, p. 220

A. Monroe Aurand, 'Popular Home Remedies and Superstitions of the Pennsylvania Germans', extracted on   www.horseshoe.cc

Thomas W. and Hatsumi Maretzki, 'Taira: An Okinawan Village' in *Six Cultures: Studies of Child Rearing*, ed. Beatrice B. Whiting, p. 459

Susan Milord, *Hands Around the World*, p. 65

Karen Sullivan, ed., *Natural Home Remedies*, pp. 35, 92, 106, 121, 147

Karen Hurrell, *Natural Home Remedies*, pp. 36, 38

Chapter 12: **A Sudden Death**

Meredith F. Small, *Our Babies, Ourselves*, pp, 134, 221

Michel Odent, letter to *The Lancet*, 25 January 1986

Deborah Jackson, *Three in a Bed*, pp. 106–130

C.J. Bacon, 'Infant mortality in ethnic minorities in Yorkshire, UK', *Early Human Development*, 38, 1994, pp. 159–60

M. Gantley et al., 'Sudden infant death syndrome – links with infant care practices', *British Medical Journal*, 2 January 1993

Dr Benjamin Spock, *Baby and Child Care* (1995), The Bodley Head, London 1961, p. 173

Brigitte Jordan, *Birth in Four Cultures*, p. 43, note 20

Sylvia Close, 'Sleep positions and the new baby', *New Generation*, December 1990, p. 45

Liz Hunt, 'Cot deaths halved by back sleeping advice', *The Independent*, 31 January 1992

Celia Hall, 'Campaign seeks reasons for 55% fall in cot deaths', *The Independent*, 30 March 1993

M. Gantley, D.P. Davies, A. Murcott, 'Sudden infant death syndrome – links with infant care practices', *British Medical Journal*, 2 January 1992, pp. 16–20.

Lennart Righard, 'Sudden Infant Death Syndrome and Pacifiers: A Proposed Connection Could Be a Bias', *Birth* 25:2, June 1998, p. 129

J.K. Grether et al., 'Sudden infant death syndrome among Asians in California', *Journal of Pediatrics* 116:4, 1990, pp. 525–8

M. Gantley, 'Ethnicity and sudden infant death syndrome: anthropological perspectives', *Early Human Development* 38, 1994, pp. 203–8

Dr Jim Sprott, 'Success of Mattress-Wrapping', 12 October 1997, www.pnc.com.au

Lois Rogers, 'Bed-sharing may cut cot deaths', *The Sunday Times*, 8 October 1995

Peter Fleming et al., (CESDI, SUDI research team), *Sudden Unexpected Deaths in Infancy*, The Stationery Office, London, 2000, p. 85

Anne Hubbell Maiden and Edie Farwell, *The Tibetan Art of Parenting*, pp. 94–5

Bryan Christie, 'The sinister silence', *The Daily Mail*, 3 April 2000

H. Barry and L. Paxson, 'Infancy and Early Childhood: Cross-Cultural Codes: 2, *Ethnology* 1971, Vol. 10: 466–508

Christine Doyle, 'Are babies safe in bed?', *The Daily Telegraph*, 23 February 1999

Chapter 12: **Home Truths**

Julie Whitfield, 'Listening to our "Stone Age" Babies', *LLL GB News*, No. 85, Jan–Feb 1995, p. 5

Turkish proverb quoted by Norma Gleason in *Proverbs from Around the World*, p. 21

13. MIND OVER MATTER

Chapter 13: **The Roots of Illness**

Anne Fadiman, *The Spirit Catches You and You Fall Down*, pp. 5, 10

Anne Hubbell Maiden and Edie Farwell, *The Tibetan Art of Parenting*, p. 139

Nisa quoted by Marjorie Shostak in *Nisa*, p. 209

Chapter 13: **Fontanelles of Wisdom**

Anne Hubbell Maiden and Edie Farwell, *The Tibetan Art of Parenting*, p. 100

Meredith F. Small, *Our Babies, Ourselves*, pp. 11–13

Desmond Morris, *Babywatching*, pp. 25–6

Piers Vitebsky, *The Shaman*, p. 14

Beverly Chalmers, *African Birth*, p. 23

Meredith Mann Taylor, *Transcultural Aspects of Breastfeeding – USA*, p. 11

Dr Loraine M. Stern, *Does My Child Need A Doctor?*, pp. 17–18

Chapter 13: **Fairy-Tales**

Bressay lullaby quoted by Mathilde Polee and Petra Rosenberg in *The Lullaby Treasury*, p. 76

Peter Popham, 'Child lama breathes new life into Buddhism', *The Independent*, 20 December 1997

Meredith F. Small, *Our Babies, Ourselves*, p. 7

Jane Belo, 'Balinese Children's Drawing' in *Childhood in Contemporary Cultures*, ed. Margaret Mead and Martha Wolfenstein, p. 59

Joules and Ken Taylor, *Scottish Folklore*, pp. 143–4

Muslim mother quoted by J.S. Dosanjh and Paul A.S. Ghuman in *Child-Rearing in Ethnic Minorities*, p. 60

Olwen Hufton, *The Prospect Before Her*, p. 201

Robert A. and Barbara B. LeVine, 'Nyansongo: A Gusii Community in Kenya' in *Six Cultures: Studies in Child Rearing*, ed. Beatrice B. Whiting, p. 137

Robert A. LeVine et al., *Childcare and Culture*, pp. 146–7

Meredith Mann Taylor, *Transcultural Aspects of Breastfeeding – USA*, p. 11

Pamela Crimmins, 'Mothering in Morocco', *Mothering* 68, Fall 1993, pp. 108–12

Homa Hoodfar, 'Child Care and Child Health in Low-Income Neighborhoods of Cairo' in *Children in the Muslim Middle East*, ed. Elizabeth Warnock Fernea, p. 160

Chapter 13: **Spiritual Intervention**

Chagga prayer quoted by the Body Shop Team in *Mamatoto*, p. 134

!Kung San mother quoted by Marjorie Shostak in *Nisa*, p. 204

Elaine Fantham et al., *Women in the Classical World*, pp. 252–4

Margaret Stewart, *Mother and Child*, p. 45

Beverly Chalmers, *African Birth*, p. 24

Erik H. Erikson, *Childhood and Society*, pp. 156, 157

Anne Hubbell Maiden and Edie Farwell, *The Tibetan Art of Parenting*, p. 103–4

Carol Laderman, *Wives and Midwives*, p. 95

Ruth Benedict, *Patterns of Culture*, pp. 28–9

Colin Taylor, *North American Indians*, p. 47

Nikki Siegen-Smith, *Welcome to the World*, p. 47

Grey Wolf, *Native American Wisdom*, pp. 80-83

Norman Autton, *Pain – An Exploration*, p. 77

Desmond Morris, *Babywatching*, p. 92

Chapter 13: **A Charmed Life**

Inuit shaman quoted by Nikki Siegen-Smith in *Welcome to the World*, p. 46

Suzanne Dixon, *The Roman Family*, p. 101

Ainu grandfather quoted by Carleton S. Coon in *The Hunting Peoples*, pp. 314–15

Susan Milord, *Hands Around the World*, p. 79

Alice Marriott, *Indians of the Four Corners*, pp. 52, 153

Norman Bancroft Hunt, *Native American Tribes*, p. 79

Thomas W. and Hatsumi Maretzki, 'Taira: An Okinawan Village' in *Six Cultures: Studies of Child Rearing*, ed. Beatrice B. Whiting, p. 459, note

Ann Wallace and Gabrielle Taylor, *Royal Mothers*, p. 59

F. Gordon Roe, *The Georgian Child*, p. 12

Sir Hugh Platt quoted in *Brewer's Dictionary of Phrase and Fable*, p. 261
Colin Turnbull, 'The Mbuti Pygmies of the Congo' in *Peoples of Africa*, ed. James L. Gibbs, p. 305

Chapter 13: **Scratching the Surface**

Lady Mary Wortley Montagu, 'Smallpox Vaccination in Turkey' quoted in *Modern History Sourcebook*, www.fordhamedu/halsall/mod/montagu
Robert de Laroche and Jean-Michel Labat, *The Secret Life of Cats*, p. 38
Nid Amina, *Childbirth and Burial Practices among Philippine Tribes*, p. 2
Beverly Chalmers, *African Birth*, p. 24
Leon Chaitow, *Vaccination and Immunization*, pp. 4–9
'The origin of smallpox vaccine', www.homeusers.prestel.co.uk
Fiona Macdonald, *A Child's Eye View of History*, p. 53
'The First Recorded Smallpox Vaccination', www.thedorsetpage.com
Leigh Minturn and John T. Hitchcock, 'The Rajputs of Khalapur, India' in *Six Cultures: Studies of Child Rearing*, ed. Beatrice B. Whiting, p. 309
'Resistance to Smallpox Vaccination', Robert Johnston, *Query*, and Larry Cebula, *Reply*, at www2.h-net.msu.edu
Henry Robert Oswald, 'Aversion of the Islanders to Vaccination', 1837, quoted by F. Coakley at www.ee.surrey.ac.uk
Thomas W. and Hatsumi Maretzki, 'Taira: An Okinawan Village' in *Six Cultures: Studies of Child Rearing*, ed. Beatrice B. Whiting, p. 463
Dr Archie Kalokerinos, 'Every Second Child', Australia 1974, quoted by Leon Chaitow in *Vaccination and Immunization*, pp. 77–8
Susan Curtis, *A Handbook of Homoeopathic Alternatives to Immunisation*, p. 5
UNICEF, 'A World Without Polio', www.unicef.org/polio
Homa Hoodfar, 'Child Care and Child Health in Low-Income Neighborhoods of Cairo' in *Children in the Muslim Middle East*, ed. Elizabeth Warnock Fernea, p. 159

Chapter 13: **Spirit Baby**

Anne Fadiman, *The Spirit Catches You and You Fall Down*, p. 10
AusInfo, *Australian Aboriginal Culture*, pp. 11–12
Rennie Loewenthal, 'Breastfeeding in Canoa, Brazil', *Feedback LLL GB*, Spring 2000, p. 31
Meredith F. Small, *Our Babies, Ourselves*, p. xix
Thomas W. and Hatsumi Maretzki, 'Taira : An Okinawan Village' in *Six Cultures: Studies of Child Rearing*, ed. Beatrice B. Whiting, p. 460
Margaret Mead, 'Children and Ritual in Bali' in *Childhood in Contemporary Cultures*, p. 40
Amanda Hopkinson, 'Midwifery and Rural Health Care in Guatemala' in *The Midwife Challenge*, ed. Sheila Kitzinger, p. 162
Phoebe Ottenberg, 'The Afikpo Ibo of Eastern Nigeria' in *Peoples of Africa*, ed. James L. Gibbs, p. 21.

Derrick J. Stenning, 'The Pastoral Fulani of Northern Nigeria' in *Peoples of Africa*, ed. James L. Gibbs, p. 390

Hilda Kuper, 'The Swazi of Swaziland' in *Peoples of Africa*, ed. James L. Gibbs, p. 498

Desmond Morris, *Babywatching*, p. 20

Chapter 13: **When a Baby Dies**

Harriet Beecher Stowe quoted by Jon E. Lewis in *The Mammoth Book of Letters*, p. 298

Kate Gordon, *Baptism and Baby-Naming*, p. 37

Tara MacAnTsior and Branfionn MacGregor, 'Birth Customs', Gaelic Celtic Culture 6 at http://homepage.eir.com.net

Philippa Waring, *Omens and Superstitions*, p. 33

Olwen Hufton, *The Prospect Before Her*, p. 189

Mary Braid, 'The long road to freedom', *The Independent Magazine*, 7 November 1998, p. 33

Carleton S. Coon, *The Hunting Peoples*, p. 312

Alice Marriott, *Indians of the Four Corners*, p. 22

Kwakiutl mother quoted by Ruth Benedict in *Patterns of Culture*, pp. 239–40

Arthur Golden, *Memoirs of a Geisha*, Vintage 1998, p. 326

'What is Jizo', http://sera.users.50megs.com

'More about Jizo Bodhisattva', http://jizo.org

Chapter 13: **Home Truths**

Martin Wollacott, 'Hunters put their faith in the spirit world', *The Guardian*, 6 June 2000

14. HUMAN HEALING

Chapter 14: **Vital Signs**

Robert A. LeVine et al., *Childcare and Culture*, p. 194

'Medical diagnosis by smell' and 'Women synchronize their menstrual periods' at http://www.experimentarium.dk

Adam J. Jackson, *Eye Signs*, pp. 1–2

Chapter 14: **Intensive Care**

Alison Parker, 'On second thoughts . . .' *LLL GB News*, No. 63, March–April 1991

Valerie Schultz, 'Mom Medicine', *Mothering* 104, Jan–Feb 2001, p. 49

Chapter 14: **Fresh-Air Therapy**

Nicholas Culpeper, *A Directory for Midwives*, quoted by Ian Thomas, ed., *Culpeper's Book of Birth*, p. 119

Dr Pye Henry Chavasse, *Advice to a mother on the management of her children and on the treatment of some of their more pressing illnesses and accidents*, Willing and

Williamson, Toronto, Canada, 1880, p. 131 (full text at www.canadiana.org)
Christina Hardyment, *Dream Babies*, pp. 65, 139, 178, 189–90, 199, 256
Tine Thevenin, *The Family Bed*, p. 59
Ada Ballin quoted by Christina Hardyment in *Dream Babies*, p. 141
Ashley Montagu, *Touching*, p. 326
Michel Odent, *The Scientification of Love*, p. 40
Jacqueline Vincent Priya, *Birth Traditions*, pp. 110, 113

Chapter 14: Skin Deep
Ezekiel 16:4
Alice Marriott, *Indians of the Four Corners*, pp. 108, 111
Mary Martin McLaughlin, 'Survivors and Surrogates: Children and Parents from
    the Ninth to the Thirteenth Centuries' in *The History of Childhood*, ed. Lloyd
    de Mause, p. 113
Nikki Siegen-Smith, *Welcome to the World*, p. 47
The Body Shop Team, *Mamatoto*, p. 136
The Soap and Detergent Association, 'History', http://sdahq.org
Nid Amina, *Childbirth and Burial Practices among Philippine Tribes*, p. 26
Leigh Minturn and John T. Hitchcock, 'The Rajputs of Khalapur, India' in *Six
    Cultures: Studies of Child Rearing*, ed. Beatrice B. Whiting, p. 306
Carol Laderman, *Wives and Midwives*, pp. 206, 244–5
Jennifer M. Russ, *German Festivals and Customs*, p. 132
Nikki Bradford and Jean Williams, *What They Don't Tell You About Being a Mother
    and Looking After Babies*, pp. 189–90
Olwen Hufton, *The Prospect Before Her*, p. 200
Nikki Wesson, *Alternative Maternity*, p. 164
Dr Hugh Jolly, *Book of Child Care*, p. 58
Anne Fadiman, *The Spirit Catches You and You Fall Down*, p. 9
Thomas W. and Hatsumi Maretzki, 'Taira: An Okinawan Village' in *Six Cultures:
    Studies in Child Rearing*, ed. Beatrice B. Whiting, p. 468
Homa Hoodfar, 'Child Care and Child Health in Low-Income Neighborhoods
    of Cairo' in *Children in the Muslim Middle East*, ed. Elizabeth Warnock Fernea,
    p. 154
Karen Sullivan, *Natural Home Remedies*, pp. 89, 152

Chapter 14: Massage of Love
Anita Roddick quoted by Sharon Maxwell Magnus, 'Breastfeeding, bonding and
    big business', *She*, September 1990, pp. 37–8
The Body Shop Team, *Mamatoto*, pp. 138–9, 146
Tim Blanks, ed., *The Body Shop Book*, pp. 134, 138
Margaret Stewart, *Mother and Child*, p. 53
Anne Hubbell Maiden and Edie Farwell, *The Tibetan Art of Parenting*, p. 158
Terence Dixon, *The Human Race*, p. 115
Gerry Pyves, 'Therapeutic Massage – The Cinderella of the healing family?' *Cahoots*,
    July–Sept 1988, pp. 12–13

James L. Gibbs, 'The Kpelle of Liberia' in *Peoples of Africa*, p. 209

Leigh Minturn and John T. Hitchcock, 'The Rajputs of Khalapur, India' in *Six Cultures: Studies of Child Rearing*, ed. Beatrice B. Whiting, p 316

Sheila Kitzinger, *The Crying Baby*, pp. 221–2

Margaret Mead, 'Children and Ritual in Bali' in *Childhood in Contemporary Cultures*, p. 43

Peter Walker, *The Book of Baby Massage*, pp. 11–12

Ruth Benedict, *Patterns of Culture*, pp. 18–19

Chapter 14: Stroking Better

Frédérick Leboyer quoted by Jody Lee Halfmoon in 'In Mother's Arms', *The Baby Connection News Journal* 3:6, December 1988

Polly Samson, 'Baby of the New Age', *The Independent Magazine*, 20 October 1990, p. 14

Sheila Kitzinger, *The Crying Baby*, p. 221

Ashley Montagu, *Touching*, p. 348

Sarah Hobson, *Family Web – A Story of India*, p. 201

Tim Blanks, ed., *The Body Shop Book*, pp. 138, 140

Chrissie Wildwood, *Aromatherapy*, pp. 37, 165, 201

M.J. Tucker, 'The Child As Beginning and End: Fifteenth and Sixteenth Century English Childhood' in *The History of Childhood*, ed. Lloyd deMause, p. 241

Marcel d'Hertefelt, 'The Rwanda of Rwanda' in *Peoples of Africa*, ed. James L. Gibbs, p. 419

Meredith F. Small, *Our Babies, Ourselves*, p. 95

Nid Amina, *Childbirth and Burial Practices among Philippine Tribes*, p. 27

Mary Martin McLaughlin, 'Survivors and Surrogates: Children and Parents from the Ninth to the Thirteenth Centuries' in *The History of Childhood*, ed. Lloyd deMause, p. 113

Carol Laderman, *Wives and Midwives*, p. 157

Margaret Stewart, *Mother and Child*, pp. 63, 71

Chapter 14: Born Too Soon

Nisa quoted by Marjorie Shostak in *Nisa*, p. 186

Leigh Dayton, reporter, 'Microprems Part One – To be or not to be . . .' *Quantum*, Australian Broadcasting Corporation, Thursday, 25 May 2000, www.abc.net.au/quantum

Jacqueline Vincent Praya, *Birth Traditions*, p. 109

Nikki Siegen-Smith, *Welcome to the World*, p. 46

Robert A. LeVine et al., *Childcare and Culture*, pp. xiii, 134, 135, 137

Meredith F. Small, *Our Babies, Ourselves*, pp. 19–20, 36

William A. Silverman, 'Postscript to Incubator-Baby Side Shows', *Pediatrics* 66(3), September 1980, pp. 474–5

The AAP Perinatal Section Ad Hoc Committee on Perinatal History, 'Martin Couney's Story revisited', letter to the editor, *Pediatrics* 100 (1), July 1997, pp. 159–60

Eleanor Clark, 'It's a different world', *The Watford Observer*, 8 March 1996

Dr Edgar Rey quoted by Oliver Gillie, 'Nature's incubator is best for baby', *The Sunday Times*, 20 May 1984

José Díaz-Rossello, 'Caring for the Mother and Preterm Infant: Kangaroo Care', *Birth* 23:2, June 1996, pp. 108–10

Julie Anne Hayes, 'TAC-TIC therapy: a non-pharmacological stroking intervention for premature infants', *Complementary Therapies in Nursing and Midwifery* 4, 1998, pp. 25–7

Angela Smyth, 'Kangaroos know that cuddles work best', *The Independent*, 18 August 1992

Emily Smyth, 'Bosom buddies: how tiny babies thrive on contact', *The Independent*, 27 December 1988

Chapter 14: **A Special Need**
Homa Hoodfar, 'Child Care and Child Health in Low-Income Neighborhoods of Cairo' in *Children in the Muslim Middle East*, ed. Elizabeth Warnock Fernea, p. 159

Plutarch, 'The Life of Lycurgus', translated by Richard J.A. Talbert in *Plutarch on Sparta*, p. 27

Meredith F. Small, *Our Babies, Ourselves*, pp. 87–8

Margaret Stewart, *Mother and Child*, p. 30

Olwen Hufton, *The Prospect Before Her*, pp. 179–80

Mary Martin McLaughlin, 'Survivors and Surrogates: Children and Parents from the Ninth to the Thirteenth Centuries' in *The History of Childhood*, ed. Lloyd deMause, p. 114

Igor Kopytoff, 'The Suku of Southwestern Congo' in *Peoples of Africa*, ed. James L. Gibbs, p. 457

Carol Laderman, *Wives and Midwives*, p. 95

Anne Hubbell Maiden and Edie Farwell, *The Tibetan Art of Parenting*, p. 142

Robert A. LeVine et al., *Childcare and Culture*, pp. 150, 193

Chapter 14: **Home Truths**
Janet Dunbar, *The Early Victorian Woman*, p. 33

15. HAPPY TALK

Chapter 15: **A Quiet Start**
Ashley Montagu, *Touching*, p. 295

Dr Sally Ward, *BabyTalk*, p. 9

John A. Hostetler, *Amish Life*, p. 7

Meredith F. Small, *Our Babies, Ourselves*, pp. xix, 95, 101

Erik H. Erikson, *Childhood and Society*, p. 142

David Crystal, *Listen to Your Child*, p. 59

Robert A. LeVine, *Childcare and Culture*, pp. xii, xiv, 148, 210, 216, 252

Anne Hubbell Maiden and Edie Farwell, *The Tibetan Art of Parenting*, p. 147
Sarah Hobson, *Family Web*, p. 26

Chapter 15: **Show Me a Sign**
Frédérick Leboyer, *Birth Without Violence*, p. 5
Professor Colwyn Trevarthen, 'How Infants Learn Culture', a talk for the British Association, Keele, 2 September 1993
Thérèse Bertherat, *The Body Has Its Reasons*, p. 64
Terence Dixon and Martin Lucas, *The Human Race*, p. 86
Joseph Garcia, 'Sign With Your Baby – How to Communicate with Infants Before They Can Speak', Northlight Communications, Seattle 1999, www.sign2me.com
Thomas W. and Hatsumi Maretzki, 'Taira: An Okinawan Village' in *Six Cultures: Studies of Child Rearing*, ed. Beatrice B. Whiting, p. 476
Margaret Mead, 'Children and Ritual in Bali' in *Childhood in Contemporary Cultures*, p. 42
Anthony Forge, 'A Village in Bali' in *Face Vales*, ed. Anne Sutherland, p. 232
Charles Higham, *The Maoris*, p. 36
Robert A. LeVine, *Childcare and Culture*, p. 223
Ifeoma Onyefulu, *A is for Africa*
Anne Hubbell Maiden and Edie Farwell, *The Tibetan Art of Parenting*, pp. 111, 122
Leigh Minturn and John T. Hitchcock, 'The Rajputs of Khalapur, India' in *Six Cultures: Studies of Child Rearing*, ed. Beatrice B. Whiting, p. 319
'The meaning of "Namaste"', www.worldtrans.org

Chapter 15: **Talking It Over**
Ruth Benedict, *Patterns of Culture*, p. 23
Desmond Morris, *Naked Ape*, pp. 76–7
John A. Hostetler, *Amish Life*, p. 35
Ken Campbell, 'Wol Wantok' Social Innovations Award winner 1999 (CD available from King Mob, 91 Brick Lane, London E1 6QL, or ekmob@aol.com)
Terence Dixon and Martin Lucas, *The Human Race*, pp. 85, 88–92
Tom Porter quoted by Terence Dixon and Martin Lucas in *The Human Race*, p. 91

Chapter 15: **An Ear for Language**
Nisa quoted by Marjorie Shostak in *Nisa*, p. 185
Jacqueline Vincent Priya, *Birth Traditions*, p. 26
Miriam Stoppard, *Conception, Pregnancy and Birth*, p. 175
Tom Wilkie reports from the American Association for the Advancement of Sciences, 'Babies "can pick out language"', *The Independent*, 12 February 1992
'Nina bobo' ('I shall rock my little baby') quoted by Mathilde Polee and Petra Rosenberg in *The Lullaby Treasury*, p. 42
Salimbene de Adam, *Cronica* (Chronicle) quoted by Mary Martin McLaughlin, 'Survivors and Surrogates: Children and Parents from the Ninth to the

Thirteenth Centuries' in *The History of Childhood*, ed. Lloyd deMause, p. 118 and note 86, pp. 152–3

Suzanne Dixon, *The Roman Family*, pp. 104, 116

Soranus, *Gynaecology* 2.12.19, quoted by Elaine Fantham et al., *Women in the Classical World*, p. 379

Tim Radford, 'Baby talk shows skills with speech are in-built', *The Guardian*, 1 January 1999

Desmond Morris, *Babywatching*, p. 135

J.S. Dosanjh and Paul A.S. Ghuman, *Child-Rearing in Ethnic Minorities*, pp. 55–6

Chapter 15: **Going Ga-Ga**

English rhyme quoted by F. Gordon Roe in *The Georgian Child*, p. 109

Meredith F. Small, *Our Babies, Ourselves*, pp. 37, 106

Catherine Garvey, *Children's Talk*, p. 201

Terence Dixon and Martin Lucas, *The Human Race*, pp. 85, 102

Mary Martin McLaughlin, 'Survivors and Surrogates: Children and Parents from the Ninth to the Thirteenth Centuries' in *The History of Childhood*, ed. Lloyd deMause, p. 117

Martha Wolfenstein, 'French Parents Take Their Children To The Park' in *Childhood in Contemporary Cultures*, p. 109

Derrick J. Stenning, 'The Pastoral Fulani of Northern Nigeria' in *Peoples of Africa*, ed. James L. Gibbs, p. 391

Anne Hubbell Maiden and Edie Farwell, *The Tibetan Art of Parenting*, pp. 115–6, 122

Mark Zborowski, 'The Place of Book-Learning in Traditional Jewish Culture' in *Childhood in Contemporary Cultures*, ed. Margaret Mead and Martha Wolfenstein, p. 124

The Body Shop Team, *Mamatoto*, p. 137

Polly Widaldji quoted by Margaret Stewart in *Mother and Child*, p. 49

Chapter 15: **Babbling Babies**

Bronwen Burford quoted by Sharon Kingman in 'How a family learnt the language of touch', *The Independent on Sunday*, 12 April 1992

David Crystal, *Listen to Your Child*, pp. 43, 46

J. Goldbart and S. Mukherjee, 'The appropriateness of Western models of parent involvement in Calcutta, India. Part 1: parents' views on teaching and child development', *Child: Care, Health and Development* 25:5, 1999, pp. 343–4

Robert A. LeVine et al., *Childcare and Culture*, pp. xii, 197–8, 201, 218, 252

Desmond Morris, *Babywatching*, p. 135

Mark Zborowski, 'The Place of Book-Learning in Traditional Jewish Culture' in *Childhood in Contemporary Cultures*, ed. Margaret Mead and Martha Wolfenstein, p. 124

Chapter 15: **Games Parents Play**

Tunisian song quoted by Sabra Webber in 'Children's Songs and Games from

Tunisia', *Children in the Muslim Middle East*, ed. Elizabeth Warnock Fernea, pp. 451–2

Terence Dixon and Martin Lucas, *The Human Race*, pp. 102–3

Robert A. LeVine et al., *Childcare and Culture*, p. 244

Desmond Morris, *Babywatching*, p. 96

Henrietta Leyser, *Medieval Woman*, p. 132

Mary Martin McLaughlin, 'Survivors and Surrogates: Children and Parents from the Ninth to the Thirteenth Centuries' in *The History of Childhood*, ed. Lloyd deMause, pp. 118, 137, 152 note 84

Lorna Marshall, *The !Kung of Nyae Nyae*, pp. 301–13

Meredith F. Small, *Our Babies, Ourselves*, p. 33

Pete May, 'Humour them', *The Guardian*, 2 August 2000

Chapter 15: **First Words**

David Crystal, *Listen to Your Child,* pp. 43, 46, 56–7

Desmond Morris, *Babywatching*, p. 70

Naomi Stadlen, 'Mamma!' *LLL GB News*, No. 88, July–Aug 1995, p. 20

Barnabas and Anabel Kindersley, *Children Just Like Me*, pp. 12, 14, 33, 36, 42, 48, 50, 52, 54, 62, 70

Anne Hubbell Maiden and Edie Farwell, *The Tibetan Art of Parenting*, pp. 115–16

Tradition China, www.babyzone.com, February 2001

A. Monroe Aurand, 'Home Remedies and Superstitions of the Pennsylvania Germans', extracted on www.horseshoe.cc

Martin Southwold, 'The Ganda of Uganda' in *Peoples of Africa*, ed. James L. Gibbs, p. 107

Margaret Mead, 'Children and Ritual in Bali' in *Childhood in Contemporary Cultures*, p. 47

Carol Laderman, *Wives and Midwives*, p. 131

Jennifer M. Russ, *German Festivals and Customs*, p. 133

James L. Gibbs, 'The Kpelle of Liberia' in *Peoples of Africa*, p. 209

Margaret Stewart, *Nisa,* p. 48

Chapter 15: **Home Truths**

Ruth Benedict, *Patterns of Culture*, pp. 2–3

Phoebe Ottenberg, 'The Afikpo Ibo of Eastern Nigeria' in *Peoples of Africa*, ed. James L. Gibbs, p. 21

16. THE BABY GROWS

Chapter 16: **Testing, Testing**

Jean Liedloff, *The Continuum Concept*, p. 75

Meredith F. Small, *Our Babies, Ourselves*, pp. 166, 219, 221

Desmond Morris, *Babywatching*, p. 87

Robert A. LeVine, *Childcare and Culture*, pp. 49, 178, 257

Kathryn Dewey and M. Jane Heinig, 'Are new growth charts needed for breastfed infants?' *Breastfeeding Abstracts* (La Leche League International) 12:4, May 1993
Richard Ferber, *Solve Your Child's Sleep Problems*, p. 19
Edith Rudinger, ed., *The Newborn Baby*, p.35

Chapter 16: **Stages of Life**
French poem quoted by Philippe Ariès in *Centuries of Childhood*, p. 20
Anne Sutherland, 'The Gypsies of California' in *Face Values*, p. 196
Maribel Cormach Lynch and Maria Isabel La Rosa Cormack, 'Peru: the life cycle perspective', Bernard van Leer Foundation *Newsletter* No. 75, July 1994, p. 7
Carol Laderman, *Wives and Midwives*, pp. 38, 40

Chapter 16: **First Things First**
Gyatso quoted by Anne Hubbell Maiden and Edie Farwell in *The Tibetan Art of Parenting*, p. 158
Olwen Hufton, *The Prospect Before Her*, p. 208
Anne Hubbell Maiden and Edie Farwell, *The Tibetan Art of Parenting*, p. 135

Chapter 16: **All Smiles**
William Blake, 'Infant Joy' from *Songs of Innocence*
Frédérick Leboyer, *Birth Without Violence*, pp. 102–3
Desmond Morris, *Babywatching*, pp. 62, 65, 66
Desmond Morris, *The Naked Ape*, p. 137
Robert A. LeVine et al., *Childcare and Culture*, p. 49
The Body Shop Team, *Mamatoto*, p. 147
Anne Hubbell Maiden and Edie Farwell, *The Tibetan Art of Parenting,* pp. 115–16
Carol Laderman, *Wives and Midwives*, p. 202
Meredith F. Small, *Our Babies, Ourselves*, p. 145
Terence Dixon and Martin Lucas, *The Human Race*, pp. 102–3

Chapter 16: **Two Front Teeth**
Chagga saying quoted by the Body Shop Team in *Mamatoto*, p. 169
Meredith F. Small, *Our Babies, Ourselves*, p. 183
Desmond Morris, *Babywatching*, pp. 33–4
Philippa Waring, *Omens and Superstitions*, pp. 226–7
Sikh mothers quoted by J.S. Dosanjh and Paul A.S. Ghuman in *Child-Rearing in Ethnic Minorities*, pp. 60, 61
Ian Thomas ed., *Culpeper's Book of Birth*, p. 125
Phoebe Ottenberg, 'The Afikpo Ibo of Eastern Nigeria' in *Peoples of Africa*, ed. James L. Gibbs, p. 31
John Arbuthnot, *An Essay Concerning the Nature of Ailments*, quoted by Christina Hardyment in *Dream Babies*, p. 6
Homa Hoodfar, 'Child Care and Child Health in Low-Income Neighborhoods of Cairo' in *Children in the Muslim Middle East*, ed. Elizabeth Warnock Fernea, p. 155

Mary Martin McLaughlin, 'Survivors and Surrogates: Children and Parents from the Ninth to the Thirteenth Centuries' in *The History of Childhood*, ed. Lloyd deMause, p. 113

Karen Hurrell, *Natural Home Remedies*, pp. 25, 30, 37, 38

Philippe Ariès, *Centuries of Childhood*, pp. 387–8

F. Gordon Roe, *The Georgian Child*, p. 12

AusInfo, *Australian Aboriginal Culture*, p. 28

Karen Sullivan, ed. *Natural Home Remedies*, pp. 90, 120, 151

Chapter 16: **Creepy-Crawlies**

Peter Walker, *Baby Relax*, p. 13

Anne Sutherland, 'Ourselves and Others' in *Face Values*, pp. 31–2

Gayle Brandeis-McGunigle, 'Childhood and Ritual in Bali', *Mothering*, Fall 1991, p. 40

Anthony Forge, 'A Village in Bali' in *Face Values*, ed. Anne Sutherland p. 231

Brigitte Jordan, *Birth in Four Cultures*, p. 43, note 20

Olwen Hufton, *The Prospect Before Her*, p. 203

Thomas W. and Hatsumi Maretzki, 'Taira: An Okinawan Village' in *Six Cultures: Studies of Child Rearing*, ed. Beatrice B. Whiting, pp. 471–2

Meredith F. Small, *Our Babies, Ourselves*, p. 89

Colin M. Turnbull, 'The Mbuti Pygmies of the Congo' in *Peoples of Africa*, ed. James L. Gibbs, p. 305

Erik H. Erikson, *Childhood and Society*, p. 159

Chapter 16: **Standing Room Only**

Tunisian song translated by Sabra Webber, 'Children's Games and Songs from Tunisia' in *Children in the Muslim Middle East*, p. 449

Anne Hubbell Maiden and Edie Farwell, *The Tibetan Art of Parenting*, p. 127

Robert A. and Barbara B. LeVine, 'Nyansongo: A Gusii Community in Kenya' in *Six Cultures: Studies of Child Rearing*, ed. Beatrice B. Whiting, p. 146

The Body Shop Team, *Mamatoto*, p.169

Carleton S. Coon, *The Hunting Peoples*, p. 310

Mary Martin McLaughlin, 'Survivors and Surrogates: Children and Parents from the Ninth to the Thirteenth Centuries' in *The History of Childhood*, ed. Lloyd deMause, pp. 118, 152 note 83

Meredith F. Small, *Our Babies, Ourselves*, pp. 82–3, 89

Ashley Montagu, *Touching*, p. 320

Jennifer M. Russ, *German Festivals and Customs*, p. 136

Homa Hoodfar, 'Child Care and Child Health in Low-Income Neighborhoods of Cairo' in *Children in the Muslim Middle East*, ed. Elizabeth Warnock Fernea, p. 155

Tradition China, www.babyzone.com, February 2001

Margaret Mead, 'Children and Ritual in Bali' in *Childhood in Contemporary Cultures*, p. 47

Desmond Morris, *Babywatching*, p. 103

Warren R. Dawson, *The Custom of Couvade*, p. 7

Chapter 16: **Baby Extreme**

Pamela Crimmins, 'Mothering in Morocco', *Mothering* 68, July–Sept 1993, p. 110

Robert A. and Barbara B. LeVine, 'Nyansongo: A Gusii Community in Kenya' in *Six Cultures: Studies of Child Rearing*, ed. Beatrice B. Whiting, p. 147

Marjorie Shostak, *Nisa*, p. 107

Staffan Janson, 'Life and Health of Jordanian Children' in *Children in the Muslim Middle East*, ed. Elizabeth Warnock Fernea, p. 190

Homa Hoodfar, 'Child Care and Child Health in Low-Income Neighborhoods of Cairo' in *Children in the Muslim Middle East*, ed. Elizabeth Warnock Fernea, p. 156

Jean Liedloff, *The Continuum Concept*, p. 89

Meredith F. Small, *Our Babies, Ourselves*, pp. 85, 88–9, 91

Thomas W. and Hatsumi Maretzki, 'Taira: An Okinawan Village' in *Six Cultures: Studies of Child Rearing*, ed. Beatrice B. Whiting, pp. 471–2

Tara MacAnTsior and Branfionn MacGregor, 'Gaelic Culture 6: Birth Customs', at www.sundown.pair.com

Manadala, www.asianart.com

Proceedings of the Society of Antiquities of Scotland, www.alkelda.f9.co.uk

Hank Harrington, 'Encounter in Kakadu', *Environment South Australia* 7:3, January 1999, www.ccsa.asn.au

Chapter 16: **Home Truths**

Saint Augustine, Sermon XXIII, iii; 3 quoted by Richard B. Lyman Jr. in 'Barbarism and Religion: Late Roman and Early Medieval Childhood' in *The History of Childhood*, ed. Lloyd deMause, p. 89

Anne Hubbell Maiden and Edie Farwell, *The Tibetan Art of Parenting*, p. 122

Zuñi prayer quoted by Ruth Benedict, *Patterns of Culture*, p. 63

Bibliography

The Little Book of Motherhood, Penguin Books, London 1997 (no author)

The Motherhood Book – for the Expectant Mother and Baby's First Years, The Amalgamated Press Ltd, London (circa 1930, compiled by 'a distinguished group of experts and specialists in health, maternity, infant and child welfare')

Peter Adamson, *Facts for Life, A Communication Challenge*, for UNICEF, WHO, UNESCO and UNFPA, P&LA, Wallingford, Oxfordshire 1993

M.D.S. Ainsworth, *Infancy in Uganda*, Johns Hopkins University Press, Baltimore 1967.

Nid Amina, *Childbirth and Burial Practices among Philippine Tribes*, Omar Publications 1978

Barbara Aria and the Body Shop Team, *Mamatoto – A Celebration of Birth*, Virago, London 1991

Philippe Ariès, *Centuries of Childhood*, Random House, London 1996 (trans. Robert Baldick 1962 from *L'Enfant et la familiale sous l'ancien régime*, Librairie Plon, Paris 1960)

A. Monroe Aurand Jr., *Popular Home Remedies and Superstitions of the Pennsylvania Germans*, Aurand Press, Lancaster, US, 1940-45

Australian InFo International, *Australian Aboriginal Culture* (1989) 1998

Norman Autton, *Pain – An Exploration*, Darton, Longman and Todd, London 1986

Janet Balaskas, *Natural Pregnancy*, Sidgwick & Jackson, London 1990

H.E. Bates, *The Vanished World: An Autobiography*, Vol. 1, University of Missouri Press, Columbia 1969

F. Batmanghelidj, *Your Body's Many Cries for Water* (Global Health Solutions, US 1992), The Therapist Ltd, Worthing, West Sussex 1994

Ruth Benedict, *Patterns of Culture* (1934), Houghton Mifflin Co., Boston USA 1989

Thérèse Betherat, *The Body Has Its Reasons – Anti-exercises and Self-awareness*, Cedar Books (Heinemann), London 1977 (trans. Carol Bernstein from *Le Corps A Ses Raisons*, Editions du Seuil, Paris 1976)

Tim Blanks (ed.)., *The Body Shop Book* (1994), Little, Brown & Co, London 1996

Nikki Bradford and Jean Williams, *What They Don't Tell You About Being a Mother and Looking After Babies*, HarperCollins, London 1997

Dr E.C. Brewer, *Brewer's Dictionary of Phrase and Fable* (1870), Centenary edition, revised by Ivor H. Evans, Cassell, London 1970

Norma Jane Bumgarner, *Mothering Your Nursing Toddler* (1980), La Leche League International, Illinois 1986

Kitty Campion, *Holistic Herbal for Mother and Baby*, Bloomsbury, London 1996

Leon Chaitow, *Vaccination and Immunization: Dangers, delusions and alternatives*, C.W. Daniel Company, Saffron Walden, Essex 1987

Beverly Chalmers, *African Birth: Childbirth in Cultural Transition*, Berev, River Club 1990

Brock Chisholm, *Prescripton for Survival*, Columbia University Press, New York 1957

H. Chapel and Mansel Haeney, *Essentials of Clinical Immunology*, Oxford 1984

Dr Pye Henry Chavasse, *Advice to a Wife On the Management of Her Own Health*, Cassell and Company, London 1911 (8th edition, revised)

Joseph Chilton Pearce, *Magical Child – Rediscovering nature's plan for our children* (E.P. Dutton, New York 1977), Bantam, London 1980

Ros Claxton (ed.), *Birth Matters*, Unwin, London 1986

Carleton S. Coon, *The Hunting Peoples* (1971), Jonathan Cape, London 1972

David Crystal, *Listen to Your Child*, Penguin, Middlesex, England 1986

Warren R. Dawson, *The Custom of Couvade*, Manchester University Press 1929

Lloyd deMause (ed.), *The History of Childhood – The Untold Story of Child Abuse* (1974), Bellew Publishing, London 1991

William C. Dement with Christopher Vaughan, *The Promise of Sleep – The Scientific Connection Between Health, Happiness, and a Good Night's Sleep* (Delacorte Press, New York 1999), Macmillan, London 2000

Suzanne Dixon, *The Roman Family*, Johns Hopkins University Press, Baltimore 1992

Terence Dixon and Martin Lucas, *The Human Race*, Methuen, London 1982

J.S. Dosanjh and Paul A.S. Ghuman, *Child-Rearing in Ethnic Minorities*, Multilingual Matters, Clevedon, England 1996

O.B. Duane, *Feng Shui – The Origins of Wisdom*, Brockhampton Press, London 1997

Kevin Duffy, *Children of the Forest – Life with the Mbuti Pygmies* (1984), Robert Hale, London 1986

William Dufty, *Sugar Blues* (1975), Abacus Press, Kent 1980

Janet Dunbar, *The Early Victorian Woman – Some aspects of her life 1837–57*, Harrap, London 1953

John Ellis (ed.), *The Works of Anne Bradstreet in Prose and Verse*, Peter Smith, Mass., US 1962

Erik H. Erikson, *Childhood and Society*, Vintage, London 1995

Adele Faber and Elaine Mazlish, *Siblings Without Rivalry – How to help your children live together so you can live too* (1987), Avon Books, New York 1988

Carine Fabius, *Mehndi – the art of henna body painting*, Three Rivers Press, New York 1998

Anne Fadiman, *The Spirit Catches You and You Fall Down – A Hmong Child, her American Doctors and the Collision of Two Cultures* (1997), The Noonday Press, Farrar, Straus and Giroux, New York 1998

Elaine Fantham et al., *Women in the Classical World*, Oxford University Press, New York 1994

Dr Richard Ferber, *Solve Your Child's Sleep Problems* (1985), Dorling Kindersley, London 1986

Elizabeth Warnock Fernea (ed.), *Children in the Muslim Middle East*, University of Texas Press 1995

David Fontana, *Teach Yourself to Dream*, Duncan Baird Publishers, London 1996

B.M. Foss (ed.), *Determinants of Infant Behaviour*, Methuen, London 1965

Maureen Freely, *The Parent Trap – Children, families and the new morality*, Virago, London 2000

Anna M. Galbraith, MD, *The Four Epochs of Woman's Life – A Study in Hygiene* (1901), W.B. Saunders & Co., Philadelphia 1915

Kuki Gallmann, *I Dreamed of Africa* (Viking 1991), Penguin, London 1992

Catherine Garvey, *Children's Talk*, Fontana, London 1984

Jamila Gavin, *Our Favourite Stories – From around the world*, Dorling Kindersley, London 1997

Menachem Gerson, *Family, Women and Socialization in the Kibbutz*, DC Heath, Mass., USA 1978

James L. Gibbs, Jr. (ed.), *Peoples of Africa*, Holt, Rinehart and Winston, USA 1965

Norma Gleason, *Proverbs from Around the World*, Pan, London 1995

Vivien Golding, *Traditions from Africa*, Wayland, Hove, Sussex 1998

Good Housekeeping Family Centre, *Good Housekeeping's Mothercraft*, The National Magazine Company, London 1959

Kate Gordon, *Baptism and Baby-Naming*, Constable & Co., London 1998

Dr Christopher Green, *Toddler Taming – A Parents' Guide to the First Four Years* (1992), Vermillion, London 1997

Annette Hamilton, *Nature and Nurture – Aboriginal Childrearing in North Central Arnhemland*, Australian Institute of Aboriginal Studies 1981

Christina Hardyment, *Dream Babies – Child Care from Locke to Spock* (1983), Oxford University Press 1984

Charles Higham, *The Maoris*, Cambridge University Press 1981

Roger Highfield, *Can Reindeer Fly? The Science of Christmas*, Metro Books, London 1998

K. Hill and A.M. Hurtado, *Ache Life History: The Ecology and Demography of a Foraging People*, Aldine de Gruyter, New York 1996

Sarah Hobson *Family Web – A story of India*, John Murray, London 1978

Mary Hoffman and Jane Ray, *Song of the Earth*, Orion Children's Books, London 1995

David Hoffmann, *Holistic Herbal*, Element Books, Dorset 1996

Patrick Holford, *The Optimum Nutrition Bible*, Judy Piatkus, London 1997

John A. Hostetler, *Amish Life*, Herald Press, Scottdale, Pennsylvania 1983

Sarah Blaffer Hrdy, *Mother Nature* (1999), Vintage, London 2000

Olwen Hufton, *The Prospect Before Her: A History of Women in Western Europe, Vol. One 1500–1800* (1995), Fontana, London 1997

Norman Bancroft Hunt, *Native American Tribes*, Regency House Publishing, London 1997

Karen Hurrell, *Natural Home Remedies – A Step-By-Step Guide*, Element, Dorset 1997

Sally Inch, *Birthrights – A Parent's Guide to Modern Childbirth* (1982), Hutchinson, London 1985

Vicki Iovine, *The Girlfriends' Guide to Pregnancy*, Pocket Books, New York 1995

Adam J. Jackson, *Eye Signs – What your eyes reveal about your health, emotions, personality and love life*, Thorsons, London 1995

Beverley Jackson, *Splendid Slippers – A Thousand Years of an Erotic Tradition*, Ten Speed Press, Berkeley, California, 1998

Deborah Jackson, *Three in a Bed – The benefits of sleeping with your baby* (1989), Bloomsbury, London 1999;
Do Not Disturb – The benefits of relaxed parenting, for you and your child, Bloomsbury, London 1993;
Eve's Wisdom – Traditional Secrets of Pregnancy, Birth and Motherhood, Duncan Baird, London 1999

Paul Z. Jackson and Mark McKergow, *The Solutions Focus*, Nicholas Brealey, London 2001

Jessica Johnson and Michel Odent, *We Are All Water Babies*, Dragon's World, Limpsfield, Surrey 1994

Dr Hugh Jolly, *Book of Child Care – The complete guide for today's parents*, Allen & Unwin, London 1975

Brigitte Jordan, *Birth in Four Cultures – A Crosscultural Investigation of Childbirth in Yucatan, Holland, Sweden and the United States* (1978), revised and expanded by Robbie Davis-Floyd, Waveland Press, Illinois 1993

Jamal Karam, *Infant Health in Lebanon – Customs and Taboos*, Harfouche, Beirut 1965

Fauziya Kassindja, *Do They Hear You When You Cry?*, Bantam 1998

Leslie Kenton, *Nature's Child*, Ebury Press, London 1993

Olga Kenyon, *800 Years of Women's Letters* (1992), Alan Sutton Publishing, Stroud, England 1994

Barnabas and Anabel Kindersley, *Children Just Like Me*, Dorling Kindersley, London 1995

Sheila Kitzinger, *The Crying Baby* (1989), Penguin, London 1990; *The Year After Childbirth*, Oxford University Press 1994; ed. *The Midwife Challenge*, Pandora, London 1988

Gitanjali Kolanad, *Culture Shock! India*, Kuperard, London 1994

Mark Kurlansky, *The Basque History of the World*, Jonathan Cape, London 1999

Robert Lacey and Danny Danziger, *The Year 1000 – What life was like at the turn of the first millennium/An Englishman's World*, Little,Brown, London 1999

Carol Laderman, *Wives and Midwives – Childbirth and Nutrition in Rural Malaysia* (1983), University of California Press, Berkeley & Los Angeles 1987

Robert de Laroche and Jean-Michel Labat, *The Secret Life of Cats* (Casterman, Belgium 1993), Aurum Press, London 1993

Maria Leach (ed.), *Funk and Wagnall's Standard Dictionary of Folklore, Mythology and Legend*, Harper, San Francisco 1996

Penelope Leach, *Baby and Child – From Birth to Age Five* (1977), Penguin, London 1989; *Children First, What our society must do – and is not doing – for children today*, Penguin, London 1994

Frédérick Leboyer, *Birth Without Violence*, Fontana, London 1987 (translated from *Pour Une Naissance Sans Violence*, Editions du Seuil, Paris 1974)

Richard Bushey Lee, *The !Kung San – Men, women and work in a foraging society*, Cambridge University Press 1979

Robert A. LeVine et al., *Child Care and Culture – Lessons from Africa* (1994), Cambridge University Press 1998

David Levinson, *Religion: A Cross-Cultural Encyclopedia*, ABC-Clio, Santa Barbara 1996

David Levinson and David Sherwood, *The Tribal Living Book* (1984), Johnson Books, Colorado 1993

I.M. Lewis, *Peoples of the Horn of Africa – Somali, Afar and Saho* (1955), Haan Associates, London 1994

Jon E. Lewis (ed.), *The Mammoth Book of Letters – The emotional and domestic worlds of the famous through their letters*, Robinson, London 1999

Henrietta Leyser, *Medieval Women – A Social History of Women in England 450–1500*, Wiedenfeld & Nicolson, London 1995

Jean Liedloff, *The Continuum Concept* (Duckworth 1975), Penguin, Middlesex 1986

Bernard Lievegoed, *Phases of Childhood*, Floris Books, Edinburgh 1987

(trans. by Tony Langham and Plym Peters from the Dutch, *Ontwikkelingsfasen van het kind*, Uitgeverij Vrij Geestesleven, Zeist, Holland 1946)

Fiona Macdonald, *A Child's Eye View of History*, Marshall Publishing, London 1997

Fiona MacLeod (William Sharp), *By Sundown Shores – Studies in Spiritual History*, George Loring Press, Portland Maine, USA 1902

Anne Hubbell Maiden and Edie Farwell, *The Tibetan Art of Parenting*, Wisdom Publications, Somerville, Mass. 1997

Alice Marriott, *Indians of the Four Corners – The Anasazi and Their Pueblo Descendants* (New York 1952), Ancient City Press, Santa Fe 1996

L. Marshall, *The !Kung of Nyae Nyae*, Harvard University Press 1976

Caitlin Matthews, *The Little Book of Celtic Blessings*, Element, Dorset 1994

Margaret Mead and Martha Wolfenstein (eds.), *Childhood in Contemporary Cultures* (1955), The University of Chicago Press 1974

J.A.M. Meerloo, *The Dance*, Chilton, Philadelphia 1960

Susan Milord, *Hands Around the World*, Williamson Publishing, Vermont 1992

Ashley Montagu, *Touching – The human significance of the skin* (1971), Harper & Row, London 1986

Lucy Maud Montgomery, *Days of Dreams and Laughter: The Story Girl and Other Tales*, Avinel Books, New York 1990

Desmond Morris, *Illustrated Babywatching*, Ebury Press, London 1995; *The Naked Ape* (1967), Arrow Books, London 1997

Michel Odent, *Entering the World*, Penguin, London 1985 (trans. Christine Hauch from *Bien Naître*, Editions du Seuil, Paris 1976); *Primal Health – A Blueprint for our survival* (1986), Century 1987; *Water and Sexuality*, Arkana (Penguin), London 1990; *The Scientification of Love*, Free Association Books, London 1999

Modupe Oduyoye, *Yoruba Names – Their structure and meaning*, Karnak House, 1987

Ifeoma Onyefulu, *A is for Africa*, Frances Lincoln, London 1993

Aliza Orbach, *Motherhood*, (אמהות) (Fischer, Frankfurt 1997) Steimatsky, Israel 1998

Trefor M. Owen, *Welsh Folk Customs* (1959), Gomer, Llandysul, Dyfed 1987

Gabrielle Palmer, *The Politics of Breastfeeding*, Pandora, London 1988

Richard Pankhurst, *A Social History of Ethiopia* (1990), The Red Sea Press, Trenton, NJ 1992

David Pickering, *Dictionary of Superstitions* (1995), Cassell, London 1998

Mathilde Polee and Petra Rosenberg. *The Lullaby Treasury – Cradle songs from around the world*, Floris Books, Edinburgh 1997 (trans. from *Als je gaat slapen zal ik singen*, Christofoor, Zeist 1997)

Linda Pollock, *A Lasting Relationship – Parents and children over three centuries,*

Fourth Estate, London 1987

Jacqueline Vincent Priya, *Birth Traditions and Modern Pregnancy Care*, Element, Dorset 1992

M.A. Qazi, *What's In a Muslim Name?*, Kazi Publications, Chicago 1982

E. and M.A. Radford, *The Encyclopedia of Superstitions*, (ed. Christina Hole) (1948) Helicon Publishing, Oxford 1995

Nigel Rees and Vernon Noblem, *A Who's Who of Nicknames*, Allen & Unwin, London 1985

Mary Renfrew, Chloe Fisher and Suzanne Arms, *Bestfeeding: Getting Breastfeeding Right For You*, Celestial Arts, Berkeley, California 1990

Jan Reynolds, *Mother and Child – Visions of parenting from indigenous cultures*, Inner Traditions International, Vermont 1997

Chris and Melanie Rice, *How Children Lived*, Dorling Kindersley, London 1995

Gay Robins, *Women in Ancient Egypt*, British Museum Press, London 1993

Anita Roddick (with Russell Miller), *Body and Soul*, Ebury Press 1991

F. Gordon Roe, *The Georgian Child*, Phoenix House, London 1961

Clare Rose, *Children's Clothes*, B.T. Batsford, London 1989

Carol Rudd, *Flower Essences*, Element, Dorset 1998

Edith Rudinger, ed. *The Newborn Baby* (1972), Consumers' Association, London 1979

Jennifer M. Russ, *German Festivals and Customs*, Oswald Wolff, London 1982

Alison Sage, *The Hutchinson Treasury of Children's Literature,* Hutchinson, London 1995

Tepilit Ole Saitoti, *The Worlds of a Maasai Warrior – An Autobiography*, Andre Deutsch, London 1986

Ruth Samuels, *Bible stories for Jewish children*, Ktav Publishing House, New York 1954

Stephen K. Sanderson, *Macrosociology – An introduction to human societies* (Third Edition), HarperCollins, New York 1995

Marjorie Shostak, *Nisa – The life and words of a !Kung woman*, Penguin, London 1981

Nikki Siegen-Smith, *Welcome to the World – A celebration of birth and babies from many cultures*, Barefoot Books, Bristol, England 1996

Alison Sim, *Food and Feast in Tudor England*, Sutton Publishing, Stroud, England 1997

Meredith Small, *Our Babies, Ourselves – How Biology and Culture Shape the Way We Parent* (1998), Anchor Books, New York 1999

K. Soddy (ed.), *Mental Health and Infant Development*, Basic Books, New York 1956

Aletha Jauch Solter, *The Aware Baby – A new approach to parenting*, Shining Star Press, Goleta, California 1984

Dr Loraine M. Stern, *Does My Child Need A Doctor?*, Bloomsbury, London

1994

Margaret Stewart, *Ngalangangpum Jarrakpu Purrurn – Mother and Child: The Women of Warmun*, Magabala Books, Western Australia 1999

Dr Miriam Stoppard, *Conception, Pregnancy and Birth*, Dorling Kindersley, London 1993

P. Stuart-Macadam and K.A. Dettwyler, eds., *Breastfeeding: Biocultural Perspectives*, Aldine de Gruyter, New York 1995

Karen Sullivan (ed.), *Natural Home Remedies*, Element, Shaftesbury 1997

Anne Sutherland, *Face Values*, British Broadcasting Corporation, London 1978

Richard J.A. Talbert, trans., *Plutarch on Sparta*, Penguin, London 1988

Colin Taylor, *North American Indians*, Parragon, Bristol 1997

Joules and Ken Taylor, *The Little Book of Scottish Folklore*, Siena, Bath 1999

Meredith Mann Taylor, *Transcultural Aspects of Breastfeeding – USA*, Lactation Consultant Series, La Leche League International, Illinois 1985

Lenore Terr, MD, *Beyond Love And Work – Why adults need to play*, Touchstone, New York 1999

Tine Thevenin, *The Family Bed*, Avery Publishing Group, Wayne, New Jersey 1987

Ian Thomas (ed.), *Culpeper's Book of Birth – A Seventeenth-Century Guide to Having Lusty Children*, Webb & Bower, Exeter, England 1985

Pat Thomas (ed.), *Every Birth is Different*, Headline, London 1997

Maggie Tisserand, *Aromatherapy for Women*, Thorsons, London 1990

Lillian Too, *Feng Shui*, Element Books, Dorset, England 1996

Piers Vitebsky, *The Shaman – Voyages of the Soul – Trance, Ecstasy and Healing from Siberia to the Amazon*, Duncan Baird, London 1995

Peter Walker, *Baby Relax* (1985), Unwin, London 1986; *The Book of Baby Massage*, Bloomsbury, London 1988

Ann Wallace and Gabrielle Taylor, *Royal Mothers – From Eleanor of Aquitaine to Princess Diana*, Judy Piatkus, London 1987

Dr Sally Ward, *BabyTalk*, Century, London, 2000

Philippa Waring, *A Dictionary of Omens and Superstitions* (1978), Souvenir Press, London 1997

Annette Weiner, *The Trobrianders of Papua New Guinea*, Holt, Rinehart and Winston, Austin, Texas 1988

Nikki Wesson, *Alternative Maternity*, Optima, London 1989

Beatrice B. Whiting (ed.), *Six Cultures: Studies of Child Rearing*, John Wiley and Sons, New York 1963

Chrissie Wildwood, *The Bloomsbury Encyclopedia of Aromatherapy*, Bloomsbury, London 1996

Margaret Willes, *And So To Bed*, The National Trust, London 1998;

Memories of Childhood, The National Trust, London 1997

D.W. Winnicott, *Babies and Their Mothers* (1987), Free Assocation Books, London 1988

Grey Wolf, *Native American Wisdom*, Judy Piatkus, London 2000

Each of these insights, gathered as they are from observation and study ... can be useful in your life only as it resonates with your own innate wisdom.

Gyatso, Tibetan Buddhist lama, from *The Tibetan Art of Parenting* by Anne Hubbell Maiden and Edie Farwell

Index